A Concise Survey of Western Civilization

Supremacies and Diversities throughout History

VOLUME 2: 1500 TO THE PRESENT

Third Edition

BRIAN A. PAVLAC
King's College

ROWMAN & LITTLEFIELD
Lanham • Boulder • New York • London

Executive Editor: Susan McEachern
Editorial Assistant: Katelyn Turner
Senior Marketing Manager: Kim Lyons

Credits and acknowledgments for material borrowed from other sources, and reproduced with permission, appear on the appropriate page within the text.

Published by Rowman & Littlefield
An imprint of The Rowman & Littlefield Publishing Group, Inc.
4501 Forbes Boulevard, Suite 200, Lanham, Maryland 20706
www.rowman.com

6 Tinworth Street, London SE11 5AL, United Kingdom

British Library Cataloguing in Publication Information Available

Library of Congress Cataloging-in-Publication Data

Names: Pavlac, Brian Alexander, 1956– author.
Title: A concise survey of western civilization : supremacies and diversities throughout history / Brian A. Pavlac, King's College.
Description: Third edition. | Lanham, MD : Rowman & Littlefield, [2019] | Includes bibliographical references and index.
Identifiers: LCCN 2018059659 (print) | LCCN 2018059913 (ebook) | ISBN 9781538112519 (electronic) | ISBN 9781538112540 (v. 1 electronic) | ISBN 9781538112571 (v. 2 electronic) | ISBN 9781538112496 (cloth : alk. paper) | ISBN 9781538112502 (pbk. : alk. paper) | ISBN 9781538112526 (v. 1 : cloth : alk. paper) | ISBN 9781538112533 (v. 1 : pbk. : alk. paper) | ISBN 9781538112557 (v. 2 : cloth : alk. paper) | ISBN 9781538112564 (v. 2 : pbk. : alk. paper)
Subjects: LCSH: Civilization, Western.
Classification: LCC CB245 (ebook) | LCC CB245 .P38 2019 (print) | DDC 909/.09821—dc23
LC record available at https://lccn.loc.gov/2018059659

♾ ™ The paper used in this publication meets the minimum requirements of American National Standard for Information Sciences—Permanence of Paper for Printed Library Materials, ANSI/NISO Z39.48-1992.

Printed in the United States of America

Brief Contents

Contents

Diagrams, Figures, Maps, Primary Source Projects, Sources on Families, Tables, and Timelines

DIAGRAMS

FIGURES

MAPS

PRIMARY SOURCE PROJECTS

SOURCES ON FAMILIES

TABLES

TIMELINES

Acknowledgments

I was interested in history from a young age, as most kids are. Too often, as they grow older, kids lose their fascination with the past, partly because it becomes one more thing they have to learn rather than a path of self-understanding or even just "neat stuff." Wonderful teachers taught me history through the years, and partly inspired by them, I foolishly went on to study history in college. Before I knew it, history became my intended profession. Since then I have been fortunate to make a living from history.

In teaching courses over the years, I found my own voice about what mattered. Instead of simply sharing my thoughts in lectures, I produced this book. Former teachers, books I have read and documentaries I have viewed, historical sites I have visited, all have contributed to the knowledge poured into these pages. Likewise, many students, too many to be named, have sharpened both words and focus. I owe thanks to the many readers whose suggestions have improved the text. For their help to me in getting this project as far as it has come, I have to thank a number of specific people. I appreciate my editor, Susan McEachern, who gave the book her time and consideration and offered a third edition, and her associates Katelyn Turner and Jehanne Schweitzer. Various people have offered useful suggestions for this edition: Cristofer Scarboro, Charles Ingram, Nicole Mares, Megan Lloyd, and especially the two readers, Ian Crowe and John Williams. Finally, most of all, my spouse, Elizabeth Lott, has sustained me through all the editions and permutations. Her skills in grammar, logic, and good sense have made this a far better book.

The final version is never final. Every new history source I read makes me want to adjust an adjective, nudge a nuance, or fix a fact. With every edition of this text, I find room for improvement. Should any inaccuracies or errors have crept in, please forgive the oversight and contact me with your proposed corrections.

How to Use This Book

Learning is difficult. If it were easy, everyone would be educated. In this age of multimedia, reading still remains one of the best ways to learn something. Of course, reading well is not always easy. You cannot read a nonfiction informative work such as this in the same way as you would a Harry Potter novel. Those novels, though, are full of information with strange new terms, from *muggles* to *Hogwarts*, that people learn easily and absorb into their knowledge. The same can be true of learning history once it interests you.

The pictures on the covers of the various editions of this textbook illustrate people in the past writing something. They have produced the sources that we use today to understand our heritage and ourselves. History is a product of people, by people, and for people. We create it, preserve it, and share it. The purpose of this text is to help you integrate the history of the Western past into your meaning of life.

I hope to make learning history as enjoyable as possible, even to those who are not in love with the past. As a survey, this book offers one person's opinion about what is good, bad, useful, and wasteful to know about our wider civilization. This book does cover the minimum historical information that educated adults should know—just compare it to other texts. Also, in the author's opinion, it offers a tightly focused narrative and interpretive structure, in a sometimes quirky style.

This text's distinctive approach applies major themes of conflict and creativity. The phrase *supremacies and diversities* describes the unifying theme through which this text evaluates the past. Supremacies focus on the use of power to dominate societies, ranging from ideologies to warfare. Supremacy seeks stability, order, and amalgamation. Diversities encompass the creative impulses that concoct new ideas, as well as people's efforts to define themselves as different. Diversity produces change, opportunity, and individuality. A tension, of course, arises between the "supremacy" desire for conformity and the "diversity" idea of individuality. This interaction has clearly driven historical conflict and change. Other approaches might be equally valuable. Indeed, to be truly educated, you should be looking at a variety of views about the past. History is rarely simple. This version merely provides a foundation for learning more.

Fulfilling the survey function, this narrative examines political, economic, technological, social, and cultural trends, depending on the historical period. The book does not much emphasize the everyday-life aspects of people in the past. For more on this, and art and literature, see the website. Five main topical themes regularly inform how this text looks at change: technological innovation, migration and conquest, political and economic decision making, church and state, and proposals about the meaning of life. These topics have significantly altered history and are still influential in the present.

How could you best learn from this book? Read well. This time-tested advice applies to anything you might want to learn thoroughly for the rest of your life. Here are a few steps:

1. Read the text in a space and at a time conducive to reading—not in the few minutes before class, not where others will interrupt, not with television or music blaring.

2. Prudently mark up, underline, highlight, and otherwise annotate your text as you study. Use the margins for notes, questions, comments, and marks to remind yourself of some important point.

3. Critique the book as you read; enter into its conversation. You might comment in the margins or on blank pages on the following points:

    connections between themes, ideas, or subjects;
    ideas you agree with;
    ideas you disagree with;
    reactions provoked by the text;
    material of particular interest to you; and
    material you would like to know more about.

4. At the end of each section, jot down notes or write a brief comment about what you have just read. The review question at the end of each section and the space provided for a response encourage this learning skill.

5. Each chapter provides a primary source project to help you think like a historian while determining your own perspective on the past and present. In the Primary Source Projects you can compare and contrast the ideas in the sources (or in a few cases within one source). Topics include the different roles of government, the power of religion, perceptions of good or bad leadership, the role of the individual, and social values. The Sources on Families present different views on the nature and experience of that basic social unit, further described in chapter 2. Important aspects of such sources are property, choice in forming a family, sexuality, social status, raising children, breaking spousal relationships, religious support, and alternatives to the "traditional" family. Answering the given questions for the sources in the space provided will help you understand and remember them. The sources have usually been lightly edited from their cited printed versions for spelling, grammar, clarity, and length (being the only correction noted by ellipses [. . .]). More versions, questions, and information

about these sources are available at the website http://www.concisewesternciv .com/sources. A list of suggested readings of primary sources is at http:// www.concisewesternciv.com/sources/suggested.html. They are largely primary sources that provide essential points of view or capture the spirit of their times, sometimes at great length.

6. A common question students have about history is "How important is it to know dates?" Understanding dates is essential. History is all about what happens before (which can affect causation), what events are happening at the same time (which adds to context), and what happens after (which may show results). The more dates connected with historical change you know, the better you will be at historical explanation. At least attempt to memorize the dates of the major periods (although different approximate dates may be offered for the same large periods—historians do not always agree on exact beginnings and ends). The book presents dates in chapter subtitles, on most maps, throughout the text, and in the block timelines toward the end of the text. Use these block timelines to review and structure your knowledge according to theme or time period. The most important terms in the text appear in **boldface** and are listed in the block timelines. Additionally, terms representing significant ideas and ideologies are defined both in the text and again in the glossary at the back of the book; these terms are set in ***boldface italics***.

7. To further help you learn dates, names, and terms, on the last page of each chapter is a "Make your own timeline" feature. Use the terms in boldface italics from what you have just read and those in the block timelines toward the end of this text. See the sample timeline at the end of chapter 1 for an example of how you can make your own.

8. As is clear from the above, even more information is provided on the website: **ConciseWesternCiv.com**. The website offers more study guides, questions, outlines, summaries, all the maps in color, diagrams, tables, many of the figures (pictures), a history of art relevant to each chapter, and links to many more websites and primary sources. All of these materials can reinforce and expand on what you learn from the text.

Finally, connect what you learn here to the rest of your experience. The more you know, the more you can know. And according to the liberal arts credo, the more you know, the better will be your decisions about your life.

CHAPTER 1

History's Story

N ow" is over and done with. It can never take place again. Each moment is surrendered to the past, whether forgotten or remembered. In our personal lives, we treasure or bury memories on our own. Our larger society, however, has historians to preserve and make sense of our collective recollection. Historians recapture the past by applying particular methods and skills that have been nurtured over the past few centuries. Although such processes are not without challenges, the work done by historians has created the subject of this book you are reading: **Western civilization**.

THERE'S METHOD

"How do we know anything?" is our starting point. As **humans**, some of our knowledge comes from instinct: we are born with it, beginning with our first cry and suckle. Yet instinct makes up a tiny portion of human knowledge. Most everything we come to know we learn in one way or another. First, we learn through direct experience of the senses. These lessons of life can sometimes be painful (fire), other times pleasurable (chocolate). Second, other people teach us many important matters through example and setting rules. Reading this book because of a professor's requirement may be one such demand. Third, human beings can apply reason to figure stuff out.[1] This ability enables people to take what they know, then learn and rearrange it into some new understanding.

The discipline of *history* is one such form of reasoning. History is not just knowing something—names, dates, facts—about the past. The word *history* comes from the Greek word ιστορία for "inquiring," or asking questions. The questioning of the past has been an important tool for gaining information about ourselves. Indirectly, it helps us to better define the present.

---

1. This approach assumes we can correctly understand the world. When the title character in Shakespeare's play *Hamlet* pretends insanity in order to discover truth, another character rationally concludes that though "this be madness; yet there is method in it."

Quite often authorities, the people in charge, have used history to bind together groups with shared identities. For many peoples, history has embodied a mythology that reflected their relationship to the gods. Or history chronicled the deeds of kings, justifying royal rulership. History also sanctioned domination and conquest of one people over another. Most people are raised to believe that their own country or nation is more virtuous and righteous than those others beyond their borders. The history of Western civilization abounds with examples of these attitudes.

Then, about two hundred years ago, several men began to try to improve our understanding of the past. These historians began to organize as a profession based in the academic setting of universities (at which they did not allow women to study at that time). Historians imitated and adapted the scientific method (see chapter 10) for their own use, renaming it the **historical method** (see table 1.1). In the scientific method, scientists pose hypotheses as reasonable guesses about explanations for how nature works. They then observe and experiment to prove or disprove their hypotheses. In the historical method, historians propose hypotheses to describe and explain how history changes. The two main problems historians have focused on are **causation** (how something happened) and **significance** (what impact something had). History without explanations about how events came about or why they matter is merely trivia.

Unlike scientists, historians cannot conduct experiments or run historical events with different variables.[2] Historians cannot even obtain direct observational evidence of events before their own lifetimes—there are no time machines. Instead, historians have to pick through whatever evidence has survived. They call these data **sources**. At first, historians sought out sources among the written records that had been preserved over centuries in musty books and manuscripts. Eventually historians learned to study human-made objects, ranging from needles to skyscrapers.

Obviously, not all sources are of equal value. Those sources connected directly with past events are called **primary sources**. These are most important for historical investigation. Reading them, one encounters history in the raw.[3] When evaluating these primary sources, historians face two predicaments. For one, evidence for many events has not survived at all or remains only in fragments. Much of history is never recorded in the first place and dies with people's memories. Even for recorded sources, some are eaten by rats and rot, while others are obliterated in war or trashed on purpose (such as the records of the British Empire in Operation Legacy, where officials purged files to keep them out of the hands of their colonial successors). For another, some people have forged sources, in whole or in part. Much of historical research involves questioning human character, deciding who is honest or deceitful, trustworthy or undependable. Then, through careful examination and questioning, historians try to write the most reliable and accurate explanation of past events, carefully sifting and then citing their sources.

---

2. Alternative histories are an increasingly popular genre of fiction. Similar to science fiction's guesses about the future, alternative histories are based on "what if" issues of the past: what would have happened differently if, for example, some leader had not been killed.

3. The "Primary Source Projects" and "Sources on Families" offer opportunities to wrestle with such primary sources. For more explanation, see "How to Use This Book."

Table 1.1.   The Historical Method

1. Find a problem.

2. Form a hypothesis (a reasonable or educated guess to the solution).

3. Conduct research into sources.

Questions to ask of sources:

A.   External: Is it genuine? Is it what it says it is?
   When and where was it made?
   How did it get from its original recording to the present?
   Who is the author?
   How was the author able to create the source?
   Are there any interpolations, emendations, or insertions by others?

B.   Internal: What is its meaning? How is it significant?
   What is the source's ostensible or intended purpose?
   How accurate is the author (any competence, bias, prejudice)?
   What is the source's content?
   How does it compare with other reliable sources?
   What do modern scholars say about the source?

4. Make the argument and conclusions, usually in written form.

5. Share the knowledge, usually through publication.

Note: The step-by-step process of the historical method rigorously questions sources in order to reconstruct the best version of the past.

As the last and most important part of the historical method, professional historians have shared their information with one another. They produce **secondary sources**, usually books and articles.[4] At academic conferences and in more books and articles, historians learn from and judge one another's work. They debate and challenge one another's arguments and conclusions. Often a consensus about the past emerges. Generally, agreed-on views begin to appear in **tertiary sources**, such as encyclopedias, handbooks, or this very textbook. Although tertiary sources are several steps removed, these sources offer convenient summaries and overviews but usually lack citations to sources.

Because the past is so vast, historians have always divided it up into smaller, more convenient chunks. All history is about selection, choosing what to examine. Professional historians usually specialize, becoming experts in one small slice of the past. Since so many historians publish scholarship today, hardly anyone can ever read all that has been written about any single subject. New books and articles emerge each year, especially about popular topics such as the American Civil War or Hitler. The history of even one day covered in any detail would be long and confusing; the novel *Ulysses* by James Joyce, about the events of 16 July 1904, is an

---

4. A good secondary source has footnotes (at the bottom of the page) or endnotes (at the end of each chapter or the whole book or article) that cite the other primary, secondary, and tertiary sources. The footnotes in this text merely add some tangential commentary.

interesting example. Whether writing many volumes or a slim book, it is impossible to cover every detail on even a small subject. Something is always left out.

Therefore, historians prioritize to make the past manageable. They select certain events or places as more important than others. For example, in one person's life, a onetime decision, such as which college to attend, would probably be more essential to include in her biography than a description about what she chose to eat for breakfast on the day the decision was made. The former probably deserves more attention, since that choice can change a life. The quality of a unique, decisive historical moment is usually more interesting than a quantity of mundane events. However, the description of breakfast choice might be valuable if, for example, years of eating too much bacon and eggs led to heart disease or a dose of poison killed a person. Few readers, though, would want to read a close description of every repeated meal. Selection and generalization prevent us from becoming either overwhelmed or bored.

Historians can select only a few bits of the past, leaving out the vast majority of human activities. They then categorize or organize their selections into sensible stories and arguments. For example, eating breakfast differs a lot from choosing a college or waging a war. Politics—kings, wars, treaties, and rebellions—was once considered by historians as the only important human activities worthy of investigation. Within the past century, however, historians have broadened their interests to include a wider range of human pursuits. These days, many historians examine social manners: family, sex roles, food, and fashion.[5] Even a shift in breakfast habits from waffles and bacon cooked by Mom to a drive-in processed Egg McMuffin can illustrate something about a **society**, a coherent group of people.

Historians categorize the past in three main ways. The first and most obvious division is **chronological**, using time as dividing points. The most natural division of time is the day, with its cycle of sunlight and darkness. This cycle regulates us all. Some particular days, like those on which battles are waged or a notable inspiration is put to paper, can change the course of history. A larger natural unit of time is the year, especially important for people in temperate climates who experience the change of seasons. Finally, the basic human experience stretches, for each of us, over a lifetime. Some lives are short and others seem long, but all end in death. Yet history marches on.

Aside from natural portions of time, historians divide up history into manageable blocks. In the largest artificial division, historians split the past into two periods: **prehistory** and history. Prehistory includes everything humans did up until the invention of writing about five thousand years ago in the Middle East and East Asia. We can examine human activity before writing only through physical remains and artifacts, such as bones and shaped stones.

Technology (the use of raw materials to make tools), ideology, and narrower political movements also define different eras. Many of the commonly used historical labels, terms such as *antiquity*, *medieval*, and *Renaissance*, were not drawn from the sources and lives of past people; instead, historians later coined those

---

5. For interesting perspectives on marriage, children, and sex and gender, see the "Sources on Family" for each chapter after this one.

terms. The names for the Stone Age or the Iron Age are based on the use of those materials for making tools during those times. The term *Middle Ages* draws on the perceptions of politics and culture that fall between the ancient and modern epochs. The titles of the ages of Renaissance and Enlightenment derive from artistic and intellectual achievements. Sometimes a country's dynasty or ruling family provides a useful marker, such as Victorian England. Given our preference for round numbers, a century fits into historical schemes, especially the more recent nineteenth or twentieth centuries. Historians apply such divisions to the past to show both what the people within a period shared in common and what they have to teach us. Acts of naming may simplify the complexities and contradictions of any given time period, but without choosing such terms we cannot have a discussion.

While chronology applies time to divide up the past, **geographical** divisions, where events took place on our planet, are equally common. The largest unit for human activity is world or global history (with the minor exception of recent space exploration). Historians are increasingly finding connections and continuities among civilizations around the planet. By the twentieth century, people were clearly bound together worldwide. At the opposite end of size, the smallest unit could be a town, a college, or even a home. Historians usually focus somewhere between these two extremes, most frequently dealing with a country, nation, or state. Indeed, history became a profession in modern times as academics constructed national stories for the modern nation-states.

The third method that historians use to slice up the past is a **topical** approach, separating the wide range of human activities into smaller groupings of human enterprise. For example, historians today often specialize in areas of intellectual, social, constitutional, gender, literary, diplomatic, or military history.

The timelines at the back of this book group historical activities into six different columns. First is *science* and technology: how we understand the universe and build tools to cope with it. Second is **economics**: how we create and manage the distribution of wealth. Third is **politics**: how people create systems to organize collective decisions. Fourth is **social structures**: the units and hierarchies (such as families and communities) within which people place themselves and the humble activities of daily life. Fifth is **culture**, especially those works and activities that people fashion in order to cope with, understand, or simply share their experiences of the world. Culture includes music, **art** (largely visual creations), **literature** (compositions of words read or performed), and recreation (acts ranging from sports to hobbies). Finally are both *philosophy* and *religion*: how people understand the purpose of life and the meaning of death, which usually involves the supernatural, or beliefs in a reality beyond our senses. These six topics essentially embrace all human accomplishments.

Historians, and this text, define a *civilization* as a coherent, large collection of peoples in a specific time and place who establish particular approaches to political, social, and cultural life, especially around their cities. The concept remains slippery, however. Where any civilization began (or ended), whether in time, geographic boundary, or membership, depends on who defines it and by what criteria. And generalizations of what holds a society together often ignore contradictions and minority movements. Sometimes a civilization is dominated by one powerful people or idea (Chinese or Muslim civilizations), while Western civilization developed from the interaction of several cultures. Most people have historically tended to view the world from their own vantage points. Historians naturally tend to focus on the history of the political states in which they live. Whether in the Americas, Europe, Asia, or Africa, historians have too rarely gazed across borders and boundaries to see how often and in what ways people have believed and acted in common.

This particular text reviews a civilization defined by many historians as "Western." As an academic subject it originated about one hundred years ago, after the United States had risen to become a world power. Many American historians saw a shared Western past with other European nations that had also risen to global power status. If Americans learned only US history without understanding how the United States fits into the larger culture of competing European powers, they argued, Americans would misunderstand their own heritage and the challenges of the future. The founders of classes on Western civilization deliberately wove together American with European history, showing the common origins of so much that Americans, and Europeans, took for granted. Thus, Western civilization courses and texts multiplied until a few years ago, when other historians argued in favor of world or global history courses, which try to cover all societies on planet Earth. An even newer trend is the "Big History," which covers material from the "big bang" origin of the universe through our current human predicaments.

Western civilization is worth studying because it organizes a large portion of interrelated history that is relevant to today's problems in a world dominated by Western industrialized states and ideologies. The West is not necessarily better in creativity or virtue than many other civilizations that arose around the world, even if many past and even present historians have thought so (for more about studying Western Civ, see the epilogue). This text will often point out where the West borrowed knowledge and when its moral virtue fell short of its proclaimed ideals. It also developed deeply contradictory ideas within itself, many of which still battle with each other today. Undoubtedly, the West became more powerful, becoming the dominant society of the contemporary world. To understand it is to comprehend how many of the globe's institutions, practices, and ideologies came to function as they do, for good or ill.

The word *Western* obviously reveals a strong geographical component. The name separates it from what might be considered northern, southern, or Eastern civilizations. While historians have not created a category for northern or southern civilizations, they used to apply the term *Eastern* (or *Oriental*, from the Latin for where the sun rises) to what they now prefer to call Asian civilizations (China and India, for example). Just as the name of the "Orient" comes from the place of the rising sun over the Eurasian landmass, the old-fashioned name for the West, the "Occident," derives from where the sun sets.

This book's narrative will show how a civilization that can be called "Western" began in the specific geographical area of **western Europe**, the northwestern extension of land from the vast landmass of Eurasia and Africa, bordered by the North Sea, the Mediterranean Sea, and the Atlantic. Its first inspirations lay in the

Middle East, the region including the river systems of the Tigris and Euphrates and the Nile. The core of its culture next developed around the Mediterranean Sea, until it shifted north into western Europe between fifteen hundred and a thousand years ago. There the key components of Western civilization finally jelled. About five hundred years ago, bearers of Western civilization began to conquer much of Eurasia and many overseas territories. The interactions of the West with other peoples around the world will decide the questions of where the West begins, endures, changes, or ends.

Just as geography defines the West, so does its chronology. Setting an exact starting date presents as many difficulties as setting its contemporary borders. One self-defining moment in Western tradition appears in its calendar, today accepted by many people around the world. The Western chronology has traditionally divided history into two periods, labeled with the initials **BC** and **AD**. These large periods mark the founding of Christianity by Jesus of Nazareth about two thousand years ago (see chapter 6). Most people can readily say BC means "before Christ," but fewer can explain that AD is the abbreviation for *anno Domini*, which means "in the year of the Lord" and refers again to Jesus of Nazareth. Many current history writers, apparently uncomfortable with the religious roots of our calendar, have switched to using the terms BCE and CE, meaning "before the common era" and "common era." These terms lack any historical content other than being placeholders for political correctness. No other event changed history around two thousand years ago to make any civilization more "common." This book's use of the terms BC and AD is not intended to privilege Christianity but merely recognizes the actual origins of our dating system.

Rather than this simple duality centered on Christianity, historians more sensibly divide the Western past into three or four periods. Ancient history (which includes prehistory) usually ends around AD 500. The Middle Ages then follow, ending any time between 1300 and 1789, depending on the historian's point of view. Then early modern history might begin as early as 1400 or as late as 1660 and last until either the modern or contemporary periods take over in the past few centuries. The year 1914 seems useful as a starting point for contemporary history because of the first modern world war. To make the past still more manageable, this book divides up the past into fifteen parts, or chapters (including this introduction and an epilogue to both sum up and point forward). The above dates and eras, of course, make sense only in relation to the history of Europe. Other civilizations need other markers, although historians often try to impose Western categories on world history.

This survey assigns the beginning of Western civilization to between fifteen and eleven hundred years ago, as western Europe recovered from the disaster of the collapse of its part of the Roman Empire. Understanding how this civilization built on previous human experiences, however, requires our reaching back beyond the fall of Rome to humanity's beginnings. Therefore, this particular book covers prehistory and the West's deep roots in the Middle East and Mediterranean regions. Sometimes coverage overlaps between chapters, and it certainly intensifies as it approaches the present, because recent events impact our lives more directly.

Chapter 2 lightly skims over several million years, while chapter 14 covers only a few decades.

Covering much of Western history in fifteen chapters requires careful selection of the most resonant information. This narrative touches on the basic topics of politics, economics, technology, society, culture, and intellectual cultural trends, depending on the historical period. This story does not deal as much with the everyday-life aspects of people in the past, such as how families lived in their homes, or what they ate. Five main topical themes regularly guide the flow: (1) control over nature through technological innovation, (2) the rise and fall of communities through migration and conquest, (3) disagreements about political and economic decision making, (4) conflicts about priorities in religion and government, and (5) proposals about the ultimate meaning of life. These topics have significantly affected the past and are still influential in the present.

This book, then, covers a lot of time, over a large part of the world, involving many human events. As a concise history, it necessarily leaves out a great deal. Historians are always making choices about what they want to study, what approach they take, and what stays in. As you learn more about history, you can choose for yourself what else to learn. For a beginning, this text should ground you in the basics of this civilization called the West.

Review: *How do historians study and divide up the past?*

Response:

WHAT IS TRUTH?

History is a human production. Every idea, institution, painting, document, movement, war, or invention originated with a human being. People believe in, fight for, kill for, and die for ideas. While natural forces such as floods, drought, and disease affect people and may influence the course of history, the survivors still must choose how to react to those disasters. No "force" works by itself to change history.

True power comes from people joined together. People usually organize themselves so that a few lead and most follow. Motivations for forming larger groups could include love, favoritism, hunger, greed, blood loyalty, defense of hearth and home, and cruelty. The variety of human experiences guarantees different points of view. The challenge for historians is to sort through those views and reach the best explanation of how history changes and what it should mean to us.

People write history. In this text's version of history, choices about what to include or exclude are shaped by the broad culture of the modern West, the personal judgment of recent professional historians, and the author. In today's modern culture, factions of citizens sharply disagree about politics, economics, science, and even the meaning of words.[6] Cultural guardians argue over which sets of facts and interpretations today's citizens and students should be required to learn. Communities disagree on how to honor or mourn the past with markers, statues, and memorials. Some differences are inevitable. The vast amount of possible information imposes selection, as do individual perspectives and agendas. As imperfect people select what goes into their history, the accounts will differ from one another.

Degrees of **subjectivity** versus **objectivity** affect any accurate version of the past. Objectivity is seeing events and ideas in an impartial way, while subjectivity involves a view ranging from **bias** (inclination toward a particular point of view) all the way to **prejudice** (dismissal of other points of view). Even the historian Herbert Butterfield referred to the "magnet in men's minds" that attracts only information that already aligns with a person's political and social inclinations. No one can entirely escape being somewhat subjective. Good historians strive toward objectivity, aware of their own inclinations. Historical relativism goes so far as to claim that no objectivity exists: actual truth is impossible to find. While most history has an agenda of supporting the dominant culture, relativists would promote better knowledge of oppressed and ignored people. Unfortunately for us all, few people really learn from history; most people use history only to confirm what they already believe.

This lack of perspective has always shaped or reflected the values of whole cultures. Different societies have seen their past according to shared grand concepts, sometimes called paradigms. In our Western civilization, the ancient Greeks, Romans, and Germans believed in both the intervention of divine beings and a powerful role of unchangeable fate. The rise and fall of people, or nations, followed according to the will of the gods. The Jews saw themselves as being chosen by one all-powerful God who reserved for them a special place in history. The Christians of the Middle Ages supposed that they were caught in a battle of good versus evil. They condemned to hell their enemies, even if those enemies were fellow Christians. Intellectuals during the Enlightenment reasoned that history obeyed unalterable laws of nature. In reaction, social Darwinists and nationalists embraced the jungle's competition of claw and fang and cheered on peoples warring against one another for supremacy. All of these versions of history's purpose made perfect sense to people at the time. Their histories usually glorified their own achievements and diminished their flaws. Nor are we in our time exempt from the limitations of our own points of view, which may one day seem quaint or even wrongheaded.

As for our view of the past today, the historical method gives us much of what actually happened, as much as it can be known. The trustworthiness of history

---

6. US president Bill Clinton (r. 1993–2001) famously responded to a question about knowledge of his extramarital affair: "It depends on what the meaning of 'is' is."

depends on whether it presents **fact**, **opinion**, or **myth**. Facts are those pieces of historical information that all reasonable people agree upon. They are the data of history, drawn from a serious examination of the sources. Once proved by historians, hard facts are the most reliable and least arguable information available. They come closest to anything we can call truth.

In recent years the entire concept of truth has come even more into question. Historians used to find it self-evident that our empirical observation of the world through our senses, the scientific and historical methods, and reasoned debate of various viewpoints would arrive at indisputable truth. The challenge of historical relativism was followed by the "linguistic turn" in philosophy and literature. Their ideas insisted that a source may be read one way superficially and officially, but when deconstructed it reveals hidden signs, meanings, and systems of discourses that explain both power and resistance to it.

These postmodern approaches seemed to question whether anything could be known for certain about history. Even more, modern neuroscience seems to indicate that an individual human brain cannot tell the difference between real or false memories. As these ideas filtered into the popular culture, those with political agendas have created their own historical discourse. Revisionism used to mean a good critical reexamination of sources and historical arguments in order to improve our understanding. Now it can mean attacking accepted historical events, such as those who deny the Holocaust or the moon landing or claim that Elvis is alive or that earth has been visited by space aliens.[7] Conspiracy theories are spread and fed by social media through the Internet. Most recently, even partisan government spokespeople deny obvious lies and errors with claims of "fake news" and "alternative facts."

Yet even those facts that are agreed upon as true mean little by themselves. Only when they have been selected and interpreted do they explain historical causation and significance. Facts become what people make them into. People may blow them out of proportion or neglect them into nonexistence. To use a metaphor, facts are the bricks of historical work. Hard and rough, they can be used to frame a hearth or build a wall, but they can also be tossed aside or thrown through a window. Because of gaps in historical preservation, many details will be missing. A historian who bothers to contemplate an ancient ruin has incomplete information, since bricks have been lost, destroyed, or perhaps never even made in the first place. In contrast, a historian reviewing recent history may have too much information, piles upon piles of construction materials. Either way, we cannot really see behind the façade of the source (see figure 1.1). We try to read the minds of people in the past, attempt to see through their eyes, but perfect clarity is impossible.

Historians construct opinions choosing from whatever sources are available. These opinions are their arguments and explanations about history. Almost all history writing today consists of opinions, which historians form as they challenge one

---

7. To be clear: there exists substantial and conclusive evidence that (1) Nazis during World War II carried out the systematic murdering of millions of Jews and others, and (2) American astronauts personally explored the lunar surface between 1969 and 1972. There exists no evidence that (1) Elvis Presley did not die partly from an overdose in 1977, and (2) almost no good evidence that extraterrestrials have buzzed the skies in flying saucers, landed on earth in their chariots of the gods, or are kept in Area 51.

Figure 1.1.   What appears to be a random pile of stones in the foreground is clearly organized in the background as a cairn or burial place. Four thousand years ago at Clava, now in Scotland, people stacked the foundations of these tombs and set up the standing stones in the background for a few of their dead. The doorway is oriented to face the rising sun on the first day of winter. What beliefs they associated with death, we do not know.

another about interpretations of the past. Opinions reveal the significance of the details and show how they mattered to people in the past or to us now. Arguments among historians with differing opinions help to keep them honest. To extend the metaphor, a historian may say that one set of bricks belongs to a palace, yet another historian, looking at the same bricks, might say they come from a fortress. Who is correct?

Without conclusive evidence (blueprints, foundations, illustrations, eyewitness accounts), disputes may remain tangled. Usually the weight of public opinion leans one way or another. People will choose facts and opinions written by respectable historians or adopt positions that flatter their belief systems. Sometimes, new insights might lead to an alternative suggestion, such as a compromise—a palace-fortress. Good historians are ready to change their opinions, given solid evidence and cogent argument. This author might conceivably rewrite and improve every sentence of this book to respond to new information in the future. Every new source provides new nuance. This changeableness is not inconsistency, dodging, or flip-flopping, but rather a result of sound judgment.

To provide some coherence to what would otherwise be only a string of facts, historians build themes around what they think changes the course of history. These paradigms, theories, or grand narratives help history give meaning, making sense of the past. Story arcs explain causation and significance in terms of the rise or decline of societies, crises or stability, the primacy of foreign or domestic policy, sex or power, or any number of drives and choices. Yet they can also obscure, simplify, and mislead.

Different historians offer competing narratives about specific points in the past and the grand sweep of time. This book's themes of supremacies and diversities help to explain our complex past. Supremacies focus on how the use of power dominates societies. Those who want *supremacy* usually seek stability, order, and consolidation. They also often seek to expand their power over others by using anything from warfare to ideologies. People react to such power by accommodating and transforming themselves in compliance or by resisting in public or covert ways. Power may flow from the top down, from rulers to subjects, or from the bottom up, from the masses to the leaders. *Diversity*, on the other hand, reflects the creative impulse that produces new ideas, as well as people's efforts to define themselves as different. Those who promote diversity create change, opportunity, and individuality.

These two trends do not necessarily oppose each other. They are not a version of dialectical materialism (see chapter 11). The opposite of supremacy is inferiority; the contrary of diversity is conformity. Nonetheless, both trends involve people excluding others who do not belong to the group. People who want supreme power usually demand **universalism**, applying the same beliefs and practices to everyone. They would promote **acculturation**, where one ethnic group conforms its culture to another. Likewise, people's frequent tendency toward diversity often encourages *particularism*, requiring that various ideas and activities differ according to location. In addition, the mixture of cultures may result in *syncretism*, where elements of one join or blend with another. A tension thus may arise between the supremacy desire for conformity and the diversity push for variety, or the two may align together. One or the other, or both, intermingle in different societies and ages. Whether applied to politics, culture, or society, supremacies and diversities offer a structure in which to illustrate historical conflict and change. They are not the only way to understand history, just this book's attempt to help make sense of facts and opinions about the past.

Explanations based on these facts and opinions can sometimes mutate into myths, which then complicate a historian's task. Myths are stories that give meaning to a society's existence. Because myths obscure the facts they draw on, they complicate understanding the past. People embrace myths as true because they make sense of a confusing world. Passed on from generation to generation, myths stubbornly exist beyond rational proof (see figure 1.2). These stories justify both the worst and the best behavior of individuals, societies, and states. The myths inherent in religion and the so-called lessons of history are problematic because they shape the meaning of life. Even religion, however, may not always offer clarity. For an example with real specifics (see chapter 6 for more context), in the Gospel of John, chapter 18, verse 37, translated from the Greek, the Roman procurator Pontius Pilate asks Jesus, "What is truth?" and does not get an answer.

Figure 1.2. This round stone disk is now called the Bocca della Verità (Mouth of Truth). Historians suggest that it was a sculpture representing Oceanus, ancient god of the seas, made during the Roman Empire, and served as a drain cover. In the Middle Ages someone brought it to a church in Rome, where it now serves as a tourist attraction (cinematically seen in the movie *Roman Holiday*). If one lies while putting one's hand in the mouth, the hand gets bitten off. How can that be true?

In striving for objectivity, many modern historians try not to favor one religion or belief system as being more true than any other. Indeed, the rational and empirical historical method cannot assert any religion's validity or falsity. Religion draws on the **supernatural**, which is beyond the limits of nature, to which historians are confined. Perhaps a religion might be true. But no one religion has ever objectively been proven real in all its supernatural aspects; otherwise most people would be convinced. Faith is there for those willing to believe, or not. The historian instead examines what the followers of any religion believed and, based on those beliefs, how they affected history.

People also want to believe good things about their own society. Thus, myths are often disguised as lessons learned from history. One should be cautious about them, since such myths are often too full of comforting pride. In particular, historical figures are often mythologized into heroes. Our own society promotes potent myths about figures such as Christopher Columbus, or George Washington, or Robert E. Lee that resist change in the face of reality. Most of Columbus's contemporaries knew the world was a globe; good evidence is lacking that Washington chopped down a cherry tree and confessed it to his father. These men might be notable, but their significance should not be based on stories that mislead. Even more tricky, from opposing points of view the heroes are switched to villains. For some Native Americans, Columbus began genocide. Washington is considered a traitor by some of the British, and some Americans believe Lee committed treason. Accurate portrayals of such figures require subtlety. Cracking open myths and examining their core is essential to learning from history.

The best history makes us self-critical, not self-congratulatory. Too often, someone's victory and satisfaction is someone else's defeat and suffering. Everyone joins in to take collective credit for victories, but resulting atrocities are blamed on isolated others. The American philosopher George Santayana wrote in 1905, "Those who cannot remember the past are condemned to repeat it." Since then, many have tried to learn from history but have nonetheless committed the same mistakes as their predecessors. While those who make history could not foresee the consequences of their actions, they should at least have been aware of contemporaries whose belief systems contradicted theirs. Learning history is dangerous, especially when opinions sprout into myths.

This text will regularly offer "basic principles," clear statements of obvious common historical behavior. They are not so much "lessons" of history as contradictions of common myths and suppositions (although there are always exceptions). They should challenge you to test them against historical experience. The first basic principle is:

> **There is no such thing as the "good ol' days," except in a limited way for a few people.**

People like to believe that there was once a golden age to which we should aspire to return. Whether in first-century Rome or eighteenth- and nineteenth-century Virginia, social elites have always proclaimed myths of their own supremacy to justify their status and power. Both Rome and Virginia, of course, benefited from enslaved people who did not enjoy the same luxuries as their masters. Plenty of privileged people have always led lives of comfort and calm. If they lost those privileges, then they could legitimately claim that a way of life once was better. A limited number of people in some places did benefit from the so-called good ol' days. Yet this good life of the few has often been based on the exploitation of a much larger number of other people.

From a broader perspective, looking at the entire sweep of human history, most people have always faced difficulties. We all face our own mortality. There has probably never been a day when one individual did not kill another somewhere or when one people did not fight against another people. Disease, hunger, natural disasters—these caused and still cause much misery. If people successfully confronted one moral dilemma, they failed in another. Each age has had its trials and tribulations, as well as its ecstasies and excitements.

The challenge for this book is making sense of the Western past for someone unfamiliar with its history, through the words of one particular author and the few translated voices of people from the past. As should be clear from the above discussion, no single view can be true for everyone, everywhere, forever. This historical account will regularly note the disputes, gaps, and disagreements of modern historians about specific interpretations. Like a reviewer of a book or film, this text both describes what happens and offers some value judgments. It often criticizes the flaws, failures, and contradictions inherent in the West. As the story unfolds, it points out the diverse options created during centuries of new ideas and practices by the many peoples that make up the West. Generalizations too often obscure detail and disagreement. Further reading and learning in history should reveal where this version is more or less objective, and what it has omitted or over-interpreted. In a comparatively few pages, though, it offers a starting point to understand the essential people, events, and ideas of the West.

Historians offer the hope that we can learn from history to improve ourselves. They write some things with certainty, much with confidence, and some with caution. The ultimate challenge for each of us is to form an opinion about history. Ask yourself: What can I learn that can give life more meaning? How can I make better decisions today based on the successes and failures of our ancestors? What knowledge of our heritage should I pass on to our descendants? This book offers some perspectives to help you answer those questions.

Review: *How can we evaluate history?*

Response:

PRIMARY SOURCE PROJECT 1: THUCYDIDES VERSUS VON RANKE ABOUT THE AIM OF HISTORY

Modern historians often credit the ancient Greek writer Thucydides with the first work of critical historical writing. His work called The Peloponnesian War *describes a conflict fought during his lifetime. Thucydides thought it the most significant of all wars up until then. In this passage, he describes his approach to writing the book. More than two thousand years later, the young Leopold von Ranke produced his work on other wars, fought four hundred years before his own lifetime. He began his study of people in the Renaissance of Latin and Germanic origin with a preface that called for a new, more methodological and neutral kind of historical writing.*

Source 1: *The Peloponnesian War* by Thucydides (ca. 400 BC)

Having now given the result of my inquiries into early times, I grant that there will be a difficulty in believing every particular detail. The way that most men deal with traditions, even traditions of their own country, is to receive them all alike as they are delivered, without applying any critical test whatever. . . .

So little pains do the vulgar take in the investigation of truth, accepting readily the first story that comes to hand. On the whole, however, the conclusions I have drawn from the proofs quoted may, I believe, safely be relied on. Assuredly they will not be disturbed either by the lays of a poet displaying the exaggeration of his craft, or by the compositions of the chroniclers that are attractive at truth's expense; the subjects they treat of being out of the reach of evidence, and time having robbed most of them of historical value by enthroning them in the region of legend. Turning from these, we can rest satisfied with having proceeded upon the clearest data, and having arrived at conclusions as exact as can be expected in matters of such antiquity. . . .

With reference to the speeches in this history, some were delivered before the war began, others while it was going on; some I heard myself, others I got from various quarters; it was in all cases difficult to carry them word for word in one's memory, so my habit has been to make the speakers say what was in my opinion demanded of them by the various occasions, of course adhering as closely as possible to the general sense of what they really said. And with reference to the narrative of events, far from permitting myself to derive it from the first source that came to hand, I did not even trust my own impressions, but it rests partly on what I saw myself, partly on what others saw for me, the accuracy of the report being always tried by the most severe and detailed tests possible. My conclusions have cost me some labor from the want of coincidence between accounts of the same occurrences by different eye-witnesses, arising sometimes from imperfect memory, sometimes from undue partiality for one side or the other. The absence of romance in my history will, I fear, detract somewhat from its interest; but if it be judged useful by those inquirers who desire an exact knowledge of the past as an aid to the interpretation of the future, which in the course of human things must resemble if it does not reflect it, I shall be content. In fine, I have written my work, not as an essay which is to win the applause of the moment, but as a possession for all time.

Source 2: *History of Roman and German Peoples from 1494 to 1535* by von Ranke (1824)

Some have claimed for history the aim to judge the past, to instruct us today for the benefit of future years. The present attempt does not dare to reach such high aims: it will merely state, how it actually was [*wie es eigentlich gewesen*].

Yet how could this be newly researched? The foundation of this present text, the origin of its material are memoirs, diaries, letters, diplomatic reports and original testimonies of eyewitnesses; other writings only either when they are directly derived from those sources, or through some original knowledge appear to be equivalent to them. Every page cites the relevant works; the manner of research and the critical results will be presented in a second volume, that will be published with the present one on the same day. . . .

Intention and material give rise to the form. One cannot expect from a history the free expression, which at least, in theory, one seeks in a poetical work. And I do not know whether with fairness one could believe such is found in the works of Greek or Roman masters. Strict description of the facts, as limited and uncomfortable as they may be, is without doubt the highest law. A second, for myself, was the development of unity and the sequence of events. Instead of, as might be expected, beginning with a general description of the political relationships in Europe (which might not have confused the perspective, but certainly would have distracted the focus), I have prioritized, from every people, every power, every particular, as they were, only then to describe them thoroughly, when they enter upon the stage as significantly active or leading. It does not worry me—for how could their existence have forever remained untouched?—that already ahead of time, here and there, they must be mentioned. In this manner at least the course, which they in general held, the path that they followed, the thoughts that moved them, could all the better be delineated.

Finally, what can one say about such treatment in detail, a so essential part of historical works? Will it not appear often hard, fragmented, bland, and tiresome? There exists for this problem noble models, both old—and not to be forgotten—also new; yet I have not attempted to imitate them: their world was another one. There exists an exalted ideal to strive toward: that is the event itself in its human dimension, its unity, its fullness. I know how far I have remained from that. What else is to say? One makes the effort, one strives, in the end one has not reached the goal. If only nobody would be impatient with that! The main thing is always, we are dealing with . . . humanity as it is, explainable or inexplicable: the life of the individual, the kinfolk, the people, at times with the hand of God over them.

Questions:

- *What kind of sources does each historian draw on and what is the difficulty with them?*
- *Against what kind of history does each historian write and toward what goal(s) does each historian aspire for his own work?*
- *How do these authors' comments illustrate the value of studying history?*

Responses:

Make your own timeline! Here is an example of information you could add to the blank timelines at the end of each chapter. Just write down terms, names, dates, whatever you think important, in chronological order. Do not worry about spacing or neatness—just get it down.

Citations

Thucydides. *History of the Peloponnesian War.* Translated by Richard Crawley. New York: E. P. Dutton, 1910, pp. 13–15.

von Ranke, Leopold. *Geschichten der romanischen und germanischen Völker von 1494 bis 1535.* Vol. 1. Leipzig and Berlin: G. Reimer, 1824, pp. v–viii. (Translated by Brian A. Pavlac.)

For more on these sources, go to http://www.concisewesternciv.com/sources/psc1a .html.

CHAPTER 9

Making the Modern World

The Renaissance and Reformation, 1400 to 1648

Already in the fifteenth century, some intellectuals had begun to claim that centuries of backwardness had given way to a "modern" age. All people, of course, believe they live in modern times, and they do. For historians, this transition to a "modern" time period, or even "early modern," reflects the changing elements of society, state, and culture compared with those of the Middle Ages and before. The key to this transition was a new appreciation for classical antiquity, the culture of ancient Greece and Rome. Historians have named that perception the **Renaissance**, meaning a rebirth of attitudes drawn from Græco-Roman culture. Classical antiquity had, of course, been appreciated to one degree or another since its collapse in the West a thousand years before. Beginning around 1400, however, a renewed interest in ancient history intertwined with economic, political, and religious developments. Reflecting on the past while sailing into the unknown, the Europeans traveled out of the later Middle Ages (ca. 1300–1500) and landed in the early modern period of history (ca. 1400–1815) (see timeline C).

THE PURSE OF PRINCES

As the Europeans recovered from the onslaught of the Black Death, the resurging economics of the towns propelled them into undreamed-of wealth and success. Amid plague and peasant rebellion, a dynamic idea later called *capitalism* began to catch on. Capitalism was a new form of economic practice that went beyond the markets of farmers or fairs. The "capital" of capitalism refers to a substantial amount of wealth that is available, and necessary, for investment. Many businesses require capital to begin operation or maintain themselves. One form of capital is profit, wealth left over after all expenses have been paid. When profits could be obtained, the practice of capitalism dictated what to do with them: reinvest.

In its simplest form, then, capitalism is reinvesting profits gained from invested capital. The usual human inclination is to spend excess wealth on showiness: fine homes, gourmet foods, parties, designer fashions, and grand edifices. One can, of course, give money away or bury it in the ground. Investing profit in one's own operations or in providing start-up and operating funds for another business, however, promoted long-term growth. Successful investments in turn created more profits, which then might be invested still further. Thus, capitalism became an engine for economic progress: wealth bred more wealth. Likewise, capitalism encouraged innovation. Clever investors looked for a new enterprise, a novel endeavor, which, if successful, would bring an even greater profit.

Only much later did historians and theorists use the exact term *capitalism*. Some historians also argue that other civilizations, either Muslim, Indian, or Chinese, practiced capitalism first and that westerners learned its techniques from them. Wherever it came from, more problematic is that people today often misunderstand the term *capitalism*. Many people often confuse capitalism with free markets. While capitalism requires markets (a space for people to exchange goods and services), they do not have to be entirely free (without restrictions imposed by authorities). This leads to another basic principle:

> **There is no such thing as an entirely free market; all markets have rules and costs.**

One of the key arguments among market participants, then and now, is how many regulations or fees there should be. One of the most important rules determines how much honesty is required between buyer and seller. If the market is an actual place, there are expenses for rent, cleaning, and upkeep. Many fees are taken by middlemen. The number of rules and expenses imposed on markets make them more or less free or fair. And breaking the rules meant punishment by law (see figure 9.1).

Another ongoing difficulty with capitalism has been when people lost their capital in financial markets. If a business venture failed, not only was there no profit, but the original capital could also disappear as well. Risk has always existed with capitalism—wealth can simply vanish into thin air. On the one hand, luck, creativity, and business acumen can create huge funds from a small incentive. On the other hand, irrational exuberance, misfortune, stupidity, and economic ignorance can just as easily destroy riches. Poor investors have lost vast assets. For example, a sudden mania for tulips in the Netherlands during the 1630s drove up prices many times their previous worth. At the most extreme, one exotic bulb for a garden cost the equivalent price of a mansion. When the bubble burst, tulip bulbs once again became merely potential flowers, that is, very affordable. Yet since early capitalists succeeded more often than they failed, the European economy grew over the long term. Capitalists may have accumulated most of the new wealth, but they also provided employment and opportunities for others to become wealthier. Indeed, capitalism helped make Western civilization the most powerful culture the world has ever known, during what historians have called the **Commercial Revolution** (1350–1600).

Figure 9.1.   This woodcut from a legal handbook (ca. 1500) shows the various punishments monarchs inflicted on criminals. Top row: cutting off an ear, preparation for dunking, disembowelment, burning alive at the stake, eye gouging, hanging. Bottom row: flaying, beheading, breaking with the wheel, cutting off a hand. (University of Pennsylvania)

The encouragement of innovation and the increase in wealth after the Black Death made medieval economic methods obsolete. The guild's hierarchical, regulated structure stifled progress, as measured by the creation of new forms of business. By definition, the guild promoted one kind of industry and opposed others. The masters who ran guilds increasingly seemed to want only to hold on to their power rather than seek improvements. While guilds had served to help medieval towns thrive, they were too inflexible to adapt to capitalism's drive for change.

The Commercial Revolution put in place more modern economic methods. Replacing the guild as the important structure for business was the partnership or firm. Usually this involved a family or several families pooling their resources to provide capital. As a business evolved, different members or alliances might come and go, which also encouraged creativity.

In the fourteenth century, families began to establish **banks**, the premier capitalist institution. The new banks evolved from benches of money changers into organizations that housed money and earned profits through finance. While bankers paid interest to attract depositors, the collection and safeguarding of deposits was merely a means to accumulate capital. Bankers invested assets as loans. A system of banks also allowed money to flow more easily from one part of Europe to another without actually lugging around boxes of gold bars and bags of silver coins.

Instead, banks issued bills of exchange, the forerunner of the modern check (the idea probably borrowed from Muslim trading partners). Commencing in Italy, bank branches sprang up in cities all over Europe.

This rise of finance as a major economic activity required some religious reform. Up to this time, most moneylending in the medieval West had been carried out by Jews, since Christians interpreted their own scriptures as declaring that making profit from money was sinful usury. But if both the borrower and the lender profited from each other, Christians rationalized that it was no sin. By the close of the Middle Ages, more materialistic church leaders had redefined the sin of usury to allow more lending so that they, too, could borrow to finance palaces and church building.

To keep track of all this wealth, money counters invented double-entry bookkeeping. Since ancient times, businesses had simply entered a running tally of incomes and expenses in paragraph form, if they kept records at all. This new method, much like any modern checkbook or bank statement, arranged the moneys into two columns, which could be easily added or subtracted; a third column tracked the running sum of overall credit or debt. Instead of Roman numerals of letters (I, V, X, L, etc.), the math was more easily done with "Arabic" numbers, which Muslims had borrowed from Hindus. Thus a merchant could better account for how much the business had on reserve or owed.

As in most economic revolutions, benefits and costs distributed themselves unevenly among varied social groups. People still earned wealth through agriculture, commerce, and manufacturing, but finance began its rise to predominance. As happens so often, the rich became richer while the poor became poorer. Women were encouraged to work, although in lower-status jobs at lower wages than men were paid for the same work. Women workers' low cost and the ease with which they could be fired helped businesses maintain their profit levels. A growing class of menial laborers piled up at the bottom of the social scale as well-paid family artisans lost out to cheap labor. The wealthiest merchants began to merge with the nobility, becoming indistinguishable from them in their manner of living except for titles and family trees of noble ancestors. As a whole, though, the overall affluence and standard of living in Western society rose.

Princes who took advantage of this economic boom became the monarchs of the late Middle Ages and early modern times. The practice of **public debt**, allowed by the new banking system, financed their expansion of power. Before capitalism, a prince's debts were considered his own—he had to finance them from his dynastic revenues. Although a prince's incomes were often quite substantial, they were limited by agricultural production and a few taxes on trade. The new idea of public debt meant that bankers could finance loans to the princes, and then all of the prince's subjects had to pay the loans off through taxes and customs duties on imports and exports. Throughout history, governments have raised taxes and piled on debt as much as they could get away with. Bankers usually supported this growing debt since they made a profit off the loans. Sometimes, a prince's debts grew too large, and through bankruptcy he defaulted on his debts. Then capital disappeared, followed by business failures and unemployment. More often, however, governments settled up their loans with interest, the bankers got their profits, and the princes became more powerful while the common people paid the price. A prince might also try to raise revenues by plundering a neighboring country, but that was shortsighted. Best was to annex another province, help it prosper, and tax it.

Such control over territories caused the **Hundred Years War** (1338–1453) between France and England. King Edward of England's Plantagenet dynasty wanted to protect some independence for Flanders (for wool) and preserve what few English territories remained in the southwest of France (for wine). The latter region, called Guyenne, was the last remaining French province of Henry II's empire (most of which his son John had lost in the thirteenth century). The kings of France wanted both Guyenne and Flanders for their own. A French dynastic crisis provided King Edward a pretext for war. King Philip IV "the Fair" had died in 1314, leaving three young sons. Within a few years, they had also died without leaving any male heirs in the Capetian dynasty—a situation France had not faced for more than three hundred years. The French aristocracy, without too much fighting, decided on Philip's grandnephew, who succeeded as King Philip VI, the first king of the Valois dynasty (1328–1589). Meanwhile, however, Edward of England claimed the throne of France as a grandson of Philip IV (although through Philip's daughter).

As the name implies, the Hundred Years War took generations to grind its way toward a conclusion. Along the way, war and politics changed decisively from medieval to modern. When the war began, knights still reigned supreme on the battlefield, as they had for centuries. Over time, however, weapon makers had concocted better ways of killing knights and of protecting them. They had also devised new ways to storm castles, while architects planned better ways to defend them. At the time of the Norman Conquest in 1066, knights wore chain mail (heavy coats of linked iron rings). By the middle of the Hundred Years War, jointed plate armor enveloped knights from head to toe. Castles in the eleventh century had been simple wooden forts on hills. By the fourteenth century, they had become elaborate stone fortresses with massive towers and high walls built in concentric circles and surrounded by deep ditches.

England perfected the use of two medieval weapons in its wars with its immediate neighbors. By the fifteenth century, the English had conquered the Welsh but continued to fight off and on in the north against the Scots. These border wars changed English military technology and tactics. The English adopted a unique weapon, the **longbow**. Originally used by the Welsh, the longbow was as tall as a man and required long training and practice to pull. It could pierce armor at four hundred paces and be reloaded more quickly than its only competitor, the crossbow. English skills with the longbow were so important that in 1349 the king banned all sports other than archery. English knights had also learned from fighting the Scottish William Wallace and Robert the Bruce to dismount from vulnerable horses and defend themselves and their archers with **pikes**, long spears of two or three times a man's height. Thus, foot soldiers once more returned as a powerful force on the battlefield, as had been the Greek/Macedonian phalanx.

During the Hundred Years War, the English raided France, devastating the countryside. French knights who tried to stop the raids took a while to realize that they no longer dominated combat. The English archers and dismounted knights wreaked havoc on French armored cavalry in three mighty battles: Crécy (1346), Poitiers (1356), and Agincourt (1415). Each battle turned the tide for the English and nearly led to the destruction of the French monarchy and kingdom. In the Treaty of Troyes (1420), King Henry V of England forced the French king to skip over the legitimate royal heir, holding the title of "Dauphin," and instead grant the succession to the future child of Henry V and his French princess-bride.

Henry's sudden death, however, saved the French. He left an infant heir, Henry VI (r. 1422–1461)—always a precarious situation, as family and others fought over guardianship. The English advantage might still have prevailed over the divided and demoralized French, but then the unique **Joan of Arc** (b. 1412–d. 1431) arrived to save the French kingdom. This lowborn teenager believed that the voices of saints and angels told her to help the uncrowned French prince, the Dauphin Charles. In 1429, Charles put her in shining armor at the head of a French army, which she "miraculously" led to victories over the English. Shortly after the Dauphin gained his crown as King Charles VII (r. 1429–1461), Joan was captured in battle. The French did nothing to rescue Joan, while the English put her on trial as a heretic. The crime of wearing men's clothing doomed her, because it meant she defied the authority of the church to control her. The English burned her alive at the stake and scattered her ashes.

Meanwhile, Charles VII cleverly used the ongoing English occupation of northern France to extort power from the French nobles and townspeople. In 1438, the Estates-General gave him the right to regularly collect taxes, such as those on salt or hearths. Everyone paid the salt tax, while the rich paid more of the hearth tax since their larger homes had more fireplaces. These revenues enabled Charles VII to raise a national, professional army paid by the government rather than one composed of feudal vassals, or hired mercenaries. Such a force had not fought in Europe since the time of the Roman legions. He also invested in the new-to-Europe technology of **gunpowder**, which had found its way from China by the fourteenth century. Charles VII's armies shot guns to punch holes in knights' armor and fired cannons to pound castles to rubble. The French finally drove the English back across the Channel.

The English did not cope well with this defeat. They did become more English, as the elites stopped speaking French, their language of choice since the Norman invasion. Their government, though, briefly spun out of control. When Henry VI turned out to be mentally unbalanced, factions formed to control him. These opposing groups eventually came to blows in civil wars called the **Wars of the Roses** (1455–1487). During these, one aristocratic alliance (Lancaster) lost to another (York), which in turn lost to a third (Tudor) in 1485. King Henry VII (r. 1485–1509) of the new **Tudor dynasty** (1485–1603) provided England with a strong monarchy, exploiting the desire of the English to return to political stability in alliance with the English Parliament. In Parliament's House of Commons, Henry bonded the English monarchy with the English middle class. The Tudor kings working with Parliament gave England a strong and flexible government, able to adapt to changing times.

While English and French kings reaffirmed their ascendance, the Holy Roman emperors slipped even further into impotence. Since the end of the Staufen dynasty in 1256, powerful dynasties had fought over who would succeed as Roman king and emperor, officially chosen by seven electoral princes. The Golden Bull of 1356 established an elective monarchy for the empire. This law strengthened the territorial princes, leaving the Holy Roman emperors more as figureheads than authoritarian rulers. The election of King Frederick III in 1438 offered some stability, although no one realized it at the time. His **Habsburg dynasty** (1438–1918) monopolized the royal and imperial title, with the briefest of interruptions, until the Holy Roman Empire's end in 1806.

Realistically, the Habsburgs' power and interests lay with their own dynastic lands: **Austria** and its neighbors. Effective rule of the rest of the empire remained beyond their grasp. Frederick's son and successor Maximilian (r. 1486–1519) found too little success in wars to expand imperial domination. The spiritual and secular princes, nobility, and free cities even set up a Diet (Reichstag), the German equivalent of Parliament or the Estates-General. Although the imperial office remained weak, marriages arranged for and by Maximilian added numerous territories to the Habsburg dynasty's possessions. His own first marriage brought him parts of Burgundy and the Lowlands after his father-in-law Duke Charles "the Rash" of Burgundy died in battle with the Swiss. Marriages of his children and grandchildren added Bohemia, Hungary, and even Spain. It was said of his dynasty, "Let others wage war for a throne—you, happy Austria, marry."

Looming on Maximilian's Hungarian border, the Ottoman Turkish Empire threatened to unsettle the self-satisfied princes of Christendom. The Seljuk Turks had weakened Byzantium in the eleventh century, leading to the crusades for the Holy Land. By the late thirteenth century, attacks from the Mongols and others had weakened Seljuk rule. The new Ottoman dynasty revived Turkish power. The dynasty (as well as plush, round footstools) was named after its founder, Osman or Othman (d. 1324), who started as one more *bey*, or leader among many Turks in Asia Minor. He and his troops served at first as mercenaries, called into Europe by Byzantine Greeks as they fought with each other and with Serbians, Bulgarians, Genoese, Venetians, and Latin Crusaders in Greece. The Byzantine Empire had ceased to be innovative. Its armies could not defend its shrinking territory, whose tax base was needed to pay for the large imperial bureaucracy.

A decisive moment came in 1354, when the Ottomans seized a permanent base in Gallipoli on the Dardanelles, south of Constantinople, in Europe. From there, Ottoman armies with *ghazi* (religious warriors) expanded in two directions, into southeastern Europe and across Asia Minor. The Ottomans soon took the title of sultans, given to powerful Muslim rulers second in rank only to the caliphs. They aspired to be caliphs themselves.

Southeastern Europe fell under the rule of Turkish Muslims. One conquest was the dual province Bosnia-Herzegovina, where the Bogomils had built up a heretical kingdom united by the dualistic religion of Catharism. Once the Turks had taken Bosnia-Herzegovina, many of the Slavs there converted to Islam. Next the Turks crushed the Serbian kingdom at the Battle of Kosovo Polje (28 June 1389), a site also called the Field of the Blackbirds (after the winged scavengers who fed on the innumerable corpses of Christian warriors). Most of the divided Bulgarian Empire quickly collapsed. A crusading army with troops from western Europe actually tried to confront the Ottoman danger. The Turks slaughtered those crusaders at Nicopolis in Bulgaria (1396), the fleeing Christian knights cutting off the fashionably long tips of their shoes in order to run away more quickly.

The few remaining unconquered Byzantine territories gained a respite when the Ottomans were attacked by the great conqueror Tamerlane, or Timur "the Lame," of Samarkand in central Asia (b. 1336–d. 1405). His reputation for slaughter surpassed that of the Huns or the Mongols. Timur's defeat of the Ottoman armies in 1402 almost ended the dynasty. Three years later, however, Timur was dead, and his empire crumbled.

The Ottoman Empire reconsolidated and expanded. Jews, Orthodox Christians, Muslims, Greeks, Turks, Slavs, Arabs, and Armenians were organized into efficient groups that provided troops and taxes. The Ottomans organized interconnected bureaucracies to manage the diverse peoples and widespread territories. The Ottoman armies also relied on young Christian boys taken from the conquered lands and trained to be expert warriors called janissaries. The Ottoman sultans finally assumed the ancient title of caliph, the religious and political leader of all (Sunni) Muslims. After crushing another crusading army at Varna on the Black Sea in 1444, the Turks besieged Constantinople, the last remnant of the once-mighty Roman Empire. The massive cannons of Mohammed or Mehmet II "the Conqueror" (r. 1451–1481) shelled the city for weeks. Defeat was only a matter of time as the walls became rubble. A Byzantine soldier who forgot to close a door through the walls, though, opened the way to a speedy defeat. The last Byzantine emperor died among his troops, defending the once-impregnable walls. Thus fell the Byzantine or Roman Empire, once and for all, in 1453.

Mehmet II made Constantinople his new imperial capital, which came to be called Istanbul (from the Greek for "to the City"). He rebuilt and repopulated it (although no one told the Turks about the many underground cisterns that had been used to supply the city with water since Roman times). The Ottomans conquered diverse peoples in the Middle East and North Africa. In 1526, the Turks then seized much of Hungary from the Austrian Habsburgs. The Ottomans were then ready to advance into the Holy Roman Empire itself and perhaps from there conquer all of Christendom.

By 1600, the Ottomans were equal in power, wealth, and creativity to any of the Europeans (see figure 9.2). Their empire proved its success by conquering huge swathes of territory in the Middle East and North Africa. On the one hand, they allowed people to keep their ethnic identities while welcoming conversions to Islam or becoming more ethnically Turkish. On the other hand, they sometimes exploited ethnic conflicts to maintain their rule, encouraging minorities to dislike one another rather than their masters. Either way, the Ottoman Empire provided a powerful rival to the West.

The victories of the Ottomans ended any medieval dream of a united Christendom. Meager attempts by crusaders to help the Byzantine Empire and other Balkan Christians failed miserably. Western popes and princes worked against one another rather than against the common enemy. The various monarchs were looking out for their own narrow dynastic interests first. Western civilization remained in the hands of diverse petty and grand states of Europe.

Figure 9.2.   The Blue Mosque dominating the skyline of Istanbul reflects the glory of the Ottoman Empire around 1600.

Once the notion of a universal Christendom was gone, so was a key component of what had defined the Middle Ages. No one precise moment, event, or battle marks the transition when medieval became modern history. Today, some historians even argue that medieval times lingered into the seventeenth and eighteenth centuries. Transformations in thought and belief, however, further turned the West away from the medieval construct of priests, knights, and peasants. Indeed, Western civilization was becoming the most powerful society in world history.

Review: *How did late medieval monarchs concentrate still more power?*

Response:

MAN AS THE MEASURE

Cities in the Italian Peninsula led the way in ending the Middle Ages. Rich cities in the northern half had been prizes for foreign powers such as German kings and emperors ever since Pippin "the Short" and Otto "the Great." The economic revival of the High Middle Ages allowed cities founded by the Romans, such as Genoa, Pisa, and Venice, to expand and flourish once more. They prospered from trade and finance, persevered through politics and warfare, and won independence from both German emperors and Roman popes. They interacted with Byzantines, Turks, Arabs, and even Mongols.

Self-government was difficult, however. Strained by economic change, citizens easily fought among themselves over control of elections and laws. Class warfare between the wealthy merchants, prosperous artisans, and the poor strained the peace of the towns. In desperation for some order, tyrants known as despots seized power in many Italian towns during the later Middle Ages. These despots started as local nobles, merchants, or even mercenaries (called *condottieri* in Italian). Since these dictators removed at least one source of strife—namely, the struggle for leadership—the citizens often tolerated them, just as had happened in ancient Greece and Rome. Some despots managed to establish dynasties. Thus, these new Italian princes often cut short the towns' initial experiments in democratic, republican government.

A successful despot might provoke war across the Italian Peninsula, seeking for his city-state to dominate others. Ambitious princes began to conquer their neighboring towns, urged on by merchants wanting to eliminate competitors. The Peace of Lodi in 1454, however, granted the entire peninsula a brief respite. For the next four decades, the five great powers upheld a fragile peace. In the south, the Kingdom of Naples was the largest in area, but it was weakened by struggles over the throne between the foreign houses of Anjou (from France) and Aragon (from the Iberian Peninsula). In the center of the Italian Peninsula, the Papal States were bound loosely under the authority of the pope. Just north of Rome, in Tuscany, **Florence** dominated all its immediate neighbors (see figure 9.3). In the northwest,

Figure 9.3. The Renaissance dome of Florence's medieval cathedral rises above the rest of the city.

Milan ruled the plains of Lombardy. Finally, in the northeast, the maritime power of Venice put down a strong foothold on the mainland, adding to its other possessions stretching along the eastern coast of the Adriatic and into the Aegean Sea. Venice's unique government was an oligarchy of the most powerful merchants, who dominated their elected ruler, called the doge.

This balance of power in the Italian Peninsula ended in 1494, when the French king Charles VIII as heir of Anjou invaded to claim the Kingdom of Naples. Charles's invasion sparked decades of war throughout the peninsula (and spread a new, nasty form of the sexually transmitted disease syphilis, which may have come from the Americas, although it was commonly called the "French" disease). Wars proliferated while French kings, German emperors, Spanish monarchs, and Italian despots fought for supremacy. In the midst of these wars, over several generations, European culture left the Middle Ages and entered the early modern period of history.

The cultural shift called the Renaissance (ca. 1400–1600) also helped push Europe into modernity. The Renaissance started in Florence. While figuring out how best to succeed in their political challenges, the Florentines sought inspiration from the Greeks and Romans of ages past. They could afford spending the time and money to revive humanism from classical antiquity because of the wealth generated from their new capitalist banks. At first, humanism had merely meant an interest in "humane letters" or the reading of classical writers. Inspired by the poet Petrarch (b. 1304–d. 1374), intellectuals had begun to scour old monastic libraries for ancient manuscripts. They edited what they found, creating the intellectual tool of ***textual criticism***—comparing different versions of an author's writings found in manuscripts written by hand at different times in different places in order to recover the best, most accurate text. One famous example is Lorenzo Valla's discourse disproving in 1444 the so-called Donation of Constantine. To the disgruntlement of the church, Valla demonstrated that the document allegedly recording the Roman emperor's gift of secular power to the papacy was a forgery.

Emphasis on the Latin literature of Rome soon led these humanists to appreciate the importance of the Greek language and literature. During the Middle Ages, knowledge of Greek had been virtually lost. The phrase "It's all Greek to me" came about because medieval readers could not decipher passages of Greek quoted by ancient Roman writers. Drawing on help from scholars fleeing the collapsing Byzantine Empire, the Western curriculum expanded to include the literature of ancient Greece. While today literature in the vernacular (that spoken by the common people), like the Italian poetry of Petrarch, is more highly valued, the ancient classics in "dead" Greek and Latin were the focus of Renaissance intellectuals.

Florence's **Medici** family played a key role in supporting this intellectual revival after they took over that city's leadership. They had risen to power in local government financed by their family banking business. Over time, the Medicis survived urban rebellions, assassination plots, invasions, and banishment to found their own aristocratic dynasty. Along the way, they aspired to be patrons of the arts, those who fostered creative interaction with Greece and Rome.

On an intellectual level, Renaissance Neoplatonic philosophers reinterpreted the ideas of Plato. On a visual level, artists drew inspiration from styles of classical art and created the new painting, architecture, and sculpture of Renaissance art.

Artists such as Leonardo da Vinci, Michelangelo, and Raphael pioneered a new naturalism in painting and sculpture that emphasized a realistic view of the world and the human body (see figure 9.4). The one error they made was assuming the ancients left their marble statues unpainted and white. As a result the polychromy so popular in medieval sculpture vanished. On a literary level, intellectuals eagerly sought and read authors from classical antiquity.

One such intellectual was Niccolò **Machiavelli**. At the beginning of the sixteenth century, Machiavelli had himself been tortured and exiled from Florence for

Figure 9.4.   In this selection from the fresco of the School of Athens in the Vatican, Raphael portrays Leonardo da Vinci as Plato in the center left and Michelangelo as the architect leaning on the block in the foreground. The majestic setting and the many other great thinkers from classical antiquity reflect the Renaissance fascination with Greece and Rome. (Art Resource)

supporting the wrong political faction. In those times, suspicion of disloyalty to rulers meant having one's arms jerked out of the sockets on a torture device called the *strappado*, a modified pulley. During his exile from the city, Machiavelli consoled himself every night by reading ancient writers of Greece and Rome. Inspired by them (and to win the favor of the Medici), he wrote **The Prince** (1513). This book combined examples of classical antiquity and contemporary politics. It offered advice on how a prince should hold on to power in an occupied territory, suggesting that a ruler's primary goal ought not to be virtue, as political writers had been propounding through the Middle Ages. Instead, a prince was to wield power, using force and fear, lying or largesse, as long as he did not become hated. Many readers claimed to be shocked by this "Machiavellian" advice for amoral political behavior freed from the constraints of Christian morality. In secret, though, most princes and politicians have admired how Machiavelli accurately described brutal power politics. He aimed to end the diversity of Italian principalities by uniting them under one powerful prince. All his practical suggestions were grounded in his humanist scholarship of antiquity.

A major boost to the humanist scholarly enterprise was the invention of the **printing press** in Germany around 1450. Using a few hundred molded pieces of movable type, any sheet of text could be reproduced much more cheaply, easily, and quickly than the laboriously handwritten page of every single book in Europe up to that moment.[1] The multiplication of books further encouraged the expansion of literacy, since more publications gave more people more writing to read.

This flood of printed materials also helped spur a change in education, giving rise to new kinds of schools. The sons of nobles and wealthy townspeople, after getting an education in a primary or "grammar" school, then attended secondary schools. These advanced institutions went beyond the primary education of reading, writing, and arithmetic, but not so far as the serious scholarly study offered by the "higher education" of colleges and universities. In these secondary schools (the forerunners of American high schools), students further refined their knowledge of the classical curriculum of the liberal arts. Through reading ancient Latin and Greek authors, a student was supposed to learn how to be worthy of liberty. The well-rounded gentleman, an individual fit in mind and body, became the Renaissance ideal.

Compared to that of men, the place of women, genteel or not, remained much more restricted. Ladies were to be respected, but few opportunities opened for their advancement. Lack of access to schools and the inability to control property remained the norm. Only a rare individual like **Christine de Pisan** (b. 1363–d. ca. 1430) could make her living from writing. Widowed and with children to support, Christine managed to market her books on history, manners, and poetry to rich male patrons in France and England. She remained an isolated example of the successful woman, unfairly forgotten soon after her death. Society still measured

---

1. Printing with woodblocks, and even movable type made of wood, clay, or bronze, began centuries earlier in China and Korea. The thousands of ideograms necessary for printing limited the usefulness of the technology compared to the flexibility and cost saving offered by Western alphabets, which only had a few dozen letters.

success by a man's achieving his material best, crafting for himself a place of honor in this world. The "Woman Question" began to be asked, although the usual answer was that women remained inferior to men.

Perhaps the greatest writer of the Renaissance, if not of all time, was the English actor, poet, and playwright **William Shakespeare** (b. 1564–d. 1616). The subjects of his plays ranged over histories (such as *Henry IV* and *Henry V*), comedies (such as *Twelfth Night* and *A Midsummer Night's Dream*), and tragedies (such as *Hamlet* and *Macbeth*). His writing captures in poetry and action a sense of universal human drama and character, drawing heavily on the classics. During his lifetime, acting companies built the first public theaters since classical antiquity, including his Globe Theater in London. Theaters soon appeared in European cities, where actors revived plays from ancient writers, adapted to new audiences.

With all this focus on success in the world, the humble path of Christ seemed somehow less attractive. Yet, as Renaissance ideas spread from Italy to northern Europe, many scholars in England, the Lowlands, and Germany did bend human-ism to a more Christian view. This **Christian humanism** still emphasized the clas-sics, using one's critical mind, and taking action in the world, but it added an interest in the writings of the Christian faith. Thus, along with Latin and Greek, Christian humanists learned Hebrew in order to read both the Old Testament in its original language and the writings of rabbi commentators.

The most famous Christian humanist was **Erasmus** (b. 1466–d. 1536). He sought to promote the best, most pure form of Christianity as he understood it from his reading in the New Testament and the writings of the early church fathers. His humanist outlook gave him a mocking attitude to authority. In his *Praise of Folly* (1509), Erasmus satirized all the problems of his contemporaries, especially the hypocrisies and failures of the Western Latin Church. Questioning authority became an important intellectual tradition, although authorities have never taken kindly to it.

Although Renaissance humanists encouraged a more critical look at the world, Erasmus and many of his contemporaries credulously accepted and promoted dan-gerous changes in beliefs about witches and witchcraft (see Primary Source Project 9). Historians have yet to fully understand how and why the fear of witchcraft began during the Renaissance. Prior to 1400, the usual position of the church had been that witches did not exist. The church taught that anyone claiming to be a witch was a dupe of the devil, and any supposed magic spells were meaningless decep-tions. After 1400, however, many western church authorities changed their opin-ions to say that a real conspiracy of witches existed, organized by the devil as a vital threat to Christian society. Actually, no reliable evidence remains that any such organized plot existed or that any magic spells have ever succeeded against anyone.

Regardless, many ecclesiastical and secular leaders began the **witch hunts** (1400–1800), actively seeking out suspected witches, torturing them into confess-ing impossible crimes, and then executing them. Like the ancient Roman persecu-tion of Christians, the hunts were sporadic, intermittent, and geographically scattered: worst in the Holy Roman Empire; moderate in France, Scotland, and England; and rare in the rest of Europe. Nevertheless, tens of thousands died, with more untold numbers submitting to false accusations, having loved ones perse-cuted, or suffering from pervasive fear. Authorities most often accused older women living on the margins of society, yet also younger women, men, and even children fell victim to suspicions.

These witch hunts ended once leaders no longer believed in the reality of dia-bolic magic. Fewer bouts of bad weather, the rising power of the state, improving economies, and more rational attitudes promoted by the Renaissance, the Scientific Revolution, and the Enlightenment (see below and chapter 11) all contributed. By the eighteenth century, most leaders, both religious and political, had once more come to the sensible view that witches and witchcraft were imaginary and no threat. The witch hunts reveal a tension between secular and religious values. The Renais-sance encouraged humanist values of questioning settled religious dogma.

While scholars studied the classics and certain magistrates hunted witches, reli-gious leaders began to rethink the accepted tenets of medieval faith. The new, more worldly emphasis of humanism deviated from the basics of medieval Christianity. Humanism prioritized this world; Christianity, the next. Most people in Chris-tendom still found meaning and purpose in their faith. The ongoing need of many people for religious certainty soon broke the unified religious system of the Middle Ages. Just as westerners accepted and fought for separate political states, they embraced and died for divided religious sects.

Review: *How did the Renaissance promote the West's transition into modernity?*

Response:

PRIMARY SOURCE PROJECT 9: WITCH HUNTER VERSUS CONFESSOR ABOUT BELIEF IN WITCHES

The age of the Renaissance and Scientific Revolution was also the time of the witch hunts. In the first source, an ecclesiastical official involved in hunting describes how far persecutions had gone in a German princedom. In contrast, a priest who heard the last confessions of people condemned for witchcraft came to a very different conclusion. In his book titled in Latin Cautio Criminalis *(Warning about Criminal Procedure), Friedrich Spee harshly criticizes the process and belief sys-tem. While he had to publish his book anonymously out of fear of retribution, his arguments soon helped stop the hunts.*

Source 1: "Report on Witch-Hunts" by the Chancellor of the Prince-Bishop of Würzburg (1629)

As to the affair of the witches, which Your Grace thinks brought to an end before this, it has started up afresh, and no words can do justice to it. Ah, the woe and the misery of it—there are still four hundred in the city, high and low, of every rank and sex, nay, even clerics, so strongly accused that they may be arrested at any hour. It is true that, of the people of my Gracious Prince here, some out of all offices and faculties must be executed: clerics, electoral councilors and doctors, city officials, court assessors, several of whom Your Grace knows.

There are law students to be arrested. The Prince-Bishop has over forty students who are soon to be pastors; among them thirteen or fourteen are said to be witches. A few days ago a Dean was arrested; two others who were summoned have fled. The notary of our Church consistory, a very learned man, was yesterday arrested and put to the torture. In a word, a third part of the city is surely involved. The richest, most attractive, most prominent, of the clergy are already executed. A week ago a maiden of nineteen was executed, of whom it is everywhere said that she was the fairest in the whole city, and was held by everybody a girl of singular modesty and purity. She will be followed by seven or eight others of the best and most attractive persons. . . . And thus many are put to death for renouncing God and being at the witch-dances, against whom nobody has ever else spoken a word.

To conclude this wretched matter, there are children of three and four years, to the number of three hundred, who are said to have had intercourse with the Devil. I have seen put to death children of seven, promising students of ten, twelve, fourteen, and fifteen. Of the nobles—but I cannot and must not write more of this misery. There are persons of yet higher rank, whom you know, and would marvel to hear of, nay, would scarcely believe it; let justice be done. . . .

P.S.—Though there are many wonderful and terrible things happening, it is beyond doubt that, at a place called the Fraw-Rengberg, the Devil in person, with eight thousand of his followers, held an assembly and celebrated mass before them all, administering to his audience (that is, the witches) turnip-rinds and parings in place of the Holy Eucharist.

There took place not only foul but most horrible and hideous blasphemies, whereof I shudder to write. It is also true that they all vowed not to be enrolled in the Book of Life, but all agreed to be inscribed by a notary who is well known to me and my colleagues. We hope, too, that the book in which they are enrolled will yet be found, and there is no little search being made for it.

Source 2: Selection from *Cautio Criminalis* by Friedrich Spee (1631)

1. Incredible among us Germans and especially (I blush to say it) among Catholics are the popular superstition, envy, libels, calumnies, insinuations, and the like, which, being neither punished by the magistrates nor refuted by the pulpit, first stir up suspicion of witchcraft. All the divine judgments which God has threatened in Holy Writ are now ascribed to witches. No longer does God or nature do anything, but witches everything.

2. Hence it comes that all at once everybody is clamoring that the magistrates proceed against the witches—those witches whom only their own clamor has made seem so many.

3. Princes, therefore, bid their judges and counselors to begin proceedings against the witches.

4. These at first do not know where to begin, since they have no testimony or proofs, and since their conscience clearly tells them that they ought not to proceed in this rashly. . . .

7. At last, therefore, the Judges yield to their wishes, and in some way contrive at length a starting-point for the trials. . . .

10. And yet, lest it appear that [Gaia, a name for the accused] is indicted on the basis of rumor alone, without other proofs, as the phrase goes, lo a certain presumption is at once obtained against her by posing the following dilemma: Either Gaia has led a bad and improper life, or she has led a good proper one. If a bad one, then, say they, the proof is cogent against her; for from malice to malice the presumption is strong. If, however, she has led a good one, this also is none the less a proof; for thus, they say, are witches wont to cloak themselves and try to seem especially proper.

11. Therefore it is ordered that Gaia be haled away to prison. And lo now a new proof is gained against her by this other dilemma: Either she then shows fear or she does not show it. If she does show it (hearing forsooth of the grievous tortures wont to be used in this matter), this is of itself a proof; for conscience, they say, accuses her. If she does not show it (trusting forsooth in her innocence), this too is a proof; for it is most characteristic of witches, they say, to pretend themselves peculiarly innocent and wear a bold front.

12. Lest, however, further proofs against her should be lacking, the Commissioner has his own creatures, often depraved and notorious, who question into all her past life. This, of course, cannot be done without coming upon some saying or doing of hers which evil-minded men can easily twist or distort into ground for suspicion of witchcraft.

If, too, there are any who have borne her ill will, these, having now a fine opportunity to do her harm, bring against her such charges as it may please them to devise; and on every side there is a clamor that the evidence is heavy against her. . . .

14. And so, as soon as possible, she is hurried to the torture, if indeed she be not subjected to it on the very day of her arrest, as often happens.

15. For in these trials there is granted to nobody an advocate or any means of fair defense, for the cry is that the crime is an exceptional one, and whoever ventures to defend the prisoner is brought into suspicion of the crime—as are all those who dare to utter a protest in these cases and to urge the judges to caution; for they are forthwith dubbed patrons of the witches. Thus all mouths are closed and all pens blunted, lest they speak or write. . . .

19. Before she is tortured, however, she is led aside by the executioner, and, lest she may by magical means have fortified herself against pain, she is searched, her whole body being shaved, although up to this time nothing of the sort was ever found. . . .

21. Then, when Gaia has thus been searched and shaved, she is tortured that she may confess the truth, that is to say, that she may simply declare herself guilty; for whatever else she may say will not be the truth and cannot be. . . .

24. Without any scruples, therefore, after this confession she is executed. Yet she would have been executed, nevertheless, even though she had not confessed; for, when once a beginning has been made with the torture, the die is already cast—she cannot escape, she must die.

25. So, whether she confesses or does not confess, the result is the same. . . .

31. . . . It would be a disgrace to her examiners if when once arrested she should thus go free. Guilty must she be, by fair means or foul, whom they have once but thrown into bonds. . . .

37. Wherefore the judges themselves are obliged at last either to break off the trials and so condemn their own work or else to burn their own folk, aye themselves and everybody. For on all soon or late false accusations fall, and, if only followed by the torture, all are proved guilty.

38. And so at last those are brought into question who at the outset most loudly clamored for the constant feeding of the flames. For the fools rashly failed to foresee that their turn, too, must inevitably come—and by a just verdict of Heaven, since with their poisonous tongues they created us so many witches and sent so many innocents to the flames. . . .

46. From all this there follows this result, worthy to be noted in red ink: that, if only the trials be steadily pushed on with, there is nobody in our day, of whatsoever sex, fortune, rank, or dignity, who is safe, if he have but an enemy and slanderer to bring him into suspicion of witchcraft. . . .

Questions:

- *How does each writer define the problem about witches?*
- *What specific details does each writer use to explain the problem with witches?*
- *How does each writer hope to solve the problem?*

Responses:

Citations

"VII. The Witch-Persecution at Würzburg." In *Translations and Reprints from the Original Sources of European History*, vol. 3, *The Witch Persecutions*, edited by George L. Burr. Philadelphia: University of Pennsylvania Press, 1912, pp. 28–29.

"VIII. The Methods of the Witch-Persecutions." In *Translations and Reprints from the Original Sources of European History*, vol. 3, *The Witch Persecutions*, edited by George L. Burr. Philadelphia: University of Pennsylvania Press, 1912, pp. 30–35.

For more on these sources, go to http://www.concisewesternciv.com/sources/psc9a .html.

HEAVEN KNOWS

A religious revolution called the **Reformation** (1517–1648) fractured the medieval unity of the Christian church in the West beyond recovery. The Reformation first addressed the church's role in the plan of salvation. Yet the Reformation also reflected the ongoing political, economic, and social changes created by Europe's growing wealth and power. The calls for reform in the Western Latin Church had been long and loud since the Great Western Schism had divided the papacy between 1378 and 1417. With the concept of conciliarism crushed, calls for reform went unheeded. The papacy's long avoidance of reform made the Reformation more divisive than it might have been.

Some believers still found comfort and hope in many of the rituals and practices of the medieval church: sacraments (from baptism through the mass to final unction), pilgrimages and shrines, saints' days, the daily office, hospices, and hospitals. An increasingly popular mysticism (the idea that people could attain their own direct experience of God) led some to question the value of a priestly hierarchy. Religious women such as the recluse Julian of Norwich (d. 1416) or the wandering housewife Margery Kempe (d. 1438) continued the practice of Hildegard of Bingen by sharing vivid and novel visions of their interactions with God.

But the church's worldly interventions also alienated many. Popes had not lived down the scandals of the Avignon exile and the Great Western Schism. Even worse, the Renaissance wars in Italy led many to consider the pope to be a typical petty prince rather than a potent moral force and spiritual leader. Christendom watched scandalized as the popes deepened their political rule over the Papal States in central Italy. Papal armies were commanded first by Cesare Borgia for his father, Pope Alexander VI (r. 1492–1503), and later by a pope himself, Julius II (r. 1503–1513). Popes played power politics and lived in pomp as princes. Thus, many Christians gradually grew disillusioned with a papal monarchy. Rome seemed to represent the obstacle to reform.

A successful call for reform rose in an obscure and unexpected place: the small town of Wittenberg in the Holy Roman Empire. There, **Martin Luther** (b. 1483–d. 1546), the simple son of prosperous Saxon peasants, had risen to be a professor at the university. Additionally, Luther dedicated himself to monastic discipline in a house of Augustinian canons regular (sometimes called Austin Friars). Finally, Luther served as the pastor of a local parish church.

As a pastor, Luther became increasingly disturbed when his poor parishioners bought **indulgences** from traveling salesmen. Indulgences had originally developed out of the Western Latin Church's sacramental system of penance. When one committed sin, the church taught, one had to do penance, such as some good deed, prayers, or a pilgrimage. Toward the later Middle Ages, some clever clerics suggested that instead of having a penitent take the time and trouble for a complicated and expensive pilgrimage to Rome, why not just have that person pay the comparable amount of cash instead? Consequently, the Western Latin Church gained money, which it could use for anything it wished. Granted, the church did officially insist that indulgences could not forgive sin unless the purchaser was truly contrite. Nevertheless, the sales pitch by indulgence sellers often overlooked that quibble. Encouraged to buy these fill-in-the-blank forms, people believed that their sins (or those of their dead friends or relatives) were instantly pardoned: a popular saying went, "When the coin in the coffer rings, the soul from purgatory springs."

In Luther's home province of Saxony, the local prince-archbishop of Magdeburg had authorized a vigorous sale of indulgences. The archbishop's share of the profits paid off his debts to the pope, who had suspended canon law so that the archbishop could take possession of more than one prince-bishopric. The pope needed these funds to help build the new Renaissance-style St. Peter's Basilica on the Vatican Hill. This new edifice, the largest church building the world had yet seen, designed by the great artist Michelangelo, replaced the crumbling twelve-hundred-year-old structure built under Constantine.

Ignorant of these back-door financial deals, Martin Luther nevertheless developed his own objections to indulgences. In his own studies of the faith, he began to question the entire concept of indulgences within the plan of salvation. For Luther, sin seemed so pervasive and powerful that he felt any normal means of penance could not erase its stain on the soul. No matter how many good works he undertook or how much he attended church, Luther worried that sin made him unworthy to enter the perfection of heaven. In comparison, he felt like a lump of manure. Luther broke through his dilemma with a revelation upon reading Romans 1:17: "The just shall live by faith." He proposed that a person is assuredly saved, or justified, simply by the belief in the death and resurrection of Jesus Christ. For Luther, worship was to be a moment of faith, not a process of rituals and ceremonies. And if faith alone justified sinners, then the sacraments provided by the ordained priestly hierarchy of the church were unnecessary. Hence, Luther's declaration of "justification by faith alone" undermined the dominant position of the chief priest, the pope, as an arbiter of salvation.

Luther offered his **Ninety-Five Theses**, or arguments, about his developing theological point of view. According to tradition, he posted them on the door of the Wittenberg church on 31 October 1517. Publishers printed these theses and spread them with amazing rapidity across Christendom. Luther became the hero and voice for those who wanted to reform the Western Latin Church.

The church hierarchy largely dismissed his ideas and sought to shut him up. When the pope finally excommunicated Luther in June 1520, the defiant reformer publicly burned the papal bull along with the books of the canon law, thus dismissing the entire structure of the church. The newly elected Holy Roman emperor **Charles V** Habsburg (r. 1519–1556) then convened a Diet in the city of Worms to consider the situation. At the 1521 **Diet of Worms**, Luther refused to recant, asserting his own understanding of scripture and reason and his own conscience. He held his position with the legendary words, "Here I stand; I can do no other." The emperor allowed Luther to leave the Diet, whereupon his supporters spirited him away into hiding. Charles concluded the Diet by declaring Luther an outlaw and by pledging to kill him in order to stamp out his heretical ideas.

Since Emperor Charles V ruled over the most wide-ranging empire in history up to that time, such a threat carried weight. As the head of the Habsburg dynasty, Charles V had inherited the lands of Austria and most of the lands of Burgundy (including much of Flanders) from his grandfather, Emperor Maximilian. From his mother he received Naples and Spain, which by this time also included much of the New World (see below), and soon, possessions in Asia. The sun never set on Charles V's empire.

Surprisingly, this powerful emperor never concentrated enough power to crush Luther and his allies. First, he was weaker in reality than on parchment. The office of Holy Roman emperor had been wasting away during centuries of conflict with the popes and the German princes. Second, Charles faced turmoil in the lands he controlled as a dynast. Both Bohemia and Hungary opposed Habsburg rule. Even some in Spain, although rich from its new colonial possessions, rebelled against Charles's authority. Third, King Francis I of France started a Habsburg-Valois dynastic conflict to weaken Charles's hold on lands hemming in France from southwest and east. Even though he enjoyed the title "Most Christian King," Francis even encouraged the Muslim sultan of the Ottoman Empire to conquer Charles's ally Hungary in 1526 and besiege the Austrian capital of Vienna in 1529.

Meanwhile, the former monk set up a new Christian denomination called *Lutheranism*. While in hiding, Luther translated the Bible into simple German. In doing so, he both set the style of modern German and promoted literacy. He simplified the worship ceremonials, emphasizing more preaching, prayer, and music. Luther closed monasteries, ending monasticism in his church. That action complicated his personal life, however. A nun, Katherine von Bora, and several other nuns were both inspired by Luther's writings and disappointed with religious life. They had escaped from their nunnery in fish barrels. Then Katherine complained to Luther that since the single, celibate life of a monastic was no longer an option, nuns needed to be married and have children. So he obliged her. He married Katherine and started a family. Other Lutheran priests and bishops soon married.

For some of the common people, though, Luther's reforming efforts did not go far enough. He reined in many reformers who had started to destroy all images and fancy decorations in churches. The bourgeoisie had long wanted more asceticism from the clergy (although the burghers themselves often spent their wealth on conspicuous consumption). Many German peasants seized on Luther's rhetoric on the defiance of authority and applied it to their social and political obligations. They rebelled against their lords in 1525. As was typical of peasant revolts during the later Middle Ages, the peasants killed a few hundred landlords; the nobles then regrouped and avenged the deaths by hanging many thousands of rebels. Luther disassociated himself from the peasants, calling them "thievish, murderous hordes."

Ultimately, Luther relied on the power of Lutheran princes, both to protect him and to help spread his message. Starting with Luther's own Duke of Saxony, many northern German princes and kings in Scandinavia welcomed the Lutheran Church.

The new structures allowed them to act as popes in their own provinces. The rulers took over the administration of the former Catholic Church property and lands for themselves and had a strong hand in appointing the bishops and priests. The Lutheran Church could devote itself to spiritual matters (which did not involve land reform for peasants).

When the Habsburg Charles V tried to ban Lutheranism at a Diet in 1529, Lutheran princes protested. From that event onward, Christians who are neither Eastern Orthodox nor Roman Catholics have usually been called **Protestants**. Once debate failed, the Protestants resorted to weapons, and wars of religion (1546–1648) sporadically erupted through Europe. Charles never achieved the military victory needed to crush Luther's princely supporters. With the **Treaty of Augsburg** in 1555, Charles V capitulated to the right of princes to maintain their Lutheran churches. He resigned his throne the next year and died shortly thereafter.

Luther's successful defiance of ecclesiastical and political authority raised a question for Christianity: who had the authority to interpret and define faith? The original, traditional answer had been the church councils. Such was still the position of the Orthodox churches in eastern Europe, although they had not held a council since long before the Great Schism with the Western Latin Church in 1054. That latter church had rejected conciliarism and instead granted the papacy a monarchical authority to determine the faith.

In contrast, Luther relied solely on his own conscience, as guided by holy scripture. Yet how was his conscience necessarily better than anyone else's? Could not anyone claim to be guided by the Holy Spirit and use individual judgment to assert doctrine? Such is what happened. Religious leaders formed new sects and denominations. Success in drawing followers validated divergent religious truths. *Protestantism* became a container for multiple Christian groups, each avowing to have the one true interpretation of Christianity.

One variety of sectarians who enjoyed some success in the sixteenth century were collectively known as Anabaptists (not directly related to later "Baptists"). *Anabaptism* consisted of many different groups lumped together by enemies who disagreed with their common refusal to accept infant baptism. For Anabaptists, only mature adults ought to be baptized. These groups often drew their followers from the lower classes, who rejected religious hierarchy and ecclesiastical wealth.

Both Lutherans and Catholics joined in exterminating most of these Anabaptists through such traditional methods as torture and war. The most famous example was the siege and destruction of Münster in 1535. There the allied Lutherans and Catholics killed thousands of Anabaptists as they retook the city. The victors tortured the survivors, executed them, and then hung their remains on a church tower in cages that remain there today. Only a few groups of Anabaptists survived, often by fleeing to the New World, especially Pennsylvania, which was founded in the late seventeenth century on a principle of tolerance. Their successors exist today in such denominations as the Mennonites, Moravians, Hutterites, and the Amish or Pennsylvania Dutch.

Various reform ideas soon spread from Germany to France, one of the most powerful nations in Europe. The kings of the Valois dynasty had little need or interest in supporting any changes. The monarchy had already arranged the Concordat of 1516, which created a convenient royal co-dominion with the church in France. The agreement authorized the French king to appoint most of the bishops, abbots, and abbesses, while the pope got a large cut of the revenues.

One Frenchman, however, found himself more sympathetic to Luther's reforms than the structures of kings and bishops. **Jean (or John) Calvin** (b. 1509–d. 1564) learned of Luther's ideas in school. Inspired by them, he created his own new religious framework, called *Calvinism*, which he solidified after being called to be the leading preacher in Geneva, Switzerland. Geneva became the center of a theocracy, a government based on divine commands. While elected leaders still ran the town council, they passed laws that tried to make the townspeople conform to Calvin's beliefs. From Geneva, Calvin then sent missionaries throughout Europe.

Calvin differed from Luther in two main ways. First, Calvinism focused on **predestination** or *determinism*: the belief that God determined in advance, for all of time, who was saved and who was damned. Nothing any person did could influence God's preordained, omniscient decision. This idea went back to Augustine and had a certain logic to it: if God knows everything, then he surely knows who is going to heaven and who is going to hell. While some complained that this belief removed free will, Calvinism called believers to choose to live the exemplary life of saints, participating in baptism and the Lord's Supper. In doing so, they hoped to re-create heaven on earth.

A second difference in Calvinism was its democratic tendency; members of a church were supposed to be involved in running it. The congregation itself approved ministers or appointed the preacher instead of a distant pope or prince from above. Calvinism expanded through much of the West under the title of Reformed churches in the northern Lowlands (the Netherlands) and much of the Rhineland. In France, Calvinists were called Huguenots. In Scotland they formed Presbyterian churches, and in Wales, Congregationalist churches. In England and its colonies, most Calvinists were labeled Puritans.

When Luther first called for reform, no one thought that the authority of the pope could be overthrown by religious ideas. Yet Lutherans, Calvinists, small groups of Anabaptists, and other sects successfully defied papal control. Papal supremacy would suffer yet another loss before it reorganized and redefined itself. Amid all this religious diversity, killing for reasons of faith continued.

Review: *On what issues did the different Protestants carry out reforms?*

Response:

SOURCES ON FAMILIES: MARTIN LUTHER, *TABLE TALK* (1566)

While the great reformer Martin Luther preached and wrote about marriage and family, he also talked about it informally with students and visitors around a table in his residence. Many quotes from these informal conversations on a wide variety of subjects were compiled by recorders over the years and eventually published as his Table Talk. *The source presented here collects a variety of quotes. Of his and Katherine, or Katie, von Bora's six children together, Elizabeth died in infancy; their other daughter, Magdalene, or Lena, is featured here at about two years old and at her death at thirteen.*

"My boy Hans is now entering his seventh year. Every seven years a person changes; the first period is infancy, the second childhood. At fourteen they begin to see the world and lay the foundations of education, at twenty-one the young men seek marriage, at twenty-eight they are house-holders and patres-familias, at thirty-five they are magistrates in church and state, until forty-two when they are kings. After that the senses begin to decline. Thus every seven years brings a new condition in body and character, as has happened to me and to us all." . . .

"To have peace and love in marriage is a gift, for a good woman deserves a good husband. To have peace and love in marriage is a gift which is next to the knowledge of the Gospel. There are heartless wretches who love neither their children nor their wives; such beings are not human."

"The greatest blessing is to have a wife to whom you may entrust your affairs and by whom you may have children. Katie, you have a good husband who loves you. Let another be empress, but you give thanks to God."

"The faith and life of young children are the best because they have simply the Word. We old fools have hell and hell-fire; we dispute concerning the Word, which they accept with pure faith without question; and yet at the last we must hold simply to the Word as they do. It is moreover a trick of the devil, that we are drawn by our business affairs away from the Word in such a manner that we do not know ourselves how it happens. There it is best to die young."

To his infant child Luther said: "You are our Lord's little fool. Grace and remission of sins are yours and you fear nothing from the law. Whatever you do is uncorrupted; you are in a state of grace and you have remission of sins, whatever happens."

Playing with his child, Magdalene, he asked her: "Little Lena, what will the Holy Christ give you for Christmas?" and then he added: "The little children have such fine thoughts about God, that he is in heaven and that he is their God and father: for they do not philosophize about him."

As Magdalene lay in the agony of death, her father fell down before the bed on his knees and wept bitterly and prayed that God might free her. Then she departed and fell asleep in her father's arms. Her mother was also in the room but farther from the bed because of her grief. As they laid her in the coffin he said: "Darling Lena, it is well with you. You will rise and shine like a star, yea like the sun. . . . I am happy in spirit but the flesh is sorrowful and will not be content; the departing grieves me beyond measure. It is strange that she is certainly in peace and happy and yet I so sorrowful. . . . I have sent a saint to heaven."

"We should care for our children, and especially for poor little girls. I do not pity boys; they can support themselves in any place if they will only work, and if they are lazy they are rascals. But the poor little race of girls must have a staff to lean upon. A boy can go to school and become a fine man if he will. But a girl cannot learn so much and may go to shame to get bread to eat."

As his wife was still sorrowful and wept and cried aloud, he said to her: "Dear Katie, think how it is with her, and how well off she is. But flesh is flesh and blood blood and they do as their manner is: the spirit lives and is willing. Children doubt not, but believe as we tell them: all is simple with them; they die without pain or anguish or doubt or fear of death just as though they were falling asleep." . . .

When one day Luther's wife was upholding her authority pretty insistently he said to her with feeling: "You may claim for yourself the control over affairs of the house, saving nevertheless, my just rights. Female government has accomplished no good since the world began. When God constituted Adam master of all creatures, they were safe and governed in the best way, but the intervention of woman spoiled all: for that we have you women to thank, and therefore I am not willing to endure your rule."

Questions:

- *What are the differences between males and females within families?*
- *How does faith serve the young and old?*
- *How does husband Luther interact with his wife Katherine?*

Responses:

Citation

Luther, Martin. *Conversations with Luther: Selections from recently published sources of the Table Talk*. Translated by Preserved Smith and Herbert Percival Gallinger. Boston/New York/Chicago: The Pilgrim Press, 1915, pp. 42–55.

For more on this source, go to http://www.concisewesternciv.com/sources/sof9 .html.

FATAL BELIEFS

Although Calvinism gained popularity in England, the **English Reformation** (1534–1559) originated uniquely due to matters of state. The reigning king, **Henry**

VIII (r. 1509–1547), had strongly supported the views of the pope against Luther. The pope had even awarded King Henry the title of "Defender of the Faith," still sported by English monarchs today. A higher priority for Henry, however, was the security of the Tudor dynasty, for which he thought he needed a male heir. After twenty years of marriage to Catherine of Aragon and six births, only one child had survived, a daughter, Mary. Although a daughter could legally inherit the throne in England, Henry believed, like most monarchs of his time, that he needed a son. So he asked the pope to end his marriage, as many kings before and since have done. Contrary to the common version of history, Henry did not want a divorce (the breakup of a genuine marriage). He actually sought an annulment (the declaration that a marriage never had existed). Catherine steadfastly resisted, backed up by her nephew and Luther's overlord, Emperor Charles V. Charles just happened to have an army outside of Rome. Fearing the nearby Holy Roman emperor more than the distant English king, the pope refused to support Henry's annulment.

Still determined to father a legitimate male heir, Henry decided to break with the pope. His Parliament declared him head of the **Church of England**, and his bishops willingly annulled his first marriage and blessed his second with his courtier, Anne Boleyn. Although the pope excommunicated Henry and declared his new marriage void, that little bothered the monarch or the great majority of the English people. Both the king and many of his subjects had long disliked what they saw as Roman interference in English affairs. Moreover, many of the members of Parliament profited nicely from the subsequent dissolution of the monasteries, whose properties they bought up at bargain rates. Despite the schism, Henry remained religiously conservative, so Calvinist and Lutheran ideas gained very little influence.

Unfortunately for Henry, he did not achieve his sought-after heir with his second wife, Anne Boleyn; she managed to give birth only to a healthy daughter, Elizabeth. To make way for a new wife, Henry had Anne executed on trumped-up charges of adultery. The third wife, Jane Seymour, gave birth to his heir, Edward VI (r. 1547–1553), but died soon after. Three more marriages followed. Henry had the fourth marriage annulled and the fifth wife legitimately executed for adultery. His sixth wife managed to outlive him. Despite this rather unseemly string of marriages, most of the English people did not oppose their king. Henry had to chop off the heads of relatively few who resisted his religious transformation.

A genuinely distinctive Church of England, or **_Anglicanism_**, grew after Henry's death. His son, King Edward VI, came to the throne as a child, and his advisors began to push the Church of England further away from the Church of Rome. They began to alter significantly the interpretations of the sacraments and methods of worship to be more in line with simplifications introduced by Calvinist, Lutheran, and other Protestant reformers from the Continent.

These policies abruptly reversed when the young Edward died after a reign of only six years. A brief effort failed to put his cousin, the Protestant Lady Jane Grey, on the throne. Henry's daughter by his first marriage, Mary I (r. 1553–1558), won the day. Her religious policy forced the English church back under the authority of the pope. To do so, she persecuted clergy and laypeople, many of whom, surprisingly, were willing to die rather than go back to obedience to Rome. She burned several hundred "heretics." For these efforts the English have dubbed her "**Bloody**

Mary." Her disastrous marriage to her cousin King Philip II of Spain did not help, either. Many English hated him as a Spaniard and a Roman Catholic, and he avoided both the country and his wife. When she died without an heir, Henry's daughter by Anne Boleyn, Queen **Elizabeth I** (r. 1558–1603), inherited the crown.

Elizabeth, who had managed to survive the changes of political and religious policy, now faced a choice herself: should she maintain obedient to Rome or revive the Church of England? In 1559, with the Act of Supremacy enacted in Parliament, she chose the latter course. Henceforward, the English monarch occupied a cere-monial role as head of the Church of England. Anglicanism defined itself as Protes-tant while still Catholic, trying to maintain the best of both versions of Christianity. The *Book of Common Prayer* (1549) laid out how worship was to be carried out, but it said little of belief. One's conscience was up to oneself—a fairly tolerant attitude. Fortunately for Elizabeth, most English embraced her religious compro-mise.

In fact, Elizabeth became one of England's greatest monarchs. The late six-teenth century saw a number of powerful and effective women on or behind the thrones of Europe, provoking the Calvinist preacher John Knox in Scotland to rail against such a "Monstrous Regiment of Women," as he titled a pamphlet against them. Although the others ruled fairly competently, Elizabeth outshone them all. England flourished during her reign, culturally, economically, and politically. Renaissance culture reached its high point with Shakespeare's plays. Meanwhile, the English navy began to help its countrymen explore and start to dominate the rest of the world, taking the first steps toward founding the British Empire. It is ironic that Henry VIII thought he needed a son, when Elizabeth was "man" enough to surpass her father's accomplishments.

The one force that seriously threatened Elizabeth was *Roman Catholicism*. By the beginning of her reign, Rome had begun what historians call either the "Counter-Reformation" or the "Catholic Reformation." Many people thought the popes had been too distracted by the opulence of the Renaissance. Newly devout and energetic popes now sought to recover lands recently lost from obedience to them. They redefined their leadership over what had become the Roman Catholic Church as a branch of Christianity. Having accepted the inevitability of reform, the papacy called the **Council of Trent** (1545–1563). Leaders chose the obscure cathe-dral city at the southern edge of the Alps for a general council because it satisfied Charles V (it was in the empire), the king of France (it was not German), and the pope (its residents spoke Italian).

Some clergy at the Council of Trent wanted to compromise or adopt some ideas of the Protestants, but the council rejected that path. Instead, the Roman Catholic Church of the popes insisted on the value of justification by faith supported by good works, combined with the mediating role of the priesthood and the sacra-ments. The Tridentine Reform (named after the Latin word for Trent) limited some abuses and corruptions and established seminary schools for a better-educated priesthood. The council affirmed that their true church, through the papacy, had the final authority to define belief and interpret scripture—not Luther's conscience, or Anabaptist interpretations, or Calvin's scholarship, or anyone's literal reading of the Bible. The popes increased their interest in organizing and clarifying the smallest details of belief and practice.

New monastic orders and reformations of older ones aided the popes in reform. The Ursulines dedicated themselves to the education of girls and women. Most importantly, the Society of Jesus, or the **Jesuits**, gained sway in European affairs. Ignatius Loyola founded the Jesuits after suffering wounds as a warrior in Charles V's Spanish army. During the painful recovery from a shattered leg, he envisioned a new kind of monastic order. Instead of being confined to the cloister, Jesuits dedicated themselves to religious vocation (formed through the *Spiritual Exercises*), education (becoming teachers and guides), and missionary work (both in Europe and the world). Loyola saw his order as a spiritual army for the Roman Catholic Church, with a so-called fourth vow (after poverty, chastity, and obedience) of absolute dedication to the pope.

The Tridentine Reform set a militant tone for Roman Catholicism during the next two hundred years. Roman Catholicism aimed to recapture the allegiance of lost followers and gain more new ones. A new Roman Inquisition began its work in 1542, partly inspired by the Spanish Inquisition of Ferdinand and Isabella. The Spanish Inquisition policed converted Jews and Muslims; this new version hunted Protestants as heretics since they rejected papal teaching. An *Index of Forbidden Books* declared the reading of certain authors to be sinful. First issued in 1559 by the Holy Office in Rome and regularly reissued thereafter for four hundred years, the list restricted the circulation of banned works in Roman Catholic countries and forbade Roman Catholics from reading these prohibited books. This censorship even included all the works of Erasmus, so fearful had Rome become of any criticism.

The Roman Catholic vigor also expressed itself in a series of wars of religion that lasted until 1648. Traditionally, territorial, dynastic, and economic reasons shaped decisions for fighting wars. In this period, ideological differences between adherents of branches of Christianity became significant motives. For a few decades, people were ready to die and kill for Lutheranism, Anabaptism, Calvinism, Anglicanism, or Roman Catholicism. Monarchs thought that their subjects and their neighbors needed to conform to their own dogmas as a matter of both public order and divine virtue. People volunteered for armies in the belief that their neighbors should worship the same way they themselves did. Some also enlisted simply as a way to earn a living—soldiering was a growth industry.

In the vanguard of militant Roman Catholicism was Elizabeth's former brother-in-law, King **Philip II** of Spain (r. 1556–1598). Philip had inherited most of his Habsburg father Charles V's possessions (except the Austrian ones, which, along with the elected title of Holy Roman emperor, went to his uncle Ferdinand). In Philip's domains, Spain had one of the world's best armies; Flanders was the textile manufacturing center of Europe; and the Americas poured silver into his treasuries. Philip also briefly united Spain with Portugal, making him the ruler of the sole global power. He built a new, modern capital for himself in Madrid. Although Madrid was not conveniently connected to the waterways that bound Philip's empire together, it was easily accessible from his palace of El Escorial, a massive, gray religious retreat (see figure 9.5). Philip was hardworking but perhaps too

Figure 9.5. King Philip II of Spain often retreated to the gray abbey of El Escorial, which served also as a second palace, away from Madrid.

focused on small details. He saw himself as a divinely appointed monarch obliged to attend to every corner of his empire. At the head of a vast bureaucracy, he regulated the lace on court costumes, ordered murders of political enemies, corrected the spelling of secretaries, and held *autos-da-fé* (public burnings of heretics at which he served as master of ceremonies).

Above all, the king of Spain sent armies to fight for his vision of the Roman Catholic faith. His navy's victory over the Ottoman Turks at the Battle of Lepanto (1571) cheered the Christian West, showing that the Ottomans were not invincible. At the time, the Muslim sultan claimed the defeat meant nothing—he would just build another fleet, which he did. Despite this boast, historians have seen the defeat at Lepanto as an obvious turning point toward the long, slow decline of Ottoman dominion. Similarly, Philip's power began to diminish. He could not manage his empire from Madrid, as his territories were far too large for the available means of communication. He could not afford his government either, declaring bankruptcy three times and thereby ruining many of the bankers and merchants he needed so badly.

In particular, some of those capitalists, namely the prosperous Calvinist Dutch in the northern part of the Lowlands, resented paying for Philip's dreams of a Roman Catholic empire. In 1581, they declared independence from his rule and formed the **Dutch Netherlands** (often called Holland after the main province). They even began to construct their own democratic government (see the next chapter). The Dutch fought on and off for eighty years before they gained full independence for themselves. To stop this rebellion, Philip first sent in the Duke of Parma, whose army earned infamy for its brutality against the civilian population. In turn,

Dutch and Huguenot merchants harassed Spanish shipping. Philip next turned his attention to England, which had been supporting the upstart Dutch after the death of Philip's wife Queen Mary I. Hostilities simmered for several years as English sea dogs or privateers (informal pirates with permission from a government to raid shipping) preyed on Spanish possessions. Riches looted by the Spanish from the American natives wound up being plundered by the English instead.

Philip retaliated by instigating plots against Elizabeth's life and throne. The pope declared her an illegitimate, excommunicated heretic and encouraged the faithful to overthrow her rule. Philip and the pope supported Elizabeth's cousin, Mary Stuart, Queen of Scots (not to be confused with Elizabeth's half-sister "Bloody Mary" Tudor, the late queen of England) as the true English monarch. The unfortunate Mary Stuart had lost her Scottish Highlands kingdom through her own folly, falling under a reasonable suspicion of blowing up her husband. She fled from her own people to England. Elizabeth kept her in comfortable confinement until Mary got herself implicated in a treasonous Roman Catholic plot. Elizabeth finally ordered Mary's beheading, although it took the headsman three whacks of his axe to succeed.

Seizing upon Elizabeth's execution of Mary in 1587 as an excuse, Philip assembled the **Spanish Armada**. This fleet of 130 ships aimed to sail from Spain to the Lowlands and then ferry Parma's troops across the North Sea to invade England. It all went terribly wrong. The most famous English sea dog, Sir Francis Drake, destroyed most of the fleet in its harbor before it could set sail. A rebuilt fleet launched in 1588, but adverse weather slowed its progress. That the commanding admiral had never been to sea was not helpful, either. Easily repulsing the English in the Channel, the admiral did finally anchor his fleet off the coast of the Lowlands, only to be told, quite reasonably, that if troops there were diverted to England, the Netherlands might succeed in their rebellion. Then the English broke up the armada by pushing fire ships, empty, burning hulls, among the fleet. The panicked Spanish broke formation and came under English guns. Storms sank most of the rest.

Philip at first wrote off this defeat, much as the Ottoman sultan had his own at Lepanto. Notwithstanding Spain's appearance of strength over the next decades, it sank to a second-rank power. England, however, continued its ascendancy, becoming stronger than ever as its national patriotism became bound with its religion and its burgeoning imperialist ventures.

Meanwhile, France had not been able to help Philip II of Spain fight Spain's traditional enemy, England, since France itself almost broke apart in religious warfare. The Huguenots (the name for French Calvinists) had grown to about 10 percent of the population. Their numbers were particularly strong in the productive artisan and business classes. The Valois dynasty might have moved against them once its long conflict with the Habsburgs ended in 1559. But that same year the Valois dynasty plummeted into crisis with the unexpected death of King Henry II, killed during a joust by a piece of splintered lance that thrust through his eye into his brain. His three young sons and their mother, Queen Catherine de Medici (b. 1519–d. 1589), were trapped between two powerful aristocratic families: the Huguenot Bourbons and the Roman Catholic de Guises. Fighting over the throne using betrayal, assassination, and war, these powerful families nearly destroyed the monarchy and the country.

The Roman Catholic party almost triumphed with the **St. Bartholomew's Day massacre** (14 August 1572), during which they viciously murdered thousands of Protestants, great and small, men, women, and children, in the streets of Paris. Henry of Bourbon survived that slaughter and was soon able to gain military domination over most of the country. After the death of the last Valois in 1589, he became officially recognized as the French king **Henry IV "of Navarre"** (r. 1589–1610), founding the Bourbon dynasty. Hostility to his Protestantism still stood in the way of his acceptance by some Roman Catholics. So, in 1593, he converted to Roman Catholicism, allegedly saying, "Paris is worth a mass." He continued to protect the Protestants, though, with the proclamation of the **Edict of Nantes** (1598). This act mandated a certain level of religious tolerance. It allowed Protestants to worship freely and to fortify fifty-one cities for their own self-defense. Diversity brought some peace and security.

The last of the religious wars, the **Thirty Years War** (1618–1648), engulfed the Holy Roman Empire and drew in the entire continent. The conflict began in Bohemia, as the Austrian branch of the Habsburgs labored to convert that province back to Roman Catholicism. Leaders in Prague "defenestrated" the emperor's representatives—meaning they tossed them out the window. Habsburg armies quickly crushed the rebellious Bohemians, but other German princes who feared a resurgent imperial power soon took up arms against Austria. Two foreign Lutheran monarchs invaded the empire—first the king of Denmark, then the king of Sweden. The Protestant armies gained brief advantages through their use of well-drilled and coordinated cavalry, artillery, and infantry units, setting the tone of military tactics for the next centuries. Regardless, the Austrian Habsburgs continued to win, fortified by the resources of their Spanish cousins.

Eventually, what began as a religious war ended as a purely political conflict. France had long feared being surrounded by the Habsburg territories of Spain in the south and the Holy Roman Empire in the east. So Roman Catholic France entered the war against Roman Catholic Austria. Dynastic and national politics overruled religious fraternity. Thus, religion faded as a motive to go to war in the West.

Indeed, the **Peace of Westphalia**, which was signed in 1648, forced Europe into new, modern, international political relationships (see map 9.1). With religious diversity now irreversible, the medieval ideal of a unified Christendom was completely broken. Instead, the numerous independent states of Europe lived in an uncertain rivalry. Each became a sovereign state, free from the influence of higher authorities, although able to agree on international principles if necessary. The most important principle maintained a ***balance of power***, ensuring that the countries should league together against any single state that tried to dominate Europe. This principle kept the great powers in check and left the middle-ranked and small buffer states free to prosper.

The rest of the treaty redrew some political borders to establish a rough balance of power. Spain held on to the southern "Spanish" part of the Netherlands (soon to be known as Belgium) but lost the northern Dutch Netherlands, which everyone recognized as an independent, sovereign state. The Swiss had their independence

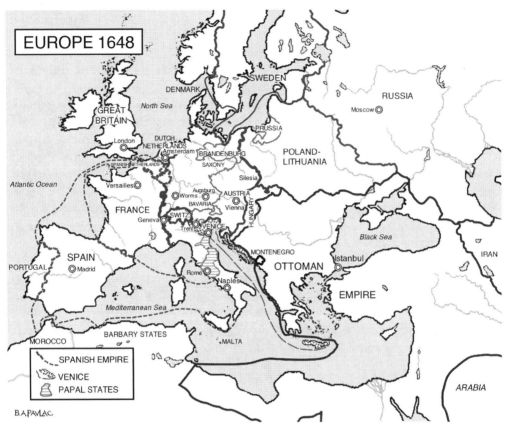

Map 9.1.   Europe, 1648.
How does the Spanish Empire dominate the western fringe of Europe?

affirmed. The Holy Roman Empire became a mere geographical expression as a synonym for Germany. The petty principalities within the empire were more sovereign than the empire itself. The Holy Roman emperor became even less relevant, a yet still weaker figurehead. While the Austrian Habsburgs kept control of the imperial office, their varied collection of hereditary territories on the empire's southeastern borders mattered far more to them than the office of emperor. Meanwhile, France chewed away a few bits of the empire, bringing its border to the upper Rhine River. Of course, neither the balance of power nor religious toleration stopped war altogether. States continued to try to expand at the expense of their neighbors.

The lack of total victory for any one side assured that religious diversity remained part of Western civilization. The pope's claim to rule Christendom became irrelevant, his prestige greatly reduced. While nations might continue to fight, hoping for power, pride, or prosperity, religion as a reason for war declined. States became the key binding agent for Europeans. The Reformation weakened the bonds between religion and the state. Many governments continued to impose religious uniformity on their own people. Indeed, many people remained satisfied with whatever tradition they were brought up in. Yet people only had to look across borders to know that others differed on Christianity and that some individuals might even be able to choose their faith or even no belief at all.

Review: How did early modern reforms among Christians culminate in wars over religion?

Response:

GOD, GREED, AND GLORY

Another change from the medieval to the modern in European history was **Western colonial imperialism**, when various kingdoms built empires based on overseas colonies. Historians today argue about what exactly made the Europeans strong enough to take the lead in a new global history after 1500. Answers used to imply, if not outright argue, *Western exceptionalism*, the idea that Europeans were somehow different from (and better than) peoples in other civilizations. More recent historians object to that characterization, especially considering the brutality with which Europeans "civilized" the world, leading to the loss of lives and liberty. Comparative historians who measure the relative accumulation of wealth, strength of government, level of cultural sophistication, status of technological development, and impulse toward creativity of various civilizations around the world over the centuries note that Europe did not rank near the top.

The Europeans benefited from excellent timing as they began their modern history with their "voyages of discovery." The explorers, of course, only "discovered" what the indigenous peoples in these faraway lands knew all along. The difference was that Europeans could exploit these foreign peoples and places as never before in their history. They declared their own Doctrine of Discovery, making up a law to justify their seizure of these new lands and their indigenous peoples. These expeditions allowed Europeans to take profit from preexisting trade networks that incorporated much of Asia and Africa, adding on the *terra incognita* or unknown lands in the Americas and Pacific. The European national governments in competition with each other over global supremacy seized their overseas empires (see map 9.2).

Europeans had three desires that fed this drive to go abroad. The first came from Christianity's own evangelistic and crusading impulses, which had already driven Western culture beyond the borders of Europe. Even before Latin Christianity began to split apart, westerners wanted to force the gospel of Christ on "heathens," as seen in the Crusades. The Reformation only encouraged the divided

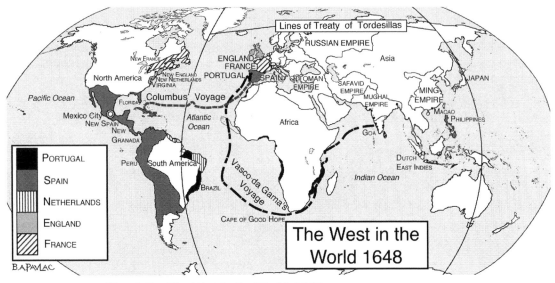

Map 9.2. The West in the World, 1648.
How did the Europeans begin to divide up the world?

Christians to convert the world, to prove their own version of Christianity as the most successful and, therefore, most divinely sanctioned. Some Europeans ventured on a path of world domination in the name of eternal salvation. Would Jesus, the Prince of Peace, have approved that his message came at the point of a sword and with the price of plundering? His followers thought so, and they had the power to do it.

God provided a spiritual motivation, while money afforded a material one. The capitalism that sprouted from the Commercial Revolution had transformed Europe from a poor offshoot on the fringes of a world trade system centered in Asia to a mainstay of economic dynamism. Financial investments from capitalists further pushed these "voyages of discovery" forward. Instead of being barriers, the deep seas and oceans soon became highways, much as rivers and coastal waters had long been.

A second motive for colonialism, then, was the opportunity for profit. Europeans wanted to travel to "the Indies," regions in distant Asia known to possess fantastic wealth in the form of spices, such as pepper, cinnamon, and nutmeg. What today sits on our shelves in small jars costing pennies was worth more than its weight in gold in 1500.

The main trade routes to the Indies had traditionally run through the Middle East. Only a rare merchant from Europe, such as Marco Polo in the thirteenth century, might travel along the Silk Road through Central Asia all the way to the Chinese Empire. During much of the Middle Ages, most western European merchants bought from the middleman merchants of the Byzantine Empire. After the Byzantine Empire's demise in 1453, the Muslim Ottoman Turks took over supply routes. The idea that the Muslims shut down the trade routes is a myth; they still wanted to trade. Rather, the western Christians resented paying these "infidel" middlemen. Europeans were looking for alternative access to the East.

Pride offered a third motive for imperialism, on both the personal and national levels. At the forefront, monarchs were drawn to the glorification that conquest always brought. New lands meant wider empires and revenues. At the lower social levels, adventuring in foreign lands raised a Renaissance gentleman's reputation and status. Any poor man might acquire treasure or farmland of his own, taken from natives who could not defend it. Thus an obscure man could rise to prominence, whether by lording it over foreigners or bringing immense wealth back home to Europe. All these contradictory motives, winning fame, fortune, and souls for Jesus, tempted Europeans out across the wide oceans.

Surprisingly, the new imperialism began with the little country of **Portugal**, founded in the twelfth century as part of a crusade during the Reconquesta of the Iberian Peninsula (see chapter 8). Over the years, Portugal had fought against the Muslims, but its armies were soon cut off from confronting the enemy by neighboring Castile's successful expansion in the Iberian Peninsula. Unable to combat the Moors in Europe, little Portugal sought another outlet for its crusading zealotry. It channeled its expansionism toward Africa, hoping both to convert the Africans and to profit from trade on that continent. Prince Henry the Navigator (d. 1460), one of the main proponents of African expeditions, also wished to find enough gold to maintain his court in proper style. His sponsored voyages discovered and colonized the islands of the Azores and the Madieras in the Atlantic. Colonists found the latter islands so heavily forested that they set a fire that burned for seven years, leaving the land covered in ash. From this new, fertile soil they grew a new wine, Madiera. Heavily populated Africa was a different matter. Instead of converting and conquering, the Portuguese only wrested away small chunks of African coastline, where they built forts to defend harbors and trading outposts. From these bases, the Portuguese began to deal in slaves, many shipped to work on sugarcane plantations in the Madieras.

Explorers soon thought that it might be possible to sail around the continent of Africa to reach the Indies. Yet sailors faced some serious challenges. First, ocean travel in the Atlantic was far more dangerous than in the Mediterranean and coastal waters. So the Portuguese adapted sailing technology from Muslim civilization in Africa and the Middle East to build ships called caravels, sturdy enough to handle the high seas. Second, navigation was aided by other Muslim achievements, such as the compass, astrolabe, and maps and charts. Thus European voyagers used the Arabs' own ingenuity against them.

On the western edge of Europe, the Portuguese were best located to launch such voyages. In 1468, the Portuguese explorer Diaz succeeded in rounding the optimistically named Cape of Good Hope, the southernmost point of Africa. It took another thirty years before **Vasco da Gama** traveled beyond that cape. In 1498, he sailed up the east coast of Africa and then ventured across the Arabian Sea to reach India, guided by Arabian pilots. He did not have much of value to trade with the Indians, but the spices he brought back profited his expedition thirty times the amount of its cost. On da Gama's next voyage, the Portuguese military technology of guns overpowered the natives. Da Gama plundered foreign merchant cargoes, blew the Arab ships out of the water, shelled cities, exploited rivalries between states, and intimidated princes. Other Portuguese followed. Soon they dominated all seagoing trade and commerce in the Arabian Sea and the Indian Ocean.

Portugal was too small to grab and keep vast territories. For five hundred years, though, the Portuguese held on to many fortified coastal enclaves: Angola, Guinea, and Mozambique in Africa; Goa in India; Timor in the Indies; and Macao in China. Only in Brazil, in the Americas, did they establish a large colony with European immigrants. Despite its overseas imperial success, Portugal itself remained on the periphery of European affairs, only rarely participating in the approaching wars among European states disputing who would dominate the world.

Even before Vasco da Gama had begun exploiting and killing Indians in India, Portugal's neighbor **Spain** had hoped to beat its rival to the Indies. Spain was a young country, founded only in 1479 when King Ferdinand came to the throne of Aragon, while his co-ruler of five years, Isabella, ruled the neighboring Kingdom of Castile. Husband and wife united their two kingdoms to create Spain, centralizing power in both their hands while weakening the nobles and other estates. Spain's hold on southern Italy was secured through Ferdinand's wars on that peninsula.

Ferdinand and Isabella rounded out their immediate realm on the Iberian Peninsula by finishing the Reconquesta crusade begun in the eleventh century. In 1492 they defeated Granada, the last Muslim principality in western Europe. Then, to impose uniformity and conformity on their tidy kingdom, they kicked out of the country all Muslims and Jews who refused to convert to Christianity. The "Sephardic" Jews settled throughout the Mediterranean countries, Christian and Muslim. Meanwhile, Spanish authorities worried about the sincerity of conversions by those Muslims and Jews who stayed behind, called, respectively, Moriscos (after the old term *Moors*) and Marranos (a word for "pig"). The monarchs set up the infamous **Spanish Inquisition** (1478–1834) to deal with their concerns. The Spanish Inquisition investigated and punished cases of people who secretly practiced Islam or Judaism, as well as some cases of sodomy or witchcraft. Over the centuries, the inquisitors ferreted out, tortured, and burned many people to death. By the early 1600s, Spain gave up worrying about whether Moriscos had been converted or not and simply expelled tens of thousands of them to North Africa. Spain's authorities enforced cultural uniformity as they built their new nation.

While Queen Isabella presided over the defeat of Muslim Granada, she gambled on an unusual plan to reach the lavish Indies. In 1492, an eccentric Italian ship captain, **Christopher Columbus**, proposed sailing westward across the Atlantic Ocean, rather than to the south around Africa (which would not succeed for six more years). Isabella's advisors were correct to warn her that Columbus's voyage should fail. Contrary to a popular yet incorrect myth, their advice was not based on a mistaken belief that the world was flat—since the time of the ancient Greeks, every educated person knew that the world was round or, more properly, a globe. Instead, Isabella's advisors were correct to point out that Columbus had underestimated the distance from his last supply point in the Canary Islands to Japan. While Columbus thought that he needed to travel a mere 2,400 miles, Isabella's advisors knew, in fact, the distance to be more than 8,000 miles. Columbus would have died at sea had he not stumbled upon the "New World." For most of his life Columbus believed that what he had claimed for Spain was part of the true Indies of the East, just as he read in Marco Polo's book. He did not want to give up a belief that seemed so close to reality. Instead, other explorers, like Amerigo Vespucci, quickly recognized that the islands of the Caribbean were the "West" Indies and that new continents lay just beyond. Therefore, mapmakers labeled the continents **North and South America** after Amerigo Vespucci, not Christopheria or Columbia after Christopher Columbus.

Columbus discovered the Americas at exactly the right moment for Europeans to exploit their advantages. There had been, of course, earlier contacts between the Old World of Eurasia and Africa with the New World of the Americas, going back even to the Vikings. In all these earlier interactions, however, the travelers lacked the interest or ability to dominate the "native" Americans who had been living there for tens of thousands of years. By 1492, however, Spain was ready to commit resources for conquest and lucky enough to have them succeed beyond expectation.

Columbus's own domination of the natives (mistakenly, of course, called Indians after the East Indies) further tarnishes his legacy. He kidnapped natives and killed to seize land at will. In his desire to acquire gold, Columbus cut off the hands of natives who failed to turn in his quotas. Those who fled he had hunted down with huge hounds who tore off their limbs while still alive. His soldiers forcibly took native women for themselves. Following Columbus, other Spanish adventurers called **conquistadors** conquered much of the Americas, supported by a firm conviction in God's blessing for their cause, rich financial backing, and a well-drilled military equipped with horses and guns.

Historians call the European takeover of the Americas and its consequences the Columbian Exchange, a mutual transfer of goods and ideas. It mostly added up to be in the West's favor, however. European settlers rushed into the Americas, grabbing control of vast expanses of land and actually and essentially enslaving native peoples. Wealth in precious metals and food products flowed into Europe, having been produced by the native peoples. Europeans ate better with foods from the New World, including peanuts, maize, potatoes, sunflowers, and tomatoes (although tomatoes were originally suspected of being poisonous because of their bright red color). Tobacco smoking provided a new social pastime. In turn, both native and immigrant Americans fed on cattle, pigs, chickens, sugarcane, coffee, rice, bananas, and even the honey of honeybees brought from the Old World to the new. Along with these new agricultural resources, the American natives gained new rulers and a new religion.

The European conquest came surprisingly easily, within a few decades after Columbus's discovery. Natives on the Caribbean islands could not organize a strong military resistance since they were still at the socioeconomic level of hunter-gatherers or simple agriculturalists. In contrast, millions of American Indians on the mainland were quite civilized and organized. Two recently formed empires maintained societies based in cities as sophisticated as any in the Old World. One of the peoples who ruled the so-called Aztec Empire, the Mexica, gave their name to modern-day Mexico. Their political power reached southward toward Central America. The Aztec capital of Tenochtitlan (today, Mexico City) arguably possessed more comforts, and certainly more people, than any one city in Spain. The Incan

Empire based in Peru controlled much of the west coast of South America. Each empire coordinated agriculture, war, and peace for millions of people, with armies well trained in conquest. These civilized societies were, ironically, even more vulnerable to conquest. They shared three serious disadvantages for competition with the Spanish: deification, ethnic conflicts, and vulnerable immune systems.

First, deification hurt the natives because they expected too much from their own human rulers, who were considered to be gods. The Aztec practice of sacrificing humans for religious reasons, carving out beating hearts with obsidian knives, also upset many subject peoples who did not believe in the Aztec gods. Even worse, the natives too often incorrectly believed the Europeans were gods themselves. The new-comers' pale skins, shiny armor, and unfamiliar horses contributed to this falsehood, which the lying conquistadors exploited to the utmost. This sham allowed Cortés in Mexico and Pizarro in Peru to get close to, capture, and then execute the native emperors (see figure 9.6). Therefore, the embodiment of both church and state collapsed with one blow. Murdered emperors left the natives disorganized and doubting.

Second, the diversity of the Native Americans helped the Spanish defeat the native political states. The Incan and Aztec Empires, like many empires, centered on specific ethnic groups that dominated others. Enemies of these empires, tribes that remained unconquered or had been recently subjugated, readily cooperated

Figure 9.6. The Spanish conquistadors are the new lords of the palace as they order the Incan ruler Atahualpa strangled by his own people. (NYPL Digital Collection)

with the Spanish against the native imperial supremacy. The Spanish played various tribal groups against one another. Then, conquistadors replaced every native civilized political structure that ruled over good farmland. Only on the fringes of the Spanish Empire did Indians retain some self-rule. They usually survived as hunter-gatherer societies, protected by mountains, deserts, or jungles.

The third and worst problem for the natives was their vulnerability to diseases carried from Europe. We understand now how many diseases are caused by germs (see chapter 11). In the sixteenth century, though, many people felt that disease was a punishment from God. Such had been the case with the Black Death, which killed a third of the European population within a few years. Little knowledge existed on how to prevent or cure illnesses. The Spanish, naturally and unintentionally, brought with them various germs from Europe, from diseases as harmless as the common cold to the more lethal measles and chicken pox and the very deadly smallpox. The Europeans bore substantial immunities to these diseases, but the native Americans had never been exposed to them. In contrast, perhaps the only illness that the Europeans may have brought back from the Americas was the sexually transmitted disease of syphilis. It first appeared in Europe at about this time and for the next few centuries disproportionately afflicted sexually promiscuous people, especially prostitutes, soldiers, and aristocrats.

In comparison, the natives of the Americas were not so fortunate. Millions became sick and died. Spreading rapidly along imperial roads, pandemics (epidemics that range over whole continents and beyond) killed large portions of the population. Large regions were completely depopulated, and native sociopolitical networks broke down.

Through exploitation of political rivalries, military tactics, and disease, Spain quickly came to dominate the Americas, wiping out much of the indigenous cultures and civilization and replacing them with its version of Western civilization. At the time, the Spanish did not realize the complete extent of the devastation or fully comprehend their own role in the plagues. But they knew how to take advantage of the situation. Empty land was theirs for the taking. In the next three centuries, perhaps close to two million Spaniards migrated to what would become known as Latin America (from the linguistic origins of Spanish and Portuguese). The Spanish reduced to servitude and enslavement those natives who survived disease and slaughter. Only insufficient numbers of colonial settlers prevented the Spanish from expanding farther north than they did.

The Spanish masters exploited the defeated. Natives dug in the silver mines (of which there were plenty, but disappointingly few sources of gold). Or they labored in the fields for long hours under the southern sun. Many died from overwork and lack of care, exploited worse than animals. Only a few voices protested, notably Bartolomé de Las Casas, the first priest ordained in the Americas. He spoke out to claim human and Christian dignity for the Indians. He and others won the argument that Indians had souls and were human, capable of entry into heaven after death. But many continued to die. Within a few decades the native population of the Americas fell from what was probably eleven million to only two and a half million.

While the depopulation guaranteed European domination, it also threatened the Western exploitation. Who would produce the silver and food that the Europeans desired and needed? How could they replace all the dead miners and peasants?

The Portuguese offered a solution with the **Atlantic-African slave trade**. In the year 1400, slavery hardly existed in Europe. Soon after, the Portuguese had gained an interest in slavery, which they had seen operating among the Africans. Beginning in 1444 they began to buy and sell black Africans, with the official excuse of the need to convert Muslim prisoners to Christianity. In reality, they wanted cheap, expendable labor. The new plantations for sugarcane, which everyone's sweet tooth craved, promoted harsh labor practices. The crop required hard, nasty, and dangerous harvesting in dank thickets, where workers hacked away at rough, sharp stalks with machetes. So over the next few centuries, Europeans of various nationalities captured and shipped millions of diverse Africans to work as slaves in the Americas. The first boatload arrived by 1510, not even two decades after Columbus's discovery. By the time the Atlantic-African slave trade ended in the nineteenth century, about ten million Africans had been shipped to the Americas, most unloaded in the Caribbean islands and Brazil, but about a fifth going to British colonies (see figure 9.7).

Thus, the new Spanish rulers forcibly converted the native American "Indians" and the imported Africans to the ways of Western civilization, which largely supported and benefited the European masters. Of course, through most of history, in most civilizations, the masses, both free and slave, have supported the few at the top. The institutionalized racism of the Americas, though, has left an especially challenging legacy. "Black" skins were identified as inferior, while "white" skins claimed superiority. The periodic revolts by both the native American and African slaves always ended with the Western masters victorious.

An improved method of investing capital, the bourse or **stock exchange**, soon financed this slave trade and other colonial investments. First appearing in Antwerp

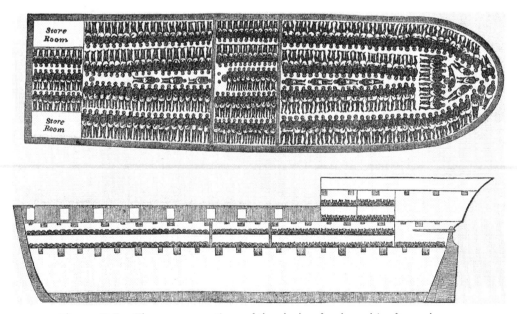

Figure 9.7. These cross sections of the decks of a slave ship, from above and from the side, show how human beings were packed for transatlantic transport. (NYPL Digital Collection)

in 1485, the stock exchange provided an alternative to banks as a place for capital to be gathered and invested. At first, members pooled their resources for new investment capital. But collective membership risked all of one's own possessions to pay debts if too many of the collective's investments failed. By 1600, joint-stock companies provided a better way to protect investments by restricting losses to only the number of shares any individual owned. This limited liability meant that some-one who prudently invested only a portion of his wealth through stock in any one venture could not be ruined. Remember, risk was always part of capitalism.

Although the New World looked like a profitable investment, it had a mixed impact on the European economy. American silver mines added tons of bullion to the treasuries of Spain, which then filtered out to the other nations of Europe and even to China through world trade. But so much silver also led to a quick and devastating inflation. A "price revolution" of swiftly rising costs of goods and services hurt the middle and poorer classes of Spain, eventually weakening the Spanish Empire. The history of capitalism is rife with both growth in wealth and suffering caused by crises in investments.

The simple idea of capitalism, reinvesting profits, offered no real guidelines on how to best keep those profits flowing to everyone's benefit. Some intellectuals attempted to figure out how to prevent economic disaster and promote economic growth. As part of the Commercial Revolution, they began to propose one of the first **economic theories**, sets of ideas that offered comprehensive explanations for how people carried out economic activity (see diagram 15.1). Since then, many theories have tried to suggest plans for action on how best to harness capitalism. Unlike scientific theories (see chapter 10), though, no economic theory has as yet sufficiently explained human economic activity.

The early ***economic theory of mercantilism*** linked the growing early modern nation-states to their new colonial empires. Theorists emphasized that the accumu-lation of wealth in precious metals within a country's own borders was the best measure of economic success. Mercantilist theory favored government intervention in the economy, since it was in governments' interest that their economies succeed. The theory argued that a regime should cultivate a favorable balance of trade as a sign of economic success. Since most international exchange took place in bullion, actual gold and silver, monarchs tried to make sure that other countries bought more from their country than they bought from other monarchs' countries. By these means, the bullion in a country's treasury continued to increase. Monarchs then obsessed about discovering mines of gold and silver, a practically cost-free method of acquiring bullion.

Because of this tangible wealth, governments frequently intervened by trying to promote enterprises to strengthen the economy. State-sponsored monopolies had clear advantages for a monarch. A state-licensed enterprise, such as importing tea leaves from China or sable furs from Siberia, could easily be supervised and taxed. Diligent inspections and regulation ensured that monopolies' goods and services were of a high quality. The government could then promote and protect that busi-ness both overseas and domestically.

Fueled by this burgeoning capital and developing theory, more adventurers sailed off to exploit the riches of Asia, Africa, and the Americas. Unfortunately for imperialists, the world was fairly crowded already with other powerful peoples. Various kingdoms and states in East Asia (the Chinese Empire, Japan), the Indian subcontinent (the Mughal Empire), and Africa (Abyssinia) had long histories, rich economies, sophisticated cultures, and intimidating armies.

Even so, Spain and Portugal boldly divided up the world between them in 1494, even before Vasco da Gama had reached the Indies, with the **Treaty of Tordesillas** (see map 9.2). The pope blessed the proceedings. The treaty demonstrated a certain hubris in those two states. They claimed global domination, notwithstanding their inability to severely damage the existing rich, powerful, well-established, and disease-resistant African and Asian kingdoms and empires. The European powers ruled the oceans but could only nibble at the fringes of Asia and Africa.

People of other Western nations did not let the Spanish and Portuguese enjoy their fat empires in peace for long. Outside the law, pirates in the Caribbean along the Spanish Main (the Central and South American coastline) and in the Indies plundered whatever they could. Some captains became legalized pirates, licensed by governments with "letters of marque." For example, raids by the English Sir Francis Drake and his sea dogs helped provoke the Spanish Armada.

By 1600, the Dutch, the English, and the French had launched their own overseas ventures, with navies and armies grabbing and defending provinces across the oceans. They all began to drive out natives in the Americas, Africa, and Asia. They also turned on one another. In Asia and Africa, the Dutch grabbed Portuguese bases in South Africa and the East Indies. The English, in turn, seized Dutch possessions in Africa, Malaysia, and North America (turning New Holland into New York and New Jersey). The English planted their own colonists along the Atlantic seacoast of North America. The French settled farther inland in Quebec. Likewise, in the Caribbean, India, and the Pacific, the French and English faced each other in disputes about islands and principalities while the native peoples were caught in the middle.

These European "illegal immigrants" seized power from the original native rulers and owners. The colonizers ravaged the native cultures, often with cruelty (scalping was invented by Europeans) and carelessness (smashing sculptures and pulverizing written works). Priceless cultural riches vanished forever. Land grabbing displaced the local farmers, while slavery (whether in body or wages) and displacement of native peoples by Europeans dismantled social structures. Where social bonds did not snap apart, European immigrants ignored and discriminated, trying to weaken the hold of native religions, languages, and even clothing styles. Robbed of their homes and livelihoods, most non-European subjects found resistance to be futile against the weight of European power.

As a result of the westerners' expansion around the world, "Europe" replaced "Christendom" in the popular imagination. Nevertheless, these diverse Europeans continued to hurl insults and launch wars against one another, which they supported through grotesque ethnic stereotypes. While the people of one's own nation were invariably perceived as kind, generous, sober, straight, loyal, honest, and intelligent, they might allege that the Spanish were cruel, the Scots stingy, the Dutch drunk, the French perverted, the Italians deceptive, the English boastful, or the Germans boorish. So Europeans remained pluralistic in their perceptions of one another while united in their desire to dominate the globe.

The elites also recognized certain common bonds in how they practiced their gentlemanly manners in ruling over the lower classes, expanded their many governments, grew their increasingly national economies, and revered the Christian religion (no matter how fractured). Some Europeans adopted a notion of the morally pure "noble savage" as a critique on their own culture. Missionaries preached the alleged love and hope of Christianity, while global natives found themselves confronted by new crimes brought in by the westerners, such as prostitution and vagrancy. The confidence in civilization of Western exceptionalism made Europeans feel that they deserved superiority over all other peoples. These diverse Europeans insisted that they themselves were "civilized" and that their dominated enemies were barbaric "savages." They increasingly viewed humans through racist lenses: "white" Europeans and "colored" others, whether "red" American Indians, "brown" Asian Indians, "yellow" Chinese, or "black" sub-Saharan Africans. All these other "races" by definition were believed to be less intelligent, industrious, and intrepid. Through increasing contacts with other peoples, the rest of the world seemed truly "foreign."

This Eurocentric attitude is reflected in the early maps of the globe. Medieval maps had usually given pride of place in the center to Jerusalem. By the sixteenth century, geographers had a more accurate picture of the globe and could distinguish other continents as connected to one another by at most a narrow isthmus (Panama for the Americas, Sinai between Eurasia and Africa). Nonetheless, they "split" the continent of Eurasia into "Asia" and "Europe," arbitrarily deciding on the Ural Mountains as a dividing point (although these hills hardly created a barrier—as the Huns and Mongols had demonstrated). Westerners saw vast stretches of eastern Europe as hardly civilized at all, a tempting target for building empires. The maps had changed to show that Europeans had moved from being located in one small corner of the map to the center. The explorers who led the voyages of discovery showed audacity and heroism, added to the scientific knowledge of Europeans, and allowed some mutually beneficial cultural exchange. Wielding a newfound global power, Western civilization had conquered much of the world by the seventeenth century. More was to come in the nineteenth century.

Review: *How did the "voyages of discovery" begin colonial imperialism by Europeans?*

Response:

Make your own timeline.

CHAPTER 10

Liberation of Mind and Body

Early Modern Europe, 1543 to 1815

While people fought over forms of faith, they also pondered man's place in God's creation. Was each person's position ordained and unchangeable, or could people achieve something higher than the status into which they were born? The increasing use of the mind, as advocated by the humanists of the Renaissance, supported the latter attitude. Yet the more European intellectuals examined the writings of the Greeks and Romans about the natural world, the more they discovered flaws and mistakes. If the philosophy of antiquity could be so wrong, then how did one find truth? Western civilization provided a new method with the so-called **Scientific Revolution** (1543–1687), which unleashed an ongoing force for change and power. Ideas that freed people from ignorance about nature would in time lead them to question social hierarchies and to transform political systems.

LOST IN THE STARS

A religious problem unexpectedly triggered the invention of modern science. The Julian calendar, established in 45 BC, had become seriously out of sync with nature. As mentioned in chapter 5, Julius Caesar had reformed the calendar by adding a leap day every fourth year to compensate for the estimated 365 1/4 days of the solar year. According to the Julian calendar, the first day of spring (the vernal equinox, when the hours of day exactly equaled those of night) should occur around 21 March. By the fifteenth century, the vernal equinox fell in early April. The church feared that this delay jeopardized the sanctity of Easter (which was celebrated on the first Sunday after the first full moon following the vernal equinox). The Counter-Reformation papacy, eager to have its structures improved and reformed, called on intellectuals to come up with both an explanation about the Julian calendar's errors and a solution.

Previously, in the Middle Ages, the study of the processes of nature took the name of natural philosophy. Natural philosophy included the mystical and supernatural to contemplate and interact with divine creation. By the Renaissance, the dominant views on nature were shaped by the ancient Greek Aristotle, as adapted and transmitted by medieval Muslim philosophers and then the victory of Scholasticism. Most intellectuals accepted Aristotle's logical assertion that the earth sat at the center of the universe. According to Aristotle, the sun, the moon, the other planets, and the stars (attached to giant crystalline spheres) revolved around the earth (which every educated person knew was a globe). The Greek natural philosopher Ptolemy had elaborated on this idea in the second century AD. Aristotle and Ptolemy's earth-centered universe was labeled the Ptolemaic or **geocentric theory**. After the success of Aquinas and the Scholastics, the Western Latin Church endorsed this Aristotelian view. It liked the argument that proximity to the center of the earth (hell's location) corresponded with imperfection and evil, while distance from earth (toward heaven) equaled goodness and perfection.

The geocentric theory was not the only reasonable view of the universe, however. A few ancient Greeks had disagreed with Aristotle's concept and argued instead that the sun was the center of the universe, with the earth revolving around it (and the moon revolving around the earth). This sun-centered universe was called the **heliocentric theory** (see diagram 10.1).

Without any winning evidence either way, Renaissance intellectuals could, at first, reasonably see both the geocentric and the heliocentric as valid scientific theories. Many people today misunderstand the meaning of a **scientific theory**, probably because the word *theory* has multiple definitions. In science, a theory does not mean something "theoretical" in the sense of a possible guess that is far from certain (that would be a hypothesis). Rather, a valid scientific theory explains how the universe actually works and is supported by most of the available facts and contradicted by very few, if any. If not much is known, then several opposing theories may well be acceptable. After scientists have asked new questions and new facts have

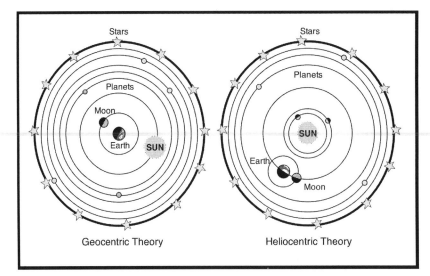

Diagram 10.1.   Geocentric versus Heliocentric Theory. Based on their observations and perspectives, ancient Greek philosophers had first proposed these theories for the structure of the universe.

been discovered, a scientific theory may either be invalidated and discounted or supported and strengthened. In this way, as scientists discovered new information, the geocentric theory eventually failed to explain the heavens, while the heliocentric theory won support.

As sixteenth-century astronomers looked at the heavens, they discovered the information that they needed to correct the calendar. They measured and calculated the movement of the stars and planets. They figured out that the year is actually 365.2422 days, a fraction less than the 365 1/4 used by the Julian calendar.

Therefore, a new calendar was proposed, one that did not add a leap day in century years that were not evenly divisible by four hundred. For example, 1900 would not have a leap day, but 2000 would. Pope Gregory XIII adopted these changes in 1582, giving Western civilization the **Gregorian calendar** to replace the Julian. He dropped ten days from that year to get the calendar back on track with the seasons: thus the day after 5 October 1582 became 15 October 1582, at least in those areas that accepted papal authority. Anglican England and Orthodox Russia waited a long time to conform to the papal view, partly because they were suspicious about anything that came from the Roman Catholic Church.

In spite of the changes to the calendar, however, the papacy fought against embracing the scientific theory that the earth revolved around the sun. In 1543, the canon and astronomer Mikolaj Kopernig in Poland (who used the Latinized name **Nicolaus Copernicus**) published a book, *Concerning the Revolutions of the Celestial Bodies*, which argued convincingly for the heliocentric theory. Copernicus knew the controversy this position would provoke and had waited to publish it until he was on his deathbed. As he expected, the Roman Catholic Church rejected his argument out of hand and put his study onto the *Index of Forbidden Books*. The papacy told astronomers they had to support the geocentric theory because it conformed to their preferred belief system of Aristotle and Scholasticism.

The Roman Catholic Church's beliefs notwithstanding, new evidence continued to undermine the geocentric theory and support the heliocentric theory. The best facts were presented by **Galileo Galilei** (b. 1564–d. 1642) of Florence. In 1609, he improved a Dutch spyglass and fashioned the first functional telescope, which he turned toward the heavens. Galileo discovered moons around Jupiter, mountains and craters on the moon, sunspots, and other phenomena that convinced him that the heavens were far from Aristotelian perfection. His publication the next year, *The Starry Messenger*, supported the Copernican theory. It sparked a sensation among intellectuals, while it also angered leaders of the Roman Catholic Church. Clergy warned Galileo his ideas were dangerous. Therefore, he kept silent until he thought a pope had been elected who would support his inquiries. Cautiously, he framed his next book, *Dialogue on the Chief World Systems* (1636), as a debate in which the Copernican view technically lost but the Aristotelian view looked indefensibly stupid.

The papacy saw through the device. The Roman Inquisition called in the seventy-year-old and questioned him, using forged evidence. The inquisitors threatened Galileo with the instruments of torture, probably including pincers, thumbscrews, leg screws, and the rack. They defined disagreement with the Roman Church as heresy, and thus Galileo was automatically a heretic. Galileo pled guilty, and the Inquisition sentenced him to house arrest for the rest of his life. The aged scientist nonetheless continued experiments that helped lay the foundation of modern physics. His studies increasingly showed that Aristotle was incorrect about many things, not only the location of the earth in the universe.

A person born in far-off England during the year Galileo died, **Isaac Newton** (b. 1642–d. 1727), assured the doom of Aristotle's views about nature. Newton first studied the properties of light (founding modern optics) and built an improved reflector telescope, which he also turned to the heavens. From his studies of the planets, Newton accepted the Copernican/heliocentric theory, but he still wanted to find an explanation for how the moon, planets, and stars stayed in their orbits while apples dropped from trees to the ground.

Supposedly inspired by an apple that fell off a tree onto his head, Newton worked to measure moving bodies, in the process inventing calculus as a tool. He finally arrived at an explanation for how the universe works, published in the book *Principia* (1687). In that treatise, Newton's theory of universal gravitation accounted for the movements of the heavenly bodies. He showed that all objects of substance, all things with the quality of "mass," possess gravitational attraction toward one another. So the moon and the earth, just as an apple and the earth, are being drawn toward each other. The apple drops because it has no other force acting upon it. The moon stays spinning around the earth because it is moving fast enough; its motion balances out the earth's gravitational pull. The delicate opposition of gravity and velocity keeps the heavens whirling.

With the publication of the *Principia*, many historians consider the Scientific Revolution to have triumphed, having created the modern, Western idea of science. Some recent historians note here the "disenchantment" of nature: instead of natural philosophy's embrace of the mystical and supernatural to contemplate and interact with divine creation, science focused on cold, hard facts. Traditional authorities, such as Aristotle, were to be doubted until proven. No longer relying on divine revelation or reason (the big debate of the Middle Ages), trustworthy knowledge was obtained through a specific tool of reason called the **scientific method**. Between the years of Copernicus and Newton's books, other intellectuals such as Francis Bacon and René Descartes had worked out this basic set of scientific principles (see table 10.1).

Table 10.1.   The Scientific Method

1. Find a problem.
2. Form a hypothesis (a reasonable or educated guess to the solution).
3. Conduct experiments (repeatedly) and/or observations (extensively).
4. Make the argument and conclusions, usually in written form.
5. Share the knowledge, usually through publication.
6. Others repeat the experiments and/or observations and share confirmations, modifications, or refutations.
7. Form scientific theories based on overwhelming evidence or laws proven by universal evidence.

Note: The step-by-step process of the scientific method rigorously uses experimentation and observation to explain how nature works.

The scientific method also compensated for the human frailties of individual scientists. For example, Newton wrote serious commentaries about the biblical book of Revelation, tried vindictively to destroy the careers of academic rivals, and fudged some of the data in his *Principia*. With the scientific process, however, human scientists applied the method to test their conclusions and produced better information about the natural world than had ever before been available in history. As a result, the Scientific Revolution had enormous consequences for Western civilization. Science became such an essential part of the Western worldview that it forms another basic principle:

> **Science is the only testable and generally accessible method of understanding the universe; every other means of explanation is opinion.**

That does not mean that all science is always correct. Many assumptions (especially about human nature) can be affected by bias or can change due to new information. Even mistakes can be useful tools to push investigations toward a more accurate understanding of nature.

As they experimented, scientists created tools to help them (see figure 10.1). One result was an acceleration in the invention of technology, which made life easier, safer, and more productive. Most people in the world around 1600 lived much the same way as they had for several thousand years. By the late seventeenth century, though, **scientific academies** (such as the British Royal Society) institutionalized scientific inquiry and its application to economic growth. Scientists were not mere theoreticians but innovators and inventors, from thermometers to timepieces, pumps to pins. These inventions were soon translated into the physical power used to dominate the globe. Medical and agricultural advances based on science followed. By 1800, westerners were living much more prosperous and comfortable lives, largely because of science.

The success of the Scientific Revolution was not complete or universal. Its attitudes only slowly spread from the elites through the population. Many westerners rejected the scientific mind-set of skepticism because they preferred specific religious doctrines or general superstitious attitudes. Moreover, science does not answer basic questions about the meaning of life and death. Honest scientists cannot proclaim certainty about the permanence of their discoveries: when presented with new information, true scientists should change their minds. And theories can come and go. For example, by the time of Newton, no reasonable scientist supported the geocentric theory because too little evidence supported it and too much contradicted it. Even the heliocentric theory has since been severely modified—while the sun *is* the center of our solar system, it is certainly *not* the center of the universe. In turn, new science led Newton's own theory of universal gravitation to be overturned (see chapter 13). By the nature of discoveries and revisions, science constantly changes life in Western civilization.

Figure 10.1. A seventeenth-century scientist, fashionably dressed and armed with a sword, examines a barometer that measures air temperature to help forecast the weather. (Treasures of the NOAA Library Collection)

Review: How did the Scientific Revolution change traditional views about nature?

Response:

FROM THE SALONS TO THE STREETS

Historians have decided that 1687, the year of Newton's *Principia*, marks the beginning of a major intellectual movement known as **the Enlightenment** (1687–1789). During this time, scientific academies and universities adapted and spread many scientific ideas. Some men chattered about these ideas in the new coffeehouses. In addition, a few wealthy and curious women gathered a variety of interesting people to discuss the issues of the day in their **salons** (pleasant rooms in their fine homes). Beginning in Paris, salon hostesses such as Madame Goffrin or Madame Rambouillet guided the witty conversation of clergymen, politicians, businessmen, scientists, and amateur philosophers, writers, and popularizers known as *philosophes*. The *philosophes* took what they learned, especially the lessons of science, and publicized it.

Philosophes made Paris the cultural capital of Western civilization. For about a century, French culture reigned supreme among the elites of the West. The French language took over intellectual life and international communication, replacing the Latin of the Middle Ages and the Renaissance. Europeans who wanted to seem sophisticated imitated French styles of cuisine, clothing, furnishings, luxury goods, and buildings. Salons and *philosophes* spread French taste across Europe. Along the way, these intellectuals explained to society how the new science and economics impacted life. Four major concepts summarize their Enlightenment views: **empiricism**, **skepticism**, **humanitarianism**, and **progress**.

The first of these concepts, *empiricism*, came from the starting point of science: observations by our senses are both accurate and reasonable. Knowledge obtained from studies of the natural world could consequently help explain human activities. This effective idea contradicted many past religious authorities, who had depended on divine revelation for their knowledge. Those supernatural, metaphysical, or spiritual answers were too open to dispute, too difficult to prove. Of course, humans do not always draw the correct conclusions from their observations, nor does the natural world always correspond to human experience. Regardless, *philosophes* were convinced that applying the tools of science to human character would help improve society.

One proponent of empirical thinking was John Locke of England. He proposed that the human mind was like a *tabula rasa* (blank slate) on which all learned information was written. His most famous empirical argument justified England's Glorious Revolution (see below) toward more democratic politics. Locke argued against books such as Thomas Hobbes's *Leviathan*, in which large sections on a Christian Commonwealth and the Kingdom of Darkness argued for absolutism.

Another famous example of an empirical argument became the *theory of classical liberal economics*. This theory contradicted the prevailing theory of mercantilism, arguing instead for making capitalism "free market" or **laissez-faire** (as coined by contemporary French economists). Classical liberal theorists justified their case on their observations of the behavior of peoples and institutions, from smugglers to ministers of state, from banks to empires. They argued against the theory of mercantilism, where government officials made key economic decisions by granting monopolies and raising tariffs. Instead, they theorized that rational individuals looking out for their own "enlightened" self-interest would make better economic choices. The most famous formulation came from the Scotsman Adam Smith in his book *The Wealth of Nations* in 1776. He saw that individual actions would accumulate to push the economy forward, as if collectively by a giant "invisible hand." Like most economic theories, classical liberal economics has serious flaws, as later history showed. For a long time, though, it made more sense than the likewise flawed theory of mercantilism.

The second Enlightenment concept, *skepticism*, followed from Descartes's principle of doubting everything and trusting only what could be tested by reason. A popular subject for skepticism was Christianity, with all its contradictions, superstitions, and schisms. Skepticism soon promoted the fashionable belief of *deism*. This creed diverged from orthodox Christianity. Deists saw God as more of a creator, maker, or author of the universe, and not so much as the incarnate Christ who redeemed sinful man through his death and resurrection. It was as if God had constructed the universe like a giant clock and left it running according to well-organized principles of nature. Thus, for many deists, Christianity became more of a moral philosophy and a guide for behavior than the overriding concern of all existence.

Many leading intellectuals embraced *agnosticism*, thus going even further down the road of doubt. Agnostics considered the existence of God impossible to prove, since God was beyond empirical observation and experimentation. Agnostics were and are concerned about this life, ignoring any possible afterlife. A few among the elites, such as the Scottish philosopher and historian David Hume, journeyed all the way to *atheism* and denied outright the existence of God. Many agnostics and atheists, moreover, attacked Christianity as a failed religion of misinformation, exploitation, and slaughter.

For the first time since the Roman Empire's conversion, Christianity was not the belief of all the leading figures of Western civilization. This trend would only continue. A natural result was that **religious toleration** became an increasingly widespread ideal. The most famous *philosophe*, Voltaire (François-Marie Arouet, b. 1694–d. 1778), thought religion useful, but he condemned using cruelty on earth in the name of saving souls for heaven. The spread of *toleration* meant that people of one faith would less often torture and execute others for having the "wrong" religion. Instead of Christian doctrine being compulsory, it increasingly became one more option among many. Religion became a private matter, not a public requirement.

Nonetheless, while many elites were turning away from traditional religion during the eighteenth century, most of the masses experienced a religious revival. Following a lull after the upheaval of the Reformation, large numbers of westerners embraced their Christian beliefs even more passionately. Furthermore, Christianity continued to fragment into even more branches. During the "Great Awakening" in America of the 1730s and 1740s, revivalist Methodists broke off from the Church of England, which they considered as too conservative or moderate. New religious groups such as the Society of Friends, nicknamed Quakers, left Europe to settle in the new American colony of Pennsylvania, founded explicitly for religious tolera-tion. Quakers expressed their faith in meetings of quiet association. In Germany, followers of **Pietism** sought to inspire a new fervency of faith in Lutheranism, dedi-cating themselves to prayer and charity. Ironically, if one counted believing Chris-tians and compared the numbers to those of nonbelieving rationalists, the Enlightenment remained more an age of faith than of reason. These measures lead to another basic principle:

> **Every religion has elements that are nonsensical to a rational outsider; nonsense or not, belief in some form of religion ful-fills a vital need for most people.**

Enlightenment *philosophes* clearly stated the first part of the principle; the histori-cal record proves the second part.

Religious toleration reflected the Enlightenment's third big concept, **humani-tarianism**, the attitude that humans should treat other humans decently. Ostensi-bly, the Christian faith and Christ's command about loving one's neighbor had a strong humanitarian component. Throughout history, however, Christian society clearly fell short of that ideal, with crusades, inquisitions, witch hunts, slavery, and cooperation with warmongers, for example. Some Christian preachers had even claimed that suffering was a virtue, calling on the faithful to wait until they died before they received any reward of paradise.

Beyond the suffering of hard conditions, active cruelty saturated eighteenth-century Western society. People visited insane asylums to watch inmates as if they were zoo exhibits. Curiously, zoos also started at that time out of scientific interest; they likewise cruelly confined wild animals in unnatural, small, bare cages. Popular sports included animal fights where bulls, dogs, or roosters ripped each other to bloody shreds. The wealthy ignored the sufferings of the poor, worsened through economic upheavals and natural disasters. Public executions frequently offered Sunday pastimes for large crowds, who watched as criminals were beheaded, burned, disemboweled (intestines pulled out and thrown on a fire), drawn and quartered (either pulled apart by horses or the dead body chopped into four pieces after partial strangulation and disembowelment), beaten by the wheel (and then the crippled body tied to a wheel and hung up on a pole), or simply hanged (usually to die by slow strangulation) (see figure 9.1). The corpses dangled for weeks, months, or even years, until they rotted to fall in pieces from their gibbets.

With the Enlightenment, the elites began to abolish such inhumanity. The new humanitarianism's virtue did not require divine commandments as its foundation. Instead, this principle of morality declared that human beings, simply because they were observably human, should be respected. Rulers passed laws to end the prac-tices of torture and to eliminate the death penalty, or at least to impose it only for the most heinous of crimes. Soon, long-term imprisonment became the common, if expensive, method of punishing criminals. Some reformers actually thought that prisons might even rehabilitate convicts away from their criminal behavior.

Even more novel, leaders began to use social reforms to prevent crime in the first place. They reasoned that poverty and ignorance contributed to the motivations of criminals, so by attacking those social ills, crime rates could be expected to decline. The idea of promoting a good life in this world, summed up in Thomas Jefferson's famous phrase, "life, liberty and the pursuit of happiness," came, for some, to be considered a basic human right.

Another radical idea of the humanitarians was the abolition of slavery. In the Enlightenment, for the first time in history, most leaders of society actually began to feel guilty about enslaving other human beings. Slaves were so expendable that as much as a quarter of the human beings bought from slavers in Africa did not live through the Atlantic crossing, chained and stacked in the filthy holds of tiny ships (see figure 9.7). Abolitionists argued for human rights for all people of whatever "color" and against the enormous profits made by those who traded in enslaved persons and those who used them on plantations and in households. Not everyone supported abolition, as some intellectuals helped better define modern racism: the idea that people inherit unchanging qualities according to their "race," and the "white" Europeans were superior to the "black" Africans, with others in between. Some historians argue that growing industrialization (see the next chapter) made traditional slavery less necessary. Yet Western civilization became the only civilization to end slavery on its own. Western powers slowly abolished formal, state-sanctioned slavery during the nineteenth century. Most slaveholders, though, only freed their enslaved people when forced to by government authority and were often well-compensated for their financial loss. Unfortunately for the newly freed, they were not given much land to farm, money to start businesses, or education to succeed in the cities.

In spite of this new recognition of humanity, half of the species, namely women, continued to suffer sexist subordination. A handful of reformers did suggest that wives should not be under the thumb of their husbands. **Mary Wollstonecraft**'s book *A Vindication of the Rights of Woman* (1792) put forth well-reasoned demands for better education of the "weaker" sex. Her notoriously unconventional lifestyle, however, undermined her call for justice. She conducted an unhappy and notoriously public love affair that produced an illegitimate daughter. As a result, many people dismissed her propositions. Long after the Enlightenment, few opportunities opened for women. True women's rights in politics, the economy, and society would have to wait many decades.

The notion that human conditions should improve, namely *progress*, was the fourth big concept of the Enlightenment. In contrast, the Judeo-Christian concept of history had direction, but not necessarily any sense that life would improve. Christians thought that at some point, either today or in the distant future, the natural world would end and humanity would be divided into those sent to hell and those united with God in heaven. The *philosophes* argued instead for a betterment of people's lives in this world, as soon as feasible, based on sound scientific conclusions drawn from empiricism. They argued that material and moral development should even happen in their own lifetimes.

As one form of progress, the Enlightenment promoted new forms of communication while fighting against government censorship. Free thought was useless without free speech and a free press. **Encyclopedias**, such as the *Britannica* (first published in 1760 and still going today) or the French *Encyclopedia or a Systematic Dictionary of the Sciences, Arts and Crafts* (begun in 1751 and finished with its first edition in 1780), offered concrete resistance to lapsing back into ignorance. In thirty-five volumes, the French *Encyclopedia* provided a handbook of all human knowledge, indeed, a summary of the Enlightenment. According to its editor, Denis Diderot, the project was supposed to bring together all knowledge, especially about technology, so that humanity could be both happy and more virtuous. Progress became reality as more people learned to read and more written materials appeared for them to read. The new literary form of **novels** (which means "new") also entertained people about the possibilities of change. Novels are book-length, fictional stories in prose about individuals who can pursue their own destinies, often against difficult odds. Samuel Richardson's *Pamela, or Virtue Rewarded* and Daniel Defoe's *Robinson Crusoe* told such tales. **Newspapers** also began publication. They informed people of recent developments in politics, economics, and culture. Armed with these foundations of information, society could only move forward.

Progress, humanitarianism, skepticism, and empiricism were agents for change in Western civilization. The *philosophes* wrote about new expectations for human beings in this world, not necessarily connected to traditional Christianity. Building on Renaissance humanism, the Enlightenment offered a rational alternative to the Christian emphasis on life after death. Actions based on reason, science, and kindness could perhaps transform this globe, despite the flaws of human nature. The question was, who could turn the words into action and actually advance the Enlightenment agenda?

Review: What improvements did Enlightenment thinkers propose for human society?

Response:

SOURCES ON FAMILIES: JEAN-JACQUES ROUSSEAU, *ÉMILE, OR ON EDUCATION* (1762)

Rather than write another philosophical tract, the philosophe *Jean-Jacques Rousseau presented his theories about education, marriage, and love in the form of a novel. He describes in detail how his protagonist, the orphan Émile, should be brought up. In the last chapter he extensively discusses the nature of women and the best way they should be raised, before describing how his hero meets and marries his designated helpmeet, Sophy. Some of his contemporaries criticized Rousseau for long living out of wedlock with a woman and having sent their children to an orphanage rather than raise them himself.*

Sophy should be as truly a woman as Émile is a man, i.e., she must possess all those characters of her sex which are required to enable her to play her part in the physical and moral order. Let us inquire to begin with in what respects her sex differs from our own.

But for her sex, a woman is a man; she has the same organs, the same needs, the same faculties. The machine is the same in its construction; its parts, its working, and its appearance are similar. Regard it as you will, the difference is only in degree.

Yet where sex is concerned man and woman are unlike; each is the complement of the other; the difficulty in comparing them lies in our inability to decide, in either case, what is a matter of sex, and what is not. . . .

In the union of the sexes each alike contributes to the common end, but in different ways. From this diversity springs the first difference which may be observed between man and woman in their moral relations. The man should be strong and active; the woman should be weak and passive; the one must have both the power and the will; it is enough that the other should offer little resistance.

When this principle is admitted, it follows that woman is specially made for man's delight. If man in his turn ought to be pleasing in her eyes, the necessity is less urgent, his virtue is in his strength, he pleases because he is strong. I grant you this is not the law of love, but it is the law of nature, which is older than love itself.

If woman is made to please and to be in subjection to man, she ought to make herself pleasing in his eyes and not provoke him to anger; her strength is in her charms, by their means she should compel him to discover and use his strength. The surest way of arousing this strength is to make it necessary by resistance. . . . This is the origin of attack and defense, of the boldness of one sex and the timidity of the other, and even of the shame and modesty with which nature has armed the weak for the conquest of the strong. . . .

The Most High has deigned to do honor to mankind; he has endowed man with boundless passions, together with a law to guide them, so that man may be alike free and self-controlled; though swayed by these passions man is endowed with reason by which to control them. Woman is also endowed with boundless passions; God has given her modesty to restrain them. . . .

Thus the different constitution of the two sexes leads us to a third conclusion, that the stronger party seems to be master, but is as a matter of fact dependent on the weaker, and that, not by any foolish custom of gallantry, . . . but by an inexorable law of nature. For nature has endowed woman with a power of stimulating man's passions in excess of man's power of satisfying those passions, and has thus made him dependent on her goodwill, and compelled him in his turn to endeavor to please her, so that she may be willing to yield to his superior strength. Is it weakness which yields to force, or is it voluntary self-surrender? . . .

The experience we have gained through our vices has considerably modified the views held in older times; we rarely hear of violence for which there is so little occasion that it would hardly be credited. Yet such stories are common enough among the Jews and ancient Greeks. . . . If fewer deeds of violence are quoted in our days, it is not that men are more temperate, but because they are less credulous, and a complaint which would have been believed among a simple people would only excite laughter among ourselves; therefore silence is the better course. There is a law in Deuteronomy, under which the outraged maiden was punished, along with her assailant, if the crime were committed in a town; but if in the country or in a lonely place, the latter alone was punished. "For," says the law, "the maiden cried for help, and there was none to hear." From this merciful interpretation of the law, girls learnt not to let themselves be surprised in lonely places.

This change in public opinion has . . . produced our modern gallantry. Men have found that their pleasures depend, more than they expected, on the goodwill of the fair sex, and have secured this goodwill by attentions which have had their reward. . . .

The consequences of sex are wholly unlike for man and woman. The male is only a male now and again, the female is always a female, or at least all her youth; everything reminds her of her sex; the performance of her functions requires a special constitution. She needs care during pregnancy and freedom from work when her child is born; she must have a quiet, easy life while she nurses her children; their education calls for patience and gentleness, for a zeal and love which nothing can dismay; she forms a bond between father and child, she alone can win the father's love for his children and convince him that they are indeed his own. What loving care is required to preserve a united family! And there should be no question of virtue in all this, it must be a labor of love, without which the human race would be doomed to extinction. . . .

Questions:

- *What does the source assert as the main differences between men and women?*
- *How does the source claim that "violence" against women (or sexual assault) has changed from ancient times to the author's?*
- *What does the source say are conditions necessary for women to raise families?*

Responses:

Citation

Rousseau, Jean-Jacques. *Émile*. Translated by Barbara Foxley. New York: E. P. Dutton, 1911, pp. 321–26.

For more on this source, go to http://www.concisewesternciv.com/sources/sof10
.html.

THE STATE IS HE (OR SHE)

Since the late sixteenth century, various works by political theorists had been articu-
lating how government could contribute to progress. Some intellectuals suggested
rather radical ideas, which are explained in the next section. Most, however, justified the increasing powers of **absolute monarchy**. This idea reflected a new intensity of royal power, the most effective form of absolutism to date.[1] Political theorists
and *philosophes* asked how people should be ruled in a fashion that improved
society. Many, such as Thomas Hobbes or Jean Bodin, answered that as much power
as possible should be put in the hands of a dynastic prince. Diets and parliaments
were seen as chaotic and inefficient.

While the term *absolutism* is embedded in the seventeenth and eighteenth
centuries, the basic concept dates back almost to the beginning of civilization. Rulers had always been naturally inclined to claim as much authority as possible. Yet
ancient and medieval rulers lacked the capacity for effective absolutism. A king like
Charlemagne sought to order society, but other forces—the aristocracy, the weak
economy, primitive transportation and communication, the low level of education,
as well as foes he needed to slaughter—made society too resistant and slow to feel
the power of government.

Early modern arguments for absolutism relied on two main justifications. The
first one, popular from the late fifteenth to the early eighteenth centuries, was rule
by ***divine right***. This idea drew on ancient beliefs that kings had special connections to the supernatural. Even the early medieval Germanic kings like the Merovingians appealed to their divine blood to justify their dynasty. The Carolingians and
Christian dynasties afterward based their views on Old Testament kings like David
and Solomon. It was a comforting thought that God had selected monarchs through
royal bloodlines. Kings mirrored the God who ruled the universe: as he reigned in
heaven completely, so monarchs on earth had the right to unconditional domination. The pomp and God-given prestige of kings sometimes made the papacy and
religion less important. This dynastic argument was so strong that even women
were allowed to inherit the throne in many countries.

With the rising skepticism of the Enlightenment, the justification for absolutism
eventually changed. Once deists doubted God's active intervention in our planetary
affairs, justifying monarchy by divine selection lost its resonance. Therefore, the
second argument sanctioning royal absolutism turned on rational utility. This
enlightened despotism asserted that one person should rule because, logically,
unity encouraged simplicity and efficiency. Moreover, this absolute rule should benefit most of the subjects within the state, not merely enhance the monarch's own
personal comfort or vanity.

---

1. The famous phrase from Lord Acton, "Power tends to corrupt, and absolute power cor-
rupts absolutely," leaps to mind. But he was writing decades later.

Historians usually credit France with becoming the first modern European state because of its royal revival of royal absolutism. By ending the civil wars of the late sixteenth century, King Henry IV rode a tide of goodwill and a widespread desire for peace to become an absolute monarch. He revised the taxes, built public works, promoted businesses, balanced the budget, and encouraged culture. He allegedly originated the famous political promise that there would be a chicken in every pot (at least on Sunday). In an age when most peasants rarely ate meat, that was quite a goal. Living well in this world was becoming more important than living well for the next.

Henry's assassination by a mad monk in 1610 threatened France's stability once again. Henry left only a child, Louis XIII, on the throne. As illustrated before, a child ruler has often sparked civil wars, as factions sought to replace or control the minor. This consequence highlighted a major flaw of monarchical regimes dependent upon one person: what if the king were incompetent or a child? The system could easily break down.

Appointing competent and empowered bureaucrats to rule in the king's name solved this weakness. Louis XIII gained such a significant and capable minister with **Cardinal Richelieu** (d. 1642).[2] Instead of serving the papacy, as his title would suggest, Richelieu became the first minister to his king. As such, he worked tirelessly to strengthen absolute government in France. As a royal servant, the cardinal ruled in the king's name. Also, because as a cleric he was required to live in celibacy, he did not pose a threat in creating his own rival dynasty, as the Carolingian mayors of the palace had done under the Merovingians. When Louis XIII came of age, he continued to relish all the privileges of being a king while Richelieu did all the hard work.

Therefore, the king's minister continued to deepen the roots of monarchical authority. Richelieu strengthened the government with more laws, more taxes, a better army, and a streamlined administration. By executing select nobles for treason, he intimidated all of the nobility. Although he was a Roman Catholic cardinal, Richelieu made decisions for reasons of state, not faith. He helped the German Protestants during the Thirty Years War because weakening the Habsburg emperors benefited France. While he took away some of the privileges granted to French Huguenot Protestants by the Edict of Nantes, his motivation was political. He interpreted the rights of Protestants to self-defense and fortified cities as impinging on the king's claim to a monopoly on force—only agents of the king could kill. In a notorious example of manipulation, the cardinal allowed a panic about demon-possessed nuns in order to interfere in the Huguenot town of Loudun.

Both Richelieu and his king died within a year of each other, again leaving a child as heir, **Louis XIV** (r. 1643–1715). Once more, the crown almost plunged into a crisis over a child king. Nevertheless, Louis XIV managed to hold on to the throne under the protection of another clerical minister, Cardinal Mazarin. Once

---

2. Versions of Alexandre Dumas's *The Three Musketeers* often portray Richelieu as a villain who seeks the throne for himself. Realistically, it would have been impossible for him to become king. Historical evidence, and the novel, shows him to be a Machiavellian manipulator, but for the benefit of the French crown.

he reached maturity, Louis XIV became the most powerful king France had ever known. Louis XIV differed from Louis XIII in that he himself actually wanted to rule. He took charge, depicting himself as shining over France as the "Sun King." According to Louis's vision, if the land did not have the sunlight of his royal person, it would die in darkness. He allegedly claimed, "L'État, c'est moi" (I am the state).

Louis XIV's modernizations were numerous. He met with his chief ministers in a small chamber called a **cabinet**, thus coining a name for executive meetings. These cabinet ministers then carried out the royal will through the bureaucracy. Instead of relying on mercenaries, France raised one of the first modern professional armies, which meant that paid soldiers were uniformed and permanently housed in barracks. Since so many troops were recruited from the common classes, this army continued the decline of the traditional responsibilities of medieval knights for warfare. Being a noble no longer meant military service. To pay for these royal troops, Louis intervened in the economy with the intention of helping it grow. His ministers adopted a version of the economic theory of mercantilism, whose advocacy of government intervention naturally pleased the absolute monarch. The government targeted industries for aid and both licensed and financed the founding of colonies.

Louis XIV's most noticeable legacy (especially for the modern tourist) was his construction of the palace of **Versailles**, which became a whole new capital located a few miles from crowded, dirty Paris. There he collected his bureaucracy and government and projected a grand image of himself. Actually, the palace was rather uncomfortable to live in. The chimneys were too short to draw smoke properly, so rooms were smoky and drafty. The kitchens were a great distance from the dining room, so the various courses, from soup, fish, poultry, and so on, got cold before they could be eaten. Yet Louis nourished a palace culture, with himself as the royal center of attention. Aristocrats and nobles clamored to reside in his palace, maneuvering to attend to both the intimate and public needs of the most important person in the country. They dressed him, emptied his chamber pots, danced at his balls, bowed down at his entrances, and gossiped behind his back. Naturally, this luxurious living required huge amounts of money from the nobles and the taxpayers. Likewise, the brilliance of the court did not entirely blind the members of the aristocracy to their long-standing prerogatives; but for a moment, absolutely, Louis was king.

Historians usually qualify Louis's greatness because of two ambivalent decisions. For one, Louis XIV revoked the Edict of Nantes. He did not comprehend the advantage of tolerating religious diversity in his realm. His view was *un roi, une loi, une foi* (one king, one law, one faith). This action raised fewer outcries than it might have decades earlier; many people had transferred their desire for religion into loyalty to the state. Still, outlawing Protestantism in France hurt the economy, since many productive Huguenots left for more tolerant countries, especially the Netherlands and Brandenburg-Prussia. For his own purposes, though, Louis XIV achieved more religious uniformity for Roman Catholicism.

The second troublesome choice of Louis's reign was his desire for military glory, *la gloire*. He thought he should wage war to make his country, and consequently himself, bigger and stronger. He aimed to expand France's borders to the Rhine

River. Such a move would have taken territories away from the Holy Roman Empire. Other tempting targets were the rich Lowlands, both the Spanish Netherlands held by the Habsburgs and the free Dutch Netherlands. Yet Louis was no great general himself; he entrusted that role to others. He himself stayed far away from the battle-front even while he committed France to a series of risky wars. Unfortunately for his grand plans, other European powers, particularly Britain and Habsburg Austria, resolutely opposed France, fearing a threat to the balance of power.

By the time Louis XIV died in 1715, France had sunk deeply into debt and lay exhausted. This situation reveals another flaw of absolutism: if anyone disagreed with government policies, little could be done to change the monarch's mind. In France, the Estates-General, the representative parliamentarian body created in the fourteenth century, had not met in more than a century. At most, people could request change by presenting a petition to the monarch. Furthermore, Louis and other absolute monarchs easily tired of criticism. They tended to insulate them-selves and heard advice only from handpicked, obsequious bureaucrats and self-seeking sycophantic courtiers. Despite this limitation, Louis set the tone for other princes, kings, and emperors. Any prince who wanted respect needed new palaces, parties at court, and military victories. Princes all across Europe imitated the Sun King.

One of the Sun King's most interesting imitators came from a place that seemed insignificant at the beginning of Louis's reign. Far off eastward, where Europe turns into Asia, a new power called **Russia** was rising. Western Europeans had not taken much note of Russia up to this point. A Russian principality around Kiev had almost started to flourish in the Middle Ages, but then the **Mongols** conquered it. The Mongols were yet another group of Asiatic horse riders, like the Huns and Turks. They invaded eastern Europe briefly in the 1300s, adding Russia to their vast Kha-nate Empire. During the 1400s, the dukes of Moscow managed to throw off the Mongol yoke and slowly freed their Russian brethren and neighboring ethnic groups from Mongol domination.

By 1600, the duchy of Moscow had expanded to become the Russian Empire, ruled by the **tsars** (sometimes spelled *czar*, the Russian word for emperor, derived from "Caesar"). Russia was a huge territory by 1613 when the Romanov dynasty came to power. The Romanovs provided continuity and stability after a period of turmoil. Like other imperialist European powers, the Russians started to conquer Asians who were less technologically advanced than Europeans. Unlike the other European powers, though, Russians did not need to cross oceans; they only had to cross the Ural Mountains into Asia. Thus began the notable reversal of a historical trend. Up until 1600, horse-riding warriors from the vast steppes of central Asia, whether Huns, Turks, or Mongols, had periodically invaded Europe. Now Europe-ans began to invade Asia. By 1648, Russians had already crossed Siberia to reach the Pacific Ocean. Then they pushed southward, taking over the Muslim Turkish peoples of central Asia. Their empire transformed Russia into a great power, although western Europeans did not recognize it at first, since Russia was so far away.

The first ruler who made Europeans take notice was **Tsar Peter I "the Great"** (r. 1682–1725). Peter saw that Russia could become greater by inaugurating a policy of **_westernization_** (conforming local institutions and attitudes to those of western Europe). Thus, Russia became more and more part of Western civilization (see figure 10.2). Before Peter, the main cultural influences had come from Byzantium and Asia. Since the Byzantine Empire's collapse, Russian tsars had proclaimed themselves the successors of Rome and Constantinople and the protectors of Eastern Orthodox Christianity. Those roles offered little chance for real political advancement. The Enlightenment offered progress, which Peter learned of firsthand, having toured western Europe in 1697 and 1698. In England, France, the Netherlands, and Germany, he saw the power harnessed by the Commercial and Scientific Revolutions and decided to bring Western economics, science, and even culture to Russia. In pursuit of that last goal, he went so far as to legislate that Russian nobles speak French and shave off their bushy beards and abandon warm furs in order to dress like the courtiers of Versailles. Silk knee pants and white powdered wigs were impractical in a cold Russian winter, but if the tsar commanded, no one said "*Non*," much less "*Nyet*."

Tsar Peter's new capital of **St. Petersburg** surpassed even Louis XIV's Versailles. Peter built not only a palace but a whole city (naming it after the saint with whom the tsar shared a name was no coincidence). First, he had needed to conquer the land, defeating Sweden in the crucial Great Northern War (1700–1721). Before the war, Sweden had claimed great power status based on its key role in the Thirty Years War. Afterward, Sweden was no more than a minor power, while Russia's supremacy was assured. Then at enormous expense, forty thousand workers struggled for fourteen years to build a city on what had once been swampland. Thousands paid the price of their lives. Located on an arm of the Baltic Sea, the new

Figure 10.2. A modern statue honors Tsar Peter "the Great" of Russia (and his wild-eyed horse) in the city he founded, St. Petersburg.

Russian capital was connected by sea routes to the world. St. Petersburg perfectly symbolized the Enlightenment's confidence that the natural wilderness could be tamed into order. Peter also considered St. Petersburg his "window on the West," his connection to the rest of Europe. As much as they might wish, Europeans could never again ignore Russia after Peter; by force of imperial will, he had made his empire part of the Western balance of power.

Besides the rulers of France and Russia, many other monarchs aspired to greatness through absolutism. One of most interesting appeared in the empire of Austria, whose rulers of the Habsburg dynasty were also consistently elected Holy Roman emperors. The ethnically German Habsburgs had assembled a multiethnic empire of Germans, Czechs, Slovaks, Hungarians, Croatians, Italians, and many other smaller groups. The dynasty alone, not tradition or affection, held these diverse peoples together. In 1740, many feared a crisis when **Maria Theresa** (r. 1740–1780), an unprepared twenty-three-year-old princess who was pregnant with her fourth child, inherited the Austrian territories.

Although her imperial father had issued a law called the Pragmatic Sanction to recognize her right, as a mere woman, to inherit, he had never trained her for rulership. Instead, Maria Theresa's husband, Francis of Habsburg-Lorraine (who was also her cousin), was expected to take over Austria as archduke and become elected as emperor. Maria Theresa loved her husband (literally—she gave birth sixteen times), but Francis showed no talent for politics. Other European rulers also knew this. When Maria Theresa's father died in 1740, France, Prussia, and others attacked in the War of Austrian Succession (1740–1748). Her enemies seized several of the diverse Austrian territories and by 1742 crowned the duke of Bavaria as Holy Roman emperor—the first prince other than a Habsburg to hold the title in three hundred years.

Surprisingly, Maria Theresa took charge of the situation, becoming one of the best rulers Austria has ever had. Showing courage and resolve, she appealed to honor, tradition, and chivalry, which convinced her subjects to obey and her armies to fight. To support her warriors properly, she initiated a modern military in Austria, with standardized supply and uniforms as well as officer training schools. She reformed the economy, collecting new revenues such as the income tax and introducing paper money. This last innovation showed a growing trust of government: otherwise, why would people accept money that for the first time in civilization was not made of precious metal? The move boosted the economy, since conveniently carried paper money made it easier to invest and to buy things. Maria Theresa's confident bureaucracy reorganized the administration of her widespread lands. She also devoted attention to social welfare, leading to her declaration that every child should have a basic education, including girls. Thus, schools were built and maintained at public expense. Her revised legal codes eliminated torture, stopped the witch hunts, and investigated crime through rational methods (see figure 10.3). Her imposition of uniformity and consistency promoted the best of modern government. Admittedly, Maria Theresa did build an imitation Versailles at Schönbrunn and did live the privileged life considered appropriate to an empress (see figure 10.4). Yet people were willing to support an enlightened monarchy that also did

Figure 10.3. In the manner of the Enlightenment, reason applied even to torture. A legal handbook written for Maria Theresa shows the most efficient means of questioning someone, using a ladder for torture. She outlawed such methods soon after the handbook was published. (University of Pennsylvania)

Figure 10.4.   As a typical absolute monarch, Maria Theresa had a new palace, Schönbrunn, built for herself outside Vienna.

something for them. In the end, Maria Theresa's competent reign safeguarded Austria's great power status and its people's prosperity.

Maria Theresa's great rival was King **Frederick II "the Great"** Hohenzollern (r. 1740–1786) of **Prussia**. That kingdom had grown from the conquests of the crusading order of the Teutonic Knights along the southern coast of the Baltic Sea. During the Reformation, these German monk-knights converted to Lutheranism and established themselves as a secular dynasty. Soon after, the Hohenzollern dynasty of the March of Brandenburg inherited Prussia. The dynasty slowly built Brandenburg-Prussia up to a middle-ranked power by the early eighteenth century, becoming "kings in Prussia" by 1715. Frederick II himself had some reluctance about becoming king, and as a young man he tried to flee the overbearing rule of his royal father. The king captured Prince Frederick, forced him to watch his best friend shot for treason, and threatened to do the same to Frederick. The young Frederick bowed to the will of his father and became much more serious about his future kingship.

Frederick's father died in the same year as Maria Theresa's. In addition to the royal crown, he inherited from his father a well-drilled army and a well-coffered treasury. Frederick used them to grab the rich province of Silesia from Maria Theresa, thus starting the War of Austrian Succession. Frederick's greatest success was having Prussia survive both the War of Austrian Succession and the Seven Years War that followed, with the prize of Silesia intact. As the actual general in command of his armies, much of the credit for this went to him personally. Aside from his conquests, King Frederick II also ruled in an enlightened manner: improving finances, justice, administration, and social welfare. Therefore, by the end of his reign, Prussia was a great power, competitive with England, France, Austria, and Russia.

Austria, Prussia, and Russia sealed their enlightened cooperation with the notorious **Partitions of Poland** (1772–1795). Maria Theresa, Frederick, and their younger contemporary, Tsar Catherine II "the Great," helped themselves to choice bits of Polish territory.[3] In 1772, Poland was the second-largest European nation, next to Russia. Yet its elected kings had almost no power. The nobility claimed to run the country through their parliament, the Sejm. Nevertheless, their self-confidence had gone too far, since any one noble in the body could veto any attempt at legislation. Consequently, few laws or reforms passed, and Poland could not keep pace with the innovations of its enlightened neighbors. Considering this incompetence of the Polish government, the enlightened argued that it would be better if Austrians, Prussians, or Russians ruled the Poles. Polish forces were unable to defend and resist the occupation of their country, which only proved the point of their government's ineffectiveness. In several stages, Austria, Prussia, and Russia carved up the country. By 1795, rationalizations by absolutists had wiped Poland from the map.

Review: *How did absolutism gain ascendancy in early modern Europe?*

Response:

(PROSPEROUS) PEOPLE POWER

Fundamentally, debates about political structures are about who should decide when and how governments can interfere in the affairs of their own people and of those of neighboring states. Governments decide important issues of law (about private property and taxes, private violence and public safety, personal versus public morality and religion) and war. With absolutism, the prince (or the reigning emperor, king, queen, archduchess, prince-bishop, duke, etc.) represented the entire state, while all people therein were subjects. Monarchs reigned above the law, or were themselves, in essence, the law. Everything circled around the ruler.

While absolutism flourished, some began fighting for another view: that power should flow upward from the citizens, who needed to participate in decision making. In the Western heritage, the notion that the people should rule themselves

---

3. Catherine (r. 1762–1796) was actually a German princess, Sophie Friederike Auguste von Anhalt-Zerbst-Dornburg, brought to Russia to marry the heir to the throne. Once he became tsar, she gained her lovers' help to remove and execute her husband and then took over herself. Despite this ruthless start to her reign, she largely ruled in the fashion of enlightened despotism.

goes back to the democracies of the ancient Greece *poleis* and the Roman Republic. Citizens had organized into factions that collectively argued about a variety of policies, leaning toward tradition or innovation regarding greater or lesser government intervention and participation by the rich or poor, the fewer or the many. Those systems had failed, but they were not forgotten. Then, in the Middle Ages, elected governments in towns and cities or in communes reasserted democratic principles. Yet self-government had not actually expanded beyond the size of a local government.

The one exception was the **Swiss Confederation**. In the late thirteenth century, Swiss townspeople and peasants had the audacity to claim self-rule, without any aristocracy. The legends of Wilhelm Tell and his archery date to this period of liberation from the Habsburg dynasty. Contemporaries, however, saw the Swiss success as an unusual circumstance brought about by the Swiss pikemen's ability to defend Alpine passes. Few gave Switzerland much respect. After a brief attempt at becoming a dominant regional power, the confederation retreated into neutrality and nonintervention after defeat in a war over Italy in 1515. Even then, few understood how the Swiss state held together, divided by four languages (German, French, Italian, and Rhaeto-Romansch) and several versions of Christianity (Roman Catholicism, Calvinism, Zwinglism, Waldensianism, etc.). For all other countries, monarchy based on a subservient aristocracy and nobility seemed the superior method of rule.

Around 1600, though, a few countries began to explore democracy as an alternative structure for political power. The two basic components of all modern democracies have been ***republicanism*** and ***constitutionalism***. As in ancient Rome, republicanism was government by elected representatives, where office seekers competed for votes, served limited terms, and then were replaced, even by their political opponents. Constitutionalism meant that law limited a government's powers, whether formally written in an explicit document or merely collected as traditions and practices. Constitutional law prohibited government from violating certain specified rights of citizens. For such a democracy to function, therefore, broad obedience to standards of law and willingness to compromise with others of differing ideologies were required.

In 1581, the **United Provinces of the Netherlands** became the first modern country to give up on kings. As seen in the Reformation, the various provinces of the Calvinist Dutch Netherlands (of which the most famous was **Holland**) had declared their freedom from the Roman Catholic Habsburg king of Spain. Fighting for religious freedom for themselves, they also soon extended it to others. The majority of the Dutch were reformed Calvinists, but they also tolerated English Puritans (including the Pilgrims), Mennonites, Lutherans, and even Roman Catholics.

The industrious merchants behind the successful rebellion against the Spanish monarchy created a new form of national government. The Dutch did not simply replace one monarch with another (although the noble dynasty of Orange was interested). Instead, the great merchants, or Hooge Moogende (High Mightinesses), pooled their resources and ran the state. The new Dutch regime was an oligarchy or, perhaps, a ***plutocracy***, rule based on wealth. Only male members of the propertied classes held political offices, much like the oligarchic patricians in ancient Rome. Although Dutch people sometimes turned to the aristocratic House of Orange for leadership, the elected representatives usually ran the country, making the key decisions in war and peace. They also spent money on artists such as Rembrandt, Hals, and Vermeer.

Under this democratic government, Holland became Europe's greatest economic power for several decades of the seventeenth century. Possessing few natural resources and a tiny territory with no hope for expansion in Europe, the Dutch pursued economic power through trade. Dutch investors and politicians founded the Bank of Amsterdam in 1609 to provide capital. Cheap fly-boats hauled cargo at the best price and speed.

The Netherlands even became a world power, creating a colonial empire to rival those of the Spanish and Portuguese. The Dutch Empire stretched from the East Indies to South Africa, to the Caribbean, to the "New" Netherlands in North America along the Hudson River. A government-chartered monopoly for Asian trade, the United East India Company (using the initials VOC) paved the way for joint-stock corporations in 1602 (see figure 10.5). As colonial masters, the Dutch were less harsh than others toward the natives. The Dutch even encouraged a

Figure 10.5. An early version of a corporate logo, the "VOC" of the Dutch East India Company (Vereenigde Oost-Indische Compagnie) marks a cannon, one of the artillery pieces with which the Netherlands took over trade in the East Indies.

vibrant trading network in East Asia, unlike other Europeans whose trade exploited the colonies solely for the mother country's benefit. Still, Dutch merchants crushed any threats from Asians to their monopoly on power, killing and enslaving when they thought necessary. Not for the first time, the benefits of democracy at home did not extend to colonized native territories around the world.

Nevertheless, their economic advantage did not last long. Dutch economic supremacy ended by 1700. The Dutch were too small in population, too vulnerable to French invasion, and too easily cut off from the Atlantic by the English, who could close the Channel and patrol the North Sea. Several wars against the English saw the Dutch defeat the young Royal Navy, but when a prince of Orange became King William III of England because of his wife Mary in 1688, his policies against France actually benefited the English more than the Dutch.

The Netherlands lost supremacy of the seas but maintained its vital role in the international economy. A state did not have to be mighty to prosper. While Holland was no longer a great power after 1700, the Netherlands nevertheless remained richer and freer than most countries of Europe.

By 1700, England had taken Holland's place as the major maritime power. The accession of the Stuart dynasty of Scotland to the throne of England (1603–1714) had helped England surpass Holland. When the Tudor dynasty ended with the "Virgin Queen" Elizabeth, a quick decision by English leaders settled the crown peacefully on her cousin, King James VI of Scotland, who became King James I of England. These combined realms were officially renamed the **United Kingdom of Great Britain** a century later. The unification of these traditional enemies did not always go smoothly, especially because the English certainly dominated the arrangement. Yet the combined British energies (throwing in Wales and occupied Ireland) slowly advanced science, technology, exploration, and profit. Soon, the British controlled the largest empire in world history.

On the path to becoming a world empire, the English stumbled through the **English Revolution** (1642–1689), which democratized their politics. The revolution's roots go back to the Reformation and deep into the Middle Ages. The medieval English kings and many kings in the West had founded representative bodies to help them in their rule. The English body, Parliament, made up of elected representatives from clergy, nobility, and townspeople, consulted with kings about taxes and laws. Parliament was originally no stronger than any other medieval political body. Then the English Reformation granted it decisive power. Parliament participated in making the laws that established the Church of England. It made decisions about the dynasty, endorsing different heirs as Henry VIII went through his wives and as his children were crowned and subsequently died. These historic decisions ensured that Parliament's elected representatives enjoyed a real partnership with the royal government.

The new Stuart dynasty at first lacked an appreciation for this development. That was odd, since the first Stuart monarch, James VI of Scotland, had minimal power in his own homeland, being hemmed in by rambunctious nobles who had thrown out his mother, Mary Stuart, Queen of Scots. Yet when James VI of Scotland became James I of England (r. 1603–1625) through an act of Parliament, he became infatuated with the divine-right theories of absolutism. He even tried to lecture

Parliament about his God-granted prerogatives. James's heir, Charles I (r. 1625–1649), went even further. He temporarily refused to summon Parliament and tried ruling without them. His effort failed.

The delicate Anglican compromise that had created a national church helped prevent absolutism in England. While the government required that everyone worship in the Church of England, many believers disagreed about how that worship should be done according to *The Book of Common Prayer*. At one end of the spectrum, English Calvinists, called Puritans, wanted a more reformed church. At the other end, supporters of bishops wanted worship and belief similar to Roman Catholicism, although without the papacy.

Not even allowed into the debate were extreme Protestant sects and Roman Catholics, whose beliefs remained illegal. Some Puritans had felt so oppressed by being forced to worship in the Anglican style that they became **separatists**, rejecting not only the English faith but also England itself. One group settled briefly in the tolerant Netherlands before getting permission to settle in the New World; they became the Pilgrims of Plymouth Colony, Massachusetts, in 1620 (the ones who originated the American holiday of Thanksgiving).

The first Stuart king, James I, usually supported the Anglican compromise, even though many Puritans suspected him of being too Roman Catholic. James I's commission of a translation of the Bible into English, the King James Bible, helped to overcome suspicions concerning his religious leanings (although his favor toward certain male courtiers continued to provoke gossip and anger about his sexual inclinations).

Suspicions about the religious reliability of the Stuarts increased under Charles I, James I's son and successor. Charles I had unwisely married a French princess who held Roman Catholic masses in the royal palaces. Like his father, Charles I believed in absolutism with even less toleration for religious diversity. As head of the Church of England, Charles insisted that all of his subjects worship the same way. In 1640, he tried to impose the Anglican *Book of Common Prayer* on the Scottish Calvinist Presbyterians. The Scots rebelled.

Charles did not have the funds to fight a civil war with his usual revenues, while tradition required Parliament to participate in raising taxes. Reluctantly, Charles held elections and called Parliament into session. The parliamentarians proceeded to insist on their prerogatives to share power with the king. Charles resisted. By 1642, the king (supported by many of the nobility, great landowners, and conservative and moderate Anglicans) was at war with many of the parliamentarians (supported by lesser gentry and yeomen, the merchant classes, the large cities, and the Puritans). The **English Civil War** (1642–1651) consequently broke out.

Unexpectedly, the country gentleman **Oliver Cromwell** (d. 1658) soon became the commander of the parliamentarians. Cromwell mastered recruiting, commanding, supplying, and inspiring armies to victory. His New Model Army—using the latest military technology of combining cavalry, pikes, and muskets—reinforced the increasing role of common people in the armed forces at the expense of the nobility. Just as in ancient Greece and Rome as well as in the Middle Ages, military change transformed politics. Parliament's armies defeated the royal forces and captured the king. Parliament tried King Charles I for treason, found him guilty, and had him beheaded on 30 January 1649.

The English then faced running a government without a monarch, having declared themselves a purely republican system, or as they called it, the **Common-wealth**. Of course, democracy was difficult. Cromwell quickly became discouraged with all the infighting and quarreling among the country's leaders, so he took harsh action. He purged the government of those representatives he did not like and took over himself. Basing his authority on the command of the armed forces, he turned the Commonwealth into the first modern *dictatorship*, called the Protectorate. Cromwell suppressed Roman Catholics and rebellious sentiment in Ireland by conducting severe reprisals. He then encouraged the settlement of Protestants from Scotland and Wales into the northern counties of Ulster and also led a trade war against the Dutch. In spite of these harsh measures, many of the English saw Cromwell as a benevolent dictator.

After Cromwell died, the British had to decide how to secure stability and responsibility without the dictator's strong hand. Cromwell's son and heir lacked the ability of the father, and he willingly resigned. Unable to resist a royal dynasty, Parliament finally recalled the Stuarts, asking for the **Restoration** of the monarchy. King Charles II (r. 1660–1685) eagerly accepted. While he had the same Roman Catholic and absolutist sympathies as his father, Charles II was at least clever enough not to let those views get in the way of being king. Instead of fighting political battles with Parliament over power, Charles II relished a sumptuous court life and many mistresses. Despite all his promiscuity, Charles II had no legitimate children, so upon his death the British throne went to his brother James II (r. 1685–1688). The second James began acting like an absolute monarch. Even worse, he openly converted to Roman Catholicism and had his son and heir baptized in that faith. Unwilling to have a Roman Catholic as king, many English had had enough.

In the **Glorious Revolution** of 1688, the English established the basic democratic system. With little bloodshed, they forced James to flee to France. Parliament then invited James's Protestant daughter Mary to be their queen, with her husband, William of Orange, as co-ruling king. Although James attempted to win back the throne with an invasion of Ireland, he lost at the Battle of the Boyne in July 1689.[4] Thereafter, the English substantially took over Ireland, and Irish independence vanished for centuries.

Other Scots, meanwhile, especially those in the Highlands, disputed the claims of William and Mary and wanted their own Stuart dynasty back. Large parts of Scotland rebelled in 1715 and again in 1745 in the name of Stuart pretenders to the throne. Following the Battle of Culloden in 1746, the English crushed Scottish hopes for independence. Curiously, the English were so worried about Scottish

---

4. England was still under the Julian calendar when the battle was fought on what then was dated "Old Style" 1 July 1689. When England converted to the Gregorian "New Style" calendar, the date should have been recalculated as 11 July 1689. Irish Protestants in Northern Ireland, however, celebrate the Boyne annually on the "Twelfth" of July, partly because of another victory on that date over Irish Roman Catholics.

resistance that they also banned the Scots from wearing tartan plaids or kilts for several decades. As a consolation prize, the victorious Parliament generously approved a small measure of toleration for religious dissenters, both Roman Catholics and Presbyterian Calvinists.

Most importantly, Parliament affirmed through the Glorious Revolution that it was in charge, not the monarch, although it took several more decades for Parliament to reach its full authority. The idea of ***parliamentarianism*** meant that an elected representative body ran the government. This system used a cabinet, where the important state officials met in a small conference room to make the important decisions. Under absolutism, these cabinet members were appointees of the king; under parliamentarianism, they were elected by voters. The member who got the most support in the Parliament and who led the cabinet became the **prime minister** (in some countries later called a chancellor). Prime ministers held on to power as long as they had a majority of votes, either in parliament or the next election. The prime minister increasingly took on actual leadership of the nation, as the cabinet met more and more often without the monarch. The prime minister's faction made policy and appointed the bureaucrats and civil servants. The British kings and queens faded into figureheads, representing that old ideal of parents of the country rather than actual war leaders and judges. By keeping a royal dynasty and using it as a stabilizing force, Britain became the most important Western ***constitutional monarchy***. Such a system uses both constitutionalism (even if there is no one single document, laws limit government authority) and republicanism (even if there is a hereditary crowned head, elected representatives wield the power).

It is surprising that having suffered so much for the sake of establishing democratic government at home, the British were unwilling to grant it to their fellow countrymen abroad. Once the British acquired an empire, they lost the perspective of the ruled and relished the supremacy of the ruler. By 1763, Britain had the most significant world empire of all the European nations. The first clash among these European empires was the **Seven Years War** (1756–1763), which could be considered the first world war. Armed forces fought three simultaneous campaigns: in Europe (especially Maria Theresa of Austria versus Frederick II of Prussia), in India (where the British called it the Third Carnatic War), and in the Americas (where the American colonists called it the **French and Indian War**). In the last two theaters, the British victory was decisive. The British drove the French out of India, leaving the British as the only significant Western power there. In North America the British attacked France's Native American allies with biological warfare, intentionally giving them articles infected with smallpox. The French lost Quebec and only managed to hold on to a few islands in the Caribbean. For the next two centuries, the British Empire was the greatest empire of the world, surpassing all previous empires.

Nevertheless, wars and empires are expensive. Despite their victory, the British needed to figure out both how to pay for and how to defend their world empire. One obvious choice for revenue was the American colonists, who had gained security with the loss of the French threat to their north. The British wanted the Americans to contribute their fair share to the economic well-being of the mother country. Many Americans wanted instead to look after their own welfare, and they clearly did not want to pay any taxes. If they did, they at least wanted a voice in parliamentary decisions—thus a slogan of their rebellion became "No taxation without representation." The **American Revolution** (1775–1789) basically was fought about taxes: who pays, how much, and who decides. The English had no desire to give the American colonists any sort of representation, even though the Americans were about as sophisticated with their technology, politics, society, and even culture as the English themselves. The American lands were rich with potential, especially since the native "Indian" peoples were so easily and quickly being eliminated after losing their French allies after the Seven Years War.

The Americans created a national self-government with the Second Continental Congress, which brought together representatives from the thirteen colonies. More importantly, the colonists organized their own military forces. First, the American minutemen militias skirmished with British troops at Lexington and Concord in April 1775, sparking the **American War of Independence** (1775–1783), the military contest that ensured the success of the Revolution. With proper financing and with George Washington (d. 1799) in charge, the Americans soon had an army almost able to win European-style set-piece battles. On 2 July 1776, the Congress declared independence from Britain. Two days later the adoption of a Declaration of Independence immortalized that independence. In that document, the **United States of America**, as the joined colonies called themselves, provided a clear justification for their actions: resistance to tyranny. Of course, the Americans knew that labeling the king a tyrant was mere propaganda. Ever since the English Revolution, Parliament was actually responsible for the governance of the British Empire. Whatever the king's role, the Americans argued that governments were responsible to the governed and that people had a right to change them when necessary, even by force.

Ultimately, force decided the destiny of the United States. Facing the strongest empire in world history, the American revolt seemed doomed to fail. Canadians refused to join, although the United States' forces had tried to invade and conquer British provinces there. Some people, like Thaddeus Kosciuszko and Casimir Pulaski from partitioned Poland, helped the Americans because they were inspired by the United States' claims to liberty. Others merely wanted to hurt the British. Countries whose worldwide empires had suffered from British attacks and competition eventually allied with the Americans: the Dutch, the Spanish, and, most importantly, the French. Without the help of these foreign states, Americans would probably have lost the war for independence and would still be drinking tea and eating crumpets. Instead, after signing the Treaty of Paris in 1783, the Americans found themselves free and independent.

The difficulty of defeating the British then gave way to the challenge of creating permanent institutions of government. Fearing the "rabble," men of wealth and property remained in charge in America—there was no argument about that. Nevertheless, they decided against an American monarchy (Washington's lack of legitimate children certainly discouraged dynastic thoughts). Americans needed to construct a political system that recognized the diverse needs of so many different colonies and colonialists. At first, the Americans created a weak central government. This attempt, the Articles of Confederation, lasted only a few years before the solution proved unworkable.

So, in a rather radical step, the politicians decided to start over and found a strong central government. The leaders of the revolution, especially Washington,

Benjamin Franklin, Alexander Hamilton, and James Madison, decided on the princi-ple of *federalism* and the office of the **presidency**, which were embodied in the US Constitution adopted in 1789. Federalism meant that the dominant national government shared power with the powerful state governments, while reserving many freedoms for the people. In other words, the stronger federal regime inter-acted with strong state administrations while a Bill of Rights sheltered the people.

The federal government itself separated its powers into legislative, executive, and judicial branches. The legislature, called Congress, enacted the laws, declared war, made peace, and consented to (or blocked) important bureaucratic and judicial appointments. As head of the executive branch and independent of the legislature, a president commanded the armed forces and enforced the laws. This authority dif-fered from the parliamentarianism of other modern democracies, where the prime minister or chancellor served as both leader of the legislature and chief executive official. The judiciary resolved civil legal disputes, convicted criminals, and, through judicial review, came to interpret the laws. The big problem of US history and politics ever since has been about the competing interests of what the federal government can impose on states and/or the people, what state governments can ignore from the national government and themselves enforce on their state residents, and what the people (citizens, immigrants, natives, others, individually and collectively) can use or resist from federal and state governments as they live with one another. Nearly every serious issue since the foundation of the American republic has revolved around this tough juggling of competing powers and freedoms.

Historians have argued about whether the American Revolution was really revolu-tionary. American society before independence hardly differed from that afterward. The prosperous people with property still dominated economic, political, and social affairs, although Americans got rid of inherited titles of nobility. Still, the wealthy Americans who had been in charge before the revolution remained largely in charge after it—only the threat of tyranny from across the Atlantic had been eliminated. Perhaps the new system that enabled reform of the original founding model was the most revolutionary accomplishment. Certainly, the political system slowly welcomed more people into the process. White males without property did get suffrage by the early nineteenth century, decades before their British counterparts. Other inhabitants remained excluded far longer. Women did not gain the right to vote until 1920, Native Americans until 1924, and most African Americans until 1965.

Geography helped the United States become powerful. First, America's location in the Western Hemisphere protected the country from the warfare waged by Euro-pean states against one another. Yet at the same time, advanced sailing ships eased cultural exchange, so science, trade, and ideas flowed back and forth across the Atlantic. The United States of America remained firmly connected to Western tradi-tions. Second, America's vast unconquered wilderness offered ample opportunities for expansion and occupation, unlike in Europe, where most agricultural land had been divided up and claimed for centuries.

The available land in America, of course, had been and would be stolen from the native "Indians." In grabbing this land, "immigrant" Americans imitated other colonizing Europeans, both absolutist and democratic. Without any sense of irony or embarrassment, the Netherlands, Great Britain, and the United States fought for the right of their own citizens to participate in government while using violence to seize rulership over non-Europeans in Asia and the Americas.

Review: How did democratic forms of government spread in the early modern West?

Response:

THE DECLARATION OF LIBERTY, EQUALITY, AND FRATERNITY

The clash of republican and absolutist politics peaked in the **French Revolution** (1789–1815). British and American ideals of liberty inspired the French *philosophes* to criticize their own absolutist government, called the ***ancien régime*** by historians. If the Americans could overthrow royal "tyranny," then why could not the French? The American War of Independence provided an immediate example. France had helped America partly through a desire to hurt Great Britain. In doing so, France paid enormous sums for military endeavors while acquiring almost nothing in return from the Treaty of Paris in 1783. France won no territories, in contrast to the vast continental possessions allotted to the United States. The huge French war debts helped to drive the French government toward a crisis of bankruptcy. Because of the worsening economic situation, all social classes became dissatisfied with the government. Poor harvests in 1787 and 1788 yielded peasant anger against Versailles. The middle classes also resented their heavy tax burden and limited social mobility. The nobility and clergy objected to how the absolute monarchy had usurped many of their once-numerous privileges.

The growing grumbling targeted the monarch personally. Despite France's role in the Enlightenment, the Bourbon dynasty had never produced an enlightened despot to reform its regime. **King Louis XVI** (r. 1774–1792) was a nice man, but he showed no particular talent for governing. He was actually more interested in being a locksmith than a king. This would not have been a problem if some able bureaucrat had ruled for him, as Richelieu had for Louis XIII. Sadly, Louis XVI was neither able to find competent ministers nor able to support them for long against palace intrigues.

Remarkably faithful in his marriage vows (for a Bourbon), Louis likewise lacked an able woman to rule from behind the scenes, such as Louis XV's mistress Madame Pompadour had done. Louis XVI's spouse, the notorious **Queen Marie Antoinette**, contributed to the growing contempt for the monarchy. Although Marie Antoinette was the daughter of Maria Theresa Habsburg, she inherited none of her mother's talents for governance. She instead preferred parties, balls, masquerades, and the life of luxury that absolute monarchs enjoyed. There is no evidence, however, that she said something so callous as, "Let them eat cake [*brioche*]" when she heard that peasants were begging for bread; the quote actually came from a fictional character in a novel by Rousseau. Yet people readily believed that Marie Antoinette could have said it. Her actions and reputation hurt her royal husband's position. Louis XVI's reign again exposed both the enduring strength and the fatal flaw of absolutism: everything depended on one person.

As Louis confronted his shortage of funds, he naturally thought of the basic ways governments raised money: conquest, loans, and taxes. The first choice of war was risky, and it required money up front to equip the troops. Besides, he had no readily available excuse to attack anyone. As for the second alternative, the French banks were tapped out, while foreign banks did not want to take on the risk of French credit. That left only raising taxes. When Louis tried to raise taxes, however, the nobles who ran the courts, the *parlements*, judged that he could not do so. The nobles hoped to use this financial crisis for their own gain, restoring some of their long-lost influence. They insisted that the king would have to call the Estates-General, as Philip IV had done four and a half centuries earlier. Certainly, as an absolute monarch, Louis could have just raised taxes. Instead of acting firmly and risking some civil disturbance, the king gave in.

Since no living person remembered the Estates-General (which had last met in 1614), public officials quickly cobbled together a process from dusty legal tomes. About nine hundred representatives would be elected, three hundred from each of the three estates: first, the clergy; second, the nobility; and third, the common people (although only the top 20 percent of the bourgeoisie, such as doctors and lawyers, were actually eligible to run for election). Some members of the Third Estate complained that their vastly greater numbers compared with the size of the other two estates deserved more representation. The king gave in, again, and conceded that they were allowed to have about six hundred representatives (see diagram 10.2). While this concession might seem more equitable, it did not challenge the predominance of the first two estates. For one, they were often related to and connected to each other, so they shared the same views. For another, each estate voted in a bloc—thus the three hundred clergy had one vote, the three hundred nobles had one vote, and the six hundred commoners had one vote. Therefore, the Third Estate would probably always be outvoted 2–1.

Shortly after the representatives to the Estates-General arrived at Versailles for the opening ceremonies on 5 May 1789, the Third Estate began to agitate for voting by individual representatives rather than by bloc, aiming to at least even out the votes to 600–600. They even tried to declare themselves as a new legislature, the National Assembly. The king was upset by this wrangling and tried to discourage any more meetings by locking up the meeting hall on the morning of 20 June. Many representatives, mostly those from the Third Estate along with a few sympathizers from the other two, proceeded to a nearby indoor tennis court. There they swore

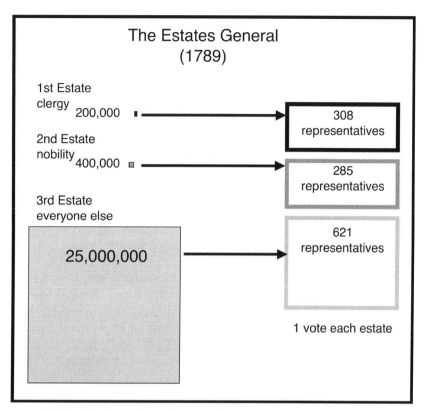

The Estates General
(1789)

1st Estate
clergy 200,000 ■ ──────────► 308 representatives

2nd Estate
nobility 400,000 ▣ ──────────► 285 representatives

3rd Estate
everyone else

25,000,000 ──────────► 621 representatives

1 vote each estate

Diagram 10.2. Even though the First Estate of the clergy and the Second Estate of the nobility comprised only a tiny proportion of the population (the small boxes as compared to the huge box of the Third Estate), each estate elected about an equal number of representatives. Since each estate voted as a bloc, the first two could always easily outvote the third. The quarrel over voting by estate versus by representative paralyzed the Estates-General.

the **Tennis Court Oath**, pledging not to go home until they had written a constitution. In fact and in law, a constitution meant the end of an absolute monarchy. Instead of sending in the troops and disbanding this illegal assembly, Louis once more gave in. Thus the bourgeoisie seized control and began a true revolution.

Things soon got out of control, as so often happens in political revolutions. While the politicians in Versailles quibbled about the wording of constitutional clauses, the populace of Paris recognized that change was at hand. They naturally feared its destructive potential. To protect themselves and their property, some Parisians began to organize militias, or bands of citizen-soldiers like the minutemen of America. Yet the Parisians lacked weapons. On 14 July 1789, a semi-organized mob approached the Bastille, a massive royal fortress and prison in the heart of the city. The crowd demanded that the Bastille release its prisoners (whom they believed were unjustly held for political reasons) and hand over its weapons to the Parisian militias.

The fortress was completely secure from the militia and accompanying rabble, so the name given to this event, the **storming of the Bastille**, is quite exaggerated.

In the hope of calming the situation and avoiding too much bloodshed from violence in the neighborhood, the fortress commander opened the gates. The mob rewarded him by beating him to death and parading his head on a pike. While the liberators gained some weapons, they found inside only a few petty criminal prisoners. Nevertheless, the attack symbolized the power of the people over the monarch. The people had openly and clearly defied royal authority and used violence on their own initiative for their own interests. The citizens of Paris tore down the fortress, stone by stone, actually selling the rubble as souvenirs. A more forceful and ruthless monarch would have mobilized his troops, declared martial law, and snuffed out this attack with notable bloodshed. What did Louis do? He gave in again.

Events were soon beyond any possible royal controls. As the peasants in the countryside heard about the storming of the Bastille, they also decided to rise up. The "Great Fear" spread as peasants attacked their landlords. The peasants killed seigneurs and burned the records that documented their social and economic bondage. The National Assembly panicked, since its members owned much of the land that the peasants were appropriating. They acted to calm things down on 4 August 1789, abolishing the *ancien régime* with its absolute monarchy and feudal privileges. A few weeks later, the National Assembly issued a **Declaration of the Rights of Man and of the Citizen** (see Primary Source Project 10). Similar to the American Bill of Rights, this document declared "liberty, property, security and resistance to oppression" for all Frenchmen. It guaranteed liberties to the citizens and restrained government. This document worked as planned: it calmed passions and allowed the forces of order to restore moderation. It also originated the phrase "Liberty, Equality, Fraternity," which became the motto for the revolution.

Much more would need to be done for these goals to be realized, but the revolution had issued a clarion call for justice. Sadly, these gains did not apply to women, as is illustrated by the masculine term *fraternité* (fraternity/brotherhood). Revolutionary men in France (just as they had in England and America) excluded females from the benefits of Enlightenment ideals. In response, Olympe de Gouges (Marie Gouze) proposed a **Declaration of the Rights of Woman and of the Female Citizen**, in which she rewrote the original as a manifesto supportive of women. For this and other writings questioning the republic, the government soon sliced her head off. A woman might be a "citizen," but the male citizens enjoyed the real protections and liberties of the law.

The royal family likewise lost their liberty and independence. In October, women who became angry at the bread shortage marched from the city of Paris out to Versailles. Thousands of marchers killed a few guards, ransacked the palace, and escorted the royal family back to Paris, to the palace of the Tuileries (near the Louvre). The people made Paris once more the capital. This action shattered any remaining royal authority. On the first anniversary of the storming of the Bastille the following summer, the king gave in and swore loyalty to the new constitution.

Two days before that oath, the National Assembly had secularized the Roman Catholic Church in France. Since the previous year, the French government had slowly been exerting its authority in the spirit of the Enlightenment and in the need of funds. The state had granted Protestants and Jews more civil rights, dissolved monastic orders not involved in education or hospitals, and confiscated many church lands and properties. On 12 July 1790, the regime restructured all the dioceses and parishes and turned the remaining clergy into civil servants. Bishops, priests, and the last few monks and nuns would henceforth be paid by the state and required to take an oath to France. Many did not, preserving their loyalty to papal authority and thus becoming liable to arrest and prison as enemies of the revolution.

Louis never reconciled himself to limited authority and the church's humiliation. A year after his constitutional oath, in the night of 20–21 June 1791, he finally stopped giving in and took decisive action. He and his family fled from their palatial house arrest. Unfortunately for him, a combination of bad luck, incompetence, and the king's own hesitant nature allowed revolutionary forces to catch the royals at Varennes. With the royal family imprisoned and back in Paris, the French decided they needed a monarch no longer. The legislature tried King Louis XVI for treason, found him guilty (by 361 to 360 votes), and then had his head cut off on 21 January 1793. He met his death on the new, lethally efficient killing machine, the guillotine, which became symbolic of the revolution. In October, Marie Antoinette followed her husband to beheading on the scaffold. While their daughter survived into old age, their son the Dauphin, or Louis XVII, disappeared and was presumed dead. Other members of the royal family fled the country. The Bourbon dynasty seemed to have ended in humiliation.

The elected bourgeois politicians now running the First French Republic faced other grave problems not easily solved by chopping off heads. The first challenge was how to make political decisions. In a fashion appropriate to democracy, they accidentally established a model of political debate and diversity. When the representatives gathered in the new republic's national convention, their seating arrangement gave us the terminology of modern political discourse. Those to the **right** of the speaker or president of the body opposed change. Those to the **left** of the speaker embraced change. Those in the middle were the **moderates**, who needed convincing to go one way or the other. Extremists on the right were **reactionaries**, and extremists on the left were **radicals** (which today is more used for any extremist of any political leaning). This vocabulary of "left" and "right" suggests that all political disagreements are about resisting or promoting change. These labels may have simplified issues, but they enabled politicians to start organizing groups around ideologies and specific policy proposals.

Review: *How did the revolutionaries in France execute political changes?*

Response:

PRIMARY SOURCE PROJECT 10: DECLARATION OF THE RIGHTS OF MAN VERSUS DECLARATION OF THE RIGHTS OF WOMAN ABOUT HUMAN RIGHTS

Historians usually see the Declaration of the Rights of Man as a foundational document for human rights. Issued by the French revolutionary government to calm civil disturbances, its basic principles embody many of the ideals of the Enlightenment. The manifesto by Olympe de Gouges points out how the rights of "Man" presumes male dominance while ignoring women's views. Olympe de Gouges had been born a butcher's daughter yet became a writer and antislavery activist. The radical Jacobins arrested and then guillotined her as a counterrevolutionary on 3 November 1793.

Source 1: Declaration of the Rights of Man and the Citizen by the National Convention (26 August 1789)

The representatives of the French people, organized as a National Assembly, believing that the ignorance, neglect, or contempt of the rights of man are the sole cause of public calamities and of the corruption of governments, have determined to set forth in a solemn declaration the natural, unalienable, and sacred rights of man. . . . Therefore the National Assembly recognizes and proclaims, in the presence and under the auspices of the Supreme Being, the following rights of man and of the citizen:

Article I. Men are born and remain free and equal in rights. Social distinctions may be founded only upon the general good. . . .

IV. Liberty consists of the freedom to do everything which injures no one else; hence the exercise of the natural rights of each man has no limits except those which assure to the other members of the society the enjoyment of the same rights. These limits can only be determined by law. . . .

VI. Law is the expression of the general will. Every citizen has a right to participate personally, or through his representative, in its foundation. It must be the same for all, whether it protects or punishes. All citizens, being equal in the eyes of the law, are equally eligible to all dignities and to all public positions and occupations, according to their abilities, and without distinction except that of their virtues and talents. . . .

X. No one shall be disquieted on account of his opinions, including his religious views, provided their manifestation does not disturb the public order established by law.

XI. The free communication of ideas and opinions is one of the most precious of the rights of man. Every citizen may, accordingly, speak, write, and print with freedom. . . .

XIV. All the citizens have a right to decide, either personally or by their representatives, as to the necessity of the public contribution; to grant this freely; to know to what uses it is put; and to fix the proportion, the mode of assessment and of collection and the duration of the taxes. . . .

Source 2: *Declaration of the Rights of Woman and the Female Citizen* by Olympe de Gouges (1791)

Mothers, daughters, sisters, female representatives of nation, organized as a National Assembly. Believing that the ignorance, neglect, or contempt of the rights of woman are the sole cause of public calamities and of the corruption of governments, have determined to set forth in a solemn declaration the natural, unalienable, and sacred rights of woman. . . . Therefore the sex that is in both beauty and courage during the sufferings of maternity recognizes and proclaims, in the presence and under the auspices of the Supreme Being, the following rights of woman and of the female citizen:

Article I. Woman is born free and remains equal in rights to man. . . .

IV. Liberty and justice consists of the freedom to do everything which injures no one else; hence the exercise of the natural rights of woman has no limits except those which the perpetual tyranny of man opposes to them. . . .

VI. Law is the expression of the general will. Every female and male citizen has a right to participate personally, or through their representative, in its foundation. It must be the same for all, whether it protects or punishes. All female and male citizens, being equal in the eyes of the law, are equally eligible to all dignities. . . .

X. No one shall be disquieted on account of his fundamental opinions; woman has the right to mount the scaffold, she should have the same right equally to mount the tribune. . . .

XI. The free communication of ideas and opinions is one of the most precious of the rights of woman, especially since this liberty assures that fathers acknowledge the legitimacy of children. Every female citizen may, accordingly, speak with freedom, "I am the mother of a child who belongs to you," without being forced by a barbaric prejudice to conceal the truth. . . .

XIV. The female and male citizens have a right to decide, either personally or by their representatives, as to the necessity of the public contribution; to grant this freely; the female citizens can accept this only when an equal division is admitted, not only in wealth, but also in the public administration. . . .

Questions:

- *About which rights are the two sources essentially in agreement?*
- *Which rights does de Gouge critique most strongly?*
- *How do both of these documents challenge the established order?*

Responses:

Citations

"Declaration of the Rights of Man." In *Translations and Reprints from the Original Sources of European History*, vol. 1, no. 5, *The French Revolution*, edited by James Harvey Robinson. Philadelphia: University of Pennsylvania Press, 1897, pp. 6–8.

Adapted from the above and Gouges, Olympe de. "Les droits de la femme" (reprod.), *Bibliothèque national de France*, 15 October 2007. Accessed 14 July 2014, http://gallica.bnf.fr/ark:/12148/bpt6k426138/f5.image.

For more on these sources, go to http://www.concisewesternciv.com/sources/psc10 .html.

BLOOD AND EMPIRES

The second problem facing the French elected representatives was war. After the French arrested their king, Louis's royal relatives and aristocrats called for an invasion to restore their fellow absolutist to power. The French government, however, declared war first. In reaction, an alliance of small and great powers formed against the French. A series of conflicts, called the **Wars of the Coalitions** (1792–1815), burdened Europe for the next generation. Ironically, considering its own democratic revolutions and empire building, Great Britain became the head of the coalition and the French Republic's most determined opponent. England feared the growth of French power more than it approved France's democratic and republican trappings. Great Britain sought to maintain the traditional balance of power among the states of Europe. France responded by taking up arms.

The revolution enabled France to create a new kind of war. During the *ancien régime*, many of the French officers in the royal army had been "blue bloods," aristocrats and nobles so named because one saw the veins through their fair, pale skin. Many nobles fled the country once revolution began. France's aristocratic enemies then expected that without God-given elite leadership, the rabble republican army would readily collapse. On the contrary, the French were inspired to shed their red blood in defense of their nation more fervently and ferociously than ever before, since it was *theirs* now, not the monarch's. They managed to turn back the first invading forces in a skirmish at Valmy on 19 August 1792. As the war ground on, talented officers rose through the ranks based on their ability, not blue-blooded connections.

The new regime called all the people to war, whatever their status. As ordered by the government, young men fought, married men supported the troops with supplies, young and old women sewed tents and uniforms or nursed the sick, children turned rags into lint for making bandages, and old men cheered on everyone else. Modern "total war" began. Key to victory were the huge new armies of inspired countrymen. The problem of feeding such large numbers of soldiers led to the invention of ways to preserve food. Scientists discovered that food boiled in bottles and tin cans would not spoil. This invention for wartime would later help feed many civilians in peacetime.

Under pressure of war and revolutionary fervor, the government became more radical and took extreme steps in changing society. This phase of the French Revolution has earned the name the **Reign of Terror** (June 1793–July 1794), or simply the Terror, an extremist period that lasted only thirteen months. The radical Jacobins (named after a club where they met) and their leader, Maximilien Robespierre, decided that they needed to purge the republic of its internal enemies. They formed the infamous **Committee of Public Safety**, which held tribunals to arrest, try, and condemn French reactionaries, in violation of previously guaranteed civil liberties. As often happens during perceived national emergencies, the government excused itself for its extreme measures. Actually, the death toll of the Terror was comparatively small (at least compared with the subsequent war casualties). In Paris, fewer than 1,300 people were guillotined. In the countryside, however, death tolls piled higher, with perhaps as many as 25,000 executed in the troublesome province of the Vendée, mostly through mass drownings.

During the Terror, radicals implemented Enlightenment ideals with a vengeance. The radicals' new Republic of Virtue threw out everything that the *philosophes* considered backward, especially if it was based on Christianity. They replaced the Gregorian calendar: the new year I dated from the declaration of the republic; weeks were lengthened to ten days; and the names of the months were changed to reflect their character, like "Windy" (Ventôse) or "Snowy" (Nivôse). Some radicals tried to abolish Christianity, turning churches into "temples of reason." Palaces, such as the Louvre, were remodeled into museums. Education was provided for all children at taxpayer expense. Slavery was abolished. Perhaps most radical of all, the government required the metric system of measurements. Tradition and custom were supplanted by the ideas of *philosophes*.

In the end, the Terror gained a bad reputation because its leaders became too extreme. They began to arrest and execute one another, accusing their former compatriots of less-than-sufficient revolutionary passion. Moderates naturally feared that they would be next. So in the month "Hot" (Thermidor) in the republican year II (or in the night of 27–28 July 1794), moderates carried out a coup d'état (an illegal seizure of power that kills few) called the Thermidor Reaction. The moderates arrested the radical Jacobin leaders and sent them quickly to the guillotine. The politicians set up a new, more bourgeois government, restricting voting and power to those of wealth. The new regime, called the Directorate, was a reasonably competent oligarchy, but uninspired and uninspiring.

Meanwhile, the military decisions forced change. The republican French armies repeatedly gained victory in battle due to competent commanders, vast numbers, and inspired morale. Therefore, instead of relying on loans or taxes, the Directorate used conquest to help pay the bills in 1796–1797. In a series of campaigns invading parts of Italy and the Rhineland, one general in particular gained the greatest fame: **Napoleon Bonaparte** (b. 1769–d. 1821). The dashing General Bonaparte soon surpassed the bland politicians in popularity, proving again that people are easily seduced by military successes. While most contemporary monarchs found it safer to stay away from the battle lines, Napoleon's generalship provided inspirational passion for the French.

Had it not been for the Revolution, Napoleon would not have amounted to anything noteworthy in history. As a Corsican and a member of a low-ranking family, he could never have risen very high in the ranks of the *ancien régime*.[5] The revolutionary transformation of the officer corps and the increased size of the French army, however, provided Napoleon an opportunity to shine. With military brilliance he maneuvered huge armies, negotiated them through foreign lands, and combined his troops to crush enemy forces in decisive blows. Soon the French dreamed not only of dominating Europe but also of restoring France's world empire. In 1798, Napoleon sailed off to invade Egypt, aiming to damage British imperial interests in the Eastern Mediterranean and the Middle East. His only success there was the discovery of the Rosetta Stone, whose inscriptions in Greek and hieroglyphics allowed modern scholars to finally translate ancient Egyptian (see figure 2.3). Soon the British navy decisively crushed Napoleon's hopes for conquest in Egypt (and seized the Rosetta Stone for the British Museum).

Napoleon nevertheless managed to rush back to France before news of his defeats could spread. Back in Paris, he seized control of the government in a coup d'état on 18 Brumaire VIII (or 9 November 1799). Imitating the Roman Republic, Napoleon declared himself the first consul and proclaimed (with about as much sincerity as Augustus Caesar had) that his leadership would restore the "French Revolutionary Republic." In a brilliant move, he held a **plebiscite** for the French people to endorse his seizure of the state. Named after the ancient Roman plebians, plebiscites are votes with no binding power. So even if the French people had voted against his constitutional changes, Napoleon could have gone ahead anyway. Napoleon's real power was based on his military command. His army could have put down any opposition. Nevertheless, the French people felt involved merely by being allowed to vote, and they indeed voted overwhelmingly for him. Many a dictator would later resort to the same method of opinion management. Plebiscites preserved the façade of popular endorsement so well that the trappings of republican government decorated Napoleon's absolutism.

Indeed, Napoleon helped establish a model for the modern dictatorship by weakening the connection between a ruler and a noble dynasty. Napoleon showed that a relatively obscure, simple person could become the leader of a great power through talent, luck, and ruthlessness rather than dynastic birth. People were willing to sacrifice their liberty in exchange for victories against neighboring states. Napoleon's rise was neither unique nor entirely modern. Many an ancient Roman

---

5. The idea that Napoleon was short was a myth largely created by British propaganda. It has given rise to many jokes and the label "Napoleon complex" for a small person compensating for lack of height with oversized aggression. In reality, he was about five feet, seven inches in height (170 cm), average for those times and taller than his opponent Lord Nelson. Historians suggest that the origins of his mythical small size lie with artistic license of cartoonists, misuse of the French term of affection "the little corporal," the contrast with the very tall imperial guards, and the difference between the length of inches in the French and English measurement systems. The "Napoleon complex" also gave rise to the idea that insane people often imagined themselves to be as powerful as Napoleon.

emperor had come from obscurity, especially in the tumultuous third century. In addition, Oliver Cromwell had enforced a benevolent dictatorship over the English.

The lure of dynasty was too powerful for Napoleon to ignore, however. He crowned himself emperor in 1804, abandoning the titles of the republic. A few years later he divorced his wife Josephine, who was too old to bear children, so that he could marry the Habsburg emperor's young daughter Marie Louise. By marrying a Habsburg princess, the once-obscure Napoleon joined the most prestigious bloodline in Europe. Furthermore, the new French empress Marie Louise soon bore her newly imperial husband an imperial son and heir.

For a time, Napoleon's political activities as ruler of France helped to cement his positive popular and historical reputation. His foundation of the Bank of France was only the start to growing a strong economy. Napoleon appeased the spiritual desires of many French citizens by allowing the Roman Catholic Church to set up operations again (although without much of its property, power, and monopoly on belief). He restored the Gregorian calendar. Napoleon himself felt that his greatest achievement was the **Napoleonic Code**, a legal codification comparable to Justinian's Code in the sixth century. Beyond simply organizing laws as Justinian had, Napoleon's lawyers tossed out the whole previous system and founded a new one based on rationalist principles and the equality of all adult male citizens. These laws were a bit like window dressing, considering Napoleon's dictatorship, and, as usual, women were granted few rights at all. Nevertheless, Napoleon provided a rationalized system that remained the foundation of French law as well as that of many other countries today in Europe (Holland, Italy) and Latin America. It even influenced the laws of Louisiana in the United States (which belonged to France until 1803). On the basis of these reforms, some historians have said that France gained an enlightened despot in Napoleon, at last.

Napoleon's military talent forged a massive empire that might have united the Continent under French power and culture. With his victory at the Battle of Austerlitz on 2 December 1805, he defeated Austria, Prussia, and Russia. He redrew the map of Europe and reduced the size of those three great powers. With the annexation of the Lowlands, Switzerland, and much of northern Italy, France itself bloated into an empire virtually the size Charlemagne's had been. In 1806, the complicated constitutional constructs that had held the territories of the Holy Roman Empire together vanished into history, although the Habsburgs conjured up a separate imperial title as emperors of their hereditary lands in Austria. Bonaparte controlled much of the rest of Europe through puppets, usually his relatives propped up on thrones. He ruled over the largest collection of Europeans up to that point in history.

Great Britain, however, refused to concede Europe to Napoleonic supremacy. Britain's worldwide possessions and growing economy gave it the ability to maintain hostilities with France until a means could be found to break up Napoleon's empire. Napoleon himself recognized the difficulty of maintaining an overseas empire. In 1803 Napoleon sold France's claims on the huge Louisiana Territory to the United States (the indigenous peoples who lived there were not consulted, of course). French armies also failed to crush a rebellion in Haiti, leading to that country's independence by 1804. And the British navy decisively crushed the French fleet on the Atlantic side of the Straits of Gibraltar at the Battle of Trafalgar on 21 October 1805. At that point, France was blockaded by the British navy and could not even control the waters off its own coast. This naval victory notwithstanding, Britain lacked the forces to invade France directly, as frustrated as naval Athens had been versus infantry Sparta during the Peloponnesian Wars.

Thus, Napoleon dominated the land, the British the sea. Neither could or would end the conflict. Instead, indirectly, the British supported a festering revolt in Spain after 1808. In turn, Napoleon tried to damage the British economy with his "Continental System," which established an embargo prohibiting all trade between his empire and any allies of the British Empire. Too many Europeans, however, had become addicted to the products of the global economy (including tobacco and coffee) that usually came through British middlemen. Napoleon's higher prices, heavy taxes, and French chauvinism (arrogant nationalism) alienated many people.

Moreover, the empires of Prussia, Austria, and Russia had merely been defeated, not destroyed. They waited for an opportunity to strike back. In 1812, Russia's refusal to uphold the embargo broke the Continental System. In reaction, Napoleon decided to teach that country a lesson: he invaded with the largest army yet assembled in human history—probably half a million men. Unfortunately for his grand plans, the Russians avoided a decisive battle. Napoleon found himself and his huge army stranded in a burned-out Moscow with winter approaching. As Napoleon retreated back to France, his forces suffered disaster. Only a few tens of thousands survived to return from the Russian campaign.

Although Napoleon rapidly raised another army, his dominance was doomed. Other generals had learned his strategy and tactics too well. Peoples all over Europe rebelled, aided by British money and troops. The insignificant War of 1812 declared by the Americans did not distract the British enough to do Napoleon any good at all. At the Battle of Nations near Leipzig, about half a million soldiers fought over French domination for three days in October 1813. More than one hundred thousand men died in one of the largest battles in history. Napoleon remained unbeaten but had to retreat from Germany. By March 1814, coalition armies had invaded France and finally forced Napoleon to abdicate.

Incredibly, Napoleon managed to overcome even this major defeat. For a few short months, Napoleon sat in imprisonment on the island of Elba off the coast of Tuscany. Then one night he escaped, and for "Napoleon's Hundred Days" he once again ruled France as l'Empereur. The countries that had so recently triumphed over him refused to accept Bonaparte back as the leader of France. British and Prussian forces finally, ultimately, once and for all overthrew Napoleon at the **Battle of Waterloo** (18 June 1815) in Belgium. This time the British shipped the captured emperor off to exile on the barren island of St. Helena in the South Atlantic, where he died a few years later of a stomach ulcer.

The French Revolution reaffirmed the basic principle that democracy is difficult. In trying to establish a republican government, the French stumbled through several failed regimes, finally unleashing a dictatorship, as had the English under Cromwell. They were not the first to experience this, nor would they be the last.

Sadly, the human tendency to want simple answers and strong leaders would repeat itself in other revolutions that quickly took the same sharp turns toward authoritarianism.

But with Napoleon's final downfall, everyone knew that an era had ended. Millions of lives and vast amounts of property had been lost in rebellion, repression, and wars, causing the suffering of whole societies. The victors faced the questions of what should be retained and what should be revised (see map 10.1). The leaders of the French Revolution had proclaimed their inspiration from previous intellectual and political revolutions. Their ideas of liberty, equality, and fraternity continued to challenge and inspire despite the French Empire's collapse. The Scientific Revolution granted Europeans new power to understand and control nature. The Enlightenment freed them to play with new ideas that overthrew authority. New governments, both absolutist and democratic, gave Western states still greater abilities to fight with one another and conquer foreign peoples. Revolutions in Britain, America, and France provided examples of how to change regimes. The legacies of scientists, *philosophes*, monarchs, republicans, and radicals worked themselves out on the ruins of Napoleon's empire. Few suspected at that time how the next century would transform the West more than any previous century had.

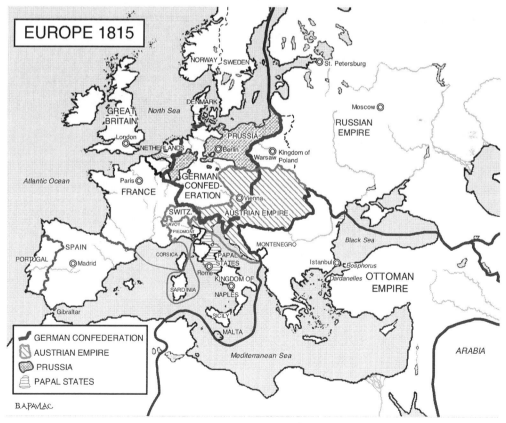

Map 10.1.   Europe, 1815.
How does the center of Europe show instability?

Review: *How did war alter the French Revolution and cause Napoleon's rise and fall?*

Response:

Make your own timeline.

1543   **1815**

CHAPTER 11

Mastery of the Machine

The Industrial Revolution, 1764 to 1914

Historians call the rough hundred years after the fall of Napoleon the **nineteenth century** (1815–1914). The period forms a convenient unit framed by the Wars of the Coalition and World War I. Between those two worldwide conflicts, Western civilization went through numerous changes in its economic practices, political ideologies, social structures, and scientific ideas. Probably the most important change was the one brought about by the **Industrial Revolution** (1764–1914), during which economies became dominated by manufacturing via machines in factories. Just as the French Revolution opened up new possibilities, so did the Industrial Revolution. The rise of new technologies and business practices fashioned the most profound economic change in human history since the invention of agriculture. The increasing sophistication of machines both supplied more power to the masters of those devices and dominated the lives of those who worked with them. Machinery also pushed Western civilization to further heights of prosperity and power. Under the leadership of new political ideologies, people increasingly abandoned the quaint agricultural ways of the past and forged the now-familiar industrialized society of our modern world.

FACTS OF FACTORIES

The basic structures of civilization had been fairly stable since the prehistoric Neolithic agricultural revolution. For thousands of years, the overwhelming majority of people, the lower classes, carried out their assigned task of producing enough food for themselves, plus a little more for their betters who did not farm. Only the few privileged people of the upper classes and middle classes were not involved in tilling the land or raising animals. The environment—insects and rodents, drought, flood, storm, frost—often threatened to destroy the farmers' crops. Whole families labored from dawn to dusk most of the days of the year just to scrape by.

Farming started to become much easier with the **Scientific Agricultural Revolution**. This revolution began around 1650 in England. Science transformed farming life, offering more control over the environment than ever before. Scientists recommended different crops to plant, such as potatoes and maize (corn), because they grew more efficiently and were more nutritious. They developed new kinds of fertilizer (improving on manure) and new methods of land management (improving crop rotation and irrigation), reducing the amount of fallow land. Fences went up as landlords enclosed their fields, consolidating them into more manageable units.

Thus, fewer farmers could produce more food than before. With fewer jobs in agriculture to keep everyone employed, a huge social crisis threatened to overwhelm England. The last traditional protections for peasants of the medieval manor disappeared. Landlords threw tenants off land that their families had worked for centuries, severing long-standing social and economic relationships. The agricultural working class broke up. Even independent family farmers with small plots of land lost out when they could not compete against the improved larger estates.

At the same time, more food and better medical science allowed rapid population growth. As in ancient Rome after the Punic Wars, large numbers of people without land began to move to the cities, hoping for work. Others left England, emigrating to find more farmland, especially in the British colonies of North America. Another outlet was a new colony in Australia, intended mainly for criminals. The first shipload of undesirables landed in Botany Bay in 1788. Yet exporting farm laborers could not solve Britain's unemployment rates and a threatening rebellion. Arriving in the nick of time was the Industrial Revolution, which turned many of the landless rural peasants into urban factory workers.

The revolution began in England, which possessed a number of inherent advantages. First, its promotion of science launched the Scientific Agricultural Revolution. Second, Britain's political system of elected representatives quickly adapted to the new economic options. Third, Non-Conformists (mostly firm Calvinists who refused to join the Church of England) put their efforts into commerce, finance, and industry. Lingering religious discrimination excluded them from civil service jobs and universities. So instead, the Calvinists' diligent "Protestant work ethic" (as later coined by sociologist Max Weber) grew the economy.

A fourth advantage for England was its diverse possessions. In the immediate vicinity, England bound Scotland, Wales, and Ireland into the United Kingdom of Great Britain. Great Britain ruled the world's largest empire in the eighteenth century, despite the loss in 1783 of the colonies that became the United States. Across the oceans, Britain held Canada, Egypt, South Africa, Australia, islands in the Caribbean (the "West Indies"), and parts of India. These far-flung territories provided many goods, from cotton to tobacco. The British navy, so successful in the Wars of the Coalitions against Napoleon, protected British merchant ships as they traded their cargos around the globe with many native peoples (and seized some of them to be sold as slaves). Businessmen concocted their deals fueled by imported sugar, tea, coffee, and cocoa.

Financial innovations gave the English yet more advantages over competitors. One was the invention of **insurance**, such as that offered by Lloyd's of London, then and today. Insurance companies would calculate risk to business enterprises, charge according to the odds that those risks would come to pass, and generally make substantial profits. By covering losses caused by natural disasters, theft, and piracy, insurance made investing less risky and more profitable. After 1694, the Bank of England also provided a secure and ready source of capital, which was backed by the government itself. The large number of trading opportunities within the empire minimized each individual capitalist's risk. Altogether, Britain possessed the best chance to seize upon the new industries.

Lastly, three new developments in energy, transportation, and machinery combined to produce the Industrial Revolution. First, improved energy came from harnessing the power of falling water with water mills. The second development, transportation, overcame the constant problem of bad roads. The technology for paved roads had been neglected since ancient Roman times. After the fall of Rome, most roads in Europe were dirt paths that became impassable mud trenches whenever it rained. Travel became significantly easier, however, with the building of **canals**, or water roads. During the eighteenth century, many canals were excavated to connect towns within the country. These canals were highly suitable in soggy England because they actually became more passable with rainy weather. Since barges were buoyant in water, one mule on a towpath could pull many more times the tonnage of goods than a horse with a wagon on a muddy path. While most canals have long since been filled in or forgotten, for a few decades they were the best mode of technologically efficient transport.

The third improvement, machines, vastly increased the power of human beings. The first mechanical devices were invented to make textiles, a huge market considering that all Europeans needed clothing for warmth, comfort, decency, and dignity. At the beginning of the Industrial Revolution, the best technology for making thread was the single spindle on a spinning wheel, as known from fairy tales. Weaving cloth was done by hand on a loom, pushing thread through weft and warp.

A series of inventions through the eighteenth century multiplied the efficiency of one woman at the spinning wheel and loom. The breakthrough occurred with James Hargreaves's **spinning jenny** (1764). Instead of one woman making one thread at a time, the new machine enabled one person to manufacture many dozens of threads at once, at lower cost per piece. Hargreaves certainly "borrowed" important concepts from other inventors and businessmen, who in turn took his jenny and made money off of it. Richard Arkwright, a former wig maker, combined his own and others' inventions into the best powered spinning and weaving machines.

Inventors protected their inventions with patents, namely government-backed certificates protecting an inventor's rights. Affording the application process, however, and then defending patent rights in court often proved too costly. The overriding economic benefits to society might also deny an inventor rights to his profits. Various inventors sued Arkwright for patent infringement and won. Nevertheless, Hargreaves died a pauper, Arkwright a wealthy knight. The bold, lucky, and unscrupulous often succeeded in making fortunes, while rightful inventors died in poverty and obscurity.

By combining all the innovations in energy, transportation, and machinery, men like Arkwright therefore launched the **factory** or (in British) the **mill system**. This Industrial Revolution was controlled by men, but it also transformed women's lives. Men did most of the inventing of and investing in machines. Men forbade women from apprenticeships, education, training, and even getting advanced technological jobs. Political, economic, and social structures continued to exclude women from positions of authority and influence. Such had been the status of most women since the beginning of civilization. As machines became more important, men claimed that women lacked a mechanically capable mind, while men alone were suited for tinkering with technology. In the nineteenth century, men remained masters of both women and the machines.

Nevertheless, the machines affected every woman's life, inside and outside the home. Since the twelfth century, women and children had earned extra income by making goods by hand through the cottage industry or putting-out method. After the eighteenth century, factory-made products cut into what women had earned this way. Losing that income soon drove women and children to work in factories, often hired because owners could pay them lower wages than men. Adding in the cheap labor of women and children, industrial production increased efficiency and lowered prices. As prices went down, demand went up, since more people could afford the machine-manufactured goods, from linen tablecloths to teacups. More-over, as new industrial forms of artificial lighting such as the arc lamp were in-vented, production could go on around the clock to get the maximum use out of the machines. Thus, capitalist industrial manufacturing emerged as investors funded the building of factories for profit.

A second wave of industrialization hit with the invention of steam power. The breakthrough came in 1769, when James Watt and Matthew Boulton assembled an efficient **steam engine**. They had adapted it from mechanical pumps used to remove water from coal and iron mines (see figure 11.1). In turn, coal became the main fuel source for these engines. Coal outmatched previous materials that people burned for energy, namely plant and animal oils, wood, or peat. The switch to the fossil fuel coal gave Europeans a decisive advantage in power over other peoples of the world. With innovation, the coal-fired steam engines vastly increased their energy output while their physical size shrank. By the 1830s, small steam engines on wagons with metal wheels running on tracks called **railroads** were transporting both goods and people (see figure 11.2). Trains on such railways soon eclipsed canals as the most efficient transportation, since they were cheaper to build and could run in places without plentiful water. Water travel remained important, though. Steam engines in ships meant faster, more certain transit across seas and oceans, further tying together markets of raw materials and factories for manufac-turing. Europeans sped up.

Some people resisted the rise of these machines, most famously the **Luddites**. Today, that label applies to anyone who is suspicious of, or hostile to, technology. The term originated from the name of a (possibly) mythical leader of out-of-work artisans. The artisans' jobs of making things by hand were now obsolete. In the cold English winter of 1811–1812, bands of artisans broke into mills, destroyed the machines, and threatened the owners. The government, of course, arrested, shot,

Figure 11.1. A massive coal breaker looms over an industrial wasteland. Inside, the coal from deep underground was broken down into smaller sizes for transport. (Luzerne County Historical Society)

or hanged the troublemakers. Great Britain had a war to win against France and was not going to let a few unemployed louts threaten enormous potential profits for the nation.

Nevertheless, the Luddite fear was natural and a foreseeable reaction to a change that left workers vulnerable. At the beginning of the nineteenth century, classical liberal economics (as described by Adam Smith) had increasingly been adopted by both business and government. Industrialization meant that only the entrepreneurial class who controlled large amounts of capital could create most jobs. Neither factory owners nor politicians felt much responsibility for those thrown out of work or paid very little (see Primary Source Project 11). Even Adam Smith had observed that capitalists would conspire to keep wages low, if the workers were prohibited from organizing to increase their wages. Some economists, such as the English banker David Ricardo, told the poor that they should just work harder and be more thrifty. **Ricardo's "iron law of wages"** exploited even those who had jobs. With this economic theory, he advised that factory owners pay workers the bare minimum that permitted survival. Otherwise, he argued, workers might have too many children, only increasing the numbers of the poor and unemployed. The dominant economic theories at the beginning of the Industrial Revolution favored the new industrial capitalists over the new factory workers.

Figure 11.2. Steam engines on railways (with windmills to pump water from far underground to store in a tank) enabled expansion across the American continent by the mid-nineteenth century. (Treasures of the NOAA Library Collection)

Review: How did inventions and capitalism produce the Industrial Revolution?

Response:

LIFE IN THE JUNGLE

The division of society into capitalists and workers led Western civilization to become more dependent on cities than ever before. The populations of industrialized cities rapidly rose upward in a process called ***urbanization***. By definition, cities had been central to civilization since its beginnings, but only a small minority of people had ever lived in them. Most people needed to be close to the land, where they could raise the food on which the few urban dwellers depended. After 1800, the invention of machines helped consolidate more people into urban life. Fewer jobs on the land meant that more people looked for work in the factories. Cities swelled into metropolitan urban complexes. The old culture of the small village where everyone knew everyone increasingly waned. This new urban living required people to abandon outmoded traditions and adopt new ways of thinking and acting.

At first, the cities grew haphazardly, in fits and starts, with little planning or social cohesion. In many districts, people did not know their neighbors, while residents could find low-paying or no jobs at all. The result was slums of badly built and managed housing. Slums became dangerous places of increased drug use, crime, filth, and disease.

People founded public health and safety organizations to manage these dangers. Firefighters became more professional. Likewise, modern **police** forces formed as a new kind of guardian to manage the lower classes. Law enforcement on the scale at which our modern urban police forces function had been unnecessary in earlier rural society. In small, stable rural villages, people had known all their neighbors, and therefore crime was limited by familiarity. In the anonymous urban neighborhood, though, crime by strangers inevitably increased. Of necessity, crime investigations required more care and scientific support. During the 1820s, Sir Robert Peel's "bobbies" (nicknamed after their founder) and their headquarters in Scotland Yard (named after the location) in London were merely the first of these new civil servants. Police forces insisted that only they could use violence within the urban community.

The concentrated numbers of new urban dwellers, which rose from hundreds of thousands into millions, also spewed out levels of pollution unknown to earlier civilization. Streets became putrid swamps, piled high with dumped rotting food and excrement. Major cities had tens of thousands of horses as the main mode of transportation, each producing at least twenty pounds of manure a day. Air became smog, saturated with the noxious fumes of factory furnaces, coal stoves, and burning trash. Infectious diseases such as dysentery, typhoid, and cholera (newly imported from India) plagued Western cities because of unsanitary conditions. Urban populations died by the thousands with new plagues fostered by industrialization.

Since disease was not confined by class boundaries to only the poorer districts, politicians found themselves pressured to look after the public health. Cemeteries were relocated from their traditional settings near churches to parklike settings on the city's fringes (in Paris, for example, the bones emptied from cemeteries were stacked up in huge underground caverns). Regulations prohibited raising certain animals or burning specific materials. The government paved roads, especially with the cheap innovative material of tar and gravel called asphalt or macadam (after its inventor, McAdam). City officials created **sanitation** organizations. Upton Sinclair's novel *The Jungle* (1906) about horrid urban living and working conditions actually led the US government to improve the regulation of food quality. People called garbagemen, refuse collectors, or sanitation engineers took trash to dumps. Freshwater supply networks replaced the old-fashioned wells, piping in clean, drinkable water from reservoirs, while networks of sewers whisked dirty water away.

In this process, Western civilization perfected the greatest invention in human history: **indoor plumbing**, namely, hot and cold running water and a toilet (or water closet) (see figure 11.3). Such mundane items are often taken for granted by both historians and ordinary people. The Romans had public lavatories and baths, some medieval monasteries had interesting systems of water supply, and a few monarchs and aristocrats had unique plumbing built into a palace here or there. But since the fall of Rome, cleanliness had been too expensive for most

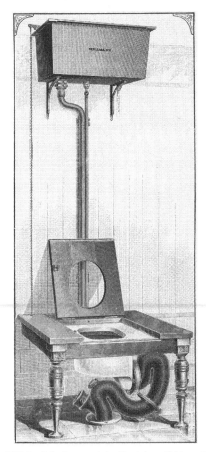

Figure 11.3. In 1888, this fancy side-flushing "Warwick" water closet offered a wood seat made of cherry, black walnut, or ash with bronzed iron legs and a cast iron "slop safe." (NYPL Digital Collection)

people to bother with. Whether rich or poor, most people literally stank and crawled with vermin. In the nineteenth century, free-flowing water from public waterworks, copper pipes, gas heaters, valves, and porcelain bowls brought the values of hygienic cleanliness to people at all levels of wealth. Of course, not all worries could go down the drain or vanish with a flush; the waste merely accumulated somewhere else in the environment. Most people, unconcerned, have easily ignored such messy realities. Regardless, more and more nineteenth-century westerners enjoyed the cleanliness and comforts of lavatories. With the new plumbing, plagues like cholera, typhoid, and dysentery began to diminish and even disappear in the West.

As industrialized cities grew in size and safety, their inhabitants accumulated wealth previously unimagined in human history. Some of those riches were spent on culture: literature, art, and music. Some were spent on showing off: bigger houses, fancier fashion, and fine dining. Because a few earned so much more than the rest, the Industrial Revolution initiated a major transition of class structures in Western society. At the bottom, supporting the upper and middle classes, was the hard labor of the **working class** (also called the proletariat after the ancient Roman underclass), made up of fewer and fewer farmers and more and more factory workers. The upper classes became less defined by birth after landownership ceased to be the most productive way to gain wealth. A successful businessman could create a fortune that dwarfed the lands and rents of a titled aristocrat. The *nouveau riche* (newly wealthy) set the tone for the new upper crust.

Meanwhile, the middle class became less that of merchants and artisans and more of managers and professionals: the white-collar worker who supervised the blue-collar workers in the factories. The colors reflect class distinctions: white for more expensive, bleached and pressed fabric, blue for cheaper and darker cloth that showed less dirt. Physicians, lawyers, and professors likewise earned enough to qualify for the "upper"-middle-class way of life. Most people came to idealize middle-class values: a separate home as a refuge from the rough everyday world; a wife who did not have to work outside the home, if at all; the freedom to afford vacations; and comfortable retirement in old age.

Essentially, these middle-class values were new, unusual, and limited only to a small portion of the population. These so-called **family values** were not at all traditional, as some social conservatives today would like people to think. Throughout civilized history, most men and women have actually worked at home or on the land close to home. And the entire family worked together: husband, wife, and children, perhaps with a few others in servile status. Most people never thought of vacation trips, only restful religious holidays. Those who survived into old age usually had to keep working to earn their keep. For a model of true traditional family life, look to the Old Order Amish or Pennsylvania Dutch, who live today in communities stretching from Pennsylvania to Missouri, Iowa, and Wisconsin. These people have consciously rejected the Industrial Revolution and its technologies. They cannot ignore it, as their young people are tempted toward the ease that the wealth of modern life provides. Nonetheless, their values of hardworking farm families reflect the family values actually passed down through the millennia of Western civilization before the Industrial Revolution.

By moving people away from farm communities, the Industrial Revolution generated serious tensions within society that few people wanted to recognize. The domestic sphere was damaged, as people worked outside the home. Social mobility became more volatile, as it was easier to rise but also to fall in class status. One major business failure could send not just the capitalist owner but also many thousands of workers into the poorhouse. For workers at the bottom of society there were few protections (see below). Businesses rotated through boom and bust, good times and bad times, hirings and firings. Whole societies became subject to market cycles, which economists have never been able to predict or prevent, despite their supposedly expert proclamations.

Over time, though, the Industrial Revolution did seem to confirm the Western notion of progress. Some people continued to suffer, and still suffer, under the system. But by and large, things for most people usually got better enough to prevent social collapse. The quality of life improved. More people had more possessions. More people became free from ignorance and disease. More people had access to more opportunities than ever before in human history. Before the Industrial Revolution, most people stayed at the level at which they were born. Capitalist industrial manufacturing, it seemed, had unleashed the possibility for anyone to live the good life, as least as far as creature comforts went. The only questions seemed to be: What did those at the bottom need to do in order to move up, and how long would they need to wait for their chance at the good life?

The modern **consumer economy**, where unknown distant workers manufactured most things that people used and purchased, only stoked impatience. Gone were the neighborhood shoemaker, blacksmith, or farmer. Instead, distant capitalists encouraged consumers to purchase possessions, even if they did not need them. To accomplish this, **advertising** became a significant tool for economic innovation. It began with simple signs in stores where products were bought. Soon, advertising was on every package and on the side of every road and byway. Advertisers began to create needs to promote consumer consumption and grow the economy. They defined new forms of proper usage for the various classes, in hygiene, fashion, and leisure. Mail-order catalogs, such as those by Montgomery Ward (1872) or Sears, Roebuck and Co. (1886), delivered thousands of products, from watches to prefabricated homes, through modern postal services. By the end of the nineteenth century, majestic department stores, such as Harrods (1849) in London, Le Bon Marché (1852) in Paris, or Macy's (1858) in New York, served as shopping meccas for the rich and middle classes in urban centers, while the lower classes could buy merchandise at the "five-and-dime" discount chains, Woolworth's (1879) or Kresge's (1899) in the United States. Even Christian holidays felt the impact, as Christmas (the celebration of Jesus's birth) began to outshine Easter (the celebration of Jesus's resurrection) because its ritual of buying and giving gifts suited consumerism. Charles Dickens's novella *A Christmas Carol* (1843) tells this tale.

Also by the late nineteenth century, a second wave of innovation intensified the revolution across much of Western civilization. The mastery of electricity and steelmaking allowed cities to grow even larger, not only across the landscape but also up into the sky. Church steeples had been the tallest urban structures since the Middle Ages. Business towers of the early **skyscrapers** began to define the modern city skyline. Previously, most residential and business buildings were limited to five stories because builders were unable to engineer useful load-bearing walls and people were unwilling to climb too many stairs. With steel-girder skeletons (1884), electric safety elevators (1887), and light bulbs (1879), buildings could be erected to ten, twenty, even sixty stories![1] Below the earth, subways (London in the 1860s, Budapest in 1896, New York in 1904) propelled workers to and from their homes and factories. Communication through telegraph (1830s), then telephone (1876), and finally radio (1906) tied the world more tightly together.

All Western economies needed power to function. Coal from the ground gained a competitor in another mineral, petroleum. This "rock oil" has since become so important to human beings that it has been shortened to the sole word *oil*. The first **oil** well in Titusville, Pennsylvania, in 1859 led the way in supplying industrial society with a sufficient amount of the material. People first valued oil as a fuel that was refined into kerosene for lamps. Kerosene replaced whale oil, which had itself replaced other plant and animal oils.

Scientists soon discovered how to easily manipulate petroleum for more than just its burning and lubricating properties. Its associated by-product, natural gas, became a common fuel for lighting, heating, and cooking. Oil's combustible properties likewise beckoned scientists to experiment with it as a fuel source for machines. Petroleum began to replace coal.

At the nineteenth century's end came an invention that would transform industrial people's mobility: the **internal combustion engine**. Several inventors between 1860 and 1885 contributed ideas to this engine, which used gasoline, originally considered a waste product from refining oil for kerosene. This new engine became a more powerful, smaller, and therefore more mobile motor than the steam engine. Karl Benz in Germany bolted the gas engine onto a frame with pneumatic tires to make the **automobile** (1886). When used to spin a propeller, a gas engine combined with large airfoils metamorphosed into the **airplane** (1903). The two Wright brothers, who owned a bicycle shop in Dayton, Ohio, assembled and launched the first modern aircraft at Kitty Hawk, in the Outer Banks of North Carolina. Both the car and the plane would revolutionize travel in the twentieth century, outpacing the success of the train.

Oil also became the foundation of a new **petrochemicals** industry. The first petrochemical businesses made dyes for coloring fabric and then fertilizers and medicines. By 1900, researchers formulated petroleum into Bakelite, the first plastic. Bakelite could take on new shapes, forms, strengths, and even colors. Plastic continued to unleash waves of inventiveness. At the time, no one worried about how the burning, refining, or disposing of petroleum products might create their own problems.

---

1. These early skyscrapers included the Home Insurance Building (1884) in Chicago, the Flatiron (1902) in New York (actually twenty-one stories with a penthouse), and the Woolworth Building (1913), also in New York.

Review: *How did urbanization develop a modern society?*

Response:

SOURCES ON FAMILIES: GEORGE SAND ON THE END OF HER MARRIAGE (1835)

The French writer Amantine Lucile Aurore Dupin (b. 1804–d. 1876) is better known by her adopted nom de plume: *George Sand. She is famous for defying gender expectations by her male name, dressing in men's clothing, writing novels, memoirs and literary criticism, smoking, and carrying on numerous affairs, most famously with Chopin. At only eighteen she had conventionally married François Casimir Dudevant, the illegitimate son of a baron, and soon bore a son and a daughter. In 1831, however, she began to explore Paris dressed as a man, publish professionally, and have affairs. In these two letters she describes the circumstances of domestic violence in 1835 under which she started to separate from her husband. The courts dissolved the marriage the next year and awarded her custody of the children (although Dudevant did briefly abduct their daughter).*

To Hippolyte Chatiron [her half-brother],

My friend, I am about to tell you some news which will reach you indirectly, and that you had better hear first from me. Instead of carrying out our agreement pleasantly and loyally, Casimir is acting with the most insane animosity towards me. Without my giving him any reason for such a thing, either by my conduct or my manner of treating him, he endeavored to strike me. He was prevented by five persons, one of whom was Dutheil, and he then fetched his gun to shoot me. As you can imagine, he was not allowed to do this.

On account of such treatment and of his hatred, which amounts to madness, there is no safety for me in a house to which he always has the right to come. I have no guarantee, except his own will and pleasure, that he will keep our agreement, and I cannot remain at the mercy of a man who behaves so unreasonably and indelicately to me. I have therefore decided to ask for a legal separation, and I shall no doubt obtain this. Casimir made this frightful scene the evening before leaving for Paris. On his return here, he found the house empty, and me staying at Dutheil's, by permission of the President of La Chatre. He also found a summons awaiting him on the mantelshelf. He had to make the best of it, for he knew it was no use attempting to fight against the result of his own folly, and that, by holding out, the scandal would all fall on him. He made the following stipulations, promising to adhere to them. Dutheil was our intermediary. I am to allow him a pension of 3,800 francs, which, with the 1,200 francs income that he now has, will make 5,000 francs a year for him. I think this is all straightforward, as I am paying for the education of the two children. My daughter will remain under my guidance, as I understand. My son will remain at the college where he now is until he has finished his education. During the holidays he will spend a month with his father and a month with me. In this way, there will be no contest. Dudevant will return to Paris very soon, without making any opposition, and the Court will pronounce the separation in default.

Dear Hydrogen [friend and neighbor Adolphe Duplomb],

You have been misinformed about what took place at La Chatre. Dutheil never quarreled with the Baron of Nohant-Vic. This is the true story. The baron took it into his head to strike me. Dutheil objected. Fleury and Papet also objected. The baron went to search for his gun to kill every one. Every one did not want to be killed, and so the baron said: "Well, that's enough then," and began to drink again. That was how it all happened. No one quarreled with him. But I had had enough. As I do not care to earn my living and then leave my substance in the hands of the devil and be bowed out of the house every year, while the village hussies sleep in my beds and bring their fleas into my house, I just said: "I ain't going to have any more of that," and I went and found the big judge of La Chatre, and I says, says I: "That's how it is." And then he says, says he: "All right." And so he unmarried us. And I am not sorry. They say that the baron will make an appeal. I ain't knowin'. We shall see. If he does, he'll lose everything. And that's the whole story.

Questions:

- *What is the difference of tone and content in the two letters and why?*
- *About what does Sand seem most concerned?*
- *What involvement do various people outside the marriage have within the married relationship?*

Responses:

Citation

Doumic, Rene. *George Sand: Some Aspects of Her Life and Writings*. Translated by
    Alys Hallard. London: Chapman and Hall, 1910, pp. 157–60.

For more on this source, go to http://www.concisewesternciv.com/sources/sof11
.html.

CLEANING UP THE MESS

Politically, the nineteenth century began not with a leap forward but with a step
backward. Elites sought to tidy up the political disorders left by the Wars of the
Coalitions during the French Revolution. After Napoleon's final defeat in 1815,
many of the victors thought that revolutionary ideas of liberty, equality, and fraternity had met their own Waterloo. The ***Romantic movement*** rejected the stark
results of the Enlightenment's rationality and of industrial technology's advance.
The romantics produced poetry, stories, and art that expressed a longing for a simpler time, whether a reimagined past or a fantasy fairyland. The French and Industrial Revolutions together brought too much change too fast. A retreat to nature
seemed preferable to the dirty, seething cities. Traditional ruling dynasts seemed
better than crude upstarts like Bonaparte. Many traditionalists hoped that all would
return to their version of normal.

The victors over Napoleon convened the **Congress of Vienna** (1814–1815) to
reorder the chaos left by France's conquest of Europe. Over the course of nine
months, hundreds of leaders and diplomats from all of Europe discussed the future
(even while dancing and drinking at the many parties). Leading the assembly in
its deliberations was Prince **Clemens von Metternich** (b. 1773–d. 1859), the first
minister for the absolutist Habsburg emperor of Austria. Metternich and others
developed the political concept of ***conservatism***, namely, the policy that advocated
preserving as much as possible of traditional political, social, and cultural structures. Under Metternich's leadership, the congress allowed only such alterations in
the old system as were necessary for European stability. It restored most of the old
dynasties to power, dumping Bonaparte's relatives and puppets and sending them
into exile or retirement. The restorations ranged from the beheaded Louis XVI's
brother as the new king of France to the pope ruling once more over the Papal
States. A few citizens protested, but all over Europe princes reaffirmed absolutism
by shredding constitutions.

The Congress of Vienna also reasserted the balance of power between the great
powers of Europe: Britain, France, Austria, Prussia, and Russia (see map 10.1).
France had too often tried to conquer Europe, so the victors strengthened states
on France's borders to help prevent any further aggression. Along the northeastern
border of France, the United Kingdom of the Netherlands combined the Dutch and
the Belgians under the aristocratic dynasty of Orange, newly elevated to royalty.
Along the southeastern border, the melded Kingdom of Sardinia-Savoy-Piedmont
barred the Alpine access to Italy. Austria held sway over the rest of northern Italy.

Directly east of France, Prussia acquired a conglomeration of territories in the Rhineland. Prussia and Austria took joint leadership of a new, albeit weakened, German Confederation that merged the hundreds of small principalities of the dead Holy Roman Empire into a few dozen. These measures effectively hemmed in France. No one thought to ask whether the peoples of these newly drawn states wanted their assigned roles in the balance of power.

In an attempt to prevent more warfare and revolutions, the Congress of Vienna also tried two new alliance mechanisms. Previously, alliances had lasted for only the duration of wartime. After 1815, nations tried to use alliances to prevent war. First was the **Holy Alliance**, binding together the absolute rulers of Orthodox Russia, Roman Catholic Austria, and Lutheran Prussia in a pragmatic burst of religious cooperation. This agreement called for the promotion of Christian charity and peace, yet it failed due to the power politics of tsar, emperor, and king.

The innovative **Quadruple Alliance** of Austria, Prussia, Russia, and Britain better maintained the reestablished order. For the first time, **collective security** provided an ongoing peacetime mechanism to prevent reckless wars between states. According to the doctrine of balance of power, states organized against one another only when one or more threatened the status quo. Collective security meant that all nations worked together regularly to maintain peace. After 1815, the regular meetings of great powers to uphold international harmony became known as the Concert of Europe. The Quadruple Alliance provided the first international peacekeeping structure to solve civil disturbances in the lesser states of Europe and to prevent dangerous unrest among the peoples.

Although the Quadruple Alliance worked relatively well, Britain slowly began to withdraw. As the only great power with a substantial overseas empire, England was uncertain about its growing rivalry with Russia, the dominant Eurasian power. Meanwhile, the restored Bourbon dynasty in France regained international respectability as it resisted reform and revolution. Thus, France gradually took England's place within the Concert of Europe. Europe settled into a few rare decades of international peace.

No Western ruler even contemplated including the distant United States of America. Yet America's example of republican government also showed many that an alternative to absolutism was still possible. While strict social hierarchies reasserted themselves in Europe, the commoners remembered their access to power under the French revolutionary regime, however brief or illusory. The French proclamations of liberty and equality had not been well implemented under Napoleon's dictatorship, but the lower classes liked those ideas all the same. The bourgeoisie continued to accumulate wealth and demand more power for themselves. The aristocracy increasingly lost its purposeful social function. Even absolute monarchs adopted many of Napoleon's and revolutionary France's methods precisely because they were so successful.

The idea of revolution simply would not disappear: people had already seen for themselves that political action could topple incompetent authoritarian regimes. Those in the nineteenth century who supported revolutions were usually categorized as liberals. The political concept of *liberalism* stood for embracing change in order to broaden, as much as reasonable, people's political, social, and cultural opportunities. Liberalism appealed to the middle classes rising with the Industrial Revolution. Its ideas promised the expansion of their political and economic power and influence.

It is important to note that the beliefs held decades ago by liberals on the left and conservatives on the right of the political spectrum were quite different from what they are today (see table 11.1). The nineteenth-century conservatives embraced absolute monarchy with its strong interventionist bureaucracy, mercantilistic economic theory, distinctions among social classes (with aristocrats at the top), and a close cooperation of state and church (called the union of throne and altar). In contrast, the nineteenth-century liberals called for constitutional and republican government, laissez-faire economic theory, equality before the law for all citizens (perhaps even including women), and separation of church and state with religious toleration. Conservatives cobbled together multiethnic states bound together by dynastic loyalty, while liberals called for nations with ethnic uniformity (about which see chapter 12). These dichotomies do not necessarily fit well with today's issues and labels. In general, only the basic attitudes of a leftist acceptance of change and a right-wing resistance to change are still true today. Political identification should always focus on specifics, not labels.

Nevertheless, the basic **political parties** of modern European democracies became organized around these two competing ideologies. Absolute monarchy with its origins in agricultural wealth was in decline while representative government empowered by capitalist manufacturing was on the rise. Political parties offered structure both to win in elections and, once elected, to cast votes in representative bodies. As more people accumulated substantial wealth and property, they wanted to influence political decisions that could affect their ability to make more money. Taxation, regulations, and monetary strength became issues of national debate. As a result, the new wealth accelerated the growth of political parties. Over the course of the nineteenth century, both sides in many countries used the methods of parliamentarianism. Liberals tried to reduce government regulations, while conservatives sought to preserve advantageous taxation. In the cities, political parties that controlled the levers of power and patronage operated so smoothly for their constituents that they themselves earned the name "machines." Political parties with their permanent leadership, mass membership, and enforcement of discipline at the polls became essential to the functioning of representative government.

Table 11.1.   Views of Western Political Parties in the Nineteenth Century

Conservatism	Liberalism
Absolute monarchy	Parliamentarianism
Social class distinctions	Equality of citizens
Aristocratic and upper-class support	Capitalist and middle-class support
Mercantilism	Laissez-faire/classical liberal economics
Multiethnic states	Nationalism
Union of throne and altar	Separation of church and state

Note: The issues important in the nineteenth century are not necessarily those that matter today. Then and now, conservatism tends to resist change, while liberalism promotes it.

Throughout the nineteenth century, the conservatives retained their dominance in most places. The propertied people of lineage wanted to stay in charge, sharing power only with the new rich capitalists. But politics changed with more frequency and without too much violence in England, which already had basic constitutional and republican structures. Majorities in Parliament bounced back and forth between the first two significant political parties, aptly named Liberals (nicknamed Whigs in England and America) and Conservatives (called Tories even today in Britain). The Whig **Reform Bill of 1832**, for instance, appeased the middle classes by removing some of the worst antiquated structures for parliamentary elections and doubling the electorate to about 20 percent of the population. Working-class citizens then launched the Chartist movement, in which they petitioned, marched, and demonstrated to get representation for themselves. Although the Chartist movement largely failed and vanished after 1848, Parliament slowly legislated reforms to further open up political participation (see figure 11.4). By 1884, the British had reached universal suffrage for men, meaning all adult male citizens had the right to vote. Despite fears about social revolution, voting and democratic institutions still left the privileged wealthy in charge, much as they always had been since the beginning of civilization. Politics opened access to power to only a few more people.

On the European continent, meanwhile, liberals resorted to revolutionary action as a force for political change. The revived absolute monarchies prohibited most possibilities for reform to be made through the ballot box. France in particular

Figure 11.4.   The British Parliament buildings were built during the nineteenth century in a romantic style imitating Gothic architecture. (Nicole Mares)

kept breaking out in revolutionary fervor. Without the same traditions and institutions as Britain had to channel the violence of political change, criticism of the regime all too easily escalated first into riots and then into rebellion. To break conservative dominance, liberals often felt compelled to resort to revolutionary violence. Armed clashes flashed on the barricades, with soldiers on one side and bourgeoisie, workers, and students on the other. This violence recast the regimes, even if it did not always improve them. And once France had erupted into revolution, more outbreaks exploded throughout the rest of Europe in 1830, 1848, and 1870.

The **Revolutions of 1830** were the first to significantly affect European politics. In July, the French people deposed the absolutist-inclined King Charles X and replaced him with the more liberal King Louis-Philippe. The United Netherlands split into the separate countries of the Netherlands and **Belgium**.[2] Even though the conservative Metternich wanted to force the new countries to reunite, the other members of the Quadruple Alliance overruled him and recognized Belgium as a sovereign state and signed a treaty that guaranteed its inviolable neutrality: any country's attack on Belgium would violate international law and trigger war with the other great powers. In eastern Europe, the Congress of Vienna had granted some autonomy to Poland as a "kingdom" technically separate yet still ruled by the Russian tsar. When the Poles tried to free themselves from Russian domination in 1830, they lost miserably. The Russian reprisal erased any political liberty the Polish had enjoyed. Other efforts by Germans and Italians in certain principalities, as well as the Spanish and Portuguese, managed to secure a handful of liberal reforms.

The **Revolutions of 1848** sparked by France were even more widespread and, initially, successful (see map 11.1). In February of that year, the French, who had tired of the Bourbons, with their tendencies to incompetence and tyranny, tossed Louis-Philippe off the throne and proclaimed the Second Republic (1848–1852). Elsewhere in Europe, many rulers briefly backed down before revolutionary demands. The Prussian king accepted a constitution. In Austria, Metternich and his mentally impaired emperor, Ferdinand I, both resigned. The new eighteen-year-old Emperor Francis-Joseph I (r. 1848–1916) promised a constitution. Different regions of the empire seized the moment to declare independence. Czechs, Hungarians, and Italians took up arms against Habsburg absolutism. Many Germans came together at a parliament in Frankfurt to better unify the German people under constitutional authority. Unfortunately for German liberals, a lack of leadership and squabbling over methods and goals slowed progress. Furthermore, European rulers soon realized that most of their military remained obedient, while liberal politicians held the allegiance of very few armed forces. By the summer of 1849, royal armies commanded by loyal generals had restored most monarchs to their absolutist thrones at the cost of much bloodshed. Despite so many failures, many people remembered that they could unite to influence a state's politics.

For example, France was not quite done with revolution. The hastily arranged democracy of the Second Republic quickly degenerated into the Second Empire (1852–1871) under the dictatorship of Louis Napoleon, the nephew of Napoleon

---

2. The new Belgium remained divided between French and Dutch (Flemish) speakers. Today many nationalists seek to further subdivide the country.

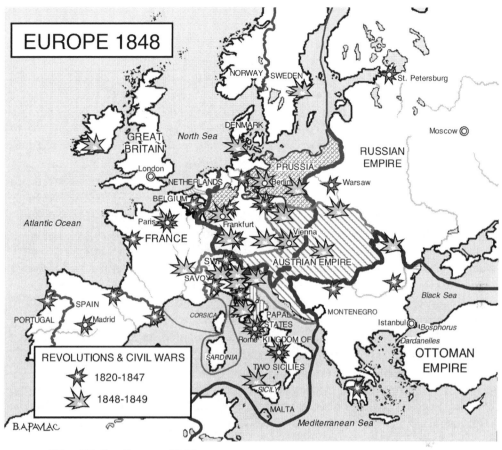

Map 11.1. Europe, 1848.
Why would some regions be prone to revolution and not others?

Bonaparte. Louis took the name Emperor Napoleon III (by number recognizing the "reign" of Napoleon's son, who had died years earlier as a pampered prisoner in the Schönbrunn Palace outside Vienna). One of Napoleon III's few major innovations was to rebuild Paris with broad boulevards. His original intention was that the wide streets would allow his troops to move quickly through the city and, if necessary, break any bourgeois barricades. The unintended consequence was to open up Paris for growth and development as one of the leading urban centers in Europe. Yet Napoleon III's imperial rule did not bring lasting peace and stability. Failed foreign policy rather than domestic insurrection, however, ended Emperor Napoleon III's reign.

In 1870 Napoleon III recklessly declared war on Prussia, which began the Franco-Prussian War (see below). France's swift and humiliating defeat led to a brief struggle over the nation's political destiny. Most of the country recognized a moderate-conservative **Third Republic** (1871–1945). At the same time, an organized group of liberals and radicals in the capital proclaimed the **Paris Commune** (March–May 1871). The commune tried to establish a socialist state of complete equality and justice. Instead, the national government's forces of moderation and conservatism crushed this effort, using Napoleon III's new wide boulevards to successfully invade the city. Frustrated Communards burned out the Tuileries, which had been the residence of kings and emperors. They also almost destroyed the adjoining Louvre Museum and all its precious art. The victorious Third Republican government killed or executed more than twenty thousand Communards and exiled another seven thousand. After this reactionary bloodletting, comparable to the radical Reign of Terror a century earlier, the French settled into a functional republican system.

After 1848, both liberalism and conservatism were quite shaken. A new generation of artists and writers offered skeptical and critical portrayals of society, called realism and naturalism, replacing the optimistic hopes of the romantics. Realists described the common social and political conditions of the day, while the naturalists focused on the most tragic and harsh aspects of the changing industrialized society. In the second half of the nineteenth century, many conservative princes and politicians shrewdly accepted both the necessity and inevitability of some change and began to adopt liberal platforms. Also, as will be explained in chapter 12, they learned to use the originally liberal idea of nationalism for their own aims. By taking the lead on constitutions, social reform, and business opportunities, conservatives could manage what they saw as the inevitable process of progress. The German philosopher Friedrich **Nietzsche** (b. 1844–d. 1900), however, doubted such progress. He proclaimed the doom of Western civilization unless it recognized the moral hypocrisy of its failed doctrines of Christianity. Nietzsche suggested that the human will's desire for power offered the only certain path for the future.

The power of the industrial age also transformed war. Armies could be raised and equipped more quickly and could attack more efficiently. The industrialization of war increased recruitment of soldiers from the lower and middle classes for the larger armies and navies. Since government decisions on war or peace might increase the risk to their lives, the common people found more reason to participate in politics. At the same time, industrialization and the resultant wealth produced smaller-scale violence over political disputes. **Guerrilla warfare** (Spanish for "little war," adopted from Spain's resistance against Napoleon) became more common. Guerrillas were irregular forces, neither recruited nor drafted, neither trained nor uniformed like the professional soldiers of modern industrial armies. Instead, guerrillas were usually volunteers defending their homeland, moving easily in and out of civilian populations. With their smaller and less-well-equipped numbers, guerrilla bands were too weak and too few to survive open battle against well-armed and drilled armies. They succeeded best in sneak attacks. For the first time guerrillas easily acquired more weapons and supplies through the manufacturing capacity and transportation options introduced by the Industrial Revolution.

The other form of political violence enabled by the Industrial Revolution was *terrorism*. Terrorists used lethal violence to achieve their political ends, usually targeting civilians (mostly because noncombatants are easier to kill than trained, equipped, and alert armed forces). Industrialization enabled terrorists to travel, both to acquire their weapons and training and then to reach their targets. Civilized regimes resented and feared the terrorists' use of violence, since the modern states considered the use of violence to be their own unique privilege. Not powerful enough to have armies or even guerrilla forces, terrorists resort to murder and mayhem on a small scale to attain political power, usually to benefit a national group or a political idea. A terrorist without an ideology was a criminal. Yet a successful terrorist could transcend into becoming a respected statesman of a body politic, just like usurpers of old.

Bombings and assassinations, consequently, multiplied in the nineteenth century. The most famous terrorists in the nineteenth century were those who believed in **anarchism**, the idea that if the growing industrialized and bureaucratized societies were destroyed, a utopian agricultural society would appear. Anarchists blew up government offices and killed leaders to undermine the structures of political trust and obedience that held societies together. Within a few years of the turn of the twentieth century, anarchists had killed a president of the United States, a prime minister of Spain, a tsar of Russia, a king of Italy, and an empress of Austria, among others. Despite these successful murders, anarchy's promise of unrestrained freedom failed to attract much support from civilized peoples, and it has faded into an insignificant ideology.

Review: How did competing political ideologies offer alternatives in the nineteenth century?

Response:

FOR THE WORKERS

Conservatives and liberals frequently confused anarchism with **socialism**, although socialism was a very different movement. Many intentionally promoted this confusion, hoping to associate the terrorist anarchists with the socialists and thus imply that the latter were violent also. Part of socialism's problem was its wide diversity of types. There existed, and still exist, many socialisms, although many Americans today often lump them all together as one collective bad thing. Quite simply, socialism in all its forms wanted to improve workers' rights and lives. Socialists tried to awaken a class consciousness, an awareness of what workers under these new conditions shared in common. Different kinds of socialism merely offered alternatives to the liberalism of the middle classes and the conservatism of the upper classes. What could be bad about that?

Well, neither liberals nor conservatives wanted to share power with the masses. They feared that giving more wealth, money, and votes to the working classes would mean less for them. If workers had an effective voice, the freedom of middle and upper classes to do what they wanted to do would be hemmed in. Wealthier elites might have to pay higher taxes; they might make fewer profits; they might have to rub shoulders with social inferiors in shops and churches; they might have to grovel for the votes of the majority of all adults.

So both liberal and conservative governments of the nineteenth century tried to prevent class conflict by resisting socialism in any form. Governments have protected ownership of property since the beginning of civilization, originally to benefit the few who possessed most of the farmland. Meanwhile, peasants called for land reform, claiming that all humanity deserved a share in creation. In the industrial age, factories became the most important places of wealth creation. Factories more obviously belonged to those whose investments financed their construction. Politicians and managers passed laws and used force to intimidate workers, usually calling it "law and order" or "protection of property rights." Workers called for a fair share of wealth, even if they lacked access to capital. Workers organized, demonstrated, and used violence to change the industrial system, calling it "people's justice." For capitalists, the profits generated by the modern industrialized state justified beatings, arrests, and executions. For workers, the exploitation suffered under the factory system excused vandalism, murders, and bombings.

The Industrial Revolution was transforming society regardless. Social roles were in flux, and traditional roles based on rural relationships were disappearing. People lost a sense of "knowing their place." Then along came the socialists, advocating social justice and trying to create a more fair society based on a more equal distribution of wealth. Many socialists also argued for granting equal rights to women and for protecting women and children from being harmed by economic necessity. Socialists rejected classical liberal economics and argued for better ways to invest capital and reap profit.

Many workers found socialism more attractive than either liberalism or conservatism because it promised to relieve their misery. Factory owners and managers vigorously exploited workers at the beginning of the Industrial Revolution. Modern lighting and machines meant factories operated around the clock, so workers sweated away in shifts lasting between ten and fifteen hours, with few breaks. Holidays were rare and weekends nonexistent. Lack of education or connections prevented laborers from finding better work than that in factories or mines. Ricardo's "iron law of wages," where owners paid workers as little as possible, resulted in whole families toiling away in factories in order to make ends meet. Also, because women and children were paid less for the same work done by men, factory owners employed larger numbers of them. The lives of worker families focused on the capitalist's factory, not the domestic fireplace. Indeed, the hearth vanished entirely for most, since available housing was in crowded, unsafe, and unsanitary tenements, ramshackle collections of small rooms.

Between the home and factory, even wretched homes were often better than the dangerous workplaces. Stale air and loud noise were common health hazards. Whirring gears and belts crushed slow fingers and tore off errant arms. Long days only increased the fatigue and carelessness that caused accidents. Injuries on the job were the victim's responsibility, since workers' compensation or even the ability to sue owners for negligence did not exist. The only alternative to working in a factory was being arrested for the "crime" of poverty and being forced to work in the poorhouse and prisons. Various works by Charles Dickens chronicle many of the awful conditions faced by the working class.

The domination of machines became more relentless at the beginning of the twentieth century. The Industrial Revolution culminated in the perfection of the conveyor-belt system and the invention of interchangeable parts. This innovation led to modern mass manufacturing with **assembly-line production**. Henry Ford made it famous in the manufacturing of his Model T car in 1905. Workers focused on narrow, repetitive tasks that reduced the time to make a car from a day and a half to an hour and a half. The myth put forward and often believed today is that Ford increased his workers' pay so that they could all afford the cars. Actually, he raised the wages because the workers needed the incentive to work through the mindless repetition of modern production. Ford's policies at his auto factories nevertheless finally began a trend toward increased wages and benefits for workers.

Such concessions were too little, too late for workers, many of whom had turned to socialism. Socialists proposed their own solutions to solve the workers' plight, since in the century and a half from the spinning jenny to the Model T, most factory owners and capitalists had been unwilling to help workers prosper. A half dozen separate socialist trends competed against the laissez-faire attitudes of the industrial capitalist manufacturers.

One, *utopian socialism*, called for business leaders to improve working conditions, often explicitly based on economic facts, historical trends, and even moral visions. Historians have labeled it "utopian" because these socialists dreamed of an ideal society, along the lines described in literature about imaginary states called utopias. In 1825, the French nobleman Count Henry de Saint-Simon published his call for socialism, *The New Christianity*, which appealed to the commands of Jesus. His followers gave voice to the original phrase of "from each according to his capacities, to each according to his work." He also called for production to be for the general welfare, not private profit.

Perhaps the most famous utopian socialist was **Robert Owen** (b. 1771–d. 1858), a Welshman who rose from poverty to become a wealthy capitalist factory owner in Scotland. The "dark Satanic mills" disturbed Owen.[3] In reaction, he began to argue that employers should treat their workers as humanely as possible. They should provide secure housing, good pay, shorter working hours, schools, banks, and shops, while children should be properly educated (see Primary Source Project 11). In consequence, he claimed, productivity would increase. Although he continued to make a profit, his attempt at model factory communities, such as at New Harmony, Indiana, were less than successful. His ideas did lead, however, to modern co-ops. Few businessmen or politicians paid attention.

The second variant of socialism, whether called **"scientific" socialism**, *Marxism*, or *communism*, would become enormously influential and creatively destructive. Karl Marx and Friedrich Engels initiated their version in 1848, the year of

---

3. The line comes from "Jerusalem," a poem by William Blake (1804), who calls on the English to do better and create a heaven on earth in their land. Later set to music, it has become an alternate national anthem for England.

so many liberal and nationalist revolutions. Their publication of *The Communist Manifesto* began with the phrase "A specter is haunting Europe—the specter of Communism." At the time, few knew what these two were talking about. The *Manifesto* called for a proletarian (working-class) revolution. First, the communist revolutionaries would destroy the current regimes, abolishing capitalist private property and bourgeois sexist laws. Then, workers would control the "means of production" (factories, offices, farms) and construct a society of equality and prosperity.

In subsequent years, Marx expanded on this program and soon conceived a whole new way of understanding history. He expounded upon "scientific" laws that explained the past and the future. Borrowing from the dialectic syllogism applied by the German philosopher Hegel to history, Marx argued that all change in civilization had been the result of class struggle, what he called ***dialectical materialism*** (see diagram 11.1). In each historical period, a dominant class (such as the patricians in ancient Rome) had controlled the means of production. An opposite, or antithetical, group then rose in response (such as the rebellious class of the plebians). Their clash over economic power generated a new ruling and new subservient class. Marx claimed that this "scientific" study of history could be used in his own contemporary age to understand the dominant bourgeoisie and the exploited proletariat. A violent class conflict was inevitable, but this time the downtrodden would seize control of their destiny. The proletarians were to organize themselves for the forthcoming revolution and guide humanity to a new, more just society. Using "scientific" socialism, Marx claimed that humanity would attain communism, defined as a condition in which the state withered away, economic exploitation vanished, and all people lived in peace and harmony. Technically, then, communism has never yet been achieved.

As an explanation of historical change, Marx's vision was sloppy. Still, his program, whether called "scientific" socialism, Marxism, or communism, held great appeal. As a comprehensive belief system, it made sense of the past, present, and future in distinctly human terms. Marx rejected a belief in the afterlife, seeing God and religion as the equivalent of drugs used to keep the masses of workers tame. Despite Marxism's atheistic attitude, his vision offered hope to the oppressed and provided an agenda as an inspirational principle for workers' organizations.

While planning for their revolution, however, Marxist organizers did not achieve much for workers' rights. Some communists actually wanted the workers' lot to get worse, hoping to spark rebellion by driving the proletariat to desperation. Still, Marxist socialism usually only contained the threat of potential violence. Even though some Marxists did associate with anarchists, these socialists actually carried out very little violence before 1917. They were supposed to wait for the collapse of bourgeois dominance to begin their revolt. In the meantime, workers still suffered.

Some "scientific" socialists began to revise Marxism because they wanted to improve the workers' conditions immediately. These revisionists agreed with Marx's historical analysis but became skeptical of the need for an actual revolution. The experience of France showed that revolutions often veered into uncontrolled violence and destruction.

The revisionists of Marxism offered a third version of socialism, called **social democracy** or ***democratic socialism***. They argued that the predicted catastrophic

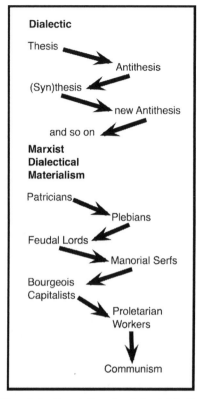

Diagram 11.1. The dialectic, dating back to Aristotle, combines two pieces of information to create a third. The German philosopher Hegel applied the process to the history of ideas, suggesting that a dominant ideology (a thesis) provoked its opposite (an antithesis) and the two clashed to combine into a new synthesis. That synthesis thus became the new thesis, which generated its antithesis, continuing the process through history. Marx applied the concept to the classes that controlled the means of production. He predicted that his contemporary situation, capitalists against the workers, would lead to a new utopia of communism and the end of history.

class struggle could perhaps be avoided through slow, gradual reforms. Social democrats began to establish political parties to help workers. Since workers were the numeric majority of the electorate in industrialized nations, social democrats worked to get members elected to representative bodies, where they could then pass legislation to incrementally improve conditions for workers. For example, the Social Democratic Party in Germany (founded in 1869) and the British Labour Party (founded between 1881 and 1906) were the results of this revisionist socialism. Most Western nations, with the notable exception of the United States of America, have prominent and competitive social democratic parties.

The atheism of most "scientific" socialists contrasted with the fourth socialist movement, namely, **_Christian socialism_**. These socialists based their efforts on the Christian call to "love thy neighbor." Jesus constantly preached about helping the poor and powerless and avoiding the sins of wealth. Pope Leo XIII in _Rerum_

Novarum (*Of New Things*, 1891) specifically tried to find a middle ground between the private property absolutists and the more radical socialists. The Roman Catholic Church declared that while private property ought to be protected, owners bore responsibility to the workers. The pope described contemporary workers as miserably exploited by the unchecked greed of capitalism. He proclaimed that the dignity of human beings requires that workers be paid a fair wage (not just a barely livable one). Christian socialists rejected the utopian dreams of new communities and the atheistic historical views of Marxists and social democrats and instead offered a more moderate, even conservative, alternative. They founded organizations for distributing charity to the poor, for helping workers reach a decent living wage, or even for forming political parties (such as the Christian Social Union in Bavaria).

Some Christian socialists joined in a fifth kind of socialism, which was to organize **labor unions** (developing as ***trade unionism*** in Britain and syndicalism in France). Labor unions originated out of self-help—workers themselves offering care for sick and old workers. Soon they tried to demand better working conditions and pay. At first, liberals and conservatives passed laws prohibiting unions from protecting workers' interests. Or, in America, companies hired workers from many different nations so that they could not converse with one another and organize into unions (see figure 11.5).

Workers organized anyway. By the end of the century, unions were trying to use the strike (work stoppage) as a way to force managers into giving them better contracts. Unions carried out tens of thousands of strikes in industrialized nations in the last decades of the nineteenth century. The strikers hoped to gain public sympathy (through marches and picketing), instigate boycotts (refusal to buy the company's products), and prevent companies from hiring non-union replacement

Figure 11.5. This sign from a Pennsylvania coal mine illustrates the diversity of nationalities brought to build America's industry. (Luzerne County Historical Society)

workers (called "scabs" by the unionists). The companies, in turn, tried to break these strikes through force and, naturally, this violence provoked more violence. Before 1914 and World War I, the government almost always sided with the capitalist factory owners when fighting erupted.

A sixth variant of socialism finally came from the liberals and conservatives who had so long and so well represented the desires of the capitalists. The liberals in particular worried about keeping votes, as they saw workers flock to the rolls of socialist political parties. At the end of the nineteenth century both conservatives and liberals finally took some steps toward meeting the needs of workers. The greatest measures were taken by the archconservative Chancellor Bismarck in Germany, who wanted economic stability and political order (see chapter 12). In the 1880s, while still vigorously opposing the growing Social Democratic Party, Bismarck passed laws that helped German workers (and attracted their votes) by providing for national health insurance, work accident insurance, and even retirement pensions (social security). His opponents attacked these policies, calling them *state socialism*. But Bismarck turned the insult into a point of pride. In turn, England ended its inhumane poor laws and legalized labor unions with their right to strike and picket. Poverty became less of a crime or a private failure and more of a social need to be addressed by legislation. Some decades later, state socialism, social democracy, and labor unions would work together to form what would be called the modern welfare state.

In many industrialized states, the passing of child labor laws (prohibiting them from working) revolutionized Western society (see figure 11.6). Ironically, many commoners had actually resisted earlier efforts of enlightened despots to provide universal education. Schooling increased the economic burden of children for their parents. Sending children to school meant they could not contribute to the family labor force until their teen years. Nineteenth-century elites also discouraged education for all people, perfectly aware that workers with education did not often want to do dirty, hard labor. They feared that workers would aspire to rise above their "assigned" social level. That is why, even in the West today, a university education is considered a ticket to a middle-class lifestyle. While education was not an immediate cure-all, a compulsory, basic grade-school education at taxpayer expense in state schools soon became the norm in the West. Literacy approached 100 percent in many Western industrialized countries by 1900.

Meanwhile, improved production through worker efficiency and new technology made **corporations** more and more powerful. Until the modern corporation, most businesses had been small, local institutions based on families or the partnerships of a few individuals. The corporation became a business where a multitude of people could pool their capital resources (stockholders) and elect representatives (a board of directors), who then appointed a chief manager (president or chief executive officer) to run the company. The corporation was an artificial legal construction: it could, like a person, own property, incur debt, sue, and be sued. Meanwhile, the people who owned that corporation were immune—only vulnerable for the amount of stock that they held. This legal status granted corporations a huge advantage over mere mortal citizens, since they could theoretically "live" forever. This was, of course, blatant hypocrisy by the ruling elites. They could form

Figure 11.6. These boys worked in and around the coal mines rather than going to school. Note that one is missing an arm, probably from an industrial accident. (Luzerne County Historical Society)

corporations that represented and united the voice of thousands of stockholders, but they would not allow unions to represent and unite thousands of workers? These corporations, fed by huge flows of capital, soon came to dominate Western economies both within their home nations and around the world.

Corporations were so successful that many quickly bloated into burgeoning conglomerates. Huge corporations combined with others as **cartels** or **trusts**. These associations conspired to establish monopolies, the control of prices and production of whole economic sectors, reducing or completely eliminating competition. Railroads, steel, oil, and even sugar came under monopolistic control in many nations. Critics in the United States called the owners "robber barons," unfairly enriched by exploited workers; the tycoons saw themselves as sharp businessmen justly compensated with unimaginable wealth. Some governments became concerned at this concentration of economic power in a few hands. The dominant "free market" economic theory of laissez-faire (or classical liberal economics) required competition to keep the system fair and efficient. Since cartels crushed competition, governments soon felt compelled to enact antitrust laws to break up the trusts and monopolies. Some capitalists cried that this intervention would ruin economic growth, but governments responded by citing the need to protect their citizens from exploitation. In America some reformers were responding to the movement of *populism*, where rural workers complained about capitalists exploiting the common man by manipulating markets and money (see chapter 12).

The question of whether profit making necessarily excludes fair treatment of workers and consumers has been a challenge faced by citizens of the West ever since the nineteenth century. What actions should citizens or their governments take to regulate or promote the rights of human individuals against legal corporations? The bundle of ideas advocated by diverse socialists still provides answers to the world today. Socialism's concept of equality originated in the suffering of the workers early in the Industrial Revolution. Therein lay its appeal, even as versions of socialism underwent varied successes and failures in the twentieth century.

Review: How did socialists address problems manufactured by the Industrial Revolution?

Response:

PRIMARY SOURCE PROJECT 11: SMILES VERSUS OWEN ABOUT THE GOOD LIFE

Two British reformers during the height of the Industrial Revolution offer different advice on how to create a just society. Samuel Smiles was a Scottish writer and editor who also briefly worked for a railroad company. The success of his advice manual, Self-Help *(1859), led him to go on lecture tours in support of his classical liberal proposals. A generation earlier, Robert Owen rose from modest circumstances in Wales to become manager and part owner of a cotton mill in New*

Lanark, Scotland. He wrote A New View *(1813) and began to lecture and call for socialist reform based on his experiences.*

Source 1: *Self-Help* by Samuel Smiles (1866)

"Heaven helps those who help themselves" is a well-tried maxim, embodying in a small compass the results of vast human experience. The spirit of self-help is the root of all genuine growth in the individual; and, exhibited in the lives of many, it constitutes the true source of national vigor and strength. Help from without is often enfeebling in its effects, but help from within invariably invigorates. Whatever is done for men or classes to a certain extent takes away the stimulus and necessity of doing for themselves; and where men are subjected to over-guidance and over-government, the inevitable tendency is to render them comparatively helpless.

Even the best institutions can give a man no active help. Perhaps the utmost they can do is, to leave him free to develop himself and improve his individual condition. But in all times men have been prone to believe that their happiness and well-being were to be secured by means of institutions rather than by their own conduct. Hence the value of legislation as an agent in human advancement has usually been much over-estimated. . . . Moreover, it is every day becoming more clearly understood, that the function of government is negative and restrictive, rather than positive and active; being resolvable principally into protection—protection of life, liberty, and property. . . . But there is no power of the law that can make the idle man industrious, the thriftless provident, or the drunken sober; though every individual can be each and all of these if he will, by the exercise of his own free powers of action and self-denial. . . .

It may be of comparatively little consequence how a man is governed from without, whilst everything depends upon how he governs himself from within. The greatest slave is not he who is ruled by a despot, great though that evil be, but he who is the thrall of his own moral ignorance, selfishness, and vice. . . . The solid foundations of liberty must rest upon individual character; which is also the only sure guarantee for social security and national progress. In this consists the real strength of English liberty. . . .

It is this energy of individual life and example acting throughout society, which constitutes the best practical education of Englishmen. Schools, academies, and colleges, give but the merest beginnings of culture in comparison with it. Far higher and more practical is the life-education daily given in our homes, in the streets, behind counters, in workshops, at the loom and the plough, in counting-houses and manufactories, and in the busy haunts of men. This is the education that fits Englishmen for doing the work and acting the part of free men. This is that final construction . . . consisting in action, conduct, self-culture, self-control,—all that tends to discipline a man truly, and fit him for the proper performance of the duties and business of life,—a kind of education not to be learnt from books, or acquired by any amount of mere literary training.

Source 2: *A New View* by Robert Owen (1817)

According to the last returns under the Population Act, the poor and working classes of Great Britain and Ireland have been found to exceed fifteen millions of persons, or nearly three-fourths of the population of the British Islands.

The characters of these persons are now permitted to be very generally formed without proper guidance or direction, and, in many cases, under circumstances which directly impel them to a course of extreme vice and misery; thus rendering them the worst and most dangerous subjects in the empire; while the far greater part of the remainder of the community are educated upon the most mistaken principles of human nature, such, indeed, as cannot fail to produce a general conduct throughout society, totally unworthy of the character of rational beings.

The first thus unhappily situated are the poor and the uneducated profligate among the working classes, who are now trained to commit crimes, for the commission of which they are afterwards punished.

The second is the remaining mass of the population, who are now instructed to believe, or at least to acknowledge, that certain principles are unerringly true, and to act as though they were grossly false; thus filling the world with folly and inconsistency, and making society, throughout all its ramifications, a scene of insincerity and counteraction.

In this state the world has continued to the present time; its evils have been and are continually increasing; they cry aloud for efficient corrective measures, which if we longer delay, general disorder must ensue. . . .

For such has been our education, that we hesitate not to devote years and expend millions in the detection and punishment of crimes, and in the attainment of objects whose ultimate results are, in comparison with this, insignificancy itself: and yet we have not moved one step in the true path to prevent crimes, and to diminish the innumerable evils with which mankind are now afflicted. . . .

In those characters which now exhibit crime, the fault is obviously not in the individual, but the defects proceed from the system in which the individual was trained. Withdraw those circumstances which tend to create crime in the human character, and crime will not be created. Replace them with such as are calculated to form habits of order, regularity, temperance, industry; and these qualities will be formed. Adopt measures of fair equity and justice, and you will readily acquire the full and complete confidence of the lower orders: proceed systematically on principles of undeviating persevering kindness, yet retaining and using, with the least possible severity, the means of restraining crime from immediately injuring society; and by degrees even the crimes now existing in the adults will also gradually disappear; for the worst formed disposition, short of incurable insanity, will not long resist a firm, determined, well-directed, persevering kindness. Such a proceeding, whenever practiced, will be found the most powerful and effective corrector of crime, and of all injurious and improper habits.

Questions:

- *What are the institutions that affect human lives mentioned by each author?*
- *What kind of personal character and attributes are mentioned by each author?*
- *What room is there for cooperation between individuals and institutions?*

Responses:

Citations

Smiles, Samuel. *Self-Help: With Illustrations of Character and Conduct.* Revised and enlarged ed. Boston: Ticknor and Fields, 1866, pp. 15–20.

Owen, Robert. *A New View of Society: Or, Essays on the Formation of Human Character Preparatory to the Development of a Plan for Gradually Ameliorating the Condition of Mankind.* 3rd ed. London: Longman, 1817, pp. 15–16, 30, 59–60.

For more on these sources, go to http://www.concisewesternciv.com/sources/psc11.html.

THE MACHINERY OF NATURE

The technology that powered the Industrial Revolution was, of course, based on scientific principles established by the Scientific Revolution. Throughout the nineteenth century, science continued to advance in areas not focused on profits. Scientists wanted to know more about how the universe worked. While Newton had supplied many answers about the movements of the planets, scientists began investigating other aspects of the earth itself, life upon it, and even people themselves. How did nature function, especially if science left God out of the equation? Scientists were determined to find out by using observable and experimental data to explain the workings of nature.

First, another phase of the Scientific Revolution crystallized, as the new science of geology studied our planet Earth. The traditional Western explanation for the earth's history had been drawn from the biblical book of Genesis. Jews began their calendar with their calculated date of the beginning of creation, equivalent to 3761 BC. In the seventeenth century, Irish bishop James Ussher recalculated the earth's age from biblical genealogies: he concluded that God created angels and the globe of the earth on 23 October 4004 BC. At first, the influence of scripture inclined scientists to think along the lines of a *theory of catastrophism* to explain geology.

According to this theory, rare and unusual events of enormous power, resembling divine intervention, explained the features of the earth. While the theory of catastrophism provided some understanding of the earth's past, new discoveries soon called it into question.

Charles Lyell's book *Principles of Geology* provided a new theory in 1829. Lyell proposed the ***theory of uniformitarianism*** to explain the history of the earth, saying that the same (uniform) processes shaping the earth today have always acted to mold the planet. Thus, erosion and deposition, uplift and sinking of landmasses, volcanoes, earthquakes, glaciers, and so on have formed every existing landscape. He concluded that the earth was not fixed but in flux. Since many of these processes move infinitesimally slowly, the theory required that earth be at least millions of years old.

Many Christians who interpreted the Bible literally opposed this new theory, since these numbers contradicted calculations based on Genesis. Nonetheless, the practice of science increasingly left biblical explanation out of the equation. Indeed, most scientific evidence collected over the nineteenth century clearly supported uniformitarianism, while almost none backed up catastrophism. Uniformitarianism could, by measurable natural processes, account for the highest mountain and the deepest valley. Just as scientists had come to accept the theories of heliocentrism and universal gravitation, they now embraced the theory of uniformitarianism because it had explanatory power and conformed to the evidence of nature.

Fossils provided much of the evidence for research into the earth's history. Scientists found petrified remains both of contemporary-looking organisms and of strange creatures that did not seem to exist anymore. Excavations dug to build mines, canals, foundations, and so on in the industrial age unearthed more and more fossils. Scientists began to organize these fossilized bones and called the large creatures dinosaurs ("terrible lizards"). As geologists compared layers of rock in which fossils were found, science showed that dinosaurs had lived many millions of years ago before becoming extinct. But how had those monsters, or many other life forms, died out, while other just-as-ancient species still lived on the earth and under the seas?

New scientists who studied living things, biologists, tried to solve that mystery. The oldest layers of rock showed a few simple living things, such as algae. More recent rock layers showed a connected diversity of life, as evidenced by the appearance of new species (namely a scientific category of living things that could reproduce with each other). As eons wore on, some species, like the dozens of kinds of dinosaurs, had clearly gone extinct. Others, like ferns, clams, and cockroaches, had survived into the present with little change. The fossil record showed that overall, life had become increasingly diverse and complex over time. Scientists called this process of biological change ***evolution***.

Christian religious literalists opposed evolution as vehemently as they earlier had denied the age of the earth or, going back to Copernicus, the location of the earth at the center of the universe. Evolution, the age of the earth, and the earth's noncentral place in the universe, nonetheless, are scientific facts. Many nonscientists complained (and still complain) that the idea of evolution is a theory, meaning a mere guess with little supporting evidence. These people apparently misunderstand science. Scientific theories are not just good guesses; they offer comprehensive explanations of the facts. Gravity is a scientific fact, once best explained by Newton's theory of gravitation (and since modified by other theories). Evolution is a scientific fact, but in the mid-nineteenth century, scientists still sought a theory that explained how life on earth had become more diverse and complex over the eons.

Charles Darwin (b. 1809–d. 1882) provided a scientific theory to explain the fact of evolution. He pondered the issue for years after investigating the unique species of finches, iguanas, and tortoises on the Galapagos Islands off the western coast of South America, which he had visited during his voyage on the ship *Beagle* in the 1830s. Darwin finally published his book ***The Origin of Species*** (1859) only when a fellow naturalist, Alfred Wallace, had figured out the same theory. Darwin's ***theory of natural selection***, also called "survival of the fittest," proposed that the struggle of creatures for food and reproduction encouraged change. As living things adapted to their environment and competed with other living things, certain advantageous characteristics enabled them to survive. Whether by stealth, strength, speed, size, or intelligence, some organisms outlived others and lasted long enough to pass those favorable characteristics on to their own viable offspring. Over millions of millennia, small, incremental variations slowly separated offspring into more complex and more diverse species. Species that did not compete successfully, especially when a climate changed, became extinct. The theory of natural selection relies on the natural drives for food and sex as a mechanism for diversity. Thus, Darwin outlined a means whereby scientists could frame their study of life on earth. While modifications have been made to Darwin's theory (as to Newton's), all subsequent science has served only to confirm and support the scientific fact of evolution.

This science notwithstanding, some Christians became even more outraged when Darwin's second significant book, *The Descent of Man* (1871), argued that humans were descended from the same apelike ancestors as chimpanzees or baboons. Many Christians were offended by a human connection to beasts and worried what that would imply about the human soul. Without God's creation, nothing differentiated us from other soulless living things. Religious leaders preached that this godless view of nature would lead to immorality.

Their point seemed proven when social theorists used humanity's connections to animals to argue that the "survival of the fittest" was how human societies should be run. This ideology came to be called ***Social Darwinism***, which argued that human ethics should reflect selfishness, greed, and exploitation of the weak because of inherited differences. Thus, the poor deserved their poverty, or the defeated were properly conquered, while the acquisition of wealth and power proved the superiority of the upper class. This skewed rationalization encouraged laissez-faire capitalism, nationalism, imperialism, and racism. The millionaire oil magnate John D. Rockefeller himself pronounced that ruthless competition in business was not evil, but instead reflected the laws of nature and God. He himself had risen from a simple farm boy through hard work, frugality, and secret deals. These ideas in turn stimulated materialism and secularism.

Social Darwinist assertions misread natural selection with an overblown confidence in human social differences. Darwin did see some civilizations as superior to others, but people could evolve their cultures and morality. Social Darwinists, however, saw supremacy as the main survival virtue and bruising competition as the means, which ignored nature's success stories. A despised creature like the cockroach survived with speed, stealth, and the ability to eat garbage. Meanwhile, a dinosaur like *Tyrannosaurus rex*, the biggest and meanest carnivore, had become extinct because it could not adapt. Evolution has no moral direction—it is merely the description of nature's work.

Social Darwinists were only one part of a larger movement to apply science to human activity. A third advance in science during the nineteenth century emerged as intellectuals invented the scholarly subjects of the **social sciences** at the end of the century. These fields sought to analyze human beings and then propose theories and laws to explain them. The study of history was tossed into this new category, after being bolstered with statistical studies. The new subject of political science clarified the multiplying electoral systems of Western democracies. Sociology studied modern societies, while anthropology examined ancient or primitive cultures. The West's new domination of foreign cultures provided new opportunities for social scientists to compare diverse peoples.

Of great consequence was the decision of sociologists and anthropologists to scrutinize Christianity. They applied the same methodology of textual criticism used in the Renaissance to acquire the best versions of ancient texts. The Bible was clearly a collection of ancient writings, which resembled those of many other faiths around the world and could be compared with them historically. *Higher criticism* dissected the Bible, instead of viewing it as a perfect product of instantaneously inspired creation by the Judeo-Christian deity. Scholars began to read the Bible as a flawed compilation composed by human beings over hundreds of years. This method reasonably explained many of the Bible's contradictions, inconsistencies, and obscurities. From the Book of Genesis alone, odd passages such as two versions of the creation of humans, different numbers of animals Noah took into the ark, or the unusually long lives of the first humans could be attributed to fallible human editing.

The growing explanatory power of science and social sciences therefore further weakened the hold of Christianity among the elites of Western civilization. In reaction, Christians of all denominations, whether Orthodox, Roman Catholic, or Protestant, began to split into two large groups with different attitudes toward the Bible. Fundamentalists reasserted standard Christian beliefs about the divine Jesus who died to keep believers out of hell. *Fundamentalism* developed an interpretation of inerrancy about the Bible. Inerrancy claims that original biblical texts are divinely created, without error of any kind, and clearly understood under guidance of the Holy Spirit. Meanwhile, *modernism* embraced textual and higher criticism to better understand a divinely inspired Bible composed by flawed humans. Modernist scholars accepted science in its worldview and ambiguity in its faith. Overall, Christianity continued its decline as a belief system, although most people in the West remained practicing Christians.

Criticisms of religious belief by the founder of psychiatry, **Sigmund Freud** (b. 1856–d. 1939), focused on its incompatibility with science. Freud abandoned much of his Jewish heritage for a more rational look at culture's interaction with individuals. As a psychiatrist, Freud brought new insights into the debate on the origins of and treatments for mental illness. He famously argued that when a person's subconscious drives (id) conflicted with social expectations (superego) and internalized lessons (ego), then neurosis and even psychosis could result. While this scheme is not specifically accepted today by the psychiatric community, it had enormous impact at the turn of the twentieth century. Freud also shocked the "decent" society of his turn-of-the-century Vienna when he unveiled how the human sex drive (libido) could affect mental health. As a result, sex became a part of our public discourse instead of being confined behind closed doors.

Through the study of biology, science discovered more practical applications for public health, largely thanks to **Louis Pasteur** (b. 1822–d. 1895) of France. First, Pasteur explained the process of fermentation, which rescued the French wine industry. Additionally, his pasteurization process saved milk from spoiling. Finally, his *germ theory of disease* helped save lives. Pasteur's science proved that microscopic organisms, such as bacteria and viruses, caused many illnesses. Of course, the germ theory does not explain all diseases, such as most cancers or illnesses of old age. Still, it has led to a huge advancement in medical cures and disease prevention. Pasteur's studies proved the efficacy of immunization through both the old practice of inoculations (giving people a live form of a disease) and new vaccinations (giving a dead form). Antiseptics (which killed germs on the outside of the body) were soon followed by antibiotics (which killed germs inside the body). Modern scientific medicine actually succeeded at improving the health and survival of people to a degree unknown by any previous society.

Finally, physicists were also busy unlocking the secrets of the universe at the smallest level. Scientists such as Pierre and Marie Sklodowska Curie in France and J. J. Thomson and Ernst Rutherford in England formulated *atomic theory*. Drawing on ideas of the ancient Greeks, modern physicists confirmed that atoms were the smallest part of matter that possesses the properties of an element. At the time, no one could have guessed that the atomic force which bound an atom together could be unleashed to enable humans to destroy all civilization.

Overall, the nineteenth century had rapidly multiplied the options open to the citizens of Western civilization. The Industrial Revolution drove the economy, with its varied goods, services, and ideologies available to consumers of the upper, middle, and lower class. Conservatives, liberals, anarchists, and the several flavors of socialists argued for different kinds of political economy, if not revolution. New scientific ideas and inventions opened the doors to the future, while romantics and many people of faith found comfort in the past. Christianity continued to fragment. Despite and because of these internal differences, however, Western civilization would soon reign supreme over most other peoples around the globe.

Review: *How did modern science generate new and unsettling knowledge?*

Response:

Make your own timeline.

1764   **1914**

CHAPTER 12

The Westerner's Burden

Imperialism and Nationalism, 1810 to 1918

By building on the superiority in industrialization and technology achieved during the nineteenth century, Western civilization gained mastery over the world as never before. Western advances dominated the globe through a revival of colonial imperialism and a new sense of self-identity called nationalism. The West's collisions with diverse world cultures both vindicated and challenged its own cultural assumptions. The British poet Rudyard Kipling's acceptance of "The White Man's Burden" (bringing civilization to primitive natives) illustrates the culture's dialogue with itself. Race, sex roles, and nationalism became linked to political control over those perceived as inferiors. Fateful decisions led the West on a path toward the most destructive war the world had ever experienced.

"NEW AND IMPROVED" IMPERIALISM

As covered in chapter 9, Western nations had begun having success with colonial imperialism outside Europe in the late 1400s and early 1500s. The "voyages of discovery" by Portugal and Spain, followed by the Netherlands, France, and England, ended in conquests of distant foreign peoples and seizure of their lands. At that time, disease had given the Europeans a decisive advantage in their conquest of the New World, since the natives of the "Americas" lacked immunities and were killed more often by germs than by guns. At the same time, resistance to disease possessed by many peoples in the Old World of Africa and Asia meant that western-ers could gain only small footholds in those places. Many of these peoples lived in their own civilizations, which for many centuries had been more advanced techno-logically, politically, militarily, and culturally than the West. Asians and Africans mostly governed themselves, as they had since the dawn of human history. By the early nineteenth century the Portuguese, Spanish, French, and Dutch controlled only scattered remnants of their once-vast overseas possessions in Asia, Africa, or the Americas. Western colonialism's ruling over distant territories seemed destined to decline.

Only the British Empire reigned over a substantial overseas colonial empire, waving its imperial glory in all the corners of the world, despite the loss of what became the United States of America. Many British saw their imperial rule as benevolent, promoting peace and prosperity at home and around the world (see figure 12.1). Some Western nations were jealous of British success with its colonies. By 1830 Britain's old rival France became particularly resentful of this empire on which the sun never set. As a result, a revived and more powerful wave of imperialism, or *neo-imperialism* (1830–1914), rolled across the oceans (see map 12.1).

Additionally, most westerners were overly confident in their own progress. Because technology had increased their power over nature, most Europeans thought that their own "civilized" cultures surpassed those of "primitive," "ignorant," and "superstitious" "barbarian" peoples. In their view, Christianity needed to replace native beliefs for the natives' own good. While many Western leaders were hardly religious, they could appeal to Christian voters by supporting missionary work to convert "heathens." These missionaries naturally needed protection from headhunters, cannibals, or fierce natives who held their own religious beliefs. So European governments sent in troops. The West's nationalistic pride, smug cultural superiority, and international security demanded global empires.

The Scientific and Industrial Revolutions empowered this new burst of Western imperialism. First, scientific medicine enabled westerners to better survive foreign

Figure 12.1.   The Europeans claimed to bring education and civilization, as in this German school in the colony of Southwest Africa (modern-day Namibia). At the same time as African children were being educated, German troops were waging a war of extermination against whole tribes. (Art Resource)

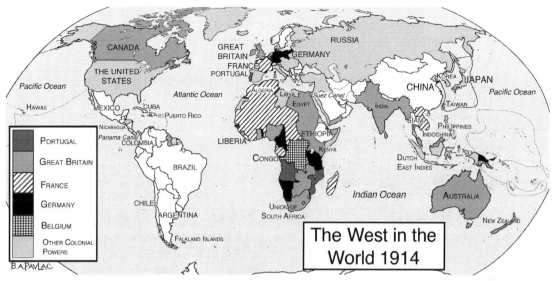

Map 12.1. The West in the World, 1914.
What countries managed to remain free of Western imperialism?

climates and their diseases, such as malaria or sleeping sickness. Knowledge about germs and infection, inoculation and vaccination, and the discovery that taking quinine (made from cinchona in Peru) prevented malaria all increased westerners' resistance to previously lethal diseases.[1] Second, modern Western military force and technology outmatched indigenous Africans and Asian armies. Even in the previous century, Asians and Africans armed with bow, spear, and sword could not compete with Western soldiers shooting muskets. By 1850, a few thousand well-trained modern troops equipped with quick-loading rifles and artillery could crush countless tribal peoples. Third, the new industrial economy compelled westerners to acquire new resources to feed the machines of industry. The round-the-clock factories required raw materials to process, while finished products demanded new markets. Businessmen and the politicians backing them thought that empires would provide both. Additionally, emigrants settling on the vast tracts of underused farmland in distant colonies could provide another outlet for the excess population of Europe, easing social tensions at home.

Consequently, economists revised the old economic theory of mercantilism for the new circumstances. While the mercantilism of the seventeenth century had asked for government intervention to foster a favorable balance of trade, the economic ***theory of neo-mercantilism*** of the nineteenth century restricted itself to asking for government intervention in order to help build empires and open foreign markets. At home, the government was to continue its laissez-faire policy and allow individuals and corporations free use of their private property. But as mer-

---

1. In the British Empire they put the quinine into tonic water and mixed it with gin (alcohol flavored with juniper oil) to create the gin and tonic. Decades earlier, cheap gin had produced a serious intoxication problem among the lower classes. The new gin and tonic made the drink respectable. Modern tonic water, though, does not contain enough quinine to prevent malaria.

chants wandered into the deepest, darkest outlands, they also needed the muscle of Western military forces to protect both their persons and their newly "acquired" possessions from the natives. It may seem a bit inconsistent for business leaders to call for government to stay out of economic decisions in one circumstance (domestic) and call for government support in another (international), but they have done so consistently since the nineteenth century.

Supported by technologically advanced armies and navies, the West sailed with new determination and spread around the world. Most non-Western peoples lost control of their lives and countries. Sometimes, enterprising businessmen simply took what they wanted. British agents stole tea from China to brew drinks, rubber from Brazil to make tires, and cinchona from Peru to extract quinine against malaria. They then grew these plants on plantations in British-controlled South and Southeast Asia. Other times, entrepreneurs used fraud, bribery, or threats to convince native chiefs to sign treaties that surrendered land rights to the Europeans. As a last resort, armies would simply mow down local resistance. As justification, the imperialists mouthed altruistic intentions of stopping violence and warfare among the natives. They might even protest that they were drawn into empire against their will, forced to make hard, violent choices. Further, Europeans often exploited native ethnic differences, exaggerating them to set the ethnic groups against one another. Such tactics revived the classic method of divide-and-rule. The westerners almost always profited and prevailed.

The intensity of domination varied in three degrees. First, in **spheres of influence**, the natives were still ultimately in charge. In these areas, one Western state would form an alliance and a close working relationship with the native regime to keep other Europeans out and arrange the best deals for itself. Second, in **protectorates** the native leaders still held a great deal of authority, at least when it came to running their own society. The Western power became decisive only in foreign affairs and in many economic decisions. Third, in complete colonization, native structures and societies were substantially eliminated, and Western people moved in and took over.

This had been the case centuries before, during the colonization of the Latin American states, the United States, Canada, Australia, and New Zealand. Immigrant Europeans shoved the comparatively few aboriginals onto the worst lands. The Dutch colony of **South Africa**, located on the Cape of Good Hope since 1652, also saw Europeans seize from the local peoples the best grazing and farm land. The descendants of the Dutch colonialists began calling themselves **Afrikaaners**. They saw themselves as Africans, just as the descendants of English colonialists in America viewed themselves as Americans. Meanwhile, the original natives in that region of Africa, San and Khoekhoe, were weakened by smallpox, war, and enslavement.[2]

---

2. How various peoples adopt or are given names determines their status. The San (meaning foragers) were hunter-gatherers, similar to other bushmen or pygmies elsewhere in Africa. The Khoekhoe, whose name means "people people," were pastoralists who often took on a paternalistic and exploitative position over the San. The Dutch insultingly named both Hottentots, probably after their common "clicking" language, now called Khoesan.

In most new colonies formed under neo-imperialism after 1830, the natives retained little power and little hope that conditions would improve. In most of Africa, the Pacific Islands, and parts of Asia, the minority population of Europeans who possessed the majority of the land and authority restricted the natives to a subservient role—foreigners in their own country. Recent historians, however, see native peoples acting as subalterns, officially subservient to the westerners yet subversive beneath the surface. Westerners at the time merely interpreted natives' lack of enthusiasm for empire as laziness and stupidity.

Some nineteenth-century science supported Western supremacy through *racism*. Such scientists divided up the human species into several "races," based on what they thought were shared bloodlines (a special, imagined quality inherited from common ancestors), as demonstrated by such anatomical differences as eye shape, nose length, or skin color. Their studies also "proved" that some races were superior to others. All this science has since been proven bogus. Humans belong to the same species, and racial differences are insignificant. But the Europeans who believed in racism constructed the idea that they were at the top, part of the "Caucasian race" (named both because some scientists considered that the people who lived in the Caucasus Mountains were the "prettiest" and because many believed humans first appeared there). Social Darwinism argued that the dominance of Europeans allegedly proved their racial superiority. Being Western was to have a "white" complexion (which, of course, is not actually white, even for albinos, who have some pink from blood vessels showing through the skin). For many, being a person of "color" (for example red, yellow, brown, or black) excluded them from acceptable society. Thus, no matter how hardworking or educated colonized races could become, their unchangeable skin color kept them inferior.

The transformation of South Africa opened the door for neo-imperialism. After some interventions during the wars of the French Revolution, the British took over the colony from the Dutch after the Congress of Vienna in 1815. British settlers moved in, confirming a mixed society where the few Europeans dominated the large numbers of transported Asian workers and the many native Africans who still lived there. But the Dutch and English did not get along very well. In 1835, because the British outlawed slavery in the South African colony, thousands of Dutch Afrikaaners left the colony on the Great Trek. They journeyed hundreds of miles inland to escape what they saw as British oppression. The Afrikaaners seized new fertile land and enslaved the native black Africans who had survived recent wars against one another. The Dutch Afrikaaners set up the Transvaal and the Orange Free State as two sovereign Western countries in southern Africa. The Western technology and methodology of these farmers (called Boers) made the land produce great wealth.

The South African conflicts focused the attention of Britain's rivals upon the continent. At the beginning of the nineteenth century, only a few European imperial possessions clung to Africa's fringes, many originating as bases for the Atlantic-African slave trade to the Americas. The French led the new wave. Their neo-imperialism began in 1830 with "the flyswatter incident." When a French diplomat arrogantly refused to discuss repaying a debt owed to Algerians, the Ottoman governor slapped him in the face with a flyswatter. Outraged by this insult to French *honneur*, France conquered the Algerian provinces and made them part of France.

Thousands of French immigrants then began buying land and settling in. They had launched a "*mission civilisatrice*," or mission to civilize the barbarians.

It took a few more years for European interest to penetrate the rest of Africa, especially the interior south of the Sahara. At the beginning of the nineteenth century, the Europeans called Africa the "Dark Continent," partly because they knew so little about it beyond their coastal bases. By midcentury, missionaries and explorers were bringing back fascinating accounts. Most famous were dispatches from the journalist Henry Stanley as he searched for the Scottish explorer, missionary, and humanitarian Dr. David Livingstone, allegedly lost in the Congo in 1871. Stanley's dry remark upon finding him, "Dr. Livingstone, I presume," is a statement of the obvious (finding the only European man amid so many Africans). More important, Stanley published exotic tales of African riches practically free for the taking. Stanley laid the foundation for the seizure of the Congo River basin by King Leopold of Belgium. Livingstone had wanted to minister to the spiritual and physical needs of the natives; Leopold desired to exploit the region as his own pet colony, plundering it of rubber and ivory. To deal with Congolese who did not cooperate, the Belgians hacked off their hands, following the example of Columbus. Others they raped, terrorized, or shot. Over the next few decades, the Belgians' brutal treatment of natives reduced the population from more than thirty million to less than ten million.

Western neo-imperialism soon overwhelmed the rest of Africa as other leaders began to follow Leopold's example. The fate of one hundred million Africans changed with the stroke of a pen in 1884. The leaders of Europe convened a meeting in Berlin to discuss the recent Belgian takeover of the Congo. At this Congress of Berlin they defined the ground rules for their **Partition of Africa** (1884–1914). Each interested power was permitted to move in from a specific area of coastline and stake claims to whatever territories it could. During this "Scramble for Africa," the invading nation was to notify other European governments so that they did not stumble into war with one another. The conquest of more than ten million square miles of African lands quickly followed.

Even the traditional rivals France and Britain managed to forget many of their ancient grievances with each other. The French were crossing the African continent from west to east, while the British linked a chain of territories from north to south. This competition between Britain and France intersected in the Sudan. The French and British competition there almost sparked a larger war. The French began to dig the **Suez Canal**, an artificial waterway to link the Mediterranean and the Red Sea. After the French investors ran into difficulties, the British rushed into Egypt in 1882 (see figure 12.2). They wanted to finish the Suez Canal, which offered a much shorter route to British India than sailing all the way around Africa. Then, in 1885, a Muslim revolt led by the "Mad Mahdi" drove the British out of Egyptian-dominated Sudan. The British General Gordon and his troops died defending Khartoum, Sudan's capital. After the French showed some interest in claiming the Sudan, the British invaded again in 1898. They avenged Gordon by killing thousands of Muslims with machine guns and retook the country. A small French force (mostly of Senegalese troops) slogged across the continent to confront the British at Fashoda

Figure 12.2.   This cartoon shows the new protector of Egypt: a confident British soldier holding a gun, with a Turk and his sheathed sword at his feet. Ironically, no Egyptians are visible—only the ancient Sphinx and pyramids in the distance. (Art Resource)

on the Nile (today Kodok in the South Sudan). Instead of fighting, the two commanders toasted each other and parted on friendly terms; diplomats then carved up the region for France and Great Britain. This cooperation in Africa soon led to the Entente Cordiale, a general British-French alliance.

While the British ended up with the best share of Africa, they faced an unanticipated challenge to their new supremacy in South Africa again. The discovery of diamonds in 1867 brought in many new European settlers to the British colony, looking to make quick and easy fortunes. In 1877, the British felt bold enough to seize bankrupt Transvaal (also known as the South African Republic by its Boer citizens of Dutch ancestry). The Boers submitted partly out of fear of the neighboring Zulu kingdom. After the British victory in the Anglo-Zulu War (1879) removed that threat, the Boers fought back against British occupation and won Transvaal's independence back by 1881. Then, in 1886, the discovery of gold in Transvaal unleashed a new crisis. Many *uitlanders* (European foreigners) flooded into Boer territories in a gold rush. As the British adventurers and then British officials threatened to take over Transvaal and its ally the Orange Free State, Afrikaaners preemptively launched the **Boer War** (1899–1902), which unexpectedly challenged British military supremacy. The Boers fought an effective guerrilla campaign until the British defeated them with a new radical measure, the **concentration camp**. The British rounded up large numbers of civilians whose only crime was being the wrong kind of person (in this case, an Afrikaaner) and confined these men, women, and children in barracks under guard and surrounded by barbed wire. The British thus perfected the concentration camp as a technique of social conquest, which others would imitate. Tens of thousands of camp residents, young and old, male and female, died from disease and hunger. The British also burned farms and armed native Africans (at least until victory had been achieved). The British won the Boer War, but at the cost of many lives and sharp international criticism. Thus, the Boer War marked the dangerous precedent of westerners fighting other westerners over foreign plots of land.

Despite this crushing defeat, the large population of Afrikaaners still resisted British domination. So the British and the Afrikaaners compromised a few years later with the creation of the **Union of South Africa**. South Africa developed into a Western industrialized nation, although its British and Afrikaaner populations remained a minority. The 80 percent majority of the population (a few immigrants from India, some "coloreds" of mixed heritage, and the large numbers of black Africans) tried to organize their own political participation by founding the (South) African National Congress (1912). Joint British and Afrikaaner rule, however, effectively excluded these people of non-European heritage.

In the Scramble for Africa, other Western powers managed to grab different slices to appease their appetites for the moment. While Western civilization had ended the international slave trade, many millions of Africans lived in slave-like conditions under these new European masters in what had been their own countries. France appeared to hold the next-largest share after England, yet much was a wasteland of forbidding desert or impassable jungle. The Germans won a couple of key colonies, but they grumbled that theirs did not compare well enough with those of the French and English. They nearly exterminated the indigenous Herero, Khoekhoe, and Nama peoples in their colony of Southwest Africa (today Namibia). The success of other states inspired even little Portugal to join in. Portuguese armies marched inland from centuries-old coastal bases to kill and conquer. New to imperialism, the brand new Kingdom of Italy grabbed a few pieces of Somalia on the eastern Horn of Africa. Regrettably for Italian pride, the poor Italians who tried to invade Abyssinia (also called Ethiopia) had their army decisively trounced by natives armed with arrows and spears at the Battle of Adowa (1896). They were the only westerners to be defeated by Africans during this wave of imperialism. Thus, by 1914, native Africans governed only in Abyssinia and to some extent in Liberia. That country was an American protectorate run by Africans whose ancestors had, for a time, been slaves in the United States. Otherwise, very few people from the West migrated to Africa, yet westerners ruled all the rest of Africa for the next half century.

While Africans succumbed relatively quickly to Western supremacy, the Asians experienced more varied levels of resistance. The first major Asian region to fall was the Indian subcontinent. Since Britain's victories in the eighteenth century, it had been the supreme foreign power in the region, either directly or indirectly through the East India Trading Company. Still, many indigenous princes and rajahs remained independent of the growing British influence. An odd incident in 1857, however, provided the means and opportunity for British imperialists to take over much of South Asia.

A rebellion broke out when the British military introduced the latest Enfield rifle and its cartridges to their native troops, called sepoys. This ammunition was more efficient than the ball and powder of muzzle-loaded muskets. The bullet and explosive charge were wrapped together in greased paper, and a soldier needed only to bite off the paper and load the powder and cartridge in the rifle. Suddenly, the rumor spread among the natives that the grease on the paper was either beef fat or pig fat. The former was abhorrent to Hindus, who believed that cows were sacred, and the latter was repulsive to Muslims, who held that swine were unclean. Thus began the so-called **Sepoy Mutiny** (1857) or, as some Indians call it, the "First War for Independence." Sadly for an independent India, the British quickly rallied and used their superior organization and technology to crush the rebels. The British destroyed dozens of temples and mosques and killed and injured thousands of innocent civilians in revenge. One favorite death penalty was to tie a rebel across the mouth of a cannon and blow him to bits. From then on, the British reigned over most of India as an outright colony, while only a few rajahs managed to preserve their states as protectorates. The British also aggravated the traditional differences among religious groups. They set Hindu, Muslim, Sikh, and others against one another: the classic divide-and-conquer routine used by imperialists in all ages.

Most of the inhabited islands in the Pacific became colonies in the second half of the nineteenth century. Europeans wanted these islands as safe harbors to store and provide food, water, and coal for their steamships. Also, many islands were mountains of guano, or bird poop, that was useful as fertilizer. Most islanders could defend themselves only with Stone Age technology and thus quickly lost.

In East Asia, powerful states that in a previous century had possessed sufficient military technology to defend their borders now found themselves outmatched by the West. The most powerful Asian state, the Chinese Empire, had endured many invasions and rebellions since its foundation two millennia before, in 221 BC. From the cultivated Chinese point of view, all foreigners were barbarians who lacked the sophistication of Chinese culture. Chinese merchants wanted very little from the outside world, although they were willing to sell their tea, silks, and porcelain for cold, hard Western silver and gold.

The British and the Americans, meanwhile, tried to find a product that the Chinese would be willing to buy. They worried that the neo-mercantilistic balance of trade tilted too much to the Chinese advantage. Ultimately, they found a product that would break open the Chinese markets: illegal drugs, in particular, opium. This highly addictive narcotic damaged the Chinese economy, health, and morality. Nevertheless, Western merchants smuggled opium into China from the fields of western and central Asia where it grew best. Profits meant more than Chinese law. When the Chinese authorities justifiably confiscated and destroyed this dangerous drug, British merchants complained to their own regime about property rights. The

British Empire declared war on China to protect the British right to sell illegal narcotics. In the short **Opium Wars** (1839–1842), the Chinese sustained humiliating and decisive defeats by modern British military technology.

The triumphant British imposed treaties that opened up China to Western exploitation. Under the concept of **extraterritoriality**, British people and possessions were exempted from native laws and authority (much as foreign diplomats and embassies still are today). Therefore, British merchants and missionaries could do what they wanted. The treaties also forced the Chinese to hand over parts of several key ports, allowing British warships and troops to move at will throughout China to defend British citizens and interests. In the next few years, the other Western great powers bullied the Chinese into handing over these same privileges to them as well. Westerners out to make a profit attacked and undermined Chinese society.

By 1900, the United States feared that other Western states might carve up the weakened Chinese Empire into distinct economic and political zones. To keep access to markets as free as possible, the United States advocated an "open door" policy throughout China: promising mutual cooperation and no trade barriers among Western imperialists. The open-door policy merely meant that China was open to being bought and sold in little bits by westerners rather than all at once. The Chinese imperial government lacked the ability to resist. The idea of **nativism**, though, provided a rallying point. Those who took up nativism argued that the rights of earlier inhabitants needed to be protected against more recent immigrants and foreigners.

A nativist movement sparked what the westerners called the **Boxer Rebellion** (1900). The name "Boxer" came from an anti-Western society whose symbol was the raised fist. The insurgents attacked foreigners all over China and laid siege to hundreds of diplomats, soldiers, missionaries, and merchants in the foreigners' quarter of the capital city of Peking (today called Beijing). After only fifty-five days, Western armies smashed the revolt and imposed more humiliating treaties on China (see figure 12.3). Shortly afterward, in 1903, the incompetent empress who had managed Chinese affairs for decades died, leaving only a child to inherit the crumbling mechanisms of power. Without leadership, the empire fell to a republican revolt in 1911. Western imperialists stayed and provoked terrible consequences in the developing twentieth century (as explained in later chapters).

In Southeast Asia between India and China, **Siam** (modern-day Thailand) managed to negotiate for itself a sphere of influence rather than a more serious takeover. The British had conquered Burma to the west, as the French seized Indochina (what would become Vietnam, Laos, and Cambodia) to the east. Yet neither side was sure how to dominate the powerful little state of Siam, which was likely to put up a fight. Instead, Siam became a buffer between French and British colonies. It learned from both, although the westernizing influence of the governess Anna Leonowens on Kings Mongkut (r. 1851–1868) and Chulalongkorn (r. 1868–1910) has been exaggerated by modern musicals and films. Siam's forward-looking kings slowly brought Western ways into the country.

Meanwhile, Europeans confidently predicted that their humanitarian burden of looking after the less-advanced peoples of the world would last far into the future.

BARBARIE   —   CIVILISATION

Figure 12.3.   The Boxer Rebellion is critiqued by this illustration by René Georges Herman Paul for a magazine. The (here unprinted) caption reads "It's a matter of perspective. When a Chinese coolie strikes a French soldier the public cry 'Barbarity!' But when a French soldier strikes a coolie, it's a proper blow for civilization." (*Le Cri de Paris*, 10 July 1899)

This "caretaking," however, was two sided. On the one hand, Europeans could point with pride to the construction of a few railroads, roads, harbors, large colonial administration buildings, schools, hospitals, and military bases. Their laws and economics brought a Western order and growth to places once considered by Europeans to be violent, barbaric, and stagnant. Christian missionaries were winning converts. And to its everlasting credit, the West ended the international trade in African slaves and did much to stop most other slavery. All humans became more connected, for good or ill, than they ever had been before in history. The Europeans even drew on the culture of the new lands and showed appreciation for some of the "exotic" art, artifacts, and literature of "Orientals" and Africans.

On the other hand, Europeans blithely ignored the exploitation, cruelty, and hopelessness created by their supremacy. Many native peoples suffered humiliation, defeat, and death. Although their health and standard of living often improved because of participation in global trade, colonial peoples felt the consequences of business decisions made in distant lands. These global economic bonds only intensified with time. Natives often felt like prisoners in their own countries, as traditional social status and customs vanished. Europeans justifiably outlawed the custom of widow burning in India while ignoring how their own policies impoverished many other widows and families. Most of the peoples of the world had been fine without Western colonialism before the nineteenth century. No sooner had they been subjugated than they began working to regain their autonomy. Within a few decades, they would succeed.

Review: How did the Europeans come to dominate Africa and Asia?

Response:

FROM SEA TO SHINING SEA

While Europeans added to their empires, a new Western power was rising, unsuspected, in the Western Hemisphere. The United States of America, like Russia before it, initially aimed its imperialism not across oceans, but across its own continental landmass. The peace agreement with Britain after the War of Independence granted the Americans most lands east of the Mississippi River, giving the United States a size comparable to western Europe. Many Americans believed it was their obvious national purpose, or **manifest destiny**, to dominate all of North America.

Some acquisitions came relatively peacefully. No "Americans" lived west of the Mississippi in 1803. In that year, the new nation practically doubled its size with the stroke of a pen. Napoleon, after losing Haiti, gave up on his own New World empire and sold the Louisiana Purchase to the United States. Neither government in Paris or Washington, DC, of course, consulted with the indigenous peoples about who owned the land. After a second attempt to conquer Canada in the War of 1812 failed, the Americans peacefully negotiated away any rivalry with Britain over mutual borders in the north with Maine or the Oregon Territory. The United States also bought Florida from Spain. To fully control these new territories, however, the Americans would have to kill and remove many of the natives, who kept resisting throughout the nineteenth century.

The next large acquisition, from the newly independent Mexico, did not come peacefully. Even before Mexican independence from Spain, American immigrants had been moving into Mexico's province of Tejas, most of whose population was Native American, especially the Comanche. These immigrants, called Texians, swore to learn Spanish and obey Mexican laws. But when the Mexicans created a stronger federal government and outlawed slavery, the Texians successfully rebelled in 1836. At first, the United States was reluctant to annex the new independent Texas. A decade later, though, the activist President Polk did so. Armed troops shooting at one another over disputed borders triggered the **Mexican-American War** (1846–1848). The United States was quickly victorious and briefly considered, but declined, taking over all of Mexico. Instead, the Yankees only confiscated a third of

Mexico's territory, leaving the rest of the country as the United States' weak southern neighbor.

Meanwhile, the Indians, or Native American peoples, stood in the way of the United States' unquestioned supremacy of America. Most Indians had been killed or removed from the original thirteen colonies before the American War of Independence. In the 1830s, **Indian removals** forced nearly all of those who had remained east of the Mississippi River onto reservations on the western side, even though some tried to defend their treaty rights in US courts. While courts upheld their rights, American power expelled them. Next, the California Gold Rush (1848–1859) tempted Americans westward to the Pacific Coast across the Great Plains, which had been acquired in the Louisiana Purchase, and the Southwest, which had been won from Mexico. The natives who lived there fought against the newcomers, whom they saw as trespassers. Rather than enforce its own legal agreements, again the US government rapidly and repeatedly broke all treaties signed with Indian tribes. In a series of **Plains Indian Wars** (1862–1890), superior Western technology and numbers gave the "cowboys" victory over the Indians.

In the popular imagination of Western civilization, images of these conflicts were colored with contradictions. "Noble savages" might seem to be either tragic heroes or barbaric "redskin" murderers. Were "civilized" men and women on the frontier heroes who embodied liberty and self-reliance as they tamed the wilderness, or were they ruthless exterminators of women and children as they stole Indian land? Either way, by the end of the nineteenth century, European Americans in the United States and Canada had killed most Native Americans or the First Nations peoples and confined the remnants to the near-worthless reservations. The closing of the American frontier meant that settlers could no longer simply take land from the original inhabitants.

For the time being, though, with both so much good farmland available and new factories being built, immigration swelled America's population. The stresses of growth fed feelings of **populism**, which held that the masses of people have more wisdom and worthiness than the few elites. They claimed to hold simple virtues through connection to the land and traditional culture. Populists at that time resented intellectuals as "know-it-alls," capitalists as greedy predators, career politicians as corrupt, city folk as stuck up, and the Roman Catholic Church as foreign and not Protestant. Some populists adopted nativist policies that were hostile to immigrants, fearing that new foreigners would steal land and jobs.

As Americans, populists and elitists alike, finished their domination of the natives, some began to consider whether opportunities of manifest destiny extended beyond the shores of North America. Since 1823, the United States (with the support of the United Kingdom of Great Britain) had upheld the Monroe Doctrine, which prevented the Europeans from reintroducing colonial imperialism to Latin America (see the next section). Increasingly, though, the United States began to see the Western Hemisphere as its own imperialist economic sphere.

The United States gained strength through its industrialization, while Latin America remained largely agricultural. Soon US merchants and politicians applied "dollar diplomacy," using American economic power, whether through bribery, awarding of contracts, or extorting trade agreements, to influence the decisions of

Latin American regimes. Obedience to Western capitalists earned Central American governments the nickname "banana republics." At the end of the nineteenth century, American corporations imported bananas, which originated in Southeast Asia, to cultivate in Central America. Under the American business plan, peasants who had grown corn to feed their families instead became laborers who harvested bananas to feed foreigners. If workers in Caribbean or Central American states resisted, the northern giant would send troops to occupy them and protect American property and trade. As a result of these "Banana Wars," US marines in countries like the Dominican Republic, Haiti, and Nicaragua propped up corrupt dictators who exploited their people but maintained friendly relations with the "big brother" to the north.

At the same time, US interests looked to profit in the Pacific. America's first major victim was **Japan**, which almost suffered the same fate as its exploited Asian neighbor, China. The cluster of islands that the Japanese themselves called the Land of the Rising Sun had maintained an isolationist policy for centuries. Since the early 1600s, hereditary military dictators, called shoguns, lorded over a well-ordered, stable, closed society in the name of powerless figurehead emperors. In the first age of imperialism, Japan had tentatively welcomed contact with Western explorers, traders, and missionaries. The Tokugawa dynasty of shoguns, though, had then shut the borders to Western influence by the late 1600s. After that, the Japanese permitted only one Dutch ship once a year to enter the port of Nagasaki for international trade. Otherwise, the Japanese wanted to be left alone.

That isolation ended in 1853, when American warships under the command of Commodore Matthew C. Perry steamed into Tokyo Harbor. Perry demanded the Japanese open trading relations with the United States or else he would open fire with his modern guns. Ironically, the government of the Tokugawa shogun had destroyed most firearms, leaving Japan defenseless. Fearful Japan submitted to a treaty loaded with extraterritoriality exploitation, just as had China. The British, French, Russians, and all the others soon followed the Americans to share in the spoils.

Despite this forced opening of its borders, Japan ended up doing something few other non-Western countries could: it rapidly westernized. The Japanese replaced the discredited Tokugawa shogun with the figurehead emperor during the **Meiji Restoration or Revolution** (1868). Then the Japanese traveled out into the world in droves and learned from the West about what made its civilization so powerful. The British taught the Japanese about constitutional monarchy and the navy. The Americans trained them in modern business practices. The French enlightened them about Western music and culture. The Germans drilled them on modern armies. Within a generation, the Japanese revolutionized their country to make it almost like any other Western power.

The name Meiji Restoration is a misnomer, however, since the Meiji dynasty was not so much restored to power as transformed in purpose. Before the restoration, the emperors had drifted through a shadowy, ineffectual existence under the shoguns (like the mikado of the contemporary Gilbert and Sullivan operetta). Now, the emperor became a godlike figure who united Japanese religion with Japanese patriotism, much as Alexander or Augustus had done for the Greeks and Romans.

This deified monarchy was the only unmodern move made by the Japanese. Otherwise, Japan plunged into a relatively smooth Western revolution, easily crushing the few samurai who resisted. Japan's equivalent of the commercial, intellectual, scientific, industrial, and English/American/French political revolutions was all accomplished in short order. The emperor's subjects soon sought to honor him with an empire, imitating what the British had done for their kings and queens. Thus, the westernization of Japan had enormous consequences for the twentieth century.

At the turn of the twentieth century, the United States went on an imperialistic spree. Looking for an excuse, the Americans seized upon the explosion of the US battleship *Maine* in Havana Harbor to start the **Spanish-American War** (1898).[3] American victories added Puerto Rico and the Philippines as colonies and Cuba almost as a protectorate. President McKinley partly justified the seizure of the Philippines with the need to convert the native islanders to Christianity. Ignorant Americans apparently did not know that most Filipinos were already Roman Catholic. When many Filipinos fought back with a guerrilla war, US forces ended resistance by resorting to concentration camps. Hundreds of thousands of Filipinos died of disease and malnutrition in the badly managed camps. McKinley also annexed Hawaii, where American pineapple and sugarcane corporations had seized power from the native Queen Liliuokalani (r. 1891–1893). The next president, Theodore Roosevelt (r. 1901–1909), suggested a corollary to the Monroe Doctrine, that the United States would use force to counter European economic claims in Latin America (thus keeping the European imperialists out). In 1903, when Colombia refused the American offer to build a canal through its province of Panama, the United States helped provincial leaders stage a rebellion. The new leaders of Panama gave control of a canal zone to the United States. American know-how finished the Panama Canal by 1914, although that extraordinary effort killed over five thousand workers brought in from the Caribbean and Europe.

Such expansionist efforts showed how Americans could behave as badly as the rest of the westerners. Most Americans, however, have usually seen themselves as somehow different, confident in their rugged individualism, creative opportunism, and eager mobility. This concept of moral superiority to the other Western and world cultures is called ***American exceptionalism***. It is similar to the common Western exceptionalism that had supported imperialism since the Renaissance. By virtue of their superior power, the stronger deserved to rule over the weak. The American version expresses feelings that manifest destiny reflects a God-given calling and that American motives and democratic institutions are more pure and generous than those of contemporary imperialist powers. Some historians have suggested that the United States does indeed differ from European states due to its origins as a society of immigrants seeking freedom and economic opportunities in

---

3. The American battle cry of "Remember the Maine" expressed a feeling of vengeance similar to the Texan "Remember the Alamo." Unfortunately the *Maine* should properly be remembered as an example of yellow journalism where the government and media together sensationalized the incident to whip up war fever. Studies of the wreck have shown its destruction happened by accident, not nefarious Spanish conspiracy (which made no sense anyhow).

an empty place with plenty of land and natural resources (although Canada, Australia, and New Zealand offer comparable histories). History shows, however, that American success too often came from brutal means to dominate that land and seize resources, a record that most Americans do not acknowledge. It is no coincidence that the United States began its global imperialism right after the Plains Indian Wars had finally ended with the total defeat of the Native Americans. Most immigrant Americans were unaware of the consequences of acquiring so much influence over so many peoples, first at home and then abroad; they noticed only the benefits of growing wealth and prosperity. American imperialism had made the United States one of the leading Western powers by 1914, poised to become the most powerful country in the world. But with power comes responsibility, and the United States would only slowly come to learn this lesson in the twentieth century.

Review: How did the United States of America become a world power?

Response:

NATIONALISM'S CURSE

While imperialism cobbled together widespread empires, a new idea was transforming politics in Europe. As seen in the experience of the United States, Western imperialism merged with the new ideology of ***nationalism***. This idea decreed that states should be organized exclusively around ethnic groups. Nationalists believed that a collection of people sharing ethnicity, called a nationality, is best served by having its own sovereign state. The Industrial Revolution's empowerment of the masses further affected the choices of definition. Many nationalists argued that the masses of people from the bottom up should define what makes a country, especially since the aristocratic and royal dynasties who ruled from the top down often came from other ethnic groups. Some dynasties, though, took the lead in nationalism, setting the terms for determining nationalist characteristics. Nationalism's earliest proponents hoped that it would usher in an era of fraternal peace, as different nations learned to respect one another despite their cultural differences.

Tragically, the emphasis on nationalism has instead more often resulted in increased international conflict. These clashes derive from a basic principle:

The greatest problem for nationalism is how to define exactly who belongs or not.

Including some people in a group while throwing out others created tensions. Each ethnic identity varies according to its definers. Ethnicity may be based on geographic location, shared history, ancestry, political loyalty, language, religion, fashion, and any combination thereof. Language was often the starting point, as cultural builders settled on one dialect and collected stories and songs that contributed to a unique identity. The increasing level of literacy meant that education reformers imposed one form of language on all people in the "nation," enforcing linguistic conformity. Even many historians wrote to support the creation of national identities. History books named the heroes and villains, military victories and defeats on the road to the nineteenth-century nation-state. If their nation was successful, historians could celebrate all the virtues that led to national unity. If their ethnic nationality had failed to achieve statehood, historians would explain all the reasons for failure and usually blame other nationalities. In these endeavors, scholarship supported patriotism and nation forming, rather than objectivity and accuracy. As one historian has noted, nationalities are "imagined communities," where people pick and choose criteria that define belonging.

At its most extreme, nationalism blended with racism. In schools and academic institutes, in the theater and novels, nationalists transmitted the supposed identity of a particular nationality. Interest groups and political parties soon organized around nationalist and racist ideas, embracing those who belonged and hating those who did not. Political history became a victorious story of destined greatness for the winners of state building or an ongoing grievance for the losers.

At the beginning of the nineteenth century, Metternich's conservative decisions at the Congress of Vienna had dismissed nationalist dreams. Each of the five great powers present at the congress included many people who did not fit the "ethnic" name of the state. Centuries of conquest and migration had left a very jumbled Europe. In the Austrian Empire no one ethnic group was in a majority, as Germans, Magyars, Italians, and Slavs (most importantly Czechs, Slovaks, Croats, and Poles) vied for the attention of the Habsburg emperor. Russia also included many different ethnic groups, including the Asians in Siberia in the east, Turks in the southeast, and Balts in the northwest, as well as the Slavic Poles and Ukrainians in the west. Prussia did have a majority population of Germans, but Roman Catholics of the Rhineland felt no sense of "Prussianness," nor did most Danes in the north and the large numbers of Poles and Wends (non-Polish Slavs in eastern Germany). Great Britain locked many disgruntled Scots, Irish, and Welsh into a "United Kingdom" with the English. Even France, which might seem the most cohesive, had Basques in the southwest, Bretons in the northwest, and Alsatian Germans in the east, as well as speakers of various dialects and "*langues*," none of whom wanted to learn the mandated word for *patrie* (fatherland). Most of the smaller countries of Europe likewise lacked absolute ethnic homogeneity.

Liberals supported nationalism early in the nineteenth century. They bought into the English crafting of its strong mercantile economy and Industrial Revolution. They applauded the political rights proclaimed by the French Revolution. Liberals neither saw the ethnic tensions in Great Britain (with Scots, Welsh, and Irish preserving their distinctive traits) nor remembered the chauvinist oppression of French patriots. The decisions made at the Congress of Vienna, the clumsy German Confederation, and the backward multiethnic absolutist Austrian, Russian, and Ottoman Empires contradicted the bourgeois values of political participation and moneymaking opportunities. So liberal nationalists drew a simple conclusion: If the French have France, the English have England, and even the Portuguese have Portugal, why shouldn't our ethnic group have Ethnicgroupland?

Surprisingly, the nationalist spirit first coalesced into reality across the Atlantic Ocean. On the French colony of Saint-Domingue on the Caribbean island of Hispaniola, enslaved people led a nationalist revolt between 1789 and 1804 to found an independent **Haiti**. While Western powers long refused to recognize it, Haiti's successful rebellion helped inspire the upper classes of European descent to carry out their own **liberation of Latin America** (1810–1825) from Spanish and Portuguese colonial imperialism. The descendants of European conquistadors and colonizers, known as Creoles (or *criollos*), slowly found their interests diverging from either the distant imperial mother countries of Spain and Portugal or the annoying and arrogant new arrivals called *peninsulares*. Many Creoles formed juntas, groups of elites who seized power from colonial administrators. In 1811, the most famous liberator, Simon Bolívar (b. 1783–d. 1830), fought for a free Venezuela, uniting it with neighboring Colombia. Meanwhile, José de San Martín, "the Liberator," freed his homeland of Argentina along with Chile and began to fight for Peru. San Martín then retired, leaving Bolívar to complete the independence of Peru and Bolivia (later named after him). The success of other freedom fighters helped create Mexico, the United Provinces of Central America, Paraguay, Uruguay, and Brazil. By 1825, only a few islands in the Caribbean Sea remained of what had once been Spain and Portugal's vast empires in the Americas (see map 12.2). The countries claimed to aspire to democracy, but the presidential system led to strongmen called *caudillos* who generally favored some powerful interest groups to the disadvantage of both others and the citizens as a whole.

The leaders of these new Latin American nations did not have significant ethnic differences from one another, except for geographic location. The elites all still spoke the Spanish of the mother country (or Portuguese in Brazil), wore similar styles of clothing, practiced the same politics and economics, and worshiped as Roman Catholics. Lower down the political and social hierarchies lived people of diverse ancestry. At the bottom were usually the original "Indian" inhabitants and the peoples originally imported as slaves from Africa. In the middle, countries such as Mexico saw large numbers of *mestizos* (meaning of "mixed" Indian and European lineage), while other countries had mulatto people of African and European heritage. Brazil's government eventually defined people according to five categories: white, brown, black, Asian, and indigenous. Each of the new "national" countries had to deal with these ethnic diversities and fabricate its own patriotic identity as different from neighboring states.

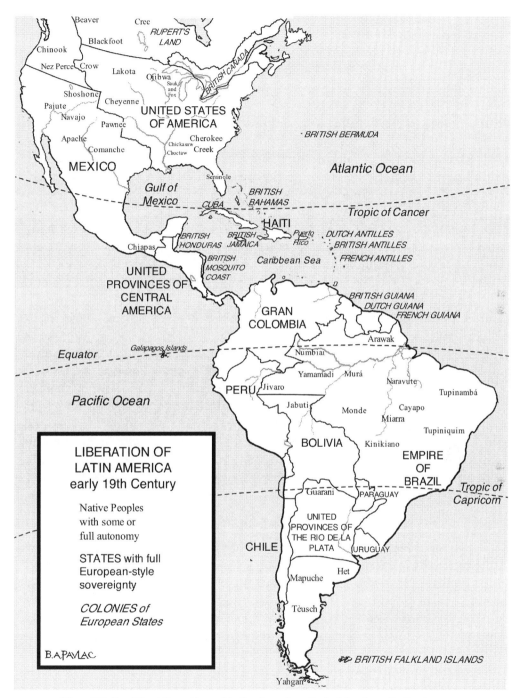

Map 12.2. The Liberation of Latin America, Early Nineteenth Century. Only a few out of many of the native still-independent peoples are named on the map. What prevented their conquest and assimilation by Westerners?

To the north, the United States endured its own major nationalist ethnic conflict with the **American Civil War** (1861–1865). This war decided whether the United States would survive united as one nation or divide into two or more countries. The country's very name, "United States," revealed the ethnic divisions at its origin. While some citizens called themselves American, more were likely to identify with their state, as a Virginian or a New Yorker. The regional differences concerning slavery sharpened these distinctions. Southerners, even those who were not slave-holders, defended their "peculiar institution" because that was how Southerners defined themselves. Under this pressure, the delicate balance among federal, state, and individual rights broke down. In the war that followed, the northern Union defeated the southern Confederacy because of the North's superior numbers, its technology, and President Abraham Lincoln's determination. Still, the reaffirmed federal unity did not entirely eliminate Southern ethnicity, since resentment still festered long after defeat. Even a century later sympathizers to the Confederacy raised statues and monuments to honor the rebellion and intimidate African American descendants of slavery. Only in 2016 did protests about some of these memorials lead to the removal of a few such symbols.

Back in Europe, the failures of the revolutions of 1848 weakened the liberal alliance with nationalism, but conservatives then adopted the idea. Nationalism appealed to the conservatives' inclination to look to the past for guidance. Indeed, nineteenth-century historians began to collect and assemble imaginative histories of ethnic groups which they argued were the forebears of modern nationalities. They collected source documents and organized them. Historians in those countries that represented a nationalist victory (for example, England or France) attributed success to cultural or racial superiority. Even historians of ethnic groups excluded from power (for example, the Irish or the Basques) adopted nationalistic perspectives, since they could glorify some distant heroic freedom that had been squelched by political tragedy or unjust conquest. The Romantic movement heavily contributed to these efforts. In addition, conservatives saw how the passion growing from nationalism could plant them or keep them in power. Conservative leaders applied ***Realpolitik***, or pragmatic politics, doing whatever was necessary to achieve a stronger state.

Italy was an early success for nationalism. Of course, there had never before been a country called Italy, at least not like the one envisioned by its nationalist proponents. Italian history began with Rome and its city-state, which quickly became a multiethnic empire. In the Middle Ages, no single kingdom ever included the entire Italian Peninsula. Since 1494, various principalities there had been dominated by foreign dynasties—the French, the Spanish, and the Austrians—while the popes clung desperately to their Papal States.

In the wake of the failed revolutions of 1848, many Italian nationalists called for a Risorgimento (resurgence and revival) of an Italian nation-state. From 1848 to 1871 the Kingdom of Sardinia-Savoy-Piedmont spearheaded unification. Conservative prime minister **Count Camillo di Cavour** (r. 1852–1861) proposed a scheme for unification to his absolutist monarch, King Victor Emmanuel II. First, they would modernize and liberalize Sardinia-Savoy-Piedmont. Then, several well-planned military actions would topple both Habsburgs in the north and the petty regimes in the rest of the Italian Peninsula (see diagram 12.1).[4]

The scheme succeeded. The king graciously granted his own Kingdom of Sardinia-Savoy-Piedmont a constitution and founded a parliament, which, weak as it was, surpassed what most Italians had had before (namely, no legislatures at all). The Piedmontese government built roads, schools, and hospitals. Other Italians began to admire the little northern kingdom. Yet Cavour's sponsorship of the republican mercenary **Giuseppe Garibaldi** almost derailed the plan. In 1861, Garibaldi and his thousand volunteers, the "Red Shirts" (named after their minimalist uniform), were supposed to invade Sicily and cause disturbances that would illustrate the need for Piedmontese leadership in Italian politics. But Garibaldi swiftly conquered the entire island. Then he sailed to the mainland, where he took control of the Kingdom of Naples and even marched on Rome itself. Piedmontese armies

Kingdom of Sardinia-Savoy-Piedmont	Kingdom of Prussia
Revolutions of 1848-1849	
King Victor Emmanuel II Savoy-Carignano 1849-1878 Prime Minister Camillo di Cavour 1852-1861	
Austro-Piedmontese War 1859-1860 Garibaldi conquers Kingdom of Two Sicilies 1860 **Kingdom of Italy** Turin becomes capital 1861	King Wilhelm I Hohenzollern 1861-1888 Minister President Otto von Bismarck 1862-1890
Florence becomes new capital 1865	*Danish War 1864*
Seven Weeks War 1866 adds Venice	excludes Austria **North German Confederation**
Franco-Prussian War 1870-1871 adds Rome which becomes new capital 1871	adds southern German states **Second German Empire** Berlin becomes capital 1871

Diagram 12.1. The national unifications of Italy and Germany in the nineteenth century share similar developments and certain wars.

4. The worst battle of the Austro-Piedmontese War was Solferino (24 June 1859), where clashed two armies commanded by emperors: Emperor Francis-Joseph of Austria against Allied French-Piedmontese forces led by Emperor Napoleon III. The evening after the slaughter, Jean-Henry Dumont, a Swiss citizen who had been trying to run a business in colonial Algeria, came across the tens of thousands of unattended dead and wounded. To better attend to victims of disaster and war, he founded the International Red Cross (1863) and got signed the first Geneva Convention (1864) to create more civilized rules of warfare.

rushed south to meet him, and Cavour managed to convince Garibaldi to turn his winnings into a united Kingdom of Italy.

From there, a few more stratagems were required to round out the new kingdom. Italy bribed France by giving it the provinces of Savoy and Nice. In 1866, Italy, France, and Prussia defeated the Habsburgs and forced them to surrender Lombardy and Venice. The last major obstacle to Italian unity was the papacy. Popes had possessed political power in central Italy since the fall of Rome in the fifth century, further consolidated by the Donation of Pippin and Charlemagne in the ninth century. A thousand years later, the popes lost their political rule. In 1870, during the Franco-Prussian War, the French troops protecting the Papal States withdrew. The royal Italian government seized control and made Rome the kingdom's capital. The resentful pope forbade Roman Catholics to cooperate with the Kingdom of Italy. Nonetheless, Italy soon took its place among the great powers (see map 12.3).

The unification of **Germany** (1862–1871) saw a similar process. Unlike Italy, there had actually been a united Germany back in the early Middle Ages, but it had quickly expanded into the loose union of the Holy Roman Empire, which also included northern Italy, Burgundy, Bohemia, and the Lowlands. The Wars of the Coalitions against revolutionary France had shattered the Holy Roman Empire, but

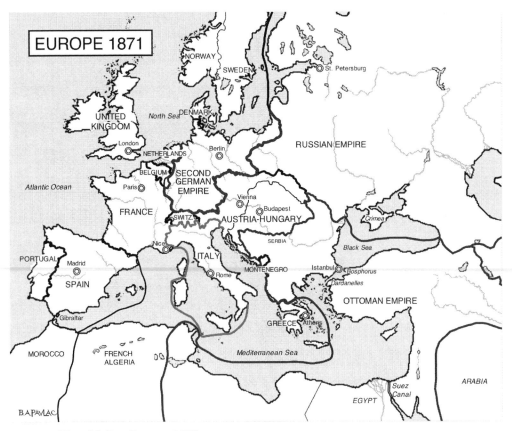

Map 12.3. Europe, 1871.
How were the number of sovereign states in Europe being reduced?

in 1815, the German Confederation replaced it. This union never functioned well, largely because of the rivalry over leadership between Prussia and Austria. The liberal attempt to create a unified Germany through the Frankfurt Parliament in 1848 failed completely. In turn, a conservative leader succeeded.

The young Prussian aristocrat **Otto von Bismarck** liked neither the Frankfurt Parliament nor the Confederation. From 1862 to 1890, he served the king of Prussia as prime minister or chancellor. Imitating Cavour, Bismarck planned and carried out the unification of Germany under the Hohenzollerns of Prussia, purposefully excluding the Habsburgs of Austria. He molded Prussia into a more modern, liberal state, albeit with a weaker parliament and a stronger executive power than in Britain. His Realpolitik, though, preferred warfare, which he called decision by "blood and iron." Bismarck knew he had to fight, especially against Austria, to overcome the resistance of other great powers to German unity. He therefore tricked his opponents into declaring wars and then defeated them one after another with the most modern army in Europe.

Bismarck's success remodeled Europe. In the Seven Weeks War (1866), the efficient Prussian army with advanced planning and rapid-firing breech-loading rifles quickly defeated Austria. Ousted from any part in a future united Germany, a weakened Austrian imperial government granted political power to the Magyars or Hungarians, transforming the Austrian Empire into the Dual Monarchy of **Austria-Hungary** in 1867. Sadly for the Slavs and others, their nationalistic hopes under the Habsburg's joint Austrian and Magyar rule remained unfulfilled.

Bismarck's next opportunity came in 1870, when the Spanish royal dynasty died out. Diplomats proposed princes from several dynasties to assume the throne. One day, Chancellor Bismarck received an insignificant dispatch or report about his king, Wilhelm I, who was vacationing at the spa resort of Ems. A petty French diplomat had pestered Wilhelm to declare that no prince of his Hohenzollern dynasty would compete for the Spanish throne. In a brilliant stroke of Realpolitik, Bismarck reworded the "Ems Dispatch" to make it seem as if the French had insulted the Prussian king. Napoleon III's insufferable pride led him to retaliate by declaring war against Prussia, just as Bismarck had hoped. Bismarck welcomed the Franco-Prussian War (1870–1871). He inspired the southern German states to join the conflict in a spirit of national unity. The combined Prussian and German forces swiftly defeated France. In the Hall of Mirrors of Louis XIV's Versailles, the German princes acclaimed the Prussian king as German emperor Wilhelm I Hohenzollern. The Second German Empire (1871–1918) quickly rose to be the most powerful country in Europe.

European nationalism, however, found difficulty including the Jews who had lived in Germany, Italy, and many other older European countries for centuries. Their life had almost never been easy, since many Christians of the Middle Ages and Renaissance were antisemites. Their animosity took the form of denying Jews civil rights; prohibiting them from most jobs; confining them in ghettoes (named after the neighborhood where since the early 16th century authorities in Venice locked Jews in every night); expelling all of them from countries such as England (1290), France (1306), and Spain (1492); or killing many of them in pogroms (from the Russian word for destroying Jews, coined in the late nineteenth century).

Following the tolerant humanitarianism of the Enlightenment, Jews actually gained civil rights during the nineteenth century. They could participate in politics and freely choose professions. After they were allowed entrance to universities, many Jews rose to prosperity and prominence in law, education, and medicine. Jews themselves had to decide how much to assimilate, or act like their Western neighbors. Three main movements, orthodox, conservative, and reformed, were developed, to various degrees asserting strong cultural identity in language, clothing, and religious worship. Many, though, ceased to keep a distinctly Jewish culture and became "secular."

Not unexpectedly, the Jews' sudden success and prominence in the nineteenth century inflamed antisemitism. Only in Russia did the government oppress Jews directly. In reaction to the assassination of Tsar Alexander II in 1881 by a terrorist bomb, the May Laws (1882) forcibly relocated millions of Jews and stripped them of many economic and civil rights. Adding to Jewish suffering, a wave of pogroms broke out, namely mob attacks that brutally tortured and murdered Jews and burned their homes. While the regime did not organize pogroms, it did little to stop them or punish the aggressors. In western Europe, the most famous example of antisemitism from that time was the **Dreyfus Affair** (1894–1906) in France. The French government tried and convicted a Jew, Captain Alfred Dreyfus, of treason for turning over secrets to the Germans. They imprisoned him on Devil's Island, a sweltering penal colony located off the coast of South America. Actually, Dreyfus was innocent. Further investigation soon found the real traitor, a well-born aristocrat named Ferdinand Esterházy. Astoundingly, a trial found Esterházy innocent in 1899. The subsequent arguments over Dreyfus's guilt or innocence exposed the fractures in France's unified national façade. After a second trial wrongly convicted Dreyfus again in 1899, only presidential intervention in 1906 freed him.

As a consequence of the hostility toward Jews that was exposed by this affair, some Jews invented their own nationalism, called *Zionism*. In 1897, the first World Zionist Congress convened in Basel, Switzerland. The delegates faced a real difficulty: how could the Jews have their own country if some people or another already occupied every livable space in the whole world? Although some Jews suggested forming a homeland in South America or Africa, most aimed for the traditional homeland of Palestine, which was at the time a province of the Turkish Ottoman Empire. The Ottomans did permit some Jewish immigration at first, since the Jews were a source of revenue. But how many Jews could poor Palestine accommodate as more arrived?

The issue of the Jews and their attempt at nationalism exposed the most difficult flaw in nationalism: how should nation-states deal with people who did not conform to nationalist standards? Every state had people of other ethnic groups within its borders. Diverse people lived next to one another everywhere, especially since the rise of mobility in modern society. Once nationalists gave up on tolerance of ethnic differences, only three choices remained: forcing conformity in outward cultural behavior, imposing confinement to certain parts of the country, or eliminating through exile or death. Any one of these choices, though, provoked conflict. Nationalism has often encouraged domination but too rarely cooperation.

Paradoxically and tragically, nationalism allied with imperialism. Just as political theorists were asserting rigidly defined states along ethnic lines, they also encouraged these nation-based states to create multiethnic overseas empires. Yet this imperialism was a contradiction. As conquered peoples everywhere learned of nationalism, they then aspired to run their own lives along ethnic principles. While imperialism has since mostly vanished, nationalism still prevails today as a concept uniting and dividing people.

Review: *How did various nationalisms unify and divide Western nations?*

Response:

SOURCES ON FAMILIES: ETHEL HOWARD, *POTSDAM PRINCES* (1915)

The years before World War I were the last heyday of many royal dynasties, a special kind of family. This memoir by Ethel Howard relates her experiences as an English governess raising the young children of Kaiser Wilhelm II of the Hohen-zollern dynasty of Prussia. Her charges ranged from the Crown Prince at fourteen, then five other boys, down to the princess Victoria Luise, or "Sissy," age three. This selection describes her appointment, then her early duties and experiences. She later went on to be a governess for the imperial family of Japan.

I was quite young at the time, and the thought of the coming parting was a nightmare to me. We were more closely knit than is common amongst most fami-lies, so much so that my father always compared us to a bundle of sticks. I had never gone abroad before, and the thought of leaving the simple and happy shelter of home for the cold and rigid ceremonial and unknown difficulties of a foreign Court appalled me. I knew little or no German, and as the hour of my departure approached I felt more and more nervous.

When, in December 1895, the dread moment arrived, my courage failed me, and I actually jumped out of the railway carriage, exclaiming, "No, I can't go so far from home, not for any Emperor!" My mother, whom I worshipped, gently pushed me in again; and so, amid blinding tears, I set forth to my new life. . . .

I was shown at once to my bedroom, which though not large was a most palatial apartment, everything in it being very beautiful, the Berlin china-ware bearing the Royal Crown, and all the linen being embroidered in the same manner.

This room was set somewhat apart from the others in the main Palace, being in fact in the visitors' wing. I was not very much impressed by the fact at the time, though I did rather wonder why (since I was obviously not a visitor) I had been put in this wing. Later I was told that it was done purposely, for the reason that the sudden introduction into the fullness of Court grandeur had frequently unbalanced people's minds—in fact, they had become temporarily insane through it. . . .

I learnt that each Prince had a military governor. . . . My work as English governess was mapped out for me, and I was given a time-table, which, however, was liable to alteration at a moment's notice, especially in the Potsdam Palace. . . . When my duties with the Princes did not claim me, I was to act as a sort of extra lady-in-waiting, attending on odd Royalties who happened to be visiting, or even on the Empress herself. . . .

I was given the early morning work, which necessitated my finishing breakfast and being ready to go out walking at 8 a.m. It was winter when I got there, and anyone who knows the intense cold of Berlin will appreciate how severe I found this morning exercise. It lasted from 8 a.m. until just before 12.30, when one had ten minutes or so to change for luncheon. . . .

The whole morning I used to spend walking with each Prince in turn, half running, as it was too cold to sit down or walk slowly; the reason for their walk and talk alone with me being that their English conversation should have my individual attention, and that they should thus perfect their knowledge of the language without too much realizing that they were doing so. . . .

In Potsdam the Princes used to be present at the terrible and formal midday meal, usually at 12:30 or 1 o'clock, but subject, like everything else, to the vagaries of circumstances. I, for one, never enjoyed it, nor, I think, did they. To this meal numerous guests were invited daily, and I often met and conversed with gorgeously arrayed officers and diplomats whose names are now household words in every land. . . .

There was nearly an hour of eating, drinking, and talking, and then we would all adjourn together, ladies first, into the room where we took coffee. Here we were often compelled to drag out another hour—a weary one to me, I must confess, as it did not seem to be correct to sit down, and after a whole morning on one's feet, and a heavy midday meal, one simply longed for a chair.

The Princes would stay talking until such time as they were carried off by their respective governors for study, and I did not see them again as a rule until after tea. . . . Then I took the Princes again for recreation, often playing games with them in the Palace garden. Supper alone with them at seven o'clock, after which I would read English story-books to them until eight o'clock, when they went to bed . . . and by that time so tired, I often went to bed very early. . . .

[I]t seemed to me that courtiers, whatever their rank, were but servants, and that wheels within wheels and petty endeavors to gain Royal favor were worth but little. I made the excellent resolution, therefore, to do what I believed to be best for the Princes, regardless of whom I might annoy. . . .

Questions:

- *What is unique about the family life of the imperial family?*
- *What made the imperial family so different from her own?*
- *What were the priorities for rearing the princes?*

Responses:

Citation

Howard, Ethel. *Potsdam Princes*. New York: E. P. Dutton, 1915, pp. 4–25.

For more on this source, go to http://www.concisewesternciv.com/sources/sof12 .html.

THE BALKAN CAULDRON

The center of nationalist and imperialist conflict at the beginning of the twentieth century was the Balkan Peninsula, that large triangle of land roughly south of a line drawn from the north of the Adriatic to the north of the Black Sea. The ethnic divisions of western Europe really seemed quite simple compared with those of the Balkans, where the migration of multiple ethnicities had left many different peoples living cheek by jowl with one another. Along the eastern coast of the Adriatic, the Albanians may have been one of the first European peoples. No one knows for sure (and many argue) about the origins of the Albanians. Then the ancient Greeks had been dominant in the far south, and the Romans conquered the area as far as the Danube. At the collapse of the western Roman Empire in the fifth century AD, many Romans left, but some Latin survivors in the region became known as the Vlachs, while others may have been ancestors of those called Romanians. Greeks, meanwhile, remained in the south. Germanic tribes briefly dominated the peninsula, but most of them eventually left for central and western Europe, only to return a millennium later in small enclaves near the Danube and in Transylvania. The Slavic peoples migrated next, including Serbs, Croats, Slovenes, Macedonians, and Montenegrins. In the seventh century, out of central Asia came the Bulgars, followed in the ninth century by the Magyars (Hungarians). By the late Middle Ages, Romany (or Gypsy folk) from south Asia wandered through the peninsula. And, as always, there were some Jews in the cities. Finally, as described earlier, the Turkish Ottoman Empire imposed its own order on the region in the Late Middle Ages, converting many to Islam (especially Bosnians, Albanians, Pomaks, and Torbeshes) and leaving governance to a relatively few immigrant Turks.

The Ottoman Empire had once been a powerful rival to the West but had declined after 1600. That multinational state did not experience anything similar to the commercial, scientific, industrial, religious, and intellectual revolutions of the Renaissance, Reformation, and Enlightenment, nor the English/American/French political revolutions. Indeed, many of its religious leaders, both Muslim and Orthodox Christian, preached against Western ways. The empire's sultans came to power through conspiracies too often carried out by the wives and eunuch custodians of the harem. Its bureaucracy operated according to complexity rather than efficiency. Its armies practiced tradition rather than innovation. The Ottoman Empire soon lacked the ability to defend itself and earned the nickname "the Sick Man of Europe."

After the failed Turkish siege of Vienna in 1683, the Habsburgs reclaimed all of Hungary, Croatia, and bits of other provinces in the Balkans from the Turks. By the eighteenth century, though, Austria was unable or unwilling to liberate the rest of the Balkans from Turkish rule. While in 1815 Austria grudgingly accepted the Ottoman Empire as a necessary part of the European state system, others saw it as ripe to be challenged.

The first nationalist movement to upset the status quo came from one of the founding peoples of Western civilization, the Greeks. Of course, there had never been a unified state called Greece before. Modern descendants of Spartans and Athenians decided in the early nineteenth century that they wanted their own country, historical precedent notwithstanding. They organized the nationalist **Greek Revolt** (1821–1829).

At first, the Western great powers accepted the absolutist Muslim monarchy's war against the Greeks, obedient to the conservative principle of preserving political stability. Many of the common people of Europe, however, saw the Greeks as romantic heroes, if not fellow westerners, and they sent aid. Some, like the poet Lord Byron, even went off to fight for them (although he died there quite unromantically of dysentery). With pressure from their own people, the great powers stepped in to provide a conservative, not a nationalist, solution. The great powers gifted the new Kingdom of Greece with an absolute monarchy, but led by a German, not Greek, king. Thus the traditional role of a king as symbolic parent and unifier of the people did not require identical ethnicity in this nation-state.

Greece's Balkan neighbors, still under Ottoman rule, could not help noticing its example. Many of the peoples in the Balkans began to embrace nationalistic ideas. ***Pan-slavism*** called for all Slavs everywhere to live together. The Russians, as the dominant Slavic group, pushed this idea the most, by embracing Poles, Ukrainians, and others. A more focused attitude of Slavic nationalism, called ***yugoslavism***, promoted the idea that the southern Slavs of the Balkans should unite. The Serbians, the largest group among these Slavs, favored this policy.

Meanwhile, the swelling Romanov Russian Empire decided to expand southward. Russia targeted the Ottoman Turkish Empire in the name of Orthodox Christian unity, pan-slavism, and imperialism. In a series of wars, the Russians fought their way south to the northern coast of the Black Sea and then around it on either side: in the west toward the mouth of the Danube River in the Balkans, and in the east across the Caucasus Mountains, where they conquered Azerbaijanis, Georgians, and Chechens.

The Russian success alarmed the other Western powers. Britain especially feared that Russian fleets might gain access to the Mediterranean from the Black Sea through the Bosphorus and the Dardanelles, thereby complicating the balance of power. After Russia occupied the Ottoman provinces of Moldavia and Wallachia (the latter a part of Romania today), the British and French Empires sided with the Ottoman Empire in the **Crimean War** (1853–1856), named after the peninsula in the Black Sea on which it was fought.

This small war is remarkably memorable. First, the traditional enemies England and France cooperated. Second, they learned to overcome the logistical difficulties of fighting so far from their homelands. Third, the work of Florence Nightingale (b. 1820–d. 1910) with the wounded started to promote modern nursing. She taught her male superiors about the benefits of hygiene, rest, and kind attention for soldiers recovering from camp diseases and modern explosive weapons. Fourth, the British poet Tennyson's poem "The Charge of the Light Brigade" tried to stir up an ideal of courage in the face of futile cavalry attacks against deadly cannon fire. And finally, soldiers brought back to Europe the habit of cigarette smoking as a more popular means of consuming tobacco than chewing or smoking cigars or pipes.

Russia's defeat in the Crimean War slowed its aggression against the Ottoman Empire only a short while. In 1876, Muslim Ottoman troops slaughtered several thousand Orthodox Christian Bulgarians because of a rebellion against the dynasty. Russia declared war, both to avenge those massacred and to help the Serbs and Montenegrins who were fighting the Ottomans, and marched Russian armies toward Istanbul. Russia quickly won a resounding victory, and Russian diplomats began to redraw the borders of the Balkans, hoping to fulfill Russia's pan-slavist hopes. The other great powers, however, again stepped in and brought the Russians to the Congress of Berlin in 1878 (not to be confused with the Congress of Berlin in 1884, which dealt with Africa). This congress forced the Russians to renounce their gains. In doing so, it created the new countries of **Serbia**, **Bulgaria**, and **Romania**, each stabilized with conservative monarchies.

It seemed only a matter of time until the Ottoman Empire was picked to pieces. The new states of Serbia, Bulgaria, and Romania were dissatisfied with their new borders. Each looked across its borders into neighboring states and saw people of the same nationality "trapped" in other countries. In Ottoman-ruled Macedonia, some of those people formed one of the first modern terrorist groups, IMRO (Internal Macedonian Revolutionary Organization). Swearing loyalty over a gun and a Bible, its members fought against both Muslim rule and the territory-hungry desires of Serbia, Romania, and Bulgaria. Meanwhile, Austria-Hungary was supposed to preserve **Bosnia-Herzegovina** as a protectorate. Instead, Austrian politicians annexed Bosnia outright in 1908; Austrian bureaucrats presented the dual province as a gift for the aged Habsburg emperor Francis-Joseph to celebrate the sixtieth anniversary of his accession to the throne.

Some Turks tried to slow the momentum toward dismemberment of the Ottoman Empire. A coup d'état by a group of westernizing nationalists called the "**Young Turks**" in 1908 encouraged *pan-turkism*, or using Turkish nationalism to strengthen the empire. Before such a policy could take effect, Italy launched the Italo-Turkish War (1911) to seize the large Ottoman province of Tripoli or Libya, just across the Mediterranean in North Africa (see map 12.4). Interestingly, Italy's venture into modern war provided the first experimental use of both airplanes and poison gas as weapons. Italy's armies managed to defeat those of the "Sick Man of Europe" in Africa.

Italy's unjustifiable attack on the Turks encouraged the other Balkan states to imitate its success. In October 1912, Serbia, Romania, Bulgaria, Montenegro, and Greece pounced on Macedonia, beginning the First Balkan War (1912–1913). The success of the Balkan states immediately raised the concern of the European powers. They convened a conference at London in the spring of 1913 to settle matters. While at the negotiating table, the greedy Bulgarians decided to try to secure what they could on their own. In June, Bulgaria launched a preemptive strike on its recent allies, beginning the Second Balkan War (1913).

When the fighting stopped in August 1913, a peace conference set up new borders. Bulgaria yielded to some losses, most importantly its Mediterranean coastline. Romania and Greece benefited nicely. Serbia ended up with the key chunk of Macedonia. Austria also encouraged the creation of **Albania** as an independent

Map 12.4. Europe, 1911.
What geographical factors led to joining or avoiding the large alliance systems?

country. This move followed nationalist principles, since the ethnic Albanians were not closely related to the Serbs—they were not even Slavs. Nevertheless, Serbia had wanted to rule over the Albanians, especially to gain a coastline and seaports on the Adriatic Sea.

Consequently, Serbian nationalists felt especially frustrated and focused much of their anger on Austria-Hungary. Elements within the Serbian secret police formed a terrorist organization, the Black Hand, to strike against the Habsburgs. They recruited ethnic Serbian college students from Bosnia. Serbian officials trained these young Bosnians in small arms so that they could carry out an assassination, a method of terrorism made popular by anarchists. The terrorists struck on 28 June 1914, as the heir to the Austro-Hungarian throne, Archduke **Franz Ferdinand**, and his wife, Sophie, visited the Bosnian capital of Sarajevo. The amateurish assassins were less than successful at first. First a bomb bounced off the archduke's car, only injuring some soldiers and civilians. Nevertheless, security remained lax. Later that day, the archduke's car made a wrong turn and stopped just where the assassin, Gavrilo Princip, was getting a sandwich. The nineteen-year-old terrorist shot Franz Ferdinand and Sophie at point-blank range. They were dead within minutes, their three young children orphaned.

The political leadership of Austria-Hungary pounced on this incident as a pretext for war against Serbia. Emperor Francis-Joseph, who did not much care for his heir, was not motivated by grief or anger. Furthermore, no firm evidence was known linking the Serbian government to the terrorists. But the Austrians thought war would solve their problems with Serbia. The Austrians' only dependable ally, the Germans, backed them up with a virtual blank check, a promise to support Austria in whatever action it might take. It took a month after the assassination for the cautious Austrians to send an ultimatum to Serbia, long after the tragedy and ensuing sympathy had faded from the front pages of newspapers. The Serbians, as expected, did not accept the whole ultimatum and mobilized their military in preparation for the expected war. On 1 August 1914, Austria-Hungary declared war on Serbia. That lit the fuse for World War I.

Overall, the nineteenth century's experience of nationalism was mixed. It did indeed promote some major peaceful arts. Nationalists identified, categorized, and recorded the language and literature, song and dance, costume and custom of the myriad ethnic groups who resided in Europe. Turning ethnicity into nationality, however, had required wars ranging from such diverse locations as the Alps or the Andes, the Rhine or the Rio Grande, the islands in the Caribbean or the Aegean. Even worse, what should have been no more than a petty third Balkan war between Austria-Hungary and Serbia instead metastasized into the worst conflict in human history, up to that point.

Review: *How did nationalism and the decline of the Ottoman Empire destabilize the Balkans?*

Response:

THE GREAT WAR

Both imperialism and nationalism came together to provide the fuel for the Great War, now known as **World War I** (1914–1918). This first of the three great global conflicts of the twentieth century deserves the global part of its title mostly because of the enormous damage it inflicted and the worldwide reach of its consequences (see timeline D). Although some battles took place in Africa, the Middle East, the South American coast, and the Pacific, the overwhelming bulk of the fighting happened in Europe, in the heart of Western civilization.

Everyone expected Franz Ferdinand's assassination to spark a war between Austria-Hungary and Serbia, yet few anticipated the conflagration that resulted. Each participant who joined in envisioned a short, sharp war, where the "guns of August" would be silenced by Christmas. Each nation confidently believed that civilization and/or God stood with her alone. Each felt aggrieved by the actions of the others. Serbia wanted to dominate the Balkans. Austria wanted a reckoning with Serbia. Russia wanted revenge against Austria. France wanted revenge against Germany. Britain wanted to maintain its international supremacy. The Ottoman Empire wanted to survive. Italy wanted an empire. Few got what they wanted.

Historians have particularly debated how Germany's war aims shaped the origins of World War I. Many German nationalists had called for an overseas empire to gain the Second German Empire its place in the sun. The clumsy efforts of Kaiser Wilhelm II (r. 1888–1918) to promote German prestige (such as comparing them to the Huns) had other Europeans viewing this latecomer to geopolitics as a bumbling upstart.

Much more responsible for nations entering the war, however, were the alliances locked in during the previous decades. On one side was the **Triple Alliance**, begun by Chancellor Bismarck to preserve the newly united Germany from French revenge for its losses in the Franco-Prussian War. Therein he bound Austria-Hungary and Italy in a mutual defense agreement with Germany. On the other side was the **Triple Entente**, which France had slowly pulled together in reaction to the

Triple Alliance. France carefully bound itself with Great Britain and Russia, although all three had many traditional and contemporary rivalries with one another. Their combined mistrust and fear of Germany, however, ultimately proved greater than their suspicions about one another (see map 12.4).

These alliances had originally been intended to prevent war by making conflict too risky. Instead, they turned into mutually supportive military cooperatives, twisting the delicate balance of power into two hostile blocs. Intensifying the alliances were military strategies connected to **mobilization**, or getting armed forces from peacetime standing to wartime footing. The vast armies supported by modern industrialization, transportation, and communication required complex timetables to get troops where they were needed either to attack or defend. Generals thus pressured politicians to begin fighting quickly, in time for mobilization to be effective.

Alliances and mobilization plans together escalated the war from a minor Balkan brawl to a clash that involved almost all of Western civilization. After Austria declared war on Serbia, Russia mobilized against Austria, wanting to support its Slavic brothers' defense. Realistically, Russia's claim to mobilize only against Austria was absurd, since the Germans knew that Russian plans were aimed against both Germany and Austria. Hence the Germans immediately demanded both that the Russians stop mobilization and that the French declare their neutrality in the conflict. These measures would have prevented a general war, but at the sacrifice of Serbia. Thus the Germans expected, even desired, the Russians and French to continue their mobilizations.

The Germans' own strategy (called the Schlieffen Plan after the general who first proposed it) was to defend against an expected slow Russian attack in the east while swiftly striking against Russia's main ally, France, in the west. After taking out Paris within a few weeks, according to the Schlieffen Plan, the Germans would then eliminate the Russian forces at leisure. Accordingly, when the French hesitated to declare themselves neutral, the Germans declared war against France. The German plan to capture Paris, though, required a quick passage through Belgium, which had been officially neutral by treaty since its creation in 1830. When German troops began invading that country, both the Belgians and the British objected to the violation of Belgian neutrality. They characterized the German's breaking the treaty as their trashing a "scrap of paper." Of course all treaties, written on pieces of paper, only last as long as they serve the interests of the signatories. Great Britain's interest in Belgium, which lay across the North Sea, was to prevent a threatening German occupation. When the Germans refused to withdraw, the British reluctantly declared war. So by the end of the first week of August, Russia, France, Great Britain, and Serbia were fighting Germany and Austria-Hungary.

Unfortunately for all the well-made plans, general staffs failed to account for the huge numbers of troops as well as variations caused by both commanders and dumb luck. The British sent troops more quickly than expected to France, Russia invaded too rapidly in eastern Prussia, and France pushed too swiftly in the Alsace. The massive German armies were slowed by unexpected Belgian resistance and then turned southward toward Paris too soon. In response, Parisians rushed enough troops to the front, some in taxicabs, to halt the German advance. Neither side could attack the other's flank since the armies were so huge. So the Germans withdrew a few miles and dug in. Swiftness transformed into stalemate as both sides huddled in trenches along a western front stretching all the way from the North Sea to the Swiss border.

Thus, the fighting on the western front unexpectedly developed into **trench warfare**. The Crimean War and the American Civil War had already pointed in this direction, but few commanders had learned from those conflicts. A few soldiers dug in and armed with machine guns could pulverize thousands of approaching enemy troops, especially when assisted by barbed wire, land mines, and artillery. Millions of troops faced one another, alternating between aimless boredom in the muddy, filthy, reeking trenches and combat in explosive terror (see Primary Source Project 12). Soldiers fell ill because of vermin and infections, including the notorious trench foot. The noise and concussive force of exploding munitions caused a new malady among the troops called shell shock (today classified as posttraumatic stress disorder). The German attempt to take the city of Verdun alone cost hundreds of thousands of lives on both sides over several months of constant bombardment. Although the French managed to repulse the German attack, the Battle of Verdun weakened the French so much that they could hardly launch any more offensives themselves. The British launched the Battle of the Somme in the north to help relieve the pressure on the French at Verdun. On the first morning of the offensive, thirty thousand British soldiers were slaughtered in about an hour. Both sides applied new weapons to break the stalemate. But airplanes, poisonous gas, and even tanks (armored vehicles) proved unable to capture victory for either side.

The western front got most of the press, while massive destruction afflicted other fronts as well. Great armies rumbling back and forth across hundreds of miles of territory ravaged Poland and the Balkans. In East Africa, some German forces held out for the entire war. Already in the fall of 1914, the Germans pressured the Ottoman Empire into joining their side. Instead of opening up decisive fronts against Russia, however, the Ottoman Empire found itself vulnerable. After a disastrous campaign along the Russian-Turkish border in the Caucasus, the Muslim Turks suspected that the Christian Armenians were collaborating with the Christian Russians. Beginning in April 1915, the Turks forcibly relocated the Armenians, marching them hundreds of miles across barren landscapes without proper supplies. These so-called **Armenian massacres** led to hundreds of thousands of deaths from exhaustion, starvation, exposure, drowning, and shooting. These incidents later led to the invention of the word *genocide*—the killing off of an entire ethnic group (although the Turkish government has continued to dispute this interpretation). Whatever one calls these atrocities, the men, women, and children remain dead.

Ultimately, the acquisition of allies became the key to victory. Germany, Austria-Hungary, and the Ottoman Empire became known as the **Central Powers**, surrounded as they were by their enemies. Italy refused to support its Triple Alliance partners and at first stayed neutral. In contrast, Bulgaria soon joined the Central Powers, still resenting its losses during the Second Balkan War and eager to crush Serbia. The so-called Allied Powers or **Allies** of Russia, France, Belgium, Great Britain, and Serbia early on outnumbered the Central Powers. Still, German military skill and industrial efficiency might have won the war for its side if the war had been short. The Central Powers' inability to find more allies doomed them in the long run.

The weight of the world slowly massed against the Central Powers as the Allies won more allies to their side. In the fall of 1914, Japan eagerly declared war on Germany and occupied most of its Asian and Pacific possessions. By 1915, the Allies had convinced Italy to attack Austria, tempting it with territory to be confiscated from its former Triple Alliance partner. The Allies pressured the Greeks and promised compensation with possessions to be seized from the Bulgarians and the Ottomans. The British tried to win the support of both Arabs in the Ottoman Empire and international Jews. In the Sykes-Picot Agreement, the British supported the creation of Arab nation-states after the war. By 1917, the British officer T. E. Lawrence (Lawrence of Arabia) had inspired an Arab revolt against the Ottomans in the Arabian Peninsula. At the same time, the **Balfour Declaration** supported a Jewish homeland in Palestine. The Allies did not care that such promises were mutually exclusive.

On the high seas, the British were also hopeful for a decisive blow against the Germans. Short of that, the British hoped that a blockade would starve out the Central Powers. In turn, the Germans tried to blockade the British Isles with another new weapon of war: U-boats or submarines. To neutral nations, submarines seemed more cruel than traditional surface warships, since large numbers of survivors after a torpedoing could not be rescued by the small, vulnerable, undersea warships.

The Germans especially annoyed the neutral Americans with their submarine warfare on commercial ships. Most notorious was a German U-boat's sinking of the passenger ship *Lusitania* (1915), which went down so swiftly that hundreds of people drowned within sight of the Irish coast. Even though the *Lusitania* was a legitimate target that was carrying contraband (weapons and military supplies) in a war zone, the many civilian deaths violated the American sense of fair play. To appease the Americans, for a little over a year the Germans limited their U-boat attacks to warships.

Early in 1917, the Germans further angered Americans with the infamous Zimmermann Telegram. In it the German government tried to convince Mexico to attack the United States. The Germans were foolish to think Mexico could have attacked the United States, since Mexicans were fighting their own civil war.[5] The British intercepted Zimmermann's telegram by tapping into the transatlantic undersea cable line and handed the telegram over to the Americans. As a result, in April 1917 the United States opened hostilities against Germany. Over the next year more than a dozen other countries, including Greece, Thailand, China, and many in Latin America, declared war against one or more of the Central Powers.

---

5. Actually, the United States had been intervening in the Mexican Revolution (1910–1920) for several years. Americans briefly supported the rebel Pancho Villa with arms and money but then abruptly stopped. In retaliation, Villa organized several raids against the United States. American troops pursued him until the United States entered World War I. A victorious authoritarian and socialist regime under the Institutional Revolutionary Party (PRI) soon dominated Mexico for most of the century.

The American men, materiel, and money came just in time. For three years, the European nations had been exhausting themselves trying to win on their own. Drained of men and resources, the home front became the last crucial area of war efforts toward victory. Out of necessity, most industrialized states had adopted **war socialism**, under which governments took control of large sectors of the economy, creating a new military-industrial complex. Central planning by government bureaucrats working with leaders of industry ensured access to raw materials and production for the armed forces. Workers gained better wages and benefits to keep up their production of munitions and provisions without striking. Safety concerns were less important. Workers injured or killed on the job or soldiers at war was the price of victory. Many women entered the public workforce in offices and factories to replace manpower serving with the armies. Consumers tolerated shortages of goods and services in order to help the troops.

To keep up flagging morale, regimes used the modern media for the spread of **propaganda**—information twisted to support a political cause. Exaggerated British propaganda convinced many Allies and Americans that the Germans were entirely monstrous "Huns," despoilers and murderers of innocent women and children. Protestors against the war or activists for women's suffrage ended up silenced and in jail. At the time, one could insightfully observe that the first casualty of war is truth.[6]

By the autumn of 1918, the peoples of the Central Powers were surprised to discover that they had lost the war, although their governments had always assured them that victory was within grasp. They had briefly hoped for victory when Russia fell out of the war in 1917, convulsed by revolution (see the next chapter). But America's finances, industrial might, and even its quickly trained armies more than made up for the loss of Russia to the Allies. By late October and early November, the Ottoman Empire, Bulgaria, Austria-Hungary, and, finally, Germany were caught up in their own revolutions, and their armies collapsed. They surrendered, one after the other.

When the killing stopped at 11 a.m. on the eleventh day of the eleventh month of 1918, more than eleven million victims of combat and disease were dead. Millions more had been wounded, some suffering vicious, horrible mutilations made possible by modern poisonous and explosive chemicals. Billions of dollars of capital had been spent and blown up. Millions of acres of territories had been ravaged; untold thousands of families had been made homeless. Dynasties had been toppled and states shattered: the Romanovs in Russia, the Hohenzollerns in Germany, the Habsburgs in Austria-Hungary, and the Ottomans in Turkey all lost their thrones. Whole populations were demoralized and on the edge of disintegration. Many thought—hoped—that this would be the war to end all wars (see figure 12.4). Sadly, it was only a prelude to worse conflicts.

---

6. These words have often been attributed to the isolationist-minded opponent of the war, American senator Hiram Johnson, who allegedly said them in a speech in 1917. No reliable source to the senator has yet been identified. Ironically, truth is also a casualty of wanting good quotations.

HOSE WHO WITH PATIENT TOIL
BUILT UP THE STATELY PILES OF
MEDIAEVAL ART ARE GONE · THEIR
NAMES ARE FORGOTTEN THEIR WORK
IS IN RUINS ·· BUT TO-DAY IS BUILD-
ING A NOBLER STRUCTURE · THE TEMPLE
OF HUMAN RIGHTS ·· THAT WILL ENDURE
FOR THOSE WHO HAVE LAID ITS FOUNDATIONS
HAVE LAID THEM IN GOOD WILL TOWARD MEN
AND HAVE LABORED FOR PEACE ON EARTH

CHRISTMAS NUMBER
1 9 1 8

Figure 12.4. The Cathedral of Rheims is portrayed as heavily damaged by shelling from German artillery in the Christmas issue of a magazine, right after war's end. Its stated expectation of better days based on human rights still has not been met. (*The Youth's Companion*, vol. 92, no. 49, 5 December 1918)

Review: *What made World War I more destructive and transformative than all previous wars?*

Response:

PRIMARY SOURCE PROJECT 12: "IN FLANDERS FIELDS" VERSUS "DULCE ET DECORUM EST" ABOUT DEATH IN WAR

The horrors of trench warfare during World War I still allowed moments of reflection, as shown by these two poems written by soldiers who had been in combat. One reaction was the Canadian John McCrae's, who calls on the living to remember the cause for which soldiers had died. The English Wilfred Owen questions the legitimacy of the war. Its title comes from the last two lines of this poem (translated as "It is pleasurable and proper to die for the fatherland"). Owen is quoting the ancient Roman poet Horace, who was encouraging young men to train for the imperial legions. Both soldier-poets died at the front.

Source 1: "In Flanders Fields" by John McCrae (1915)

In Flanders fields the poppies blow
Between the crosses, row on row
That mark our place; and in the sky
The larks, still bravely singing, fly
Scarce heard amid the guns below.
We are the Dead. Short days ago
We lived, felt dawn, saw sunset glow,
Loved and were loved, and now we lie
In Flanders fields.
Take up our quarrel with the foe:
To you from failing hands we throw
The torch; be yours to hold it high!
If ye break faith with us who die
We shall not sleep, though poppies grow
In Flanders fields.

Source 2: "Dulce et Decorum Est" by Wilfred Owen (1917)

Bent double, like old beggars under sacks,
Knock-kneed, coughing like hags, we cursed through sludge,
Till on the haunting flares we turned our backs
And towards our distant rest began to trudge.
Men marched asleep. Many had lost their boots
But limped on, blood-shod. All went lame; all blind;
Drunk with fatigue; deaf even to the hoots
Of gas-shells dropping softly behind.
Gas! GAS! Quick, boys!—An ecstasy of fumbling
Fitting the clumsy helmets just in time,
But someone still was yelling out and stumbling
And flound'ring like a man in fire or lime.—
Dim, through the misty panes and thick green light,
As under a green sea, I saw him drowning.
In all my dreams before my helpless sight

He plunges at me, guttering, choking, drowning.
If in some smothering dreams you too could pace
Behind the wagon that we flung him in,
And watch the white eyes writhing in his face, His hanging face, like a devil's sick of sin,
If you could hear, at every jolt, the blood
Come gargling from the froth-corrupted lungs,
Bitter as the cud
Of vile, incurable sores on innocent tongues,—
My friend, you would not tell with such high zest
To children ardent for some desperate glory,
The old Lie: *Dulce et decorum est*
Pro patria mori.

Questions:

- *What are the different perspectives of the poems' "narrators"?*
- *How do the poems use different imagery to convey meaning?*
- *Upon reflection, what attitudes should soldiers and civilians hold about the war?*

Responses:

Make your own timeline.

1810   **1918**

Citations

McCrae, John. *In Flanders Fields*. New York: Putnam, 1919.
Owen, Wilfred. *Poems of Wilfred Owen*. Edited by Siegfried Sassoon. London: Chatto and Windus, 1920.

For more on these sources, go to http://www.concisewesternciv.com/sources/psc12
.html.

CHAPTER 13

Rejections of Democracy

The Interwar Years and World War II, 1917 to 1945

Many people in the West thought they had won the Great War in the name of democracy. Western civilization increasingly promoted the idea that most adults in a state should share in governance, making decisions through conflict and compromise within legal and moral boundaries of behavior in established parliaments and other representative bodies. While such participatory politics had been growing in power and influence since the seventeenth century, democracy remained difficult. Democratic governments were undermined by the Great War's loss of life, economic destruction, high-handed government policies, shattering of old morals and traditions, and flawed peace process (see timeline E). The "war to end all wars" led to the even worse World War II.

DECLINE OF THE WEST?

The Scientific Revolution had offered science as the vehicle for humanity's progress toward peace and prosperity. But the modern chemical explosives and machined weapons of the Great War showed how science might instead drive nations toward death and destruction. Nor could science help much as a worldwide plague, the **influenza pandemic** (1918–1919), killed perhaps as many as forty million people worldwide, far more than the deaths caused by the recent war.[1] The flu germs swept around the globe with amazing velocity and lethality. Only the natural mutation of the germ and increasing resistance of the human immune system defeated the plague. But what could prevent a new epidemic from striking? Many people no longer had the same confidence that science could make the world a better place.

New scientific views in physics that followed those of Darwin in biology and Freud in psychiatry further weakened confidence that the world could be understood and improved. Einstein's complex **theory of relativity** (1916) replaced the

---

1. It is sometimes called the Spanish flu, since physicians first studied it in that country. That version of the flu, however, probably originated in the United States.

logical simplicity and sensible familiarity of Newton's clockwork universe. According to this new theory, a person's position of observation, or point of view, could affect such facts as the measure of time or distance. Even matter and energy were interchangeable, according to the famous formula $E = mc^2$ (energy equals mass times the speed of light squared). The physicist Heisenberg's uncertainty principle (1927) stated that one could know either the location or the direction of an atom's electron, but not both simultaneously. Another theoretical experiment for understanding the atom, Schrödinger's cat, suggests that states of matter are only determined by observation (such as not knowing whether a cat in a box is alive or dead until the box is opened). These additions to atomic theory became metaphors for increasing doubt.

The future of world peace also grew increasingly uncertain, despite the clear victory of the Allied Powers in the Great War. The American president Woodrow Wilson in particular had proclaimed that the Great War was about making the world safe for democracy. Indeed, many of the new countries created out of the peace settlement of the Paris Peace Treaties drew up democratic constitutions. They actually made reasonable attempts at practicing responsible self-government. Real participation of all adult citizens—with laws and amendments even finally granting the vote to women—reached its high point in most modern industrialized states just after the Great War. Having the structures of republican government, though, did not always result in actual practice of the democratic process.

The Great War's peace process unexpectedly undermined principles of democracy. Negotiations had started off with much optimism in Paris in January 1919. At that time, the Europeans welcomed Woodrow Wilson, the first sitting US president ever to leave the country. Since America's power had won the war for the Allies, the other leaders of the "Big Four" allies (Lloyd George of Britain, Clemenceau of France, and Orlando of Italy) grudgingly accepted his preeminence. A year earlier, in January 1918, while the war was still raging, Wilson had already set the tone for peace proposals with the declaration of his **Fourteen Points**. These ideals proposed a world of international cooperation with open and honest diplomacy, support for nationalistic principles, and avoidance of warfare. The European peoples certainly hoped, based on the sound common sense and decency of the Fourteen Points, that Wilson's American vision would establish a better future for all nations.

Wilson also envisioned a new international institution, the **League of Nations**. This organization was meant to replace the obviously failed practice of sovereign nations facing off in a balance of power, with or without alliances. Instead, the League was to promote collective security in a fashion similar to the Concert of Europe conducted by the Congress of Vienna a century before. Its standing forum of delegates would replace the need for emergency congresses or conferences convened every time an international crisis threatened to flare into war. The League offered the possibility for diverse nations with divergent interests to work together rather than against one another. Another world war, people rightfully feared, could doom civilization as they knew it.

It was too much to hope, however, that a few months of negotiations could easily overcome the grudges and disagreements amassed during a thousand years of European conflict since the Treaty of Verdun in 847. Complicating resentments further were the aspirations of oppressed colonial peoples all over the world. The League's own doom was largely determined by the exact place in which it was called into existence, namely Paris, the capital of Germany's bitter enemy. Instead of forging a new beginning for cooperation in Europe, those who wanted to punish the Central Powers outmaneuvered Wilson's good intentions. In the **Treaty of Versailles**, signed in Louis XIV's baroque palace, the Allies forced the Germans to accept primary blame for the war. That treaty also pointedly excluded Germany from the new organization of "free" peoples. Thus, one of the most important great powers was deliberately left out. The victorious Allies also shut out their former great power ally Russia because of its new communist government (see below).

The worst blow to League membership was when the United States refused to join. Many Americans had never shared Wilson's vision of world participation; they instead thought the United States should return to an isolationist attitude. These Americans tried to ignore the reality that the United States was inextricably tied up in world affairs with its colonies in the Pacific, its grip on the Caribbean and Latin America, and its worldwide economic reach. Additionally, partisan politics poisoned the process. Wilson was a Democrat, and both houses of Congress were held by Republican majorities. The Republican leaders of the Senate, which constitutionally ratified all treaties, suggested a few changes they thought would preserve American independence of action and control over its own armed forces. Wilson refused to compromise and embarked on a whirlwind campaign to win popular support for "his" treaty. The stress of traveling thousands of miles in just a few weeks brought on a stroke, which incapacitated him. His wife, Edith, practically ran the White House for months as she interpreted the bedridden president's feeble attempts at communication.

Wilson's removal from politics meant that the United States of America signed a separate peace with Germany, without the covenant concerning the League of Nations. So the United States turned its back on collective security and drifted into isolationism. Great Britain and France, nervous about the growing influence of American power, were glad at first to see the Americans leave. For the next two decades, the isolationist United States retreated behind the imaginary shelter of the Arctic, Pacific, and Atlantic Oceans. The defensive value of bodies of water, however, shrank in an age of iron-hulled motorized ships and aircraft.

Strangely, the United States had become essential to Western civilization even as it withdrew its political interests. Before World War I, most cultural, widespread economic, and social influence came from Europe. After the war, European society seemed stagnant compared to the creativity coming from Americans. During the **Roaring Twenties**, America swelled with the artistic creativity of the Jazz Age. The "Lost Generation" of American writers, disillusioned by both World War I and American materialism, led the literary elites of the West even while they drank past midnight in Paris. Since America became the main creditor nation of European war debts, New York replaced London as the capital of global finance (see figure 13.1). This cultural and economic shift to the New World remained unthreatening to the Old World because of the United States' reluctance to maintain large armed forces

Figure 13.1. New York City. A construction worker on a skyscraper in Manhattan admires the nighttime skyline. (National Archives and Records Administration)

or to throw around its diplomatic weight. American jazz music, however, hit Europe hard, thrilling those who were moved by its African-based rhythms and horrifying those who could not hear its beauty or appreciate its complexity.

Millions first heard jazz music over the new invention of **radio**, which tied the world's cultures together as never before. Although invented before the war, radio as a medium came into its own in the 1920s. Radio stations were built all over the industrialized nations. Although usage taxes (paid by owners of radio sets) supported public broadcasting in many European countries, radio's expansion in the United States was mostly financed through paid advertising. Either way, radio signals reached around the globe, especially thanks to the British Broadcasting Corporation's growth throughout the British Empire.

When not gathered at home around their radios for entertainment, Western audiences also flocked to the **movies**. Motion pictures, like radio, had started in industrialized countries before the war but became wildly popular afterward. Movie theaters or cinemas, specially built or remodeled from performance halls, showed films reporting on current events, adapted from classic plays and literature, or newly created for the silver screen. American filmmakers in the sunshine of Hollywood became the most prolific creators of that medium worldwide, soon outproducing the Europeans.

Movies became a dominant feature of Western culture. One of the first movie stars, the British-born Charlie Chaplin with his "Little Tramp" character, became an iconic figure around the globe. For the first few years, movies had no sound except as provided by local musicians in the theaters. The first movie with synchronized sound, *The Jazz Singer* (1929), portrayed the clash of old culture (a Jewish cantor) with his modernized and Americanized son (the jazz singer of the title). It symbolized the new age replacing the traditional past. Because of the success radio and movies had in English-speaking countries, English increasingly became the language of international media and culture.

The new world tied together by radio and movies seemed even smaller because of new innovations in transportation. Airplanes soared across oceans. Lindbergh captured the public imagination with the first solo flight from New York to Paris (1927). His instant fame demonstrated how radio and newsreels spread information and invented celebrities. Airlines soon began to fly paying passengers across all barriers of land and sea. The most popular and affordable transport was the motorcar or automobile, symbolic of the movement and force of the twentieth century. As the car became the backbone of industrial production, the demand for paved roads and parking began to radically transform the urban and rural landscape. Automobiles also allowed more young people to escape parental supervision, making the "backseat" a byword for sexual opportunity.

The standards of living rose briskly in most of the industrialized West during the 1920s. At first, the costs and destruction of the Great War had drained the resources of many European nations, but it only took a few years to realign their economies back to peacetime production. Then, consumer consumption became the great engine for economic growth of modern economies. More manufacturing meant better pay and benefits for productive workers. While advertising enticed westerners to purchase goods and services, easier access to credit lent them the means to do it quickly and conveniently. A rising level of prosperity nurtured an irresistible tendency toward materialism. Refrigerators and washing machines were soon not just novel modern conveniences but necessities. Even factory workers expected leisure time and vacations. By the late 1920s, members of the widening Western middle classes were enjoying themselves as never before.

For some people, that enjoyment included consuming mood-altering chemicals. Psychoactive substances such as opium (increasingly purified into morphine and heroin), cocaine, and marijuana became more accessible due to modern agriculture, processing, and transportation. As authorities in Western nations grew concerned over increasing rates of addiction and the resultant social destruction, they began to regulate and outlaw such recreational drugs. The United States went furthest, outlawing the manufacture and selling of alcohol with a law declaring Prohibition (1920–1933). Alcohol has been, of course, the most widespread recreational drug since civilization began, whether in the form of beer, wine, or distilled liquor. The American experiment with controlling alcohol consumption was unusual and ultimately unsuccessful. Unsurprisingly, recreational drug use remained prevalent in Western nations despite their official restrictions or prohibitions.

Despite a seeming prosperity, for some the rising materialism, increasing drug use, and spreading popular culture encouraged pessimism. For them, the war had killed or damaged too many promising youths, weakened traditional elites, and led to a decline in churchgoing. Oswald Spengler, in *The Decline of the West* (1922–1926), summed up people's fears. Although his book was more discussed than actually read, Spengler claimed in dense prose that Western civilization had become senile. The events of the 1930s seemed to prove his point.

The troubles began with the **Wall Street crash** (1929), which then triggered the worldwide economic collapse called the **Great Depression** (1929–1941). In the 1920s, the stock exchanges on Wall Street, the financial district of New York, had been pushing people to invest more money than ever before. The eagerness to own stock, even in companies that were overvalued, pushed the prices higher. Many people, both rich and middle class, were buying stock on credit, believing that prices would keep rising forever. Thus, billions of dollars in stock values had accumulated out of sheer optimism and greed. One Thursday morning, 24 October 1929, some investors began to doubt the alleged worth of these stocks and sold them while the market was high, hoping to cash out with big profits. As other investors tried to bail out as well, the market fell fast. Too quickly, financial institutions began to collapse, and wealth disappeared. Within a few weeks, the value of the market had fallen by 50 percent, and it continued to fall for the next three years. Billions of dollars of capital simply vanished into thin air.

Since New York had become the pivotal center for the investment of capital, the Wall Street crash smashed other Western economies. Banks called in their loans, but borrowers had little with which to pay them back. Even when banks confiscated collateral, such as homes or real estate, they still had too little cash on hand when frightened investors demanded their deposits. Forced into bankruptcy, banks failed, and the life savings of millions of people disappeared. Many businesses could not meet payrolls, saw their capital resources drained, and closed their doors. As consumers had too little disposable wealth to buy goods and services, businesses shut down because new orders dried up. More workers then had no paychecks, further weakening demand and consumption. Governments tried to defend their countries' factories and farms by erecting protectionist trade barriers of high taxes or bans on imports. These measures only damaged international trade and did little to help the domestic economies. Even food prices fell, forcing one out of every four farms into foreclosure in the United States. Millions of people went on the move looking for jobs, but too few could be found.

These effects spread through the industrialized West, hitting hardest in the United States, Japan, Germany, and Austria. The worldwide economic depression of the 1930s accelerated the abandonment of parliamentarianism in those countries where they had had too little time to take root. People began to question their government's competency or whether democracy could work at all. Great Britain, France, and a few others clung to their parliamentary democracies, while communist and socialist parties gained in elections in nearly all Western nations.

The only place where organized socialist and communist movements remained weak was in the United States. In America, the administration of President **Franklin Delano Roosevelt** (r. 1933–1945) found other solutions to the economic collapse. When FDR (as he was commonly called) ran for president in 1932, he revitalized the Democratic Party with a coalition of intellectuals, Southerners (both white and black), Jews, farmers, immigrants, and workers—all united in getting the economy moving. Roosevelt's advisors declared laissez-faire classical liberal economics as a fraud, since its free reign to the capitalists had brought on the economic collapse. Instead, he proposed a "New Deal" for Americans, with massive government intervention in the economy and the society.

The heart of the New Deal program was ***Keynesian economic theory***, which suggested a revision to the long-dominant theory of laissez-faire or classical liberal economics. Laissez-faire theory assumed that capital would always be available for investment. But the economic worldwide collapse of 1929 had eliminated many banks and much capital. To get out of such a serious economic collapse, when private capital was in short supply, British economist John Maynard Keynes recommended that governments spend money they borrowed from themselves. Such government spending could help fuel a recovery, which could then revive private capital investments. The massive public debt created by deficit spending could later be paid off through the normal taxation and borrowing from banks after people were working and investing again. Most Western governments began to adopt and use this deficit spending practice regularly.

Deficit spending by Roosevelt's administration put Americans to work at government expense at jobs that ranged from planting trees to writing plays, building bridges to digging ditches. Nevertheless, the American economy failed to fully recover during the 1930s. Majorities of Americans, however, cheered by these efforts and FDR's image of cheerful and determined optimism, voted him into office four times, more times than any other US president. Meanwhile, Roosevelt's political and economic enemies hated the growing power of the federal government and accused FDR of socialism and dictatorship.

Leaders of other democracies in the West did not enjoy the kind of popularity FDR had in America, although they did share his inability to end the Depression. Those leaders who did gain popular followings actually became dictators and often carried out real socialist policies. One after another, many westerners turned away from the enlightened participatory politics of liberal democratic parliamentarianism and handed their fates over to dictators. These dictators then tried to reshape the world into their own visions.

Review: How did the West suffer cultural confusion in the wake of war?

Response:

RUSSIANS IN REVOLT

The first great political alternative to the Western democracies arose out of World War I with the **Russian Revolution** (1917–1922). Before the Great War, the Russian Empire had already been playing catch-up, as it ponderously industrialized in imitation of its European rivals. In politics, though, the absolute monarchy of Tsar Nicholas II (r. 1894–1917) had shown little interest in democratic institutions. Revolution then forced change, as it had in France a century earlier, with results that were equally unexpected. The Russian Revolution's overpowering ideology pioneered new forms of government: the modern dictatorships of *totalitarianism* and *authoritarianism*.

These types of dictatorial regimes became commonplace after World War I. Although authoritarianism was somewhat less intrusive and effective than totalitarianism, both types adapted absolutism to a democratic age. As in an absolute monarchy, one person took charge of the state. Yet unlike the monarchies of old, the new dictators did not descend from some special god-linked dynasty but rather claimed to be singled out by "historical destiny." Napoleon Bonaparte exemplified this type of charismatic genius who seized power from incompetent politicians. Often, the lower-class birth of a dictator worked to his advantage, allowing a portrayal as a man of the people, a member of the masses who had become important and empowered with industrialization. The authoritarian leader's clothing helped to cement this new image. Gone were the crowns, ermine robes, and scepters of kings. Instead, the business suit, antiquated traditional costume, or worker's overalls and cap linked the dictator with average citizens; as an alternative, a military uniform asserted the values of discipline, obedience, and force.

As opposed to monarchs, who relied on tradition, dynasty, nobility, and religion, the modern dictator maintained power through the modern mechanism of a political party—elite followers who willingly and diligently served the leader. The party embodied the "will" of the people, who were only asked to participate in rigged elections and plebiscites. The party structure channeled the will of the dictator down to the local level. Combined with the modern technologies of mass communication, bureaucracy, and law enforcement, the masses could be mobilized to achieve national goals as never before in history.

The authoritarian and totalitarian regimes of the twentieth century sprang from both the nationalism and socialism that had arisen in the nineteenth century. Karl Marx died in 1883, never thinking that the first successful proletarian revolution might take place in Russia, because of its minimal industrialization. The Russian regime had always lumbered on under the sheer weight of its conjoined rule of tsar, Orthodox Church, and landed aristocracy.

Defeat in wars, however, triggered drastic change for Russia. The empire first showed its vulnerability when it lost the **Russo-Japanese War** (1905–1906). The Japanese surprise attack on Russian positions in East Asia expanded its own imperialism at Russia's expense. Nimble Japan successfully humiliated stumbling Russia. In reaction to the defeat of Russian armies and navies, the **1905 Revolution** broke out. The Soviets (or councils) of Workers and Soldiers organized by the socialist **Leon Trotsky** provided some real muscle behind the revolt. At first, Tsar Nicholas II made concessions, at least to middle-class demands for a representative and limited government. After loyal troops returned from the front, however, he realized he had the power to crush the rebellion after all. Consequently, Tsar Nicholas acted on a basic principle:

> **No revolution can succeed against a relatively competent government.**

The tsar broke his promises to liberalize his government, revoked the constitution, and repressed the radicals, executing some and sending many others to prison in Siberia. They and others already in exile survived to organize again.

The enormous costs of World War I offered a second chance for revolution, as the tsar's system failed in the crucible of that brutal conflict. The Russian front, as mentioned in the previous chapter, is often ignored in histories, which prefer to concentrate on the dreadful trench warfare of the western front. Yet the vast ebb and flow of armies from the mountainous Balkans to the frigid Baltic ravaged eastern Europe more horribly than the Battles of Verdun or the Somme had western Europe. The Russians did have some successes against the hapless Austrians, but as the efficient German high command took over operations on the eastern front, Russia found its troops ground up by modern weaponry. Tsar Nicholas himself went to the front to command the troops, but he lacked any skills beyond his limited ability to inspire.

Meanwhile, the capital of Petrograd (the new name for St. Petersburg, which sounded too Germanic) remained in the hands of the tsar's dilettante wife, Tsarina Alexandra. She fell under the spell of the charismatic charlatan Rasputin. That mad "monk" had convinced her that he could cure their son, the Tsarevitch Alexei, of hemophilia. People suspected that Rasputin exercised a baleful influence over Alexandra, ruling from behind the scenes. Even after a group of nobles brutally murdered Rasputin, the government still seemed adrift. The high casualties among the soldiers and increasing food shortages for the common people made Russia ripe for collapse.

The spark that set fire to the dynastic façade came from the Russian women, or "*babushkas*" (named after their headscarves). On International Women's Day, 8 March 1917, women trying to provide meals for their families became fed up with government incompetence in bread rationing and took to the streets in protest.[2] Troops sent in to put down the riots with force instead joined the *babushkas*. Within a week, Tsar Nicholas was talked into abdication. The Romanov dynasty ended; the first, and brief, Russian Republic (1917) began.

This new liberal democratic parliamentarian government was a revolutionary success in itself. Its fate, however, foreshadowed what would happen to so many other regimes after the Great War, as the newly responsible politicians failed to solve their nations' problems. Three serious issues faced Russia's new leader, Alexander Kerensky, a leftist Socialist-Revolutionary. First, the elected government shared power with a shadow regime made up of the revived Soviets of Workers and Soldiers. Second, the wrangling political parties failed to unite on a common policy to solve issues of land reform or to energize the economy. Consequently, food shortages worsened. Third, and worst of all, the government continued fighting Germany after being urged, bribed, and bullied by the other Allied Powers to stay in the war.

A clever move by the Germans guaranteed that Russia's fragile republic would fail. They sent **Lenin** (b. 1870–d. 1924) on a sealed military train from Switzerland to Russia in April 1917. Born as Vladimir Ilyich Ulanov, this revolutionary had taken on the pseudonym "Lenin" (whose meaning is unclear) and at the turn of the century had become leader of the Bolsheviks, a faction of the Russian Social Democratic Party. **Bolshevik** means the "majority," and Lenin claimed the name for his followers after winning a minor issue during a party congress held in exile in London in 1903. Actually, the other Social Democrats, the Mensheviks, or "minority," were usually in the majority on most issues. Still, Lenin knew the value of a good label. The term ***Bolshevism*** gave a Russian name to Lenin's strict, hard-line Marxism: the belief that an elite party of dedicated revolutionaries would carry out a violent revolution. Lenin had no patience with the desire of other revisionist Mensheviks and their social democracy to work with the bourgeoisie and change society gradually by applying constitutional methods. Nevertheless, until 1917 Lenin had merely offered words and ideas, having spent some of his adult career in Siberia and the rest in exile in western Europe. By sending Lenin back to Russia, the Germans hoped that his revolutionary activities would destabilize their enemy. Lenin seized the opportunity for the long-awaited proletarian revolution and fulfilled German hopes, to their later regret.

Lenin laid out his program to the masses with beautiful simplicity: "Peace, bread, and land!" He promised to end the war, feed people, and let peasants have the land they worked. He was not interested in winning elections. In mid-July, his Bolsheviks tried to seize control of the government. Although that uprising failed, Lenin had converted to his cause Leon Trotsky, who had wavered over the years

---

2. Russia still operated under the Julian calendar, so what the rest of the West counted as taking place in March was called the "February" Revolution by the Russians.

between Menshevik social democracy, Bolshevism, and his own version of Trotsky-ism. Trotsky then provided more power through the Soviets of Workers and Sol-diers. The better-planned October Revolution succeeded with barely a hitch during the night of 6–7 November 1917.[3] A large number of leftists, including Socialist-Revolutionaries, Mensheviks, and Bolsheviks, seized key public buildings. The war-ship *Aurora* in the Petrograd harbor fired the shot that launched the assault on the government sitting in the Winter Palace. After a few more shots, the revolutionaries basically strolled right into the palace, which was defended by few soldiers, includ-ing some in the grandly named Women's Battalion of Death. Later films showing heroic battles were mere propaganda. Kerensky himself had already left and eventu-ally ended up in New York, where he died in 1970.

On the morning after Lenin's coup, the leftists elected him as head of the provi-sional government. Now Lenin put into actual practice his version of Marxism, soon called **Leninism**. Bolshevism moved from theory to practice. First, Lenin's dictator-ship began with disbanding the new representative assembly the day after it opened in January. Second, he quickly outlawed and destroyed all the other political parties who had helped in the October Revolution. Terror and violence by secret police and revolutionary-inspired informers kept people in line. Third, Lenin declared a policy of **war communism**, which nationalized business and industry, both domes-tic and foreign owned. The land reform went through, at least by taking properties away from the bourgeoisie and the Orthodox Church. Fourth, he reduced the work-day to eight hours. Fifth, Lenin relocated the capital from Petrograd to Moscow, seeing Petrograd as too exposed to foreign intervention.

At the time, the forces of opposition were indeed dangerous. The first problem was Germany. Lenin ended Russian participation in World War I with the Treaty of Brest-Litovsk in March 1918. It gave away one-third of the Russian Empire's Euro-pean possessions, although most of those areas (Finland, the Baltic states, Poland, and the Ukraine) were mostly inhabited by non-ethnic Russians. Then the "Whites" (a loose alliance of nationalists, monarchists, republicans, and socialists) counterat-tacked the "Reds" (the Bolsheviks and their fellow travelers) from all directions of the compass. The Bolsheviks in turn murdered the imperial family, who had been under house arrest in the distant Ural Mountains. They shot in cold blood the former tsar, his wife, and their five children (including little Anastasia, contrary to the claims of later pretenders and cartoons).

For a while, it seemed as if the Whites might succeed in their counterrevolution, especially as they were briefly helped by foreign intervention. The Poles provoked their own war, hoping to expand their border to include territories once belonging to the greater Poland-Lithuania. Even more dangerously, Allied armies (British, French, Japanese, and American troops) seized Russian ports in the north along the western Arctic coast, in the south along the Black Sea coast, and in the east on the Pacific coast of Siberia. Their ostensible reasons were, first, to help fight Germany; second, to prevent munitions sent to the Russian Republic from falling into Bolshe-vik hands; and finally, simply to crush the Bolsheviks themselves. At one point, five

---

3. Again, because of the Julian calendar, Russia's "October" Revolution took place in what the rest of the West called November.

thousand American troops occupied the northwestern ports of Russia, while nine thousand were in eastern Siberia. American soldiers invaded Russia, shot at Russians, and killed some.

Still, the Bolsheviks won the civil war by 1920, despite Allied intervention. The counterrevolutionary Whites lacked any common political program, military coordination, or revolutionary fervor. The Reds had better lines of internal communication, the support of many of the peasants, and united, strong resolve under the leadership of Lenin and Trotsky, who had commanded the Red Army.

Following the first Bolshevik victory, the country lay in ruins, with millions dead, millions more threatened with famine and disease, and the economic structures in shambles. Here Lenin showed his true genius by introducing the New Economic Policy in 1921. This policy reversed the extreme nationalization program of war communism. The NEP allowed most businesses to be privately owned again and to generate private profits in relatively free markets. By the mid-1920s, Russia had gained stability and caught up with its prewar economic status.

The new success of the country was reinforced in 1922, when Lenin declared Russia to be the **Union of Soviet Socialist Republics**, or **USSR** (1922–1991). At the core of this new political structure was the Russian Federative Soviet Republic. It included much of the old Russian Empire, including Siberia. Some of the other socialist republics somewhat contributed ethnic diversity, such as Ukrainians, Belarusians, Uzbeks, Turkmen, and Kazakhs. The collective state of the USSR defied and, indeed, superseded nationality with a new ideology based on proletarian revolution. The central Communist Party controlled the government bureaucracy and elections, while the Politburo, its highest organ, directed the people in a socialist transition to the utopia of communism prophesied by Karl Marx. Most inhabitants accepted the new stability of their self-proclaimed "workers' paradise."

The victory of the communists in the Russian Revolution inspired imitators and raised alarm in Western nations. In the chaos of the Great War's end, communists briefly seized power in Hungary and parts of Germany. In 1920, the Party of Institutionalized Revolution settled Mexico's decades of political instability. This Mexican socialist regime carried out land reform on forty million acres and nationalized foreign companies. Even though Mexico found itself too poor to compete with industrialized states, Western nations feared that more socialist revolutions could threaten their own status.

During this **Red scare** (1918–1922), Western politics became dominated by *nativism*, a fear of foreigners and immigrants. Western nations controlled their borders, suppressed radical political parties, arrested and deported suspected subversives, and fired left-wing teachers and civil servants. In 1919, the US government founded a new national police agency, the Federal Bureau of Investigation (FBI), to fight domestic communism. In hindsight, such fears were unrealistic. By the mid-1920s, communism had gained hardly any additional believers.

In Communist Russia, the man who had guided the revolution to its success was also faltering. Lenin ruled in a modest fashion, often out of the public eye. He began to fall ill from a series of strokes in 1922. His wife, Krupskaya, did her best to convey the increasingly debilitated leader's wishes (as Edith Wilson had done for her husband only a few years before). Lenin was dead by January 1924. His mummi-fied corpse, displayed in a glass case within a tomb in Red Square, became the sacred shrine for his Bolshevik revolutionary success. The Bolsheviks now had to find a replacement for Lenin while lacking a political mechanism for choosing a successor.

The logical choice was Leon Trotsky, a key figure in the revolutions since 1905. He had much practical experience as an organizer of the Soviets and the Red Army. He was energetic, intellectually brilliant, and rhetorically inspiring. Yet some criti-cized Trotsky for arrogance, his Jewish heritage, and his ideological impurity: he had only converted late to Bolshevism. Strangely enough, others deemed him too radical as he pushed a program to start communist revolutions around the world.

In the end, Lenin's successor was a man called "Steel" or **Stalin** (b. 1879–d. 1953). Born Joseph Vissarionovich Dzugashvily in Georgia in the Caucasus Moun-tains, Stalin had played only a marginal role in the early revolutionary period. In the new Soviet Union, though, he rose to become general secretary for the Commu-nist Party. In that position, Stalin directed the hard drudgery of bureaucracy neces-sary for the functioning of any complex modern state. He also found jobs and arranged promotions for his own friends and supporters. Stalin's position of first advocating socialism in one state, Russia, before taking on world revolution made him appear more moderate.

Stalin quickly secured his own dictatorship. As general secretary of the Commu-nist Party since 1922, Stalin's design of the constitution in 1924 enabled him to take control of both party and state by 1927, ratified by constitutional revision in 1936. He convinced the Politburo to throw Trotsky out of the party and even exile him from Russia. Trotsky fled to socialist Mexico City, where in 1940 an assassin, on Stalin's orders, bashed in Trotsky's head with an ice axe.

Once in complete control, Stalin added his own variant to what Marx and Lenin had implemented before him. **Stalinism** probably would have horrified both of them. The experimentation of the early years abruptly ended. Instead, Stalin estab-lished an absolute personal dictatorship, supported by the cult of his own perso-nality. The dictator eliminated all his rivals, culminating in the **Great Terror (1936–1938)** that echoed the Reign of Terror of the French Revolution. Stalin arrested tens of thousands of "Old Bolsheviks," those who had fought alongside Lenin and Trotsky. All women, who under socialist principles of equality had risen to positions of authority, were removed. He liquidated half of his officer corps. Many of these victims were purged through show trials, where they publicly con-fessed to crimes of espionage or counterrevolutionary activity of which they could not possibly have been guilty. Stalin had many victims officially executed; others simply "disappeared." Stalin sent thousands to internal exile, in prison labor camps in Siberia called gulags.

The propagandized benevolent image of Stalin countered this campaign of fear. Stalin made sure that his own face, name, and reputation shone brighter than every-one else's, including Marx and Lenin. The entire history of the revolution was rewritten to emphasize Stalin's alleged central role. Numerous holidays, ceremon-ies, and programs were dedicated to Comrade Stalin, who, with paternal caring similar to that of the tsars of old, looked after his proletarian flock.

People put up with this megalomaniacal side of Stalin's regime partly because of his success with another key part of Stalinism: modernization. The Soviet Union had already advanced further than it had under the tsars, but that achievement was not good enough for Stalin (see figure 13.2). He felt that his state was decades behind other advanced countries and wanted to make up the difference quickly. In 1928, he ended the New Economic Policy, Lenin's experiment with free-market

Figure 13.2.   A poster from the Soviet Congress of 1934, held by Stalin, celebrates the revolution, boasting that under the leadership of Lenin, Russia would march to victory. (Art Resource)

capitalism and private ownership. Instead, a series of **Five-Year Plans** revived central planning of the economy to a degree never before experienced. The government bureaucracies transformed the economy in the minutest detail, emphasizing heavy industry. Forced laborers hastily built new cities in Siberia, such as the poorly planned Magnitogorsk, which went from a population of a few bears to two hundred thousand people in ten years.

Stalin borrowed freely from the United States. The steel works in Magnitogorsk were modeled on those of Gary, Cleveland, and Pittsburgh, along with their freely flowing industrial pollution in air and water. Large-scale, mechanized, industrial farming in the American heartland inspired ***collectivization*** of agriculture in Russia. The state confiscated the peasants' land, and communal groups then farmed the land. Many peasants resisted surrendering the land they had only recently gained. The regime machine-gunned such opponents or sent them to prison camps. In turn, many peasants slaughtered their own animals or burned their own crops in retaliation, thus contributing to a major famine. In all, the application of the Five-Year Plans killed perhaps ten million people and caused suffering for millions more.

In the long term, Stalin was successful, if success is measured by power. The land was cleared; homes grew out of wilderness; factories hummed with machinery. Stalin's policies also provided access to education and health care for all citizens. The standard of living for most Soviet comrades far surpassed that of the tsar's subjects. Stalin had transformed a weary, second-rate great power into the second most powerful nation in the world, next only to the United States of America. "Nothing succeeds like success," quip the Americans. Many westerners, disillusioned by their own infighting of splintered parties and the failures of capitalism in depression and inflations, admired what Stalin had accomplished. They joined socialist and communist organizations in their own countries, confident that these ideas embodied the future. It was easy to ignore the millions of dead: the pointless World War I, the heartless flu—death had taken so many in the past decades. At least these Russians, some said, had died for the worthwhile cause of progress. Unfortunately, no one could ask the dead for their opinion.

Review: *How did the Bolsheviks establish a new kind of state and society?*

Response:

LOSING THEIR GRIP

During the years after World War I, the colonial empires of the Western powers began to weaken. Exhausted by the efforts of global war, the European powers did not even realize that the strength of their imperial embrace was wavering. In reality, profits and tax revenues from maintaining empires failed to cover the costs of investments and government payments. Leaders slowly came to believe that modern colonialism was not worth the costs in taxes and lives. Meanwhile, their distant subjects were also growing restless, and stronger.

At war's end, though, the European leaders still clung to continuing their own empires, and the new League of Nations helped them with that effort. The League took charge of the colonial territories of the defeated Central Powers and handed them out to the victorious Allies, calling them **mandates**. The British and French Empires received most of the former German colonies of Africa and the southern Pacific as well as much of the non-Turkish regions of the dismantled Ottoman Empire. The Belgians took over Rwanda and Burundi, near King Leopold's original colony of the Congo. The Belgian colonial rulers pitted the very similar Hutu and Tutsi peoples against one another in order to better control the colony. As far as the imperialist planners of Western nations were concerned, at first it seemed that the twentieth century would continue just as the nineteenth had.

Colonial peoples saw this sharing of the spoils as a betrayal of President Wilson's idea of self-determination in the Fourteen Points. The West believed itself to have exported its glorious Western civilization to peoples who still lived in darkness. Those peoples who lived in the allegedly dark places of the globe did not see it that way. The victors callously ignored delegations from colonial areas. The Wafd (or "Delegation") Party from Egypt could not make its plea for independence heard. The Chinese argued in vain for concessions on extraterritoriality. Western leaders even snubbed Japan, their ally in the Great War.

For the next few decades, westerners remained confident they could hold on to and continue to convert the rest of the world to their way of life. Even though profits from colonial areas were slim to nonexistent, confident investors still hoped to make money. They believed they could adapt the colonial lands to the world economy, mostly to benefit the various mother countries. For example, confident British imperialists thought a handful of Oxford-educated civil servants and trained police officers could handle populations in South Asia that outnumbered them by thousands to one.

This imbalance in numbers tilted ever more against the West. Europe's own prosperity had caused a **population explosion** in the nineteenth century, when the inhabitants doubled in number, even with immigration to the Americas and colonial possessions. By 1914, however, imperialism had brought these industrial and scientific advantages to the four corners of the world. Soon the peoples of Asia and Africa also underwent their own population explosions (which to some extent still continue). In contrast, modern industrial society led in the West to smaller families. Compulsory education raised the cost of having children, since they could not contribute to the family's labor resources. Better workers' benefits also reduced the need to have enough children to support parents in their old age. So population growth slowed, stopped, and even began to recede in European countries throughout the twentieth century. Soon the "white" portion of world population began to shrink, as it is still shrinking today, compared with the "colored" portion. Europeans already in the 1920s noticed the trend and began to fear a Yellow Peril, a threat that Asians might regain their independence or even come to dominate the West. These fears found expression in suspense novels about the inscrutable evil genius Fu Manchu or the conquering "Yellow hordes" in the *Buck Rogers in the 25th Century* comic strip.

Contrary to Western stereotypes, the colored peoples of the world were neither stupid nor evil. Certainly, they had not gone through a commercial revolution, a scientific revolution, or an industrial revolution on their own. With imperialism, however, the lessons learned from those tumults were available to anyone with an open mind (and at less risk and lower costs). Once they had recovered from the initial shock of the Western invasions and subjugations, colonized peoples began to wield the westerners' own ideas against them, especially that of nationalism. Self-government was not only for Belgians or Italians but also for Chinese or Congolese. Meanwhile, the Bolsheviks in Russia promoted themselves as the friends of "oppressed peoples" (covering up their own russification of non-Russian subjects). Soviet calls to resist capitalist and imperialist exploitation found willing listeners. Thus, the pressures of the native peoples for self-government grew relentlessly.

The British Empire, which set the example for imperialism in the nineteenth century, led the way in its decline in the twentieth. Immediately after the Great War, its imperial structure began to crumble. The trouble began closest to home as the "**Irish Problem**" flared up for the British. In Ireland, the political party **Sinn Fein** ("Ourselves Alone") had worked toward independence from Britain since the turn of the century. In 1916, their Easter Rising in Dublin had been bloodily crushed. As soon as the war was over, many Irish formed the so-called Irish Republican Army (IRA). At first, the IRA used terrorism, but soon it organized enough to fight a civil war against the special British police troops, the "Black and Tans." The growing violence convinced Great Britain to withdraw. Both sides agreed to a semi-independent Irish state in 1920. In 1938 this state became the completely sovereign Republic of Ireland.

The fighting did not stop, however, as some Irish thought the victory incomplete. The sore spot remained in the counties of **Northern Ireland**, also called Ulster, which stayed part of the United Kingdom of Great Britain. Back in the 1600s, Protestant Scotch-Irish families had settled there and ever afterward formed the majority. Since they had been in Ireland as long as white people had in North America (or Afrikaaners in South Africa), they considered themselves Irish, even if they identified with the Protestant English and Scots more than the Roman Catholic Irish. The moderate majority throughout Ireland accepted this division of the island, but some few demanded the whole island be under one independent government. So Irish Catholics in the south began killing other Irish Catholics over this disagreement. The Irish Republican Army broke apart in this second civil war. By 1922, the moderates' acceptance of a divided island had won. Over the next five decades, only a few underground terrorists occasionally and ineffectively surfaced with a bombing or assassination to protest the ongoing political division of the island.

Of greater consequence to the decline of British power (although less violent) was the breakaway of the empire's four self-governing white **dominions**. Great Britain settled the three most important dominions, Canada, Australia, and New Zealand, in the same way as they had the American colonies. British immigrants stole the land from the natives, whether called the First Nations and the Inuit of Canada, the Aborigines of Australia, or the Maori of New Zealand. They wrote fraudulent treaties, forced the natives from their lands, confined them to reservations, and discriminated against them in the towns of "white" society. By 1900, white populations had transformed these dominions into Western, modern, industrialized states that were comparable economically and socially to any in Europe. In the fourth significant dominion, the Union of South Africa, the white ethnic British and Dutch Afrikaaners co-ruled the land, even though they were in the minority to the various tribes of black Africans.

All four of these states were tired of being bossed around by a Parliament sitting in London. As British dominions, they had been automatically drawn into World War I, where too much of their own people's precious blood had been spilled far from home on the battlefields of Europe. The dominions saw too many differences in economic policy as well, especially as the Great Depression overwhelmed the globe. In 1932, these four states negotiated an equal partnership in the newly formed **British Commonwealth**. This new structure offered its members economic cooperation, not political compulsion. As for the United Kingdom, the British Empire clearly dropped in its status as the ranking world power after losing direct and immediate access to the resources of Canada, Australia, New Zealand, and South Africa.

The British Empire suffered still more setbacks in the Middle East and South Asia. In 1922 the British finally granted independence to Egypt, a territory they had snatched from the Ottomans in the late nineteenth century. The British kept ownership, though, of the crucial Suez Canal until 1956. To compensate for the loss of Egypt, the British grabbed on to mandates carved out from the destroyed Ottoman Empire. Drawing arbitrary borders of straight lines on the map, British geographers contrived the countries of **Iraq** and Transjordan. They put in charge new kings, Faisal and Abdullah of the Hashemite dynasty. These two Saudis had been allies of the British during the Great War but had never before lived among the Arabs in Iraq or Transjordan.

The appointed king of newly created Iraq ruled over diverse peoples: a handful of Jews and Christians, and the Sunni Arabs in the center of the country, who traditionally hated the Shiite Arabs in the south. Also, the non-Arab Kurds in the north were frustrated that they had not gained their own country of Kurdistan (which would have taken parts of Turkey and Iran as well). The British helped Faisal fight insurgencies, using airplanes with poison gas against rebel Kurds and Arabs. By 1926 they had tired of fighting. The British withdrew, although they kept key military and economic privileges. The next year, petroleum was discovered under Iraq's sands. Although modern British technology was necessary to pump the oil from the ground and refine it, Iraq was ultimately sole master of this resource, which made it a power to be respected and feared in the region.

Britain's other mandates in the Middle East were as troublesome as Iraq. The British cut the Ottoman province of Jordan into two parts, Transjordan and **Palestine**. The latter was beginning to receive the Jewish immigrants encouraged by the Balfour Declaration made during the Great War, which had committed Britain to allowing a Jewish "homeland" there. The native Arabs quickly grew resentful at the growing numbers of new Jewish neighbors. By 1936, violence between Jews and Palestinian Arabs had intensified into a near civil war, with the British caught in the middle. By 1939, a fateful year, the British stopped all Jewish immigration in order to keep the peace with the Arab majority.

Meanwhile, the "jewel in the crown" of the British Empire, the Indian subcontinent, was also hostile to continuing English rule. The British mistakenly believed their regime was doing the Indians a favor. They correctly argued that India's vast area had never actually possessed a unified native government. Often Indians had been ruled by foreign conquerors, of which the British were merely the latest. Instead of being grateful, however, Indians resisted with their own version of Western nationalism. The **Indian National Congress**, founded in 1886, began as a body to help maintain British dominion but soon worked to get rid of the same.

After 1915, the British Empire was shaken to its roots by the return to India of **Mohandas Karamchand Gandhi** (b. 1869–d. 1948). In his youth Gandhi had tried to assimilate. After studying law in London, Gandhi first tried to practice law in South Africa. Originally, Gandhi had been just one more Indian trying to make himself over as British. Then the injustice of being thrown off a train because he was not a white European radicalized him. Gandhi learned that for people of color, the Western ideals of liberty and equality were empty promises. After he had organized the Indian community in South Africa to fight for civil rights, he returned to his native India in 1915.

By then, Gandhi had rejected westernization as materialistic, immoral, and godless. He began to transform into a traditional Indian holy man, with enough success to earn him the honorific title "Mahatma" (Great Soul). He discarded Western pinstriped suits, starched collars, and ties and instead wore loose, homespun robes and shaved his head. He cultivated asceticism and simplicity. Certainly, some aspects of his life took on a touch of the unusual, such as his concern with vegetarianism or his practice of resisting sexual temptation by (literally) sleeping alongside naked young women. Most importantly, though, Gandhi took Indian religious ideas and turned them into a political philosophy. He claimed that *satyagraha* (soul force) could defeat the greatest empire in history, and his soul force was based on civil disobedience. Indians, he felt, would wake up British sensibilities with their own ideals of decency and fair play.

A massacre by the British of hundreds of peaceful protesters in 1919 at Amritsar (or Jallianwala Bagh), boycotts of manufactured goods, protests of taxes on salt, and peaceful marches against discrimination all worked to Gandhi's advantage. In turn, the British periodically imprisoned him. His nonviolence left him immune to criticism about means, while his fasts, simplicity, and eccentricity made him resistant to personal attacks. News spread by the international press made Gandhi a popular hero around the world. Only the most stubborn of the British, like Winston Churchill, thought that England could hold on to India for much longer.

Meanwhile, the other European imperialist powers failed to recognize the precariousness of their own situations. France continued to hope to "civilize" its Caribbean, African, and Asian subjects. Belgium continued to exploit the Congo. The Italian, Dutch, Portuguese, and Spanish outposts limped along. Ignoring calls to recognize humanity in all people, certain westerners began to glorify attitudes of imperialism even more than the many nationalists had in the nineteenth century. These beliefs helped hatch a new ideology based on racism and violence.

Review: *How were the Western empires slowly weakening?*

Response:

FASCIST FURY

The brief spirit of international cooperation seen in the League of Nations was soon overwhelmed by the intensification of nationalism and imperialism. Bolshevism had adapted to nationalism and imperialism under Stalin. A new political ideology, *fascism*, now furiously swept across much of eastern Europe, as yet another alternative to both communism and capitalism. Like the Bolsheviks, fascists rejected the actual practice of parliamentarian democracy, which they saw as more about political opponents quarreling than solving serious problems. Despite this agreement on method, both Marxists and fascists were essentially different from each other. Fascism focused on national unity. Instead of Marx's ideology of how class conflict drove historical change, fascists argued for ethnic conflict.

In the fascist point of view, the stronger people should dominate while the weaker died out. The fascists cited the **eugenics** movement, which twisted scientists' revelations about heredity. Supporters of eugenics called for breeding policies to eliminate undesirables from the human gene pool. In the fascist analysis, the clash of peoples, whether between large races, smaller nations, or tiny tribes, changed the course of the world.

Fascist ideology called for a **corporate state** that unified the leader and people of one ethnic group. Fascists believed that since both workers and property owners belonged to the same ethnic people, they should cooperate in harmony under the beneficial guidance of the leader of the corporate state. Their protection of private property, properly used, made allies of the economic elites, while socialist language won over the workers. Even the old nobility might be welcomed back as guardians of the national heritage.

Fascists also exalted violence. They embraced militarism, reflected in their love of uniforms, banners, and parades. Other militaristic virtues such as obedience, discipline, and endurance of hardships replaced liberal ideals such as creativity, freedom of conscience, or expanding opportunity. Fascism went beyond typical militarism and praised violence as the greatest glory of man, whether applied to the conquest of other peoples or to the forceful repression of domestic differences. Fascist bullies frequently hurt others just to prove their own superiority, even if it disturbed law and order.

The departure point of this new ideology of hate and hurt was Italy. That country's imperial inferiority complex had combined with embarrassment over its lackluster performance in World War I. At the war's end, Italians found their "victory" to be hollow and bitter. They had never really won any great battles. Their few acquisitions of territory from the dismembered Austrian Empire caused more problems than they were worth, since they actually added troublesome ethnic minorities from German South Tyrol and Slavic Istria. Italy had failed to gain anything from the Ottoman Empire, and the papacy, still bitter over the loss of the Papal States, continued to frustrate national politics. Italian politics was bogged down with postwar economic readjustment causing unemployment and strikes, while the traditional socialist, liberal, and conservative parties could not cooperate with one another.

Out of this swamp, a former anarchist and socialist, **Benito Mussolini** (b. 1883–d. 1945), rose to become the first theorist and practitioner of fascism. Mussolini declared that he had the answer to Italy's civil disorders, even while his fascist thugs added to the turmoil. When the fascists staged a massive March on Rome in October 1922, Mussolini waited in the background, ready to flee the country if anything went wrong. He need not have worried. The democratic parties simply abandoned responsibility when confronted by the bold assertions of the fascists, as republicans had done when faced by the Bolsheviks in Russia during 1917–1918. The king of Italy readily appointed Mussolini as prime minister. Mussolini used this position to become "Il Duce" (the leader) of both his party and all Italy.

It took several years, however, for the Italian fascists to reach their destination of authoritarian power. They bullied, assaulted, and murdered their opponents. They stripped Italians of civil liberties and political responsibility. Meanwhile, their propaganda showcased their job programs, swamp drainage, housing construction, and arrests of undesirables. Many people even came to believe that Mussolini made the notoriously late Italian trains run on time. He did not. Yet hopeful Italians and optimistic foreign observers convinced themselves that Italy was on the rise. Mussolini even reconciled the pope to modern Italy by signing the Lateran Concordat, establishing the Vatican City and a few other palaces and properties as an independent territory under papal sovereignty. Italians achieved a certain perverse pride in the rise of their national standing again. By 1927, Mussolini could do whatever he wished.

What Il Duce wished was to revive the Roman Empire. His fascist version, though, lacked the original's tolerance for diversity. Instead, Mussolini wanted Italians to impose their culture on all their subjects. On the European continent, he was already forcing Slavs in Istria and Germans in the South Tyrol to become Italians by forbidding their languages and even translating their family names into Italian. On the continent of Africa, he harshly repressed independence efforts in Italy's colonies of Libya and Somalia. Then some Italian troops in Somalia violated the border of neighboring Abyssinia (more often called Ethiopia) in December 1935. Mussolini could not tolerate black Africans shooting at white Italians. He also sought to avenge the humiliating defeat of Adowa, where Italy had lost to the Abyssinians in 1898. Thus, in the summer of 1936, Mussolini launched the **Italo-Abyssinian War** (1936–1937).

In response, Haile Selassie, the emperor of Abyssinia, appealed to the League of Nations to stop this aggression against one of its own members. The only action the League made in Abyssinia's defense was to impose economic sanctions against Italy with a trade embargo on many products. These sanctions, however, neither included oil, which powered Italy's modern military machines, nor curtailed the United States, which continued to trade with Italy. As a result, with modern trucks, tanks, and planes, the Italian forces decisively defeated Abyssinia's less mechanized forces. By the summer of 1937, with all of Ethiopia occupied, the League lifted the insignificant sanctions, thus essentially endorsing Mussolini's aggression.

Fascism might have remained confined to one country (and its empire), just as Bolshevism had been, without the Great Depression. The apparent failure of democratic leaders compared with Mussolini's obvious success inspired imitators: strongmen seized power throughout eastern and southern Europe. These areas were particularly vulnerable to fascism. The Paris Peace Treaties had created many small states out of the former empires of Romanovs, Habsburgs, and Ottomans. This ***balkanization*** meant that small states struggled with national identity and ethnic minorities, economic competition with neighbors, and lack of investment capital, all with little tradition of democracy. Many welcomed the simplistic nationalism of hatred and exclusion pitched by fascists.

For example, the **Kingdom of the Serbs, Croats, and Slovenes** founded at war's end soon succumbed to fascist yugo-slavism. Numerous other ethnic groups, however, such as Montenegrins, Bosnians, Germans, Italians, Magyars (Hungarians), Bulgars, Turks, Albanians, Macedonians, Pomaks, Vlachs, and Romany (Gypsies), nestled with the dominant Serbs, Croats, and Slovenes within the borders of the kingdom. Both ancient and new disagreements among these ethnic groups frustrated cooperation and effective political action. In 1929, a bitter King Alexander dissolved the parliament, suspended the constitution, and abandoned democracy. In his renamed **Kingdom of Yugoslavia**, Alexander enforced a royal dictatorship based on Serbian fascism. Rather than meekly accepting the dominance of Serbs, other ethnic groups organized an opposition. The Macedonians revived the IMRO, and the Croatians formed the new Ustaša (Insurrectionist) terrorist organizations. Working together as assassins where they had not as politicians, they blew up King Alexander on 9 October 1934 while he visited Marseilles, France. His

Serbian successor, though, maintained the fascist royal dictatorship for several more years.

In the far western part of southern Europe, the Iberian Peninsula also knuckled under to fascist dictatorships. Generals seized power in Portugal in 1926, and their military successors continued to rule there until 1974. In contrast, neighboring Spain briefly experienced an expansion of democracy. In 1931, a peaceful revolution had thrown out the capricious and arbitrary king and established the Republic of Spain. At first, liberals and democratic socialists dominated the government. Then anarchists and communists (influenced either by Trotsky or Stalin) won elections and formed a coalition called the "Popular Front." These reform-minded leftists soon encroached on the traditional prerogatives of the Roman Catholic Church and Spanish aristocrats. Conservatives called on Generalissimo Francisco Franco to overthrow the legitimate government. Franco began the **Spanish Civil War** (1936–1939) by leaving his outpost in the Canary Islands, first to invade Spanish possessions in North Africa and then mainland Spain itself. Franco outmaneuvered his conservative allies and founded a fascist movement under his personal control, which he called the Falange (phalanx). Fascist Italy and Germany helped him with money, supplies, seventy thousand Italian "volunteer" soldiers, and planes and pilots from the German Luftwaffe (air force).

Surprisingly, the legitimate Spanish republican government was able to slow the advance of Franco's fascist armies. A few foreign believers in democracy and socialism, such as the writers George Orwell and Ernest Hemingway, volunteered to aid the republicans, served in their militias, and publicized their cause. The Soviet Union aided the republicans with some money and advisors. The help by authoritarian Bolsheviks, however, probably hurt more than it helped the Spanish republicans. No Western democratic government supported the leftist Spanish Republic.

Desperate for support, the republicans made a deal with the **Basques**, a people who have claimed to be the longest residents of Europe. Through centuries of domination by Romans, Visigoths, Moors, Castilians, and modern Spaniards, the Basques had managed to maintain their language and culture despite having little political power. In October 1936 the Republic of Spain allowed the establishment of the "Republic of Euzkadi," an autonomous region of Basque self-government. To the fascistic nationalists under Franco, such diversity in Spain was intolerable. On 27 April 1937, German bombers unleashed the first successful strategic bombing raid in modern history on the Basque capital. By the end of the day, the city was in ruins, with more than two thousand dead. The terror felt by the people, if not the world, was expressed in Picasso's famous painting, named after the Basque capital: *Guernica*. The Republicans, increasingly divided along ideological and ethnic lines and without allies, could not hold off the fascist onslaught. In March 1939, Franco finally took Madrid and established a dictatorship that would last for the rest of his life, thirty-six more years (see figure 13.3).

By 1939, only two countries in southern and eastern Europe remained democratic. The first country was Turkey, on the southeastern fringe of Europe. The Paris Peace Treaty with the defeated Ottoman Empire left only a weak and small Turkish state. Alone among the losers of World War I, however, the Turks resisted the treaty

Figure 13.3. The Valley of the Fallen. Franco's fascist memorial to the dead of the Spanish Civil War was built with the forced labor of the republican and socialist defeated. Disagreements between supporters of the left and right or nationalism and regionalism about whether the monument memorializes fascism too much continue to disturb politics in Spain.

imposed upon them. An army officer, Mustapha Kemal, overthrew the Ottoman sultan and abolished the sultanate on 1 November 1922, ending the one cultural institution that claimed to unite all Muslims. He renamed himself **Atatürk** (b. 1881–d. 1938), which meant "father of the Turks," to symbolize his role as a new founder for the Turkish people. He led Turkish armies to drive out invading Italians and Greeks while the British and French dithered. Atatürk then westernized his nation and set up a secular state.

While Atatürk largely succeeded at founding a stable democratic government, nationalistic resentments led the Turks to solve some ethnic conflicts by expulsion. Turkey expelled most of its Greek and Bulgarian citizens, while Greece and Bulgaria returned the favor by ejecting many of their Turks. Greeks had been living in Asia Minor since the sixth century BC. With these forced removals, twenty-five centuries of Greek civilization in the important region of Ionia ended abruptly. Nearly two million people were exchanged with much hardship, although fortunately few slaughters. At the time, few other countries followed this relatively bloodless model of solving ethnic claims.

The brand new country of **Czecho-slovakia** remained the only other state in southern and eastern Europe to resist authoritarianism.[4] Czecho-slovakia itself seemed like a miniature version of the vast multiethnic Habsburg Austro-Hungarian Empire, out of which it had been carved and cobbled together. The rivalry between the two dominant ethnic groups of Czechs and Slovaks mirrored the conflict between Austria-Hungary's Germans and Magyars, while the Sudeten Germans mirrored the place of the Croats as a large third force. A minority of Magyars along the Hungarian border wanted to join Hungary, as Serbs had wanted to leave Austria and join Serbia. Nevertheless, Czecho-slovakia provided democratic representation and relatively fair treatment for all ethnic groups. The Sudeten Germans' fascination with fascism, however, would later destroy Czecho-slovakia (see below).

Thus, by 1939, all of southern and eastern Europe had come under authoritarian or totalitarian regimes: Latvia, Estonia, Lithuania, Poland, Austria, Hungary, Romania, Bulgaria, Yugoslavia, Albania, Greece, Italy, Spain, and Portugal. Those countries in Europe that did not have fascist regimes at least had fascist political parties. Even distant Japan (see below) prostrated itself before a clique of fascist generals. The tide of history clearly seemed to be carrying dictatorship, not democracy. Soon enough, the most fascistic of all fascists would begin a war intending to dominate Europe, if not the world.

Review: How did fascism spread across the West?

Response:

HITLER'S HATREDS

The most notorious and successful of fascists was, of course, **Adolf Hitler** (b. 1889–d. 1945). In 1933 he became "Der Führer" (the Leader) of the **Third Reich**

---

4. The Czecho-Slovak State, as the peace treaties named it, had been organized by exiles in Cleveland, Ohio, and Pittsburgh, Pennsylvania. The official name of the country between the wars often used the hyphen to separate the two dominant ethnic groups.

(Third Empire), supposedly succeeding the Holy Roman emperors and the Hohenzollern kaisers. At first, Hitler peacefully extended the borders of his German state to its largest expanse since the fifteenth century. Then, in 1939, he launched a war that conquered most of the heartland of Western civilization.

Today it seems incomprehensible that Hitler could have attained such great power so quickly. Indeed, no one who had known Hitler during the Great War would have expected his later achievements. As the son of an insignificant Austrian civil servant, a reject from art school, and a mediocre painter of postcards, Hitler held in contempt the diverse ethnic groups of cosmopolitan Vienna. Ultranationalist ideas of *pan-germanism*, that all Germans should unite and dominate, entered his ideology. He fled his native Austria when the Habsburg regime called him to compulsory military service expected of all able-bodied male citizens. Shortly after Hitler arrived in Germany, however, he applauded the outbreak of the Great War, volunteered, and served on the front lines. Against all odds, he survived four years. During this time, he failed to distinguish himself with any leadership ability and rose only to the lowly rank of corporal.

Hitler's leadership only appeared as World War I ended and revolution threatened to tear Germany apart. During the last few years of the war, the Generals Hindenburg and Ludendorff had become military dictators, but they could not come up with a winning strategy. They had realized the war was irrevocably lost even before the Allied armies broke through German lines in the fall of 1918. Revolutions began breaking out all over Germany (see figure 13.4). The Social Democrats attempted to bring stability and to prevent a communist takeover by proclaiming a new republic. This republican Germany, governed by its elected representatives, has since become known as the **Weimar Republic**, after the city where politicians hammered out its constitution.

Gravely threatening the fragile Weimar Republic were the peace terms imposed by the victorious Allies. As mentioned at the beginning of the chapter, the whole first part of the Treaty of Versailles, which established the League of Nations, was an insult to the excluded Germans. The Germans could have expected to lose Alsace-Lorraine and a few bits of land to Belgium, but they also lost a chunk of territory to Denmark, which had not even participated in the war. In the west, they lost the Saar region to France for fifteen years. In the northeast, the city of Danzig fell under League control as a unique international city. Poland gained a section of land along the north coast of Germany. This Polish Corridor gave it access to the Baltic Sea but cut off the province of East Prussia from the rest of Germany. Even worse, the Germans were to disarm: no navy, no air force, and an army of only one hundred thousand men without tanks or heavy artillery.

As intended, such a force was insufficient to defend Germany, much less begin a war. A demilitarized Germany suited France. To further Germany's vulnerability, the western bank of the Rhineland (that side bordering France) was to be permanently demilitarized: devoid of troops and military installations. Thus, Germany could not easily invade France or Belgium, while France could march into Germany without trouble. To enforce these provisions, Allied troops were to occupy the Rhineland for fifteen years.

By Claude Shafer in the *Cincinnati Post.*

DOG-GONE IT.

Figure 13.4. This editorial cartoon by Claude Shafer, "Dog-gone it!," illustrates the dangers of unforeseen consequences. Germany did send the dog of revolution, namely the Bolshevik Lenin, to Russia. The Russian Revolution took that country out of the war, but the dog of revolution can go anywhere. After World War I, numerous revolutionary attempts broke out in Germany and elsewhere.

Worst of all, the Allies forced the Germans in part VIII, article 231, to accept guilt for the war and responsibility for causing all the war's destruction. As a consequence, the Allies felt justified in making the Germans pay reparations in compensation. The costs of the war had been so high, though, that it took two years for the Allies to add up and present their bill. In the meantime, under threat of a renewal of armed conflict and with a blockade still starving the country, the Allies forced the reluctant German representatives to sign the treaty on 28 June 1919, five years to the day after the assassination of Archduke Franz Ferdinand of Austria.

Paying close attention to these developments was the former corporal Adolf Hitler. After the war he stayed with the military, working for its intelligence agencies, gathering information on the numerous political parties that were springing up in the new Weimar Republic. He believed the propaganda that German forces would have won if socialists and Jews had not "stabbed them in the back." One day Hitler attended the disorganized meeting of a group calling itself the German Workers' Party. He soon seized control of the party, changing its name to the National Socialist German Workers' Party, or the **Nazis**. Hitler then reshaped the party's platform into ***Naziism*** or ***national socialism***, weaving together a powerful fascism with elements of racism, pan-germanism, nationalism, socialism, sexism, militarism, conservatism, and many other ideologies.

Hitler's love for Germany inspired a hatred for anything that he thought would weaken his nation in his eyes. He spelled out his chief goals in his 1924 autobiography, *Mein Kampf* (*My Struggle*). In his book Hitler argued that cultural diversity endangered Germany. He thought that Jews and Marxists threatened the superiority of the German race, or Aryans (drawn from a pseudo-scholarly name for the Indo-Europeans who had settled Europe).[5] To overcome this threat, he believed that he needed to become the dictator of Germany. A true German culture would then unify and strengthen the Germans as never before. Since other nations threatened the German purity, Germany needed to expand into eastern Europe and acquire sufficient *Lebensraum* (living space). In the same book and in speeches and writings throughout the 1920s and 1930s, Hitler laid out a vision of national revolution and international conquest. Who could not have seen his desire for war?

Nevertheless, many both in Germany and abroad did not, even when Hitler's first attempt to seize political power involved force. The opportunity seemed ideal when Germany was racked by horrible inflation. In 1921, the bill for war reparations totaled 269 billion marks (worth ninety-six thousand tons of gold or over 770 billion of today's US dollars). When the German government briefly stopped paying the reparations in 1923, the French marched across the Rhine and occupied the Ruhr, the industrial heartland of Germany. German workers went on strike, and the Berlin government simply kept printing money to keep the economy functioning. Without either gold reserves or industrial production to back it up, however, the mark fell in value. This disastrous inflation meant that one dollar, which in 1914 had bought about four marks, would buy four trillion marks in 1923. To stop the disaster, the rich Americans stepped in with the Dawes Plan: US banks would loan the money to recapitalize Germany, which would then pay the reparations to France, which could then use the money to pay back what it had borrowed from the United States during World War I. Thus, a stream of capital flowed through the economic veins of the West. The plan worked, ending the ruinous inflation.[6]

---

5. The Aryan "race" is not to be confused with the Arian heresy of Christianity.

6. Much of the original reparations were written off, and during the Great Depression Germany stopped paying anything for years. But after World War II and even more after reunification Germany finally paid off some of the bonds used to finance reparations. The final payment that closed Germany's books on the Great War was on 3 October 2010. Other bonds owed by other countries for war debts have still not yet been redeemed. Debt endures.

This inflation provoked political uprisings all over Germany. Among others, Hitler attempted a *putsch* (German for coup d'état) organized in a Munich beer hall to take over the province of Bavaria. The attempted coup failed miserably. Instead of executing Hitler for treason, however, the conservative court merely sentenced him to five years in prison. He served only nine months, using the time to write *Mein Kampf*. Released from prison with his party banned, nothing more should have been heard of him. He should not even have deserved the merest mention in this history.

But then the Great Depression brought a return of the economic collapse. The American capital necessary for the Dawes Plan disappeared. Economic collapse spread around the world as banks shut down, businesses went bankrupt, and unemployment skyrocketed. Germany suffered most of all. Hitler used the disruptions to revive his party and establish it as the center of political discourse. His Nazi party went from the ninth largest in 1930 to the single largest in parliament (the Reichstag) by 1932. Soon democracy had ceased to function in the Weimar Republic. One chancellor with emergency powers followed another as each failed to solve the economic crisis. On 30 January 1933, a coalition of nationalists and conservatives arranged for Hitler's appointment as chancellor.

Hitler then made sure that no remnants of parliamentary democracy would trouble him further. Hitler frightened the parliamentary majority into removing his rivals after a mentally imbalanced Dutch socialist committed arson on the Reichstag building. Once in Nazi hands, Hitler's Reichstag first outlawed the Communist Party (which, of course, had nothing to do with the arson but was the greatest rival to the Nazi party). In the next few months, the rump Reichstag outlawed every other political party. As for the remaining enemies of the new Nazi order? Within a few months, the Nazis started their first concentration camp at Dachau, near Munich. Into this camp, and many others that followed, the Nazis sent political prisoners (communists, socialists, and pacifists), religious prisoners (Roman Catholics, Lutherans, and Jehovah's Witnesses), behavioral prisoners (sex offenders, homosexuals), and racial prisoners (foreigners, Romany [Gypsies], and Jews).

After the communists and other political enemies had been dealt with, Hitler then had the chance to solve his "Jewish Problem," yet he hesitated. After some initial firings from government jobs, a few boycotts of Jewish businesses, and some assaults on Jews, official Nazi policies did not further harm the Jews for two years after 1933. Many Jews thought that perhaps they had seen the extent of Nazi discrimination. Nevertheless, the more fortunate Jews emigrated.

Worse did come. First, in September 1935, new laws that took away Jewish civil rights were issued from the party center of Nuremburg. Jews lost many rights of citizenship. In the next few years, more restrictions took away options for normal lives. The regime exaggerated the Jews' ethnic differences, preventing any possible assimilation. Jewish businesses were marked, then closed; Jewish physicians could not practice on Germans; Jewish lawyers were dismissed from courts; all male Jews had to take on the name "Israel" and female Jews the name "Sarah." During the night of 9–10 November 1938, thereafter remembered as Kristallnacht (Night of the Broken Glass) or the Novemberpogrom, an organized Nazi assault smashed businesses, burned synagogues, looted homes, desecrated cemeteries, and mur- dered hundreds of Jews (although many of the deaths were officially listed as sui- cides). Those Jews who still wished to emigrate were allowed—if they could pay and if they could find a place to go. Few other countries wanted Jews. Even the British invitation to Palestine was withdrawn in 1939. The international outcry was minimal. The great powers were more concerned with Hitler's other plans that were slowly becoming more obvious.

Review: *How did Hitler rise to power and change Germany?*

Response:

SOURCES ON FAMILIES: JOSEPH GOEBBELS, "GERMAN WOMANHOOD" (1933)

The Nazis considered their takeover of the German government at the end of Janu- ary 1933 as a revolution that ended the so-called Weimar regime and began a national revival along racist principles. On March 18, the propaganda minister Joseph Goebbels opened an exhibit in Berlin on "Die Frau" (which can be trans- lated as the "Mrs.," "wife," or "woman"). In his speech, Goebbels laid out the Nazi vision for the role of women in the new Third Reich.

German Women, German Men!

I would like to see this moment as a fortunate coincidence, that I should pres- ent my first public speech directly to German women since taking over the Ministry of the People's Enlightenment and Propaganda. If I should acknowledge [the histo- rian] Treitschke's saying, that "men make history," I do not thereby forget, that it is the women who raise our youngsters to be men. It is certainly known to you: the national-socialistic movement, as the only party, keeps women far from being directly involved in daily politics. The party has, as a result, been in many ways bitterly attacked and demonized, and all that is an injustice. It is not because we do not respect women, but rather because we respect them so much, that we have kept them far from the parliamentarian/democratic quarrels which have shaped politics for the last fourteen years in Germany. Not because we see in women some- thing useless, but rather because we see in her and her mission something useful for a different purpose, than that which men fulfill.

. . . Nobody, who understands modern times, could conceive of the ridiculous idea to drive women out of public life, out of jobs, professions, being breadwinners.

But it must not be left unsaid, that matters which are appropriate to men, must stay with men. And to such belongs politics and the military. . . .

If we took a fleeting glance at the last few years of German decline, then we would come to the fruitful, almost overwhelming conclusion, that so little were German men determined to prove themselves in public life as men, so much more did it fall to women to take on man's duty instead. A feminization of the man always leads to a masculinization of the woman. . . .

At the risk of sounding reactionary and traditionalistic, let me say it clearly and baldly: the first, best, and most suitable place for a woman is in the family, and the most wonderful task which she can fulfill, is to give children to her country and people, children, who carry forward the generations and the immortality of the nation. . . .

The liberal attitude toward family and child is complicit in Germany sinking so low within a few years, so that already today one can speak of the impending extinction of our people. While in the year 1900 one mature person had seven children, today one can expect only four children. If such birth rates remain the same, the ratio in the year 1988 would be one-to-one.

We are not willing to stare blankly and with crossed arms at the collapse of our culture and the destruction of our genetic substance passed on through our bloodlines. . . .

The new German women's movement begins here. If the nation again has mothers, who profess themselves freely and proudly to motherhood, then the nation cannot perish. If the woman is healthy, so are the people healthy. Woe to the state which forgets to care for the wife and mother.

Questions:

- *What does the source declare as the main role of women within society?*
- *What evidence does the source bring to support this need?*
- *How much are these values based in tradition or racism?*

Responses:

Citation

Goebbels, Joseph. "Deutsches Frauentum." *Signale der neuen Zeit: 25 ausgewählten Reden von Joseph Goebbels*. 8th ed. Munich: Zentralverlag der NSDAP, 1940, pp. 118–26. (Translated by Brian A. Pavlac.)

For more on this source, go to http://www.concisewesternciv.com/sources/sof13 .html.

THE ROADS TO GLOBAL WAR

World War II can easily be seen as a continuation of World War I. That first great conflict did not resolve the pesky "German problem": how do you cope with a powerful, aggressive united Germany in the heart of Europe? Legacies of imperialism and nationalism remained harmful to peace. The nationalist aspirations of many peoples in Europe and around the world remained unfulfilled. The harsh competition produced by industrial manufacturing continued to set nations against one another. War still remained a popular solution for resolving differences.

Not surprisingly, many democratic peoples around the world did not want another world war. The potential death and destruction brought on by several great powers fighting again transformed many thinking people into pacifists. The two democratic European great powers, Great Britain and France, had been badly frightened by the horrors of that first Great War and the realization of their own fragility.

Meanwhile, westernization in East Asia was laying the foundations for a new, greater war. Imperialism's intervention destabilized the two-thousand-year-old Chinese Empire. Uprisings against the imperial regime had continued after the Boxer Rebellion in 1901. By the end of 1911, rebels had toppled the last emperor of China (which the child did not even notice, as he was so isolated in the Forbidden City). The first president of the Republic of China was the Western-educated and -trained **Sun Yatsen** (b. 1886–d. 1925). Sun had for years been planting the seeds for a democratic China, organizing the **Nationalist Party** (abbreviated as GMD or KMT).[7] He had designed the party along Western lines by incorporating ideals of nationalism, republicanism, and socialism. His democratically inclined methods proved too fragile, however. A few weeks after Sun had been sworn in on 1 January 1912, a general forced him out of the presidency and took power. Even so, the new military dictator could not prevent more uprisings, leaving much of China under the sway of local warlords.

Japan took the opportunity to replace Western imperialists in China, as World War I distracted the European great powers. The Japanese had learned from Western imperialism about the importance of colonial possessions. Many Japanese leaders now felt called to rule East Asia and the Pacific. Japan joined the Allies at the beginning of World War I and took over the German extraterritorial privileges in China. Japan soon began to consider that problematic country its special protectorate.

The postwar period went less well for Japan, as the Western powers sought to rein in its expansionist tendencies. The Japanese resented the disarmament conference held in Washington, DC (1921–1922), which restricted the Japanese navy to

---

7. Chinese and Japanese personal and family names are traditionally in reverse order compared with Western names. Thus Sun was his family name and Yatsen his personal or familiar name. Also, the difference between GMD and KMT or other names comes from a change in the late twentieth century in how to transliterate Chinese characters into the Latin alphabet. In this text, the more modern is listed first, although the second version is still frequently seen.

being at a lower rank than the British and American navies. The Japanese were insulted by racist American laws limiting Japanese immigration. Then the Great Depression struck Japan in 1930 with all the fury that had wiped out businesses in the United States. Many Japanese blamed the resultant unemployment and social disorder on their European-style parliamentarianism. Consequently, many Japanese adopted Western fascism. Japanese fascists wanted to establish a new, revived, glorious Japan, this time with imperial domination of Asia. Intimidation and assassination silenced the critics as the Japanese military gradually came to dominate the government.

Japan's fascists knew their opportunity to dominate China was limited, since China had begun to achieve stability under the leadership of the Nationalists. After being ousted from the presidency, Sun rebuilt his own political base against the warlords by using the Nationalist Party and some new allies. One ally was Russia, which Sun's protégé, **Jiang Jei-shei** or **Chiang Kai-shek** (b. 1886–d. 1975), had visited in order to learn modern Soviet military organization. Sun's Nationalist Party also allied with the fledgling Chinese Communist Party. Founded in 1921 and inspired by the Bolsheviks, Chinese communism was another successful Western export to Asia. In 1927, after Sun's death, Jiang became leader of the GMD, attacked many warlords, and, unexpectedly, defeated most of them. Along the way, he also attacked his former allies, the communists, driving the survivors into a distant province in the southeast. By 1928, Jiang began to urge the Western powers to give up their oppressive extraterritoriality treaties and recognize China as an equal, sovereign great power.

The interaction of nationalism, imperialism, and communism complicated China's politics. Since the communists had withdrawn to rural southern China, one of their leaders, **Mao Zedong** (b. 1893–d. 1976), began to adapt to the needs of the Chinese peasants, especially focusing on land reform. Then the communists survived a second attack by Jiang's Nationalists through their legendary "Long March" of 1934–1945. The communists retreated for thousands of miles until they reached a haven in the far north. At the same time, the Japanese seized the province of Manchuria from China. After Jiang's government appealed to the League of Nations, an investigatory committee looked into the matter and weakly criticized the Japanese aggression. In reaction, Japan became more belligerent. In 1937, a minor incident at the Marco Polo Bridge in Beijing (named after the medieval Italian traveler to China) prompted the Japanese to launch a full-scale invasion. Japan's attack on the city of Nanking in December 1937 viciously slaughtered almost half the city's population of six hundred thousand. The violation of tens of thousands of Chinese women gave the assault its name: the Rape of Nanking. The rest of the world, including the Western powers, watched and did nothing. They did not realize that this war between two Asian great powers was the beginning of **World War II** (1937–1945), which was soon to engulf them all.

Britain and France were more concerned with German aggression in Europe, although even there they took no action. The French hoped that their Maginot Line, a series of complex and expensive fortifications begun even before Hitler came to power, would stop any possible German attack. In 1935, Hitler began to openly rearm Germany, directly violating the Treaty of Versailles. In 1936, he remilitarized the Rhineland, completely ending the imposed restrictions of the treaty. In March 1938, he bullied fascist Austria into agreeing to annexation, or **Anschluß**. When Austria's chancellor tried to hold a referendum to preserve Austrian independence, German troops simply marched into the country. Most people in Austria and abroad accepted the fait accompli. Austrians who openly objected wound up dead or in concentration camps. Then in the fall of 1938 at the **Munich Conference**, Hitler got the British, French, and Italians to sign off on his annexation of the Sudeten-land, an ethnic German part of Czecho-slovakia. After that agreement, most ethnic Germans in Europe lived under Hitler's authority. The "rump" Czecho-slovakia meanwhile had lost the ability to defend itself.

The inaction of the great powers concerning the events both in Asia and in Europe has often been attacked as **appeasement**. The word simply describes a policy of giving in to an aggressive government's demands rather than fighting. It has become a term implying weakness and failure because, with hindsight, these actions made Japan and Germany better prepared for war. At the time, though, Western leaders saw appeasement as a reasonable approach. Not every issue is worth a war. When it came to Hitler's demands, why should Germany not be armed as every other nation was? Why should Germany not reasonably occupy and defend its own territory? How could anyone say that Germany should not include all ethnic Germans?

After the easy annexation of the Sudetenland, though, Hitler's demands ceased being reasonable, even under nationalist principles. Western leaders finally recognized Hitler's desire for *Lebensraum*, despite promises of peace (see Primary Source Project 13). In the spring of 1939, Hitler enticed or coerced the Slovaks into declaring independence from Czecho-slovakia. That act provided his excuse to occupy the remaining Czechs. For the first time he had annexed substantial numbers of non-Germans, acting as an imperialist instead of a nationalist. This action finally woke up France and Britain to Hitler's expansionism. While France and Britain were not prepared to go to war for Czecho-slovakia, they did pledge their support to Poland, which seemed Hitler's next likely target (because of the Polish Corridor and Danzig). Not many noticed or cared about Mussolini's conquest of Albania in April 1939.

Hitler laid the foundation for further acquisitions in eastern Europe in a brilliant diplomatic maneuver. The deadly rivals Nazi Germany and Communist Russia signed a nonaggression pact in late summer 1939. These newfound allies secretly divided eastern Europe into spheres of influence between them. Free from worrying about a possible two-front war, which hurt Germany in World War I, Hitler could now do what he wanted. He invaded Poland on 1 September 1939, beginning the European phase of World War II.

Although Britain and France declared war two days later, there was little they could do to save Poland. Hitler's generals were able to test their *Blitzkrieg* (lightning war) tactics to great success (see diagrams 13.1–13.4). Coordination of air power and tanks solved the problem of maneuvering large armies. These tactics (and Russia's attack from the east) eliminated Polish forces in a matter of weeks.

Germany at first seemed to have all the advantages. Britain and France sat through the "Sitzkrieg" (meaning "sitting war," a word play on *Blitzkrieg*) of the

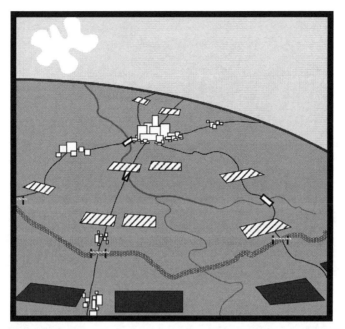

Diagram 13.1. Blitzkrieg, Phase 1. Before the Blitzkrieg-style warfare begins, black and striped military units face each other across a border.

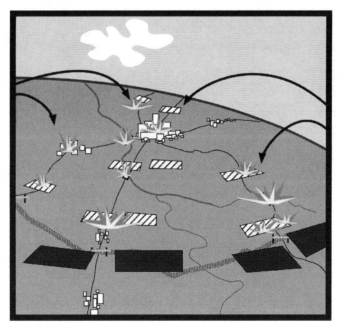

Diagram 13.2. Blitzkrieg, Phase 2. As attacking black ground forces advance, black's bombers strike far behind the lines to break up enemy units, disrupt lines of transportation and communication, and even bomb civilians in the cities, causing panic and confusion.

Diagram 13.3. Blitzkrieg, Phase 3. Attacking black tank forces both confront enemy forces and go around them cross-country. Small commando units seize or build river crossings to enable larger armies to cross.

Diagram 13.4. Blitzkrieg, Phase 4. Aerial bombing, artillery shelling, and flanking and encirclement by black armies have fragmented the defending striped forces. Infantry mops up the remains.

winter of 1939–1940, while Russia defeated plucky Finland to grab key defensive positions. With the spring thaw, Hitler surprised everyone with an attack on Denmark and Norway. Victory came quickly, first because effective use of paratroops enabled the Nazis to seize key locations. Second, native fascists, sympathetic with Nazi Aryan ideology, operated as "fifth columnists" (implying an extra group of troops on the inside) or "quislings" (named after the Norwegian fascist leader) to help the Nazis into the countries. Hitler thus solved another problem of World War I: Norway's ports on the Atlantic ensured that Germany could not be successfully blockaded, while its U-boats (submarines) could attempt to blockade Britain.

The new British prime minister, **Winston Churchill** (r. 1940–1945, 1951–1955) was barely in office when German armies attacked Holland, Belgium, France, and Luxembourg. The Germans evaded France's Maginot Line by punching tanks through the ill-defended Ardennes Forest. Like Poland, France fell in weeks. The British and a handful of allied forces managed to flee from Dunkirk (on the French coast) back to England, leaving much of their weaponry behind. By the fall of 1940, Hitler tried to soften up England for invasion with the **Battle of Britain**, the first decisive air battle in history. Britain won this battle (partly due to the new invention of radar). Since Germany lacked the air cover to protect a sea-to-land assault, Britain gained time to recover and rearm. The prospect of defeating Germany alone, however, seemed bleak.

By this time, Hitler ruled most of Europe, with the largest empire since Napoleon's. If he had remained satisfied with these gains, the course of world history would have been much different. Nothing less would satisfy him, however, than German mastery of all Eurasia. Impatient and confident in his previous successes, Hitler betrayed and attacked his ally, the USSR, on 22 June 1941. His surprise attack was at first brilliantly successful.

With Britain still at his rear, Hitler launched a two-front war. Regrettably for Hitler, serious errors slowed his invasion of the Soviet Union. Britain was strong enough to help Russia with supplies. The vastness of Russia, as Napoleon had learned, made it nearly impossible for armies to find and defeat all the Russian forces. At first, many peoples in Russia actually welcomed the German armies as liberators from the brutality of Stalin. Quickly, though, the Germans showed that they were Nazis, dedicated to enslaving or killing all non-Aryans. Peoples of the Soviet Union learned that there was something worse than Stalinism.

As the German offensive against Russia bogged down in the muddy fall of 1941, several eager Nazis returned to their obsession about the Jewish Problem. They came up with a **Final Solution**: killing all Jews. As a result, the Nazis built several special camps in occupied Poland to which they shipped the Jews from their ghettoes. In camps like Auschwitz, Treblinka, and Sobibor, the Nazis stole the Jews' last possessions, killed them in gas chambers, and burned their corpses in crematoria. The resulting deaths of millions of Jews have been named the **Holocaust** (Greek for burnt sacrifice) or **Shoah** (Hebrew for disaster). Some people these days, calling themselves "revisionist historians," deny the reality of this slaughter. They say it didn't happen; the Nazis did not try to execute all the Jews. Such people are either fools or liars. The Final Solution was as real as the rest of World War II. It is an indisputable fact of history. Given enough time, the Nazis would have killed every

Jew they could have laid their hands on, followed by the extermination of other racial and social enemies. The only thing that stopped this Nazi genocide was losing the war.

Germany lost this war because, just as during World War I, its opponents built alliances to outnumber and outfight it. Before the war, Hitler built superior alliances. Germany had named itself and its allies the Axis Powers, including hapless Italy, energetic Japan, and reactionary Spain, which, however, stayed out of the war. During the war, the only truly willing allies were the resentful states of Hungary (angry about its small size after World War I), Bulgaria (simmering over its losses in the Balkan Wars), and Finland (having suffered Stalin's attack in 1939). In the end, the lack of cooperation among the Axis Powers doomed them. If Japan had invaded Russia, a two-front war might have brought down the Soviet Union. Instead, Japan decided to attack Great Britain and the United States of America.

Axis attacks made building a coalition of opposing Allies much easier. After Hitler had treacherously attacked Russia, Churchill quickly allied with Stalin, despite concern about communism. Churchill also successfully cultivated the American president, Roosevelt (see Primary Source Project 13). Churchill and FDR went so far as to sign the **Atlantic Charter** in the fall of 1941. This document proclaimed their mutual support and set generous goals for a postwar world, even though the United States was not yet in the war. Indeed, most Americans were isolationist, thinking it just fine if communists and fascists and Asians fought each other.

Then, on 7 December 1941, the Japanese launched planes from aircraft carriers and bombed the American military base at **Pearl Harbor** in Hawaii. They also attacked other British and American bases in the western Pacific. The attack on Pearl Harbor, though bold and successful in its immediate goal, was a strategic blunder. Attacking Britain made some sense: England could barely defend itself, much less its worldwide possessions. Bringing the United States into the war, however, doomed Japan. Americans saw the planes flown against Pearl Harbor as unjustified, especially since the bombing had taken place before a formal declaration of war. In the words of one of their own commanders, the Japanese had awakened a sleeping giant. The outraged Americans would never have stopped fighting to avenge the death of 2,600 soldiers and sailors until Japan was utterly defeated.

The entry of the United States into World War II was the beginning of the end. The vast industrial potential of the country and its determination to avenge Pearl Harbor guaranteed an Allied victory. Then, a few days after Pearl Harbor, Hitler made the worst mistake of his career. Without any real necessity, he declared war on the United States. This relieved Roosevelt of a huge dilemma. He had wanted to help Britain in Europe but could not easily ask Congress to authorize what would be a two-front war. Thus, even though America was committed to the War in the Pacific because of Pearl Harbor, Hitler's overconfident declaration brought the United States into the European conflict as well.

America was strong enough to fight, and win, a global war alongside the other Allies (see map 13.1). The United States fully unfolded its vast economic power, helping to equip the Allies and fighting major conflicts both in Europe and in Asia at once. By the summer of 1942, the Japanese were overstretched by the conquest of most British, Dutch, and American possessions in the Pacific. Counterattacking

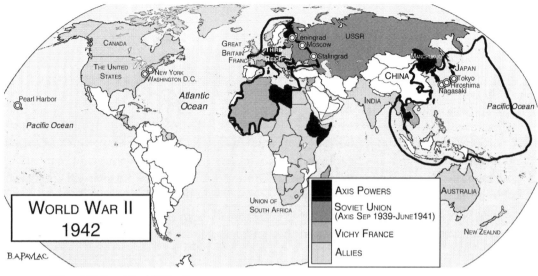

Map 13.1. World War II.
What geographical challenges did the Axis Powers face in their quest for world domination?

American forces began hopping from island group to island group, learning their own jungle combat and using aircraft carriers to help cut Japanese communications and supplies. The battles in the Pacific were small in scale compared with the hundreds of thousands of men on the Russian front, but the fighting was brutal and nasty. Jungle heat and tropical disease sorely afflicted both sides. Still, defeat was inevitable, even though the Japanese resisted to the last soldier on almost every island.

In the fall of 1943, the tide turned in Europe, as American forces began to liberate North Africa and the Russians enmeshed the Germans in the Battle of Stalingrad. By early 1944, German armies were in slow yet inevitable retreat. D-Day, or the Normandy invasion by the Allies (6 June 1944), saw the largest sea-to-land assault in human history. Axis regimes ran out of fuel and raw materials to produce armaments and also suffered from a lack of workers to use them. Allied heavy bombers, the British by night and the Americans by day, were sparking firestorms, setting entire cities on fire. In one night of bombing, a modern city could be reduced to rubble, while tens of thousands of civilians, including old men, women, and children, died in their bomb shelters from heat or suffocation.

Nazi scientists had, for a while, hoped for "wonder weapons" to bring victory. Jets and rockets were put into action too little, too late. Another possibility had been a city-destroying device: an **atomic bomb**. German leadership in the study of physics had given the Nazis a great head start in the science for such a weapon. Instead, America built the bomb first. The most brilliant physicist of the century, Albert Einstein, had fled from Nazi Germany to America because of Hitler's persecution of Jews. Einstein wrote to President Roosevelt to encourage America to construct an atomic bomb before the Nazis could. The Nazis never came close to building such a weapon. By May 1945, Germany had been conquered. Hitler was

dead from suicide, his body only partially cremated in a ditch because his last followers lacked enough gasoline.

After the defeat of Germany, Japan still fought on. In July 1945, American scientists successfully tested their "Trinity" atomic device, applying a divine name to a
weapon of mass destruction. On 6 August, America dropped one bomb on Hiroshima; on 9 August, another bomb on Nagasaki followed (see figure 13.5). The
bombs accomplished what previously had taken hundreds of bombers dropping
thousands of bombs. The two cities were incinerated in a flash: tens of thousands
of people killed, many thousands more wounded—and suffering from the little-
known phenomenon of radiation. Japan finally surrendered on 14 August 1945.
Thus, the worst instantaneous destruction in human history ended the worst war
in human history. The United States stood at the helm of Western civilization, now
able to lead it into the rest of the century.

Figure 13.5.   A lonely church on a hill remains from the devastated city
of Nagasaki after the second atomic bomb was dropped on Japan by the
United States.

Review: How did the German and Japanese desire for world empires shape World War II?

Response:

PRIMARY SOURCE PROJECT 13: HITLER VERSUS FRANKLIN D. ROOSEVELT ABOUT THE JUST SOCIETY

As nations prepared for World War II, leaders offered their ideological perspectives for fighting. Chancellor and Führer Adolf Hitler of Germany asserted his peaceful intentions but noted threats to his people. Once the war had begun, President Franklin Delano Roosevelt called on Americans to support nations fighting against Hitler. He also set forth his view of measures needed for a just society.

Source 1: Speech to the Reichstag by Adolf Hitler (30 January 1939)

When, six years ago this evening, tens of thousands of National Socialist fighters marched through the Brandenburg Gate in the light of their torches to express to me, who had just been appointed Chancellor of the Reich, their feeling of overwhelming joy and their vows as faithful followers, countless anxious eyes all over Germany and in Berlin gazed upon the beginning of a development, the end of which still seemed unknown and unpredictable. . . .

But one thing remains unforgotten: It seemed that only a miracle in the twelfth hour could save Germany. We National Socialists believed in this miracle. Our opponents ridiculed our belief in it. The idea of redeeming the nation from a decline extending over fifteen years simply by the power of a new idea seemed to the non-National Socialists fantastic nonsense. . . .

To the Jews and the other enemies of the State, however, it appeared to be the last flicker of the national power of resistance. And they felt that when it had disappeared, then they would be able to destroy not only Germany but all Europe as well. Had the German Reich sunk into Bolshevik chaos, it would at that very moment have plunged the whole of Western civilization into a crisis of inconceivable magnitude. . . .

Gentlemen, we are faced with enormous and stupendous tasks. A new history of the leadership of our nation must be constructed. Its composition is dependent on race. . . .

What is the root cause of all our economic difficulties? It is the overpopulation of our territory. . . .

But to assume that God has permitted some nations first to acquire a world by force and then to defend this robbery with moralizing theories is perhaps comforting and above all comfortable for the "haves," but not for the "have-nots." . . . Nor is the problem solved by the fact that a most important statesman simply declares with a scornful grin that there are nations which are "haves" and that the others on that account must always be "have-nots." . . .

[I]n connection with the Jewish question, I have this to say: It is a shameful spectacle to see how the whole democratic world is oozing sympathy for the poor tormented Jewish people, but remains hard-hearted and obdurate when it comes to helping them, which is surely, in view of its attitude, an obvious duty. The arguments that are brought up as an excuse for not helping them actually speak for us as Germans and Italians. . . .

Today I will once more be a prophet. If the international Jewish financiers in and outside Europe should succeed in plunging the nations once more into a world war, then the result will not be the bolshevization of the earth, and this the victory of Jewry, but the annihilation of the Jewish race in Europe! . . . At the moment Jews in certain countries may be fomenting hatred under the protection of the press, of the film, of wireless propaganda, of the theater, of literature, etc., all of which they control. . . .

Source 2: Annual State of the Union Report to Congress by Franklin Delano Roosevelt (6 January 1941)

I have recently pointed out how quickly the tempo of modern warfare could bring into our very midst the physical attack which we must eventually expect if the dictator nations win this war.

That is why the future of all the American Republics is today in serious danger.

That is why this Annual Message to the Congress is unique in our history. . . .

The need of the moment is that our actions and our policy should be devoted primarily—almost exclusively—to meeting this foreign peril. For all our domestic problems are now a part of the great emergency. . . .

I also ask this Congress for authority and for funds sufficient to manufacture additional munitions and war supplies of many kinds, to be turned over to those nations which are now in actual war with aggressor nations.

Our most useful and immediate role is to act as an arsenal for them as well as for ourselves. They do not need man power, but they do need billions of dollars worth of the weapons of defense. . . .

Certainly this is no time for any of us to stop thinking about the social and economic problems which are the root cause of the social revolution which is today a supreme factor in the world.

For there is nothing mysterious about the foundations of a healthy and strong democracy. The basic things expected by our people of their political and economic systems are simple. They are:

> Equality of opportunity for youth and for others.
> Jobs for those who can work.
> Security for those who need it.
> The ending of special privilege for the few.
> The preservation of civil liberties for all.

The enjoyment of the fruits of scientific progress in a wider and constantly rising standard of living . . .

In the future days, which we seek to make secure, we look forward to a world founded upon four essential human freedoms.

The first is freedom of speech and expression—everywhere in the world.

The second is freedom of every person to worship God in his own way—everywhere in the world.

The third is freedom from want—which, translated into world terms, means economic understandings which will secure to every nation a healthy peacetime life for its inhabitants—everywhere in the world.

The fourth is freedom from fear—which, translated into world terms, means a worldwide reduction of armaments to such a point and in such a thorough fashion that no nation will be in a position to commit an act of physical aggression against any neighbor—anywhere in the world.

That is no vision of a distant millennium. It is a definite basis for a kind of world attainable in our own time and generation. That kind of world is the very antithesis of the so-called new order of tyranny which the dictators seek to create with the crash of a bomb.

To that new order we oppose the greater conception—the moral order. A good society is able to face schemes of world domination and foreign revolutions alike without fear.

Since the beginning of our American history, we have been engaged in change—in a perpetual peaceful revolution—a revolution which goes on steadily, quietly adjusting itself to changing conditions—without the concentration camp or the quick-lime in the ditch. The world order which we seek is the cooperation of free countries, working together in a friendly, civilized society.

Questions:

- *According to the speakers, what are the dangers facing their nations?*
- *How does each speaker propose to overcome those dangers?*
- *How do the speakers see themselves and their nations at turning points?*

Responses:

Make your own timeline.

1917   **1945**

Citations

"Speech Delivered by Adolf Hitler before the German Reichstag on January 30, 1939." N.p., n.d. Internet Archive. Accessed 1 September 2014. https://archive .org/details/SpeechOfJan.301939.

Roosevelt, Franklin D. *Annual Message to Congress, January 6, 1941*. Records of the United States Senate; SEN 77A-H1, Record Group 46, National Archives.

For more on these sources, go to http://www.concisewesternciv.com/sources/psc13 .html.

CHAPTER 14

A World Divided

The Early Cold War, 1945 to 1980

T he resounding victory of the Allies in World War II did not lead to international stability, as expected and hoped for. Instead, a new kind of conflict,
the **Cold War** (1948–1991), dominated most of the latter half of the twentieth century. The Cold War resembled the long geopolitical competition between
France and England that had lasted from the fourteenth to the nineteenth century.
This time, two new primary enemies, the United States and the USSR, wrestled for
world domination and threatened everyone else as never before. Their ideological
points of view made it difficult to compromise or cooperate. During this colossal
conflict between different aspects of Western civilization, the Cold War drew nearly
every person on the planet into the influence of Western science, politics, economics, and culture.

FROM FRIENDS TO FOES

After the devastation of World War II, the first challenge for all states was the restoration of order and the reconstruction of economies. Much of Europe and Asia lay in
ruins. Among the survivors, tens of millions of people had been displaced as soldiers, prisoners, forced laborers, or refugees. The millions of Germans who fled
or were forcibly ejected from areas subsequently occupied by Russia, Poland, or
Czechoslovakia gained little sympathy. Some nations began to carry out ethnic
removals to bring about nationalistic conformity. Yugoslavia kicked out Italians.
Even Bulgaria and Greece seized the opportunity to expel thousands of Turks, even
though Turkey had remained neutral during the war. Never before had such numbers of people been forced to migrate. Most displaced persons lacked homes and
jobs, although many states became much more ethnically uniform, as nationalistic
ideals demanded. The Allied armies that occupied the defeated nations organized
the slow rebuilding of their societies and suppressed the fascist policies that had
caused the war.

The victorious Allies showcased the defeat of the fascists by conducting trials
for war crimes against humanity. The slaughter and genocide of civilians during the

war were considered so horrific that the victors undertook the unusual measure of convening international courts. As a result of the **Nuremburg Trials** in Germany, twenty-five captured Nazi leaders were hanged. Over the next several years a few dozen lower-ranking Nazis also faced judgment and execution.

Not all fascist criminals came to justice, however. Some Nazi sympathizers, collaborators, and even high-ranking officials managed to escape, many fleeing to sympathetic fascist regimes in Latin America, sometimes with the knowledge of local governments. In particular, Nazi scientists, especially those responsible for work on rockets and jets, were smuggled to one victor or another. In Asia, the trials for Japanese war criminals were much less thorough. Emperor Hirohito of Japan had declared himself no longer a god, so the American occupiers retained him in office and absolved him of all blame for the war and atrocities committed by Japanese soldiers. Comparatively few Japanese war crimes were exposed or punished, especially since the United States was becoming less concerned about its wartime enemy, Japan, than about its wartime ally, Russia.

That the victorious wartime alliance fell apart so quickly surprised and confused many. Certainly the victory in World War II created a unique geopolitical situation. The great powers, powerful countries who could assert military action around the world, had dominated international politics since the nineteenth century. By the end of World War II, though, England and its British Empire were clearly exhausted by the effort. France needed to rebuild, as did China, after suffering hard occupations. Of course, defeated Germany, Italy, and Japan lay in ruins and were occupied by the Allies. Only the United States and the Soviet Union remained capable of effective global action. Indeed, they had risen to the status of **superpowers**. They had large populations (over a hundred million), were industrialized, occupied vast continental landmasses, were rich in agricultural land and natural resources, and possessed massive military forces. The other declining great powers could not hope to match them.

Almost equal in power, the United States and the USSR were nevertheless divided by opposing ideologies (see diagram 14.1). The Soviet Union was a totalitarian dictatorship with a secret police, the KGB; the United States worked along more

	Politics	Economy	Society	Culture	Belief
USSR	totalitarian soviet one party	centralized, state-planned economy communism	classless society (party elites vs. masses) free public education	rigid censorship state-controlled press and arts	atheism persecuted Russian Orthodox
USA	democratic vs republican two parties	mixed economy: laissez-faire capitalism & socialism	upper middle lower classes private & public education	limited censorship free press profit-making arts	religious toleration separation of church & state nominally Christian

Diagram 14.1. This comparison and contrast between the United States of America and the Union of Soviet Socialist Republics notes how they represented different aspects of the Western heritage which competed for people's allegiance during the Cold War.

republican and constitutionalist principles. The USSR used centralized state planning for its economy (often called communism); the United States practiced capitalism in a mixed economy of some socialistic regulation and competitive, semi-free markets.[1] Russia proclaimed itself to have outgrown nationalistic and class divisions (although its party elites led a substantially better life than its common workers); the United States, despite a growing middle class, remained divided into significant economic disparities between rich and poor, often based on sex, ethnicity, and race. The Russian government rigidly controlled and censored its media; businesses, through their advertising dollars, influenced the American media. The Union of Soviet Socialist Republics proudly proclaimed itself to be atheistic (ostensibly believing in the dogmas of Marx, Lenin, and Stalin) and restricted worship by Orthodox Christians; the United States of America asserted religious freedom and toleration, while the majority of citizens attended diverse Christian churches. Communist Russia lost sight of the individual in its mania for the collective—many suffered so the group might succeed; capitalist America awkwardly juggled individual rights and communal responsibility.

The differences in these practices and ideologies did not necessarily mean that a conflict was inevitable. Both sides could have decided to live and let live. Yet both sides envisioned their own path as the only suitable way of life for everyone on earth. Each state tried to dominate the world with its own vision of order, echoing the clashes of the past, whether between the Athenian creative individualism versus Spartan disciplined egalitarianism of the Peloponnesian Wars or revolutionary France against commercial Great Britain during the Wars of the Coalitions. The world split up between them. The United States and its allies often called themselves "the West." The Soviet Union and its allies were often called the "Eastern bloc" because of their center in Eastern Europe or from their association with China in East Asia. A more accurate terminology arose of the "First World" (the nations associated with the United States), the "Second World" (the nations associated with the Soviet Union), and the "Third World" (Latin America and the soon to be newly liberated colonial areas of Asia and Africa).

The splits between these blocs widened during Allied planning conferences as World War II wound down. First, in February 1945 at the Soviet Black Sea resort of **Yalta**, the "Big Three"—Stalin for the Soviet Union, Roosevelt for the United States, and Churchill for Britain—began to seriously plan for the postwar world after their inevitable victory. They agreed in principle that Europe would be divided into spheres of influence, thus applying the language of imperialism to Europe itself. Southern Europe went to the British, while much of Eastern Europe came under the Russian sphere. Under the guidance of the British and Russians, self-government in different nations was supposed to be restored. The only sphere the United States committed itself to was joining Britain and Russia in occupying Germany.

---

1. As part of this ideological war, the term *capitalism* was redefined to oppose the "communism" of central planning of the economy by government. Thus, today many people define capitalism as the private ownership of the means of production instead of its simpler definition as the practice of reinvesting profits. Soviet-style "communism" likewise differed from Marx's ideal of common ownership.

After Germany's defeat but before Japan's surrender, the "Big Three" met again at **Potsdam** near Berlin in July 1945, although two of the leaders had been replaced. Stalin still represented the USSR, but Churchill had been voted out as prime minister and replaced by Labour Party leader Clement Atlee. In the United States, **Harry Truman** (r. 1945–1953) succeeded to the American presidency following the death of FDR in April. These three men shaped up plans for German occupation (adding France as a fourth occupier), *denazification* and the war crimes trials, restoration and occupation of a separate Austria, and peace treaties for the minor Axis members. While many questions remained open, the settlements seemed to be going well.

One more hope for a unified future of the world was an institution that had been created by the victorious Allies to prevent new conflict, the **United Nations Organization** (UN). The United Nations Charter was first signed in San Francisco on 26 June 1945, as war still raged in Asia. The five victors of World War II (the United States, the USSR, Great Britain, France, and, generously, China), became the permanent members of the Security Council, with veto power over the organization's actions. The UN could provide some international regulations and help with health-care issues. More importantly, when the Security Council agreed, the UN's members could quickly and easily commit military forces. Its hope was to use collective security to maintain peace. The UN's peacekeeping role has indeed managed to keep many wars and rebellions from growing worse around the world. From the Congo to Cyprus, peacekeepers have saved lives, but the UN can solve an issue only if and when all five permanent members of the Security Council agree unanimously.

Soon enough, the superpowers diverged, as the temptations of occupation proved too strong for Stalin. Stalin soon began *sovietization* of the states in his sphere of influence (Poland, Czechoslovakia, Hungary, Romania, Bulgaria, and its occupied zones of Germany). Believing it his right to have friendly neighbors in Eastern Europe, Stalin helped communist parties take over governments, which then claimed to be people's democratic republics. As in the Soviet Union, these regimes lacked opposition parties but still conducted elections. The new communist leaders terrorized their people into fearful obedience. They reeducated, arrested, or executed "class enemies" such as fascists, but also liberals, conservatives, and socialists. They even purged their own followers, putting communist comrades in show trials just to show that no one was safe. Using the excuse of rebuilding from the war's devastation, communist governments nationalized businesses and property. As the Soviet armies stayed and the new leaders of Eastern European states took direction from Moscow, these "satellite" or "puppet" states were becoming protectorates rather than merely falling under a sphere of influence. These changes led the retired British prime minister Winston Churchill to use the metaphor of the "Iron Curtain" separating communist oppression from "Christian civilization" (see map 14.1).

At first, Americans ignored Churchill's warning. Nonetheless, growing communist-backed insurgencies in Greece and Turkey encouraged the Americans to adopt Churchill's concerns. Soviet intervention in these new areas convinced American leaders that Stalin was expanding beyond the provisions of Yalta and Potsdam. President Truman decided to carry out a policy called **containment** to try

Map 14.1. Cold War Europe.
How did Europe divided between NATO and the Warsaw Pact reflect the
interests and fears of the USA and the USSR?

to limit the influence of the Soviet Union in several ways. In his speech creating the
Truman Doctrine, he promised aid to governments resisting hostile seizures of
power by foreigners or even by armed minorities of natives. He explicitly contrasted
the freedom of the United States with the tyranny of Russia. The United States
followed up with military aid to the Greeks and Turks, who crushed the insurgencies. Through the Marshall Plan (or European Recovery Program) the United States
also provided money to European states struggling with a lack of capital in the wake
of the war. A small American investment of $13 billion helped rebuild Europe and
weaken the appeal of communism. To further combat communism, a new American
Central Intelligence Agency (CIA) gathered information and carried out covert
operations outside the United States (including supporting armed intervention,
sabotage, and assassination).

These heightening tensions solidified into an enduring dispute centering on
occupied Germany. As the war ended, both Germany and Austria had been divided
into four zones, each run by one of the victorious powers, Britain, France, the
United States, or the Soviet Union. The victors also quartered and occupied the
capital cities, Vienna and Berlin, located in the middle of their respective Soviet
zones. While the four Allies quickly granted some self-government to Austria, they

could not agree about Germany. The three Western occupiers wanted Germany to become more independent as soon as possible. Meanwhile, the Soviet Union plundered its East German occupation zone for materials to use in rebuilding its own devastated territories. It also feared that a united Germany could one day invade Russia again.

In June 1948, when the British, French, and Americans took steps to allow a new currency in the Western zones, the Russians initiated the **Berlin blockade** (1948–1949), shutting down the border crossings in violation of treaties and agreements. The Allies could have, with legitimacy, used force to oppose these Russian moves. Instead of becoming a "hot" war, with each side unleashing firepower against the other, the war remained "cold." Each side held to a basic principle:

> **Nobody wanted World War III because it would mean the end of the world.**

With "weapons of mass destruction" (as they were later called) of atomic, biological, and chemical (or ABC) technology, the superpowers could exterminate huge numbers of people. Even a small military action against the Russians would have, of course, created a counterattack, with the two superpowers in a shooting war. If it escalated to the use of ABC weapons, World War III (a war including several great powers and superpowers against one another) could have wiped out all humanity or at least destroyed all modern civilized ways of life. Only in fiction did people launch nuclear war, whether realistically predicting the catastrophic results as in the movie *On the Beach* or in James Bond movies where evil madmen plot world destruction.

A nonconfrontational solution to the blockaded city, the **Berlin airlift**, succeeded in the short term. The Western allies supplied the city, using airplanes to fly over the Russian barricades. Over nine hundred flights per day provided seven thousand tons of food and fuel to keep the modern city of two million people going for over a year. Enormous sums of money were spent, and men died (in several plane crashes), but no shots were fired. Then one day, the Russians opened the border again. Soon afterward, the Allied occupied zones became the new Federal Republic of Germany, or West Germany, based on the capitalist and democratic values of the Western allies. Subsequently, the Russians turned their sovietized occupation zone into the German Democratic Republic, or East Germany (see figure 14.1).

Both sides built new alliance systems. The **North Atlantic Treaty Organization (NATO)** bound together most Western European states, along with Canada and the United States, in a mutual defense pact. Sweden and Switzerland retained their neutrality. Russia arranged the **Warsaw Pact** with its satellite states (Poland, East Germany, Czechoslovakia, Hungary, Romania, and Bulgaria) to better coordinate their military forces in opposition to NATO. These military alliances, ready to fight World War III, faced one another across the barbed wire and barricades that ran through the heart of German field and forest. Still, the divisions solved the "German problem," at least temporarily.

Figure 14.1.   The glass stone mural "The Way of the Red Flag" of 1969, by a collective led by Gerhard Bondzin and placed on the side of the Culture Palace in Dresden, proclaims the values of the communist German Democratic Republic. A heroic female victory figure strides forward in front of various workers. At the top, the words read, "Despite everything, we are the victors of history."

Nevertheless, an arms race continued to threaten the world. By 1949, the Russians had their own atomic bomb. Then, by 1952, the United States developed the hydrogen or **H-bomb**, on which most modern thermonuclear weapons are based. Each H-bomb could have the explosive power of hundreds of times the Hiroshima and Nagasaki atom bombs (each of which destroyed an entire city). Aided by information gained through espionage, however, the Russians soon tested a thermonuclear weapon of their own. With or without spying, nuclear proliferation remained inevitable. With enough time, effort, money, and access to supplies, any nation can harness science to build nuclear as well as biological, chemical, and any number of conventional weapons. Throughout the Cold War, both sides kept shortsightedly relying on some fleeting technological advantage, only to see it vanish with the next application of scientific effort by the other side.

At first, complexity and cost usually meant that nuclear weapons remained in the hands of great powers. The British were next with nuclear bombs in the 1960s, quickly followed by the French. Soviet ally China came next. By the 1990s, India tested its prototype bomb, which prompted Pakistan to produce its own. It is unclear when South Africa and Israel got theirs, probably sometime in the 1970s, although South Africa has given up its technology, as have former Soviet republics such as Ukraine. Recently, North Korea has built atomic weapons and ICBMs to carry them, while diplomats and inspectors have been trying to keep Iran from joining the "nuclear club."

These smaller states, though, each held only a handful of nuclear weapons. In comparison, the two superpowers each held enough to destroy their enemies many times over. As technicians perfected **ICBMs** (intercontinental ballistic missiles) by the late 1950s, any target on the globe was vulnerable to vaporization. By 1977, the superpowers had stockpiled tens of thousands of nuclear devices—with the equivalent of about fifteen tons of TNT per person on the planet.

During the Cold War, the superpowers never pressed the button to end human history with the explosion of nuclear weapons. Instead, they relied on **deterrence** (preventing war through the fear that if one side started nuclear war, the other would finish it). The American policy of deterrence was aptly called MAD, the acronym for "mutually assured destruction." Both sides did play at brinkmanship (threatening to go to war in order to get your opponent to back down on some political point). In reaction to this threat to civilization, some citizens of Western states began calling for nuclear disarmament. Governments also realized that they could not endlessly build risk into global politics. As a result, some areas became off limits for weapons (Antarctica, the ocean floors, and outer space). Other countries were discouraged from acquiring their own weapons through nonproliferation treaties beginning in 1968. Throughout the 1960s and into the 1980s the two superpowers negotiated on limits or mutual inspections of numbers and use of arms.

For the next several decades after the Berlin blockade, the Cold War was on. This third great world war of the twentieth century was unique in the history of politics. Like its predecessors, World Wars I and II, the Cold War cost enormous amounts of money, destroyed a lot of territory, cost many lives, and changed the destinies of nations. Unlike those other two conflicts, the main opponents, the Soviet Union and the United States, did not actually fight each other, despite a string of international crises. Instead, they encouraged other people to do the killing, sometimes supplying intelligence, equipment, advice, and even soldiers to client states. These proxy wars killed perhaps fifteen million people over several decades. Although the Cold War was an ideological civil war of the West, it weighed on every international and many a domestic decision of almost all countries in the world.

Review: How did the winning alliance of World War II split into the mutual hostility of the Cold War?

Response:

PRIMARY SOURCE PROJECT 14:
KHRUSHCHEV VERSUS NIXON ABOUT COMPETITION

Vice President Richard Nixon helped to open an American exhibit at a trade fair in Moscow in 1959. He and the Soviet premier Nikita Khrushchev engaged in spontaneous conversations about the different worldviews of America and the Soviet Union. Because some of the discussions took place around consumer products such as refrigerators and dishwashers, the exchanges became known as the "Kitchen Debate." The news conference was shown on American and Soviet television a few days later.

Source: The Kitchen Debate between Khrushchev and Nixon (24 July 1959)

Khrushchev: . . . Regarding our wishes, we wish America the very best to show its goods, products, and abilities, great abilities and we will gladly look and learn. Not only will we learn but we also can show you what we do. This will contribute to improved relations between our countries and among all countries to assure peace throughout the world. We want only to live in peace and friendship with Americans, because we are the most powerful nations. If we are friends then other countries will be friends. If someone tries to be a little bellicose then we can tug his ear a little and say "Don't you dare." We can't be at war. These are times of atomic armament. A fool may start this war and a wise man won't be able to end that war. Hence these are our guiding principles in policy domestic and international. We wish you success in demonstrating America's capabilities, and then we will be impressed.

This is what America is capable of? And how long has she existed? 300 years? 150 years of independence and this is her level of achievement. We haven't quite reached 42 years, and in another 7 years, we'll be at the same level as America, and after that we'll go farther. As we pass you by, we'll wave "Hi" to you. [He waves and laughs.] And then if you want, we'll stop and say, "Please come along behind us." . . .

Another speaker: Mr. Vice President, from what you have seen of our exhibition, how do you think it's going to impress the people of the Soviet Union? . . .

Nixon: I, very early in the morning, went down to visit a market, and where the farmers from various outskirts of the city bring in their items to sell. . . . I can only say that there was a great deal of interest among these people, who were workers and farmers, etc. I would imagine that the exhibition from that standpoint will, therefore, be a considerable success. As far as Mr. Khrushchev's comments just now, they are in the tradition we learned to expect from him of speaking extemporaneously and frankly whenever he has an opportunity.

And I am glad, and I am glad that he did so on our color television at such a time as this. . . . [T]his, Mr. Khrushchev, is one of the, one of the most advanced developments in communication that we have, at least in our country. It is color television of course. It is, as you will see in a few minutes, when we will see the very picture of your speech and of my comments that has been transmitted. It's one of the best means of communication that has been developed.

And I can only say that if this competition which you have described so effectively, in which you plan to outstrip us, and particularly in the production of consumer goods, if this competition is to do the best for both of our peoples and for people everywhere, there must be a free exchange of ideas. There are some instances where you may be ahead of us—for example in the development of your, of the thrust of your rockets for the investigation of outer space. There may be some instances, for example, color television, where we're ahead of you. But in order for both of us [Khrushchev starts to speak] for both of us, for both of us to benefit, for both of us to benefit. . . .

Khrushchev: What do you mean ahead? No, never. We've beaten you in rockets and in this technology.

Nixon: You see, you never concede anything.

Khrushchev: We're ahead of you, too.

Nixon: Wait'll you see the picture.

Khrushchev: Good. . . . We always knew that Americans were smart people. Stupid people could not have risen to the economic level that they've reached. But as you know, we are not fools. "We don't beat flies with our nostrils!" [Laughter.] In 42 years we've made progress. So let's compete! Let's compete. We can produce the most goods for the people. That system is better and it will win.

Nixon: Good. Let's have a, let's have a far more communication and exchange in this very area that we speak of. We should hear you more on our televisions. You should hear us more on yours. . . .

Nixon: You must not be afraid of ideas.

Khrushchev: We are telling you not to be afraid of ideas! We have no reason to be afraid. We have already broken free from such a situation, and we are not afraid of ideas.

Nixon: Well, then, let's have more exchange of them. We all agree on that, right? . . .

Khrushchev: Yes, I agree. But first I want to clarify what I'm agreeing on. Don't I have that right? I know that I'm dealing with a very good lawyer. Therefore, I want to be unwavering in my coalminer's girth, so our miners will say, "He's ours and he doesn't give in to an American lawyer."

Nixon: No question about that.

Khrushchev: You're a lawyer of Capitalism, I'm a lawyer for Communism. So let's compete.

Nixon: All that I can say, from the way you talk and the way you dominate the conversation, you would have made a good lawyer yourself. But what I mean is this: here you, here you can see the type of tape which will be trans—which will transmit this conversation immediately and this indicates the possibilities of increasing communication. And this increase in communication will teach us some things, and it will teach you some things, too. Because, after all, you don't know everything.

Khrushchev: If I don't know everything, then you know absolutely nothing about Communism, except for fear! . . . I want you, the Vice President, to give your word that this speech of mine will be heard by the American people, reported and telecast on the TV in English. Will it be?

Nixon: Certainly it will. . . . [shaking hands on it] And . . . everything that I say will be recorded, and translated and will be carried all over the Soviet Union. That's a fair bargain.

Khrushchev: That's agreed! All your words will be recorded in Russian. We're businessmen. We came together on this immediately.

Questions:

- *What details does Khrushchev use to support his ideology?*
- *How do the speakers express ideas of competition?*
- *How do the speakers use and understand processes of communication?*

Responses:

Citation

Nixon-Khrushchev Kitchen Debate, July 1, 1959. C-SPAN. Accessed 18 August 2014, http://www.c-span.org/video/?110721-1/nixonkhrushchev-kitchen-debate.

For more on this source, go to http://www.concisewesternciv.com/sources/psc14 .html.

MAKING MONEY

Rather than fight the Cold War, most Americans would probably have preferred to concentrate on expanding the US economy. But the traditional American isolationism was doomed not only by the events of World War II but by the worldwide economy led by the United States after the war. Some Western economies grew so fast that they needed to import immigrant workers for their factories. Western capitalists regularly took advantage of these workers by paying them less than they would union-organized Western laborers, but even so, such low wages far exceeded what the foreigners could have earned in their own native lands. Notably, West Germany's *Gastarbeiter* (guest workers) from the Balkans helped the German economy grow. Their labor served both West Germany and their home countries. Guest workers typically sent money back to families in their homelands, building capital for those economies. Their lives in Germany remained isolated, however, segregated from the main German culture. For a long time the Germans thought the workers would eventually go home again, and so they ignored issues of integrating the *Gastarbeiter*. Instead, many stayed from one generation to the next. Economic necessity, rather than defeat in World War II, created an ethnically mixed Germany.

Other European nations accepted immigrants from their colonies as cheap labor. So many came to England that in 1962, 1968, and 1971 the British Parliament restricted holders of British passports from moving from other parts of the Commonwealth to the mother country. Nevertheless, the numbers of foreign-born residents in Western European states began to surpass the number of comparable immigrants in the United States, a nation traditionally much more favorable to immigration. Throughout Europe the guest workers too often lived in shabby, crowded apartments lacking services and facilities, isolated from the main ethnic groups of the nation. This segregation allowed foreign workers and their families to maintain many of their own cultural traditions. Since many Europeans long ignored these new residents as an invisible underclass, the lack of integration and acculturation practically guaranteed eventual social disruptions of clashing cultures.

Coming out of World War II, the United States had the strongest internationally oriented economy, with dominant influence in the International Monetary Fund (IMF) and General Agreement on Tariffs and Trade (GATT). By the 1960s, though, the other great powers, especially Germany and Japan, had recovered from the devastation of the war. They then began to offer serious economic competition to the Americans. Both Germany and Japan used a socialistic cooperation of government, management, and workers to a degree that the Americans, with their antagonism between the interests of owners and unions, could not.

The rapid increase of wealth in the West was a significant victory for certain socialist ideas. After World War II, social democratic and Christian socialist parties came to power in many Western countries. Their gradual, legal, revisionist, state socialism created the modern **welfare state**. Germany rebuilt itself in record time, using the idea of a social-market economy. As in a free-market economy, German businesses were regulated as little as possible. At the same time, the German state enforced socialist welfare programs, which provided workers with protections for illness, health, old age, and joblessness, while labor unions gained representation on the boards of corporations. Sweden had also been building an egalitarian welfare state since the 1930s. By the 1970s it reached the high point of its "Swedish model" of generous pensions and unemployment compensation, plentiful public housing, strong trade unions, and some nationalization of industries, all paid for with high taxes.

For a while Great Britain went furthest along the road toward the modern welfare state, although its loss of empire made adjustments difficult. The British swept away "poor laws" (which had condemned poor people to prison for debt) and instead initiated programs to provide a minimum decent standard of living for most people. Government support and regulation established national health-care programs, pensions, and unemployment insurance. Public education of high quality, through the university level, was available for free or at modest cost. Programs sent aid for housing and food directly to families. Many essential businesses, especially coal, steel, and public transportation, were nationalized and taken over by the government, to be run for the benefit of everyone, not just stockholders. Unfortunately for economic growth, government management did not provide efficiency, and some of these firms could not compete well in world markets.

All over the West, standards of living rose. The social "safety net" provided more chances for the poor to rise out of poverty. Reliable supplies of electricity and installation of indoor plumbing became nearly universal. The middle class broadened out to include many of the working class, because social-welfare legislation and union contracts gave workers decent wages and benefits. More people gained access to labor-saving appliances such as washing machines and automatic dishwashers. Home ownership increased. Meanwhile, the well-to-do continued to prosper (even if they disliked paying taxes that were redistributed by the government to help the middle and poor classes).

This vast increase in wealth also led to an amazing lifestyle change in industrialized nations, especially the United States. Instead of the duality of city and countryside that had marked the living patterns of civilization since its beginning, most people began to live in a novel kind of place, the suburbs. *Suburbanization* blended traditional urban living with rural landscapes. The wannabes of the middle class sought open space (the yard with lawn) and separate dwellings (the stand-alone home), as well as shopping amenities (the shopping mall). Many jobs, however, continued to be located in the cities (see figure 14.2). Thus, commutes multiplied over vast miles of roads. To meet this need, production of motor vehicles in the United States soon reached the equivalent of one car for every man, woman, and child. Huge amounts of new construction catered to automobiles, from superhighways to parking lots. Europe also suburbanized, although more slowly, as it lacked open spaces that could be developed. Europeans also tended to favor mass transportation by bus, tram, or train over commuting by private automobile. Both Western and Eastern European societies aimed to provide consumer products, whether through capitalistic or communistic means of production.

While suburbs had many admirable comforts, their cost tore at the social fabric of the West, especially in the United States. By definition, living in suburbs required a good income. Local zoning laws enforced a middle-class and white racial exclusivity on suburbs. American inner cities of the East and Midwest to which blacks had

Figure 14.2.   Railroads brought acres of cows to the stockyards in Chicago (here in 1947), where workers slaughtered meat for America. Better truck transportation and refrigeration would soon allow owners to build slaughterhouses outside of cities in rural areas.

migrated from the South before and after World War II became virtual ghettoes as whites fled to live in suburbs. White men, both middle and working class, could earn enough in the 1950s and 1960s to allow their wives to stay home as domestic managers. Meanwhile, many stay-at-home women felt isolated in their suburban luxury. The economic shift of the 1970s (see below), however, soon forced women to find jobs, since two incomes became necessary to support the suburban lifestyle, and that meant absentee parents. Increasingly, children were left home alone. Television provided mindless entertainment for some. Along with traditional alcohol, drugs such as marijuana, cocaine, heroin, and psychedelics continued to be bought and then consumed behind closed doors. In dealing with increased drug use, many governments decided to take a criminal direction rather than a medicinal one, leading to larger and larger numbers of incarcerated. A "war" on drugs failed to achieve victory. By the end of the century, in contrast, governments such as those of Switzerland and the Netherlands, or the US state of Colorado, experimented with legalization and toleration of some recreational drugs, especially marijuana.

An expanded middle class and suburbanization had enormous consequences. The incredible affluence of the West led to a cultural revolution, as the children born after the World War II generation started to come of age. Often called "baby boomers" in the United States, these large numbers of young people had more education, opportunities, and wealth than ever before. They criticized the elites of the "establishment" as hypocritically too interested in power, wealth, and the status quo rather than social justice. In turn, the "establishment" criticized young people as too obsessed with sex, drugs, and rock 'n' roll. The popularity of movies, television, and recorded music indulged trends toward a counterculture. Rock 'n' roll provided a new international youth culture that gained momentum with the worldwide sensation of the British music group **The Beatles** (1962–1970). On the one hand, some Western cultural conservatives worried that the long-haired rockers were as bad as communists. On the other hand, communists condemned the Beatles as sex-crazed capitalists.

A **sexual revolution** arose as part of the new counterculture. Greater freedom in sexual activity became possible with improvements in preventing pregnancy. In the late 1950s, pharmaceutical companies introduced reliable contraceptives in the form of an oral pill. "The Pill" allowed more people to have sex without the risk of pregnancy, while medically supervised abortions could end pregnancy with relative safety for a woman. The revolution also encouraged more sex outside the confines of traditional marriage. Sex became a more noticeable part of literature instead of being sold under the table. Courts refused to enforce censorship laws against serious novels like Henry Miller's *Tropic of Cancer* or art films like *I Am Curious, Yellow*. Everything from girlie magazines like *Playboy* to explicit pornography became more accessible.

This increasing extramarital sexual activity brought unforeseen medical risks. The Pill could have side effects, such as blood clots. Even more serious were venereal or sexually transmitted diseases (STDs). For a few years in the middle of the century, the traditional sexual diseases of syphilis and gonorrhea had become treatable with modern antibiotics, so people did not have to worry about sexually transmitted diseases. But new diseases began to develop as multitudes of human bodies came into more intimate contact. Acquired Immune Deficiency Syndrome (AIDS) became a worldwide scourge in the 1980s. Since it was spread in the West at first by male homosexual sex, AIDS became a target of cultural conservatives, who saw the disease as a divine retribution against homosexuals. Despite these prejudices, persons attracted to the same sex, gays and lesbians, began to seek acceptance in Western society instead of being confined to the "closet."

The sexual revolution also spurred Western women to claim legal and economic equality with men. As mentioned above, married women were already moving into the workforce again as middle-class standards became more difficult to afford on one income. Women were also progressively more dissatisfied with the title of "housewife," which gained so little respect in the culture at large. The *women's liberation* movement of the 1960s addressed important issues, such as the rights of women to go to university, serve on juries, own property, and be free from legal obedience to their husbands' commands (as many legal systems still mandated well into the 1970s). Despite the notable defeat of the Equal Rights Amendment in the United States, most women in the West achieved substantial equality before the law and opportunity for economic access in the 1970s.

Women's liberation, however, faltered after these initial successes. The women's movement fragmented as women of color, or religion, or class, or different sexual orientation disagreed with the white middle-class women who had first led the reforms. Around the world today, families and societies still deny women education or force them into marriage or prostitution according to long traditions of "civilization." In spite of this subjugation of women, the term *feminism* has often become associated with hatred of men rather than its best definition of advocating women's equal access to political, economic, and social power structures.

In the United States of America, the struggle for **civil rights** for minorities coincided with the struggle for women's rights. The "race issue," oversimplified as "black" versus "white," divided Americans. The population of African origin, the former slaves and their descendants, lived under nominally "separate but equal" policies, which in reality imposed second-class status on blacks in the United States. Beginning in the 1950s, court challenges, demonstrations, marches, sit-ins, boycotts, and the nonviolence of Dr. Martin Luther King Jr. (b. 1929–d. 1968) challenged segregation laws. The Civil Rights Acts of 1957, 1960, and 1964 gave blacks real political participation not seen since the Reconstruction period after the American Civil War. Sadly, right after these gains, more riots burst out in American cities, and King himself was assassinated. But the possibility for Americans of African heritage to achieve the "American dream" was finally, at least officially, possible.

The inhumane horrors of World War II further motivated some westerners to try to make human rights a permanent part of the international social agenda. Eleanor Roosevelt, the widow of FDR, had pushed the United Nations in that direction already in 1948 with the Universal Declaration of Human Rights. Enforcing the noble goals of equality presented a still unfinished task.

The Union of South Africa, with its minority of "whites" (those descended from British or Dutch settlers) and majority of "coloreds" (Indian and mixed ancestry) and "blacks" (native African) offered a contrast. At the beginning of the Cold War, the ruling party had intensified racist discrimination through a legal system called

apartheid (1948–1993). This set of laws deprived the darker-skinned peoples of their right to vote, choose work, and live or even socialize with anyone of the wrong "race." Fear of the natives' long-standing political organization, the African National Congress, encouraged the South African government to imprison and persecute their leaders, including Nelson Mandela. By the 1970s, in the wake of the American civil rights movement, worldwide criticism and boycotts had somewhat isolated the racist regime. Still, many Western governments, in the name of Cold War solidarity, ignored boycotts organized by human rights groups.

Just as some westerners were concerned about the rights of their fellow humans, others focused on the "rights" of the planet itself. Since the beginning of the century, petroleum, usually just called oil, provided the most convenient source of power. Refined into either diesel fuel or gasoline, it was cheaper and easier to use than coal. Natural gas, a by-product of drilling for oil, also found numerous uses because of its efficiency in burning. Burning coal or oil, though, added noticeably to worsening air pollution. Petrochemicals were also fouling the waters of rivers and coastlines and killing wildlife. The heavily populated and highly industrialized West produced more waste and garbage than had all the humans in all of previous history. A growing awareness of the dirty results of urbanization and industrialization spawned *environmentalism*, or looking after the earth's best interests. Earth Day was first proclaimed in 1971. Political parties usually called **Greens** were organized chiefly around environmental issues, winning representation in parliaments in some European countries by the end of the century. Meanwhile, many governments responded to environmental degradation by regulating waste management and encouraging recycling. The damage to nature slowed its pace, and in a few areas the environment even improved.

As an alternative to oil, some suggested **nuclear energy**, power based on the same physics that had created atomic and nuclear weapons. Nuclear power plants used a controlled chain reaction to create steam, which drove the turbines and dynamos to generate electricity. Many Western nations began building nuclear power plants, hoping for a clean, efficient, and cheap form of power that did not depend on Middle Eastern oil sheiks. Disasters, however, helped to reduce enthusiasm for the technology. First, at **Three Mile Island** in Pennsylvania (1979), a malfunctioning valve cut off coolant water to the hot reactor, causing part of the radioactive pile to melt down. If the situation had not been solved, a catastrophic explosion might have created the equivalent of an atomic bomb. Still, today, hundreds of thousands of tons of highly radioactive debris remain to be cleaned up. Then, at **Chernobyl** in the Ukraine, on 26 April 1986, two out of four reactors at a nuclear complex did explode. Only a handful of people were killed outright, but thousands needed to be evacuated and were forbidden to return to their now-contaminated homes. Hundreds of children subsequently developed birth defects, thyroid diseases, and immune system damage. Most recently, an earthquake and tsunami damaged a plant in Fukushima, Japan (2011), which continues to leak radioactivity into local ground water and the ocean. While none of these accidents was a worst-case disaster, they were enough to discourage the construction of more nuclear power plants in many Western nations. The disposal of nuclear waste products, dangerously radioactive for generations to come, likewise remains unsolved.

Concern about the physical world mirrored a continued interest in the human spirit. Religious divisions, sects, and options multiplied. Perhaps the nuclear arms race, which had created a situation in which the world could end with the press of a few buttons, made people appreciate the fragility of human existence. Indian-inspired cults and practices such as yoga, Hare Krishna, or transcendental meditation made their way into Western belief systems. Other leaders reached into the ancient polytheistic religions or combined Christianity with hopes about space aliens. The ability of some cults to convince their members to commit mass suicide regularly shocked people. At the same time, established world religions took root in the West. Muslim immigrants set up mosques in every major city. The first traditional Hindu temple in Europe was dedicated in London in 1995. The variety of concepts available to individuals and communities seeking supernatural answers to the meaning of life reached into the thousands.

In the United States, where religions were most freely practiced and most diverse, large numbers of Western believers still sought out not only churches but also mosques, temples, and meeting halls. Christianity became even more infected with materialism as televangelists took to the airwaves and raised millions of tax-free dollars from people who felt closer to God through their televisions than at the neighborhood church.

In contrast, church attendance declined in Western Europe. Religiously in-spired laws, such as enforced prayer in schools or no sales on Sunday, disappeared in most Western nations. In Eastern Europe, communist regimes shut down Ortho-dox churches, turning them into museums, storehouses, or abandoned ruins. Even after the end of Soviet oppression, relatively few believers returned to the Orthodox faith. The Roman Catholic Church, which had once dominated Western civilization, seemed to be drifting toward irrelevance. The Second Vatican Council (1963–1965) briefly encouraged many with its new *ecumenism* and liturgy in the language of the people rather than Latin. But soon quarrels over how much the Roman Catholic Church should modernize sapped away momentum. Pope John Paul II (r. 1978–2005) and his compelling personality inspired Roman Catholics and others. The first non-Italian pope since the Renaissance, John Paul II traveled the world and revitalized the international standing of Roman Catholicism. Even his efforts, though, could not reverse the trends in Europe toward unbelief. Whether the cur-rent Pope Francis I (r. 2013–) from Argentina can do better is an unfolding mystery.

In wealth, opportunities, and creativity, the West held its own in the Cold War conflict with "godless communism." The standard of living in communist states seemed meager in comparison, despite the advantages of basic health care, educa-tion, and job security for those loyal to the approved ideology. Both sides had used their industrialized economies to pay for the ongoing conflict of the Cold War. As it stretched into decades, the decisive question became one of who could afford to "fight" the longest.

Review: How did the postwar economic growth produce unprecedented prosperity and cultural change?

Response:

SOURCES ON FAMILIES: SHIRLEY CHISHOLM, SPEECH ON EQUAL RIGHTS (1969)

The proposed Equal Rights Amendment to the U.S. Constitution was an attempt to change the fundamental law of America in response to women's rights. In this address to the House of Representatives, Congresswoman Shirley Chisholm (r. 1969–1983) explains why the amendment is necessary. Chisholm was the first African American woman to win a congressional seat and the first to run for president within a major party. The amendment was approved by Congress in 1972 but failed to receive enough ratifications from states.

Mr. Speaker, when a young woman graduates from college and starts looking for a job, she is likely to have a frustrating and even demeaning experience ahead of her. If she walks into an office for an interview, the first question she will be asked is, "Do you type?"

There is a calculated system of prejudice that lies unspoken behind that question. Why is it acceptable for women to be secretaries, librarians, and teachers, but totally unacceptable for them to be managers, administrators, doctors, lawyers, and Members of Congress?

The unspoken assumption is that women are different. They do not have executive ability, orderly minds, stability, leadership skills, and they are too emotional.

It has been observed before, that society for a long time discriminated against another minority, the blacks, on the same basis—that they were different and inferior. The happy little homemaker and the contented "old darkey" on the plantation were both produced by prejudice.

As a black person, I am no stranger to race prejudice. But the truth is that in the political world I have been far oftener discriminated against because I am a woman than because I am black.

Prejudice against blacks is becoming unacceptable, although it will take years to eliminate it. But it is doomed because, slowly, white America is beginning to admit that it exists. Prejudice against women is still acceptable. There is very little understanding yet of the immorality involved in double pay scales and the classification of most of the better jobs as "for men only."

More than half of the population of the United States is female. But women occupy only two percent of the managerial positions. They have not even reached the level of tokenism yet. No women sit on the AFL-CIO council or Supreme Court. There have been only two women who have held Cabinet rank, and at present there are none. Only two women now hold ambassadorial rank in the diplomatic corps. In Congress, we are down to one Senator and ten Representatives.

Considering that there are about 3½ million more women in the United States than men, this situation is outrageous.

It is true that part of the problem has been that women have not been aggressive in demanding their rights. This was also true of the black population for many years. They submitted to oppression and even cooperated with it. Women have done the same thing. But now there is an awareness of this situation, particularly among the younger segment of the population.

As in the field of equal rights for blacks, Spanish-Americans, the Indians, and other groups, laws will not change such deep-seated problems overnight. But they can be used to provide protection for those who are most abused, and to begin the process of evolutionary change by compelling the insensitive majority to reexamine its unconscious attitudes.

It is for this reason that I wish to introduce today a proposal that has been before every Congress for the last 40 years and that sooner or later must become part of the basic law of the land—the equal rights amendment.

Let me note and try to refute two of the commonest arguments that are offered against this amendment. One is that women are already protected under the law and do not need legislation. Existing laws are not adequate to secure equal rights for women. Sufficient proof of this is the concentration of women in lower paying, menial, unrewarding jobs and their incredible scarcity in the upper level jobs. If women are already equal, why is it such an event whenever one happens to be elected to Congress?

It is obvious that discrimination exists. Women do not have the opportunities that men do. And women that do not conform to the system, who try to break with the accepted patterns, are stigmatized as "odd" and "unfeminine." The fact is that a woman who aspires to be chairman of the board, or a Member of the House, does so for exactly the same reasons as any man. Basically, these are that she thinks she can do the job and she wants to try.

A second argument often heard against the equal rights amendment is that it would eliminate legislation that many States and the Federal Government have enacted giving special protection to women and that it would throw the marriage and divorce laws into chaos.

As for the marriage laws, they are due for a sweeping reform, and an excellent beginning would be to wipe the existing ones off the books. Regarding special protection for working women, I cannot understand why it should be needed. Women need no protection that men do not need. What we need are laws to protect working people, to guarantee them fair pay, safe working conditions, protection against sickness and layoffs, and provision for dignified, comfortable retirement. Men and women need these things equally. That one sex needs protection more than the other is a male supremacist myth as ridiculous and unworthy of respect as the white supremacist myths that society is trying to cure itself of at this time.

Questions:

- *How does the source present the intersection of ethnicity, class, and gender?*
- *What specifics does the source present on the serious problem of prejudice?*
- *What objections and obstacles to the amendment does the source indicate?*

Responses:

Citation

Chisholm, Shirley. Extensions of Remarks: May 21, 1969. *Congressional Record* (Bound Edition), 91st Congress, 1st Session, Volume 115, Part 10, (May 15, 1969–May 26, 1969): 13380–81.

For more on this source, go to http://www.concisewesternciv.com/sources/sof14 .html.

TO THE BRINK, AGAIN AND AGAIN

The history of the Cold War involved a series of international crises and conventional wars around the world, where East and West confronted each other, fortunately without erupting into a "hot" war, which could be World War III and the end of civilization. The first major crisis after the Berlin blockade centered on China. Further putting the seal on the hostility between East and West was the "loss" of China to communism. As World War II ended, everyone expected Jiang's Nationalist Party to rebuild China from the devastation of the war. Because of this expectation, he gained a seat on the Security Council of the United Nations as a great power victor of World War II.

But westerners did not understand how divided China had become between Nationalists and Communists since the 1930s. Many Chinese reviled Jiang's government as incompetent and corrupt while admiring Mao's Communists as both dedicated guerrilla fighters against the Japanese and supporters of the common peasants. Despite American mediation, civil war broke out in 1947. Most Western observers assumed the Nationalists would win since they controlled far more territory, weapons, and resources. The Communists, not having enough resources at first to engage in open battle, relied on guerrilla warfare. They expanded slowly their operations until they could field a national army. The Communists then drove Jiang and his allies off the mainland of China to the island of Taiwan (Formosa), where Jiang's followers proclaimed it as **Nationalist China**. Protected by the United States, Jiang ran the small island country as his own personal dictatorship until his death in 1975. Meanwhile on the Asian mainland, Mao proclaimed the state of the **People's Republic of China** (1 October 1949), a new rival to the West even as it drew on the Western ideas of Marxism and revolution.

Many Western intelligence analysts had long believed that Mao was merely Stalin's puppet. Instead, Mao began to forge his own unique totalitarian path. With the **Great Leap Forward** in 1958, Mao tried to modernize China, forcing it into the twentieth century and equality with the Western powers. Lacking capital or resources beyond the labor potential of an enormous population, Mao's crude methods turned into a disaster. Instead of investing in Western-style industrial and agricultural technology, he told his people to try to manufacture steel in their backyards and plant more seeds in fields. Chinese peasants obeyed their leader's ignorant suggestions. In the resulting famine, tens of millions died of starvation. Although Communist Party moderates soon ended these catastrophic policies, in 1965 Mao went over their heads to proclaim the **Great Proletarian Cultural Revolution** (1965–1969). He encouraged young people to organize themselves as Red Guards who attacked their elders, teachers, and all figures of authority except for Mao. The Red Guards killed hundreds of thousands and shattered the lives of tens of millions by sending them to "reeducation" and prison camps. Although these policies were all aimed to make China's power competitive with the West, China took decades to recover from Mao's mistakes.

China's first major confrontation with the West took place over the division of Korea. The Allies had liberated Korea from Japan in 1945 but had not been able to agree on its political future. So they artificially divided the country: the Russian forces left behind a Soviet regime, the People's Republic of Korea (North Korea), and the Americans installed an authoritarian government, the Republic of Korea (South Korea). Unhappy with this arbitrary division of their nation, northern forces, with the permission of Stalin and Mao, tried to conquer the south in 1950. The United States convinced the United Nations to defend South Korea, a member state, against aggression, beginning the **Korean Police Action** (1950–1953). In the name of the UN, America provided the bulk of the money and sent the most arms and soldiers, although other Western nations also contributed. An American-led invasion drove back North Korean forces, but then, in turn, hundreds of thousands of Chinese "volunteers" (so named by the Chinese Communist government that claimed no direct involvement) pushed back the UN forces to the original division along the thirty-eighth parallel. After several years of inconclusive fighting, a treaty reinstated the division of the peninsula between the Communist-aligned north and the Western-aligned south.

Worried Americans saw the communists' actions in Berlin, Greece, Turkey, China, and Korea as part of an effort by the Soviet Union to gain world supremacy. A new Red scare tore through the West. This postwar reaction seemed credible, given the power of Stalin's armies and their sway over Eastern Europe. In reality, communist states were divided among themselves, and communist movements were weak outside of the Russian sphere. Communist Party successes in elections in the West were miserable. Nevertheless, in America, the Red scare created *McCarthyism*, a movement named after a senator who used the fear of communism to destroy the careers of people he labeled as "commie pinko" sympathizers. But all the fear and hearings were wasted effort since communist organizations in the United States were never a serious threat to America's security or its way of life.

In contrast, the military might of the Soviet Union unquestionably allowed it to remold Eastern Europe. After Stalin's death, his successor, **Nikita Khrushchev** (r. 1953–1964), disavowed Stalin's cruelties and called for "peaceful coexistence" with capitalist countries (see Primary Source Project 14). That brief moment of optimism ended in 1956, however, when the Hungarians tested the limits of Khrushchev's destalinization by purging hard-line communists and asking Russian troops to leave the country. The Russian leadership interpreted these moves as a **Hungarian Revolt**. The tanks of the Warsaw Pact rolled in, and, since Hungary was clearly in the Soviet Union's sphere of influence, NATO could do nothing. Two hundred thousand people fled the country before the Iron Curtain fell again.

Berlin, for a second time, next focused Cold War tensions. The ongoing four-power occupation of Berlin had turned into a bleeding wound for communist East Germany. Many in the so-called workers' paradise were envious of their brethren in the West. East Germans knew that if they moved to West Germany, they were accepted as full citizens with special benefits. Thousands were soon leaving East Germany through Berlin. To stem the tide of emigration, the Russians gave permission to the East Germans to build the **Berlin Wall** (1961–1989) (see figure 14.3). The wall became a militarized barrier to keep East Germans from West Germany. Since preventing the Berlin Wall from being built might have meant World War III, there was little the West could do. The Communists claimed that the Berlin Wall was a necessary bulwark to keep out Western imperialism and capitalism. Most people, however, recognized it as a symbol of the prison mentality of Soviet power. When American president John F. Kennedy visited in 1962, he proclaimed that all freedom-loving people should be proud to say, "Ich bin ein Berliner."[2]

Khrushchev's fall from power and replacement by Leonid Brezhnev again suggested to some that the enduring rivalry of the Cold War might calm down. Then Czechoslovakia experienced a virtual repeat of the Hungarian Revolt of 1956. Czechoslovakia and its politicians tested Brezhnev's renewed proclamations of tolerance by initiating in 1968 broad liberalizing reforms called the **Prague Spring**.

---

2. Literally translated, the sentence could mean "I am a jelly doughnut." Some grammarians fuss that to convey the meaning, "I am a person from Berlin," Kennedy should have said, "Ich bin Berliner." Regardless, the Berliners cheered.

Figure 14.3. The sign at Checkpoint Charlie in divided Berlin, where people could pass through the Iron Curtain, offers only a mild warning.

When the Soviets decided the Czechs had gone too far, the tanks once again lumbered into the country, ending the revolt. Many Czechoslovakians were killed and imprisoned. And again, the West could do nothing without triggering World War III. The new Russian leader proclaimed the Brezhnev Doctrine, clearly stating that once a state had become "communist," its Warsaw Pact comrades would enforce Soviet allegiance to ideology by force if necessary.

In this Cold War over different ideologies, even science became part of the ammunition. During the **Space Race** (1957–1969), both sides seized on efforts toward the legitimate scientific goals of space exploration to win advantage and prestige over each other. The Russians gained the first victory, surprising the usually technologically more advanced Americans with the launch of the first functional satellite, **Sputnik** (4 October 1957). The nearly two-hundred-pound device, the size of a beach ball, sent a simple radio signal as it circled the globe every ninety-five minutes. The Russians then proceeded to beat the Americans by sending the first animal, the first man, and the first woman into space. President Kennedy then decided to leap ahead of the Russians. He called on America to land a man on the moon by the end of the 1960s. Just as in a war, large forces were mobilized at high cost, great minds planned strategy, and people died (although in accidents, not by gunfire). In the end, the Americans won the race, as Neil Armstrong became the first person to walk in the lunar dust on 21 July 1969 (see figure 14.4). Hundreds of millions of people watched on live television. Western science proved its ability to move us beyond our earthly home. In the end, the moon turned out not to have much practical value. With the Space Race "won," lunar flights ended by 1972. But the Cold War continued, with other crises and costs on other foreign fronts.

Figure 14.4.   In July 1969 the American *Apollo 11* mission landed on the moon. Here the lunar module *Eagle* is seen returning from the moon's surface while the earth rises in the distance.

Review: *How was the Cold War fought in the West and around the world?*

Response:

LETTING GO AND HOLDING ON

The strains of World War II and the Cold War weakened the great powers of Europe so completely that they were forced to dissolve their colonial empires. The rise of the superpowers of America and the Soviet Union meant that the European ability to dominate the world was definitely finished after 1945. No longer could a European state send its gunboats, at will, to intimidate darker-skinned peoples. The colonies had failed to fuel the European states' economic growth. The costs of building the economic infrastructure and providing order and prosperity in both homeland and colony were finally deemed too expensive. The only motives slowing down the release of colonies were pride that the empires instilled and the sense of responsibility for all the peoples whose native societies had been replaced by European structures.

The colonial peoples of Africa and Asia began to increase their efforts toward independence. Some peoples fought for **decolonization**; others negotiated it; a few had it thrust on them before they were ready. All then faced the difficult challenge of finding prosperity in a world economy run according to the elites of Western civilization. Most were hastily freed with little preparation within imperialist-imposed borders that seemingly arbitrarily combined and separated ethnic groups. A few examples may illustrate the diverse ways imperial colonies became new nations.

The British let go of their colony of India immediately after World War II in, for them, a peaceful separation. As the war ended, the exhausted British caved to the demands of Gandhi and Nehru for decolonization and negotiated a transition to Indian self-government. The British decided to split the colony into two countries, recognizing the conflicting interests of Muslims and Hindus. The bulk of the subcontinent was to be **India**, run by the Indian Nation Congress, while the Muslim League was to control **Pakistan**, a new, artificially drawn country. Pakistan took its name from the initials of several of its peoples (Punjabi, Afghans, Kashmiri, and Sindi, translating as "Land of the Pure"). Pakistan's peoples were united by Islam but geographically divided into two parts, West Pakistan and East Pakistan, separated by a thousand miles and very different languages and traditions.

A stroke of the pen led to Indian and Pakistani independence from Britain, after midnight on 14 August 1948. Tragically, horrible violence broke out as millions of Muslims fled to Pakistan and Hindus escaped to India, each side killing hundreds of thousands along the way. Gandhi made some efforts to bring about peace and tolerance. These were too much for a Hindu fanatic who assassinated Gandhi on his way to a prayer meeting (30 January 1949). Both states continued to quarrel over the control of Kashmir (from where cashmere wool comes). India became "the world's largest democracy," although electoral violence and assassinations of politicians intermittently continued. Meanwhile, Pakistan's prevailing political system has been military dictatorships. The state fell apart during a civil war in 1971, at which time India helped East Pakistan to become the independent state of Bangladesh, now notorious as one of the poorest countries on earth. By the 1990s, India and Pakistan remained hostile and distrustful toward each other, each armed with nuclear weapons in a standoff reminiscent of the US and the USSR during the Cold War.

A country that had to fight for its independence was **Algeria**. The native-organized resistance movement, the National Liberation Front (FLN), in 1954 began a campaign of terrorism against French colonists living there. The ruling French colonists struck back with their own use of terror: shootings by the military, torture of suspects, secret executions, mass arrests, and concentration camps. Even in Paris, police allegedly drowned Algerian demonstrators in the Seine. Existentialist philosophers, such as Jean-Paul Sartre and Albert Camus (himself born in the colony), debated over which path to take toward a resolution. The protracted violence in both Algeria and France ended the Fourth Republic in 1958. For the first time, a government's failure to handle a colonial conflict had brought down a European constitution. The World War II hero Charles de Gaulle subsequently helped France reorganize under the Fifth Republic.

As a newly empowered president, Charles de Gaulle (r. 1959–1969) dismantled France's empire. At first, he tried to organize colonies in a French Community, similar to the British Commonwealth, but only with moderate success. As deaths in Algeria piled up into the hundreds of thousands, de Gaulle finally allowed Algerians to vote for independence in 1962. Unfortunately for the Algerians, they could not develop a functional democracy. The FLN set up a one-party state that lasted for decades. After experimenting with democracy, a rival Islamic party finally won an election in 1990. Then a mysterious group of politicians and generals, called "the Power," seized control. The civil war that followed killed over 150,000 people, many of whom had been hacked to death. Amnesties and reconciliation policies slowly ended the violence, at the price of the killers on both sides going unpunished. Recently, human rights advocates criticize the continuing authoritarianism of the ruling FLN party.

The British colony of **Kenya** showed how a country could win independence by using both violence and negotiation. By 1952, the Kikuyu tribe resented colonial exploitation enough to begin the "Mau Mau" revolt against British rule. A few dozen deaths of Western colonists prompted the British to declare a state of emergency. The British crushed the Mau Mau revolt by executing hundreds of suspected terrorists and rounding up hundreds of thousands more to live in either outright concentration camps or "reserves." There, many British and African guards humiliated, raped, and tortured their prisoners, often forcing them into hard labor and depriving them of food and medicine. Tens of thousands died.

By 1959, the British ended the campaign, and in 1963, they handed over rule to the new president, Jomo Kenyatta, a Kikuyu they had until recently held in prison for seven years. Kenyatta practiced a relatively enlightened rule, sharing involvement in government across ethnic lines. Since his death in 1978, the country has held together despite political rivals accusing each other of corruption and incompetence.

Surprisingly, **Congo** is as of the present still intact, after having suffered the worst experience both of colonization and of decolonization. After decades of plundering, the Belgian colonial rulers simply abandoned the colony in June 1960. The new Democratic Republic of the Congo lacked a single native college graduate, physician, lawyer, engineer, or military officer. The charismatic Patrice Lumumba became president but was assassinated with the connivance of the CIA and British MI6 in January 1961 because they thought he was a communist. The country immediately dissolved into chaos. Rebel groups tried to seize different provinces that were rich in minerals. At first, the United Nations had some success in creating stability by sending in troops, but the effort waned the following year after UN secretary general Dag Hammarskjöld's death in a plane crash, perhaps because it was shot down. Colonel Joseph-Désiré Mobutu seized power in 1965. Weary of the conflict, Western powers accepted his claim to rulership and supplied him with technology, training, and cash. Mobutu developed a personal and corrupt dictator-ship. He tried to discourage tribal identification and instead nourished a Congolese nationalism, *zairianization*. He rejected European names, renaming his country as Zaïre in 1971, the capital Leopoldville as Kinshasa, and himself as Mobutu Sese Seko kuku Ngbendu wa Za Banga. Mobuto's absolutism ended only in 1997, when international pressure after the end of the Cold War allowed a successful rebellion backed by the president of neighboring Rwanda. Wars by armed groups killed mil-lions until about 2003. The renamed Democratic Republic of the Congo still suffers from too much illegal mining and deforestation, militia warfare (often using child soldiers), rape, disease, poverty, famine, and refugees, as well as state-manipulated media and a corrupt and authoritarian central government that has nonetheless never gained sufficient power to control the entire country.

Even though almost all of Africa and Asia had been freed of official imperialism by 1965, the former imperialist powers still intervened in their former colonies' affairs. The Commonwealth (which had dropped the adjective "British") and the French Community offered weak structures of unity between former colonies and masters. France in particular kept many military arrangements with its former colo-nies, sometimes sending troops to protect the regimes from insurgencies (as against Tuareg rebels in Mali in 2013), other times toppling dictators (as in Chad in 1975 or the Central African Republic in 1979).

African states faced even more daunting new economic challenges in a world system largely run by Western nations. Economic growth was hindered by minerals and agricultural products fetching low prices in the marketplace, poor decisions by corrupt strongman leaders, and economic aid that benefited industrialized coun-tries more than African ones. Former colonies often grew cash crops for export to the West, such as bananas or cocoa, instead of staple foods to feed their own peo-ple. Farming only a single crop (monoculture) left the population deprived of a varied diet and the crops vulnerable to blight. Their model and competition were the nation-states of Europe, which they were ill equipped to imitate or compete with, especially because of their ethnic diversity.

Further replacing the nineteenth-century colonization was the twentieth-century "Coca-colanization," a term combining the most famous American soft drink with the word "colonization," implying a takeover through commerce, not direct imperialism. Western products were marketed to meet the desires of the world's consumers. Natives abandoned regional and ethnic drinks, food, and cloth-ing for American icons such as soda pop, hamburgers, fried chicken, t-shirts, and blue jeans. Public health advocates recently have been trying to slow consumption of carbonated sweetened drinks by taxing them.

From the 1970s on, **global debt** also hampered the worldwide economy, as many countries in Africa, Asia, and Latin America borrowed heavily from Western banks. The loans were supposed to be invested in industrialization but were too often instead wasted in corruption or on building from poor designs. As Third

World countries could not pay off their debts, Western banks threatened to fore-close. An increasing stress between rich nations and poor nations, therefore, bur-dened international relations. What little industry in former colonies existed was still owned and controlled by, and for, Western businesses, who kept the profits. The Third World countries also lacked support systems for sufficient education and medical care compared with industrialized nations. What little health and prosper-ity existed, though, allowed populations to soar, often faster than jobs could be created. The population explosion fueled a cycle of urban poverty and criminality.

The new leaders of new nations too often seemed less interested in good gover-nance and more involved in **kleptocracy**, using political power to increase their own wealth. The world economy was also skewed so that whenever things went wrong, the military was tempted to seize power. Many regimes repeatedly alter-nated between military dictatorship and civilian government. The few elected lead-ers who lasted in power often became dictators. Transitioning to modern statehood so fast, the former colonies continued to prove that democracy was difficult.

The most problematic area of declining colonialism turned out to be in the Middle East. Most colonies there had either won independence before or shortly after World War II or had never been completely dominated, like Saudi Arabia or Iran. In the third quarter of the twentieth century, the most accessible oil reserves were located in the Middle East, in nonindustrialized countries that required far less fuel for themselves than the energy-hungry West. The desire to control the petroleum reserves in the Arab states kept Western powers intimately involved in Middle Eastern politics. Arab opposition to the new, largely Western state of **Israel**, founded in 1948, also hindered the West's easy access to oil.

Israel grew out of Zionism, the organized movement for Jewish nationalism begun in 1898. The Balfour Declaration during World War I had encouraged Jews to move to Palestine, a British mandate and the site of the Jews' ancestral homeland of Judaea. The horror of the Holocaust, the Nazi attempt to exterminate the Jews during World War II, created much sympathy for creating a Jewish state. The British, caught between increasingly violent Jewish and Muslim terrorist attacks, handed over the problem to the United Nations in 1947. A UN commission proposed divid-ing up the territory into two new countries of roughly equal size: Israel (most of whose citizens would be Jews) and Palestine (most of whose citizens would be Arabs). The Jews eagerly accepted the proposal and declared their independence on 14 May 1948.

The Palestinian Arabs refused the commission's proposal, which they consid-ered to be giving away their homeland. On their behalf, the states of the Arab League launched the first Arab-Israeli War (1948–1949), intending to destroy the new Jewish state. They lost. Victorious Israel seized part of what the commission had apportioned to a Palestinian state, while Jordan and Egypt took control of the rest. The state of Palestine vanished from the map before it even had a chance to begin. Hundreds of thousands of Palestinians suddenly had no country, forced to live as refugees under the rule of Egypt and Jordan (who refused to integrate them) or in exile in Lebanon and Syria in camps (without rights, seemingly without a future).

Meanwhile, Israel organized itself as a Western state, not surprisingly since so many Jews had lived in the West. It had a parliamentary government dominated by a socialist party and a conservative party (with other, smaller, liberal and religious parties). Its economy was thoroughly Western, based on markets, investments, private property, and the welfare state. Some Israelis did experiment with socialist living in communes called kibbutzim, but these were more important for building a strong sense of community than for contributing to the overall economy and social structure. Most Israelis believed in Judaism, although the level of devotion varied widely. The government practiced religious toleration, a benefit for the 10 percent of its citizens who were Muslim Arabs. Jews revived the virtually dead language of Hebrew as a living tongue, both for reading their scriptures and for daily interaction. Ongoing immigration by Jews from all over the world, including some from non-Western countries in North Africa, Russia, India, and even Ethiopia, caused tensions within the Israeli state, especially between the secularist and traditionalist religious factions.

Ongoing hostility from its Arab neighbors, however, meant that Israel had to fight for its existence, supported by most states of the West. The next war between Israel and the Arabs, the **Suez Crisis** of October 1956, also marked the last time the Europeans acted as independent great powers. In that year, Egypt nationalized the Suez Canal and closed it to Israeli shipping, violating British property rights and international agreements. The British and French, in collusion with the Israelis, launched a surprise attack on Egypt. Overwhelmed by the successes of the enemy invaders, Egypt appealed for help from the Soviet Union. The United States feared that the Suez Crisis might escalate to involve the superpowers. The United States ordered its NATO allies to go home. The former great powers of France and Great Britain could no longer intervene at will in world affairs.

The ongoing opposition to Israel by Arab states and Palestinians continued, however. By 1964 some Palestinians, who remained homeless and without a state, unified different political factions under the **Palestine Liberation Organization (PLO)**. The PLO began a more aggressive terrorist campaign, intending, ultimately, to destroy Israel. In turn, the Israelis carried out a preemptive strike against their Arab neighbors and won a significant victory in the Six-Day War of 1967. Israel conquered the Golan Heights from Syria, the West Bank from Jordan, and the Gaza Strip and the entire Sinai Peninsula from Egypt. These acquisitions, however, left millions of Muslim Arabs living without any civil rights under Israeli domination, as if under colonial power. Israel had no idea what to do about this situation, besides settling for a military occupation that deprived the stateless Palestinians of civil rights.

The brief Yom Kippur War in 1973 was the last war so far to attempt Israel's destruction. The Arab states attacked by surprise on the Jewish holy day and made some significant gains, especially in the Sinai. The Arab states also tried to weaken support for Israel among its Western allies by using their dominance in the petroleum trade group, the Organization of Petroleum Exporting Countries (OPEC). They imposed an oil embargo on Western states that supported Israel. While this embargo and the resulting fuel shortages did damage Western economies briefly,

Israel survived. Subsequent peacemaking efforts, usually mediated by the United States, have failed to fully remove hostility in the region.

The legacy of occupation and ongoing economic and political interests (especially access to natural resources) kept Western states involved in Africa, Asia, and the Middle East. The direct imperialism of colonial possessions had largely vanished by 1965. Although neo-imperialism had begun with noble aspirations and patriotic fervor only a century before, it had obviously failed. The Europeans had used their power around the world to compete with one another, build up their own economies, and spread their culture. After letting their colonies go, the West continued to cope with the ongoing political and economic ties of Europeans living in foreign parts and non-Western immigrants moving to Europe. Since the West controlled the bulk of the world's wealth and power, it could hardly avoid responsibility for some of the legacy of its century of colonialism.

Review: *How did the decolonization of Africa and Asia succeed yet force choices between communist or Third World status?*

Response:

AMERICAN HEGEMON

The unquestioned leadership of the West lay, of course, with the United States of America. In some ways, the United States fit the definition of an empire, as one people that ruled over a variety of other peoples. It did let go of its colony of the Philippines in 1946 and turned Hawaii into its fiftieth state, but it held on to several other colonial possessions in the Pacific (Guam, the Northern Mariana Islands, and Samoa) and the Caribbean (Puerto Rico, the Virgin Islands). As the strongest shield against communism and the wealthiest warrior for capitalism, America's unique superpower status enabled it to dominate other nations without directly reducing them to colonies and protectorates. Within its sphere of influence, though, the United States intervened militarily and economically around the world. Closest to home, within the Western Hemisphere, the United States particularly intensified its involvement with Latin America. In reaction, Latin Americans tended to blame the "Yankees" rather than themselves for their political, economic, and social problems.

Among these problems were great social inequities derived from class and ethnic divisions, dating back to Latin America's westernization as part of the Spanish and Portuguese empires. Creoles, those of European descent, exploited those of Native American or African ancestry. Since the Creole elites feared the results of votes by the alienated poor majorities, they avoided expanding democratic participation beyond their own ranks. Many countries alternated between corrupt civilian leaders and juntas (cliques of military officers ruling as dictators). Meanwhile, the dominant Roman Catholic hierarchy, usually drawn from the ruling elites, too often accepted exploitation of the lower classes. The priests preached to the peasants and the poor to accept their lot as something unchanging, promising rewards only after death.

Inevitably, however, Western modernity penetrated the traditional conservative Latin American culture. While increased food production and improved health care caused a population explosion, many people remained impoverished because of a lack of jobs. Just outside most urban centers, shantytowns of the suffering poor multiplied. They, as well as dissatisfied members of the middle class, began to listen to communist revolutionary ideas. Some Roman Catholic priests in the 1970s even began to preach ***liberation theology***, which called for social justice in this life instead of waiting for the next. The papacy of John Paul II discouraged such meddling and ordered ministers to be silent. The juntas silenced opponents through violence. For example, in 1980 they assassinated Archbishop Oscar Romero of San Salvador as he presided at the Eucharist in a hospital chapel. Long considered a saint by the common people throughout Latin America, the Vatican finally canonized him on 13 October 2018.

The history of **Argentina** reflects many of the tensions between ruling elites holding on to power and the masses seeking opportunity and fairness. As World War II ended, a junta with fascist inclinations ruled Argentina (making it hospitable to fleeing war criminals like Joseph Mengele, the "Butcher of Auschwitz"). But one member of that junta, **Juan Perón** (b. 1895–d. 1975), toyed with socialist ideas. His wife, **Evita Duarte**, who had risen from a broken lower-class family to fame in the movies, helped her husband appeal to the masses, especially *los descamisados* ("shirtless ones," those too poor to afford even a shirt). Perón seized power in 1945, and for the next ten years he nationalized businesses, increased social welfare benefits, censored the media, criticized the Roman Catholic Church, and used violence and force to maintain power. A new junta drove Perón into exile in September 1955, emboldened by Evita's death in 1952, economic failures, and an oblique excommunication by the pope.[3] Succeeding governments that rejected socialism likewise failed to make Argentina prosper. Memories of Perón allowed him to return to power from exile in October 1974, but he died within a year. His second wife tried to rule as his successor, but a coup replaced her in March 1976. The ensuing regime tried to adopt strict laissez-faire policies.

---

3. The government's forcing a bishop and a deacon from office prompted the excommunication. The clerics had protested the Peronist regime's legalization of prostitution, restriction of the church's role in education, reduction of religious tax exemptions, and recognition of equal rights for illegitimate children. While the excommunication did not mention Perón by name, it provided one more excuse for a coup attempt in July that killed hundreds.

As the economy continued to fail, however, the government launched the so-called **Dirty War** against left-wing political opponents. The military secretly arrested suspected radicals, tortured them, and then murdered hundreds, often by tossing victims out of helicopters over the Atlantic Ocean. Instead of joining a conspiracy of silence, hundreds of mothers and grandmothers began picketing before the presidential palace, asking for their lost children.

The government then tried to use a patriotic success to distract people's attention. Argentine forces invaded the nearby Falkland Islands, possessed by Great Britain but claimed by the Argentines (who called them las islas Malvinas). Fewer than three thousand British citizens inhabited the islands (with almost half a million sheep). Surprisingly, the British decided to fight back. The **Falklands War** (April–June 1982) ended with almost a thousand dead but a British victory. Argentina's failure led to the collapse of the junta and the exposure of the secrets of its Dirty War. Advice of unrestrained laissez-faire capitalism from Milton Friedman's acolytes from the University of Chicago, known as the "Chicago Boys," instead led to serious unemployment, massive debt to American banks, and riots by 2001. Neo-Peronist policies of state intervention and populism advocated by the husband and wife presidents Kirchner (r. 2003–2015) stabilized and grew the economy again.

While Argentina remained free of direct political intervention by the United States, the leaders of three other Latin American nations felt the power of their northern neighbor. First, President Jacobo Arbenz Guzman of **Guatemala** passed land reform policies that threatened the profits of US banana companies that controlled almost half the country's land. In 1954, the CIA organized covert subversion and even a military invasion to depose Guzman. By 1960, a virtual civil war had broken out between the government, usually run by juntas, and various guerrilla factions, often organized by communists. By the war's end in 1996, military, paramilitary, guerrilla, and terrorist forces had killed perhaps two hundred thousand Guatemalans.

In another case, the CIA likewise helped overthrow President Salvador Allende of **Chile** in 1973, as his socialist policies began nationalizing US businesses, especially copper mining. A military junta led by Augusto Pinochet bloodily seized power.[4] Then to maintain power, his authoritarian regime suppressed opposition by torturing tens of thousands and killing (or "disappearing") several thousand more over the years. The recent president of Chile, the socialist Michelle Bachelet (r. 2006–2010, 2014–2018), was among those tortured. For a few years Pinochet gave free reign to "neoliberal" economic policies, yet their lack of success led him to nationalize industries as Allende had previously done. Pinochet ruled until 1989, when the end of the Cold War made his dictatorship less useful to the United States. In 1998, a Spanish court attempted to bring him to trial for crimes against humanity, albeit Pinochet argued for immunity first as a former head of state and then for reasons of health. Nevertheless, he was soon on trial or under investigation for many crimes. At his death in 2006, Pinochet remained unconvicted in courts of law while judged guilty by his historical record.

---

4. Many long claimed (and some still do) that Pinochet's troops murdered Allende. An official autopsy based on his body exhumed in 2011 declared his death a suicide. He had shot himself with an AK-47 given to him by Fidel Castro.

In a third instance, the removal of the president of **Panama** came with the direct intervention of the US military. In 1978 America gave the Panama Canal to Panama. In 1989–1990, however, twenty-five thousand American troops illegally invaded and literally kidnapped Panama's military dictator, Manuel Noriega (r. 1983–1989), who called himself maximum leader of the national liberation. They brought him to trial in Miami for drug trafficking (an activity he claimed to have carried out on behalf of the CIA). Various international courts found him guilty of crimes such as tax evasion, drug money laundering, corruption, and murder. Ultimately, in 2011 a French court extradited Noriega back to Panama to serve out his sentences until his death in 2017.

The most notorious US intervention was with **Cuba**, which had been a US protectorate since the Spanish-American War. In the 1950s, Fulgencio Batistá, a semi-fascist dictator, offered Cuba as a haven for both legitimate US business interests and criminal organizations. Batistá faced a rebellion led by **Fidel Castro** (b. 1927–d. 2016), the privileged son of a Cuban sugar planter, who at first had wanted to play professional baseball. Castro had converted to radical politics and began subversive activities all over Latin America. He invaded Cuba in 1956, finally achieving a surprising victory on New Year's Eve 1958. Once in control, Castro set up a one-party socialist state that made him dictator. He arrested his enemies, nationalized most foreign property, tossed out crime syndicates, redistributed land, and provided free health care and education to all the people. Thousands of Cubans fled the island, most settling in the American state of Florida. Nevertheless, Castro and the image of Castro's lieutenant Che Guevara symbolized for many Latin Americans a better, socialist future, free of Yankee capitalist exploitation.

The US reaction was to try to get rid of Castro. The CIA organized some 1,500 exiles in an attempted counterrevolution. These Cubans tried to reconquer Cuba with the **Bay of Pigs invasion** (17 April 1961), named after their landing site. Lacking open support from the United States and popular backing from the Cuban people, the invasion failed miserably and embarrassed the new administration of US president Kennedy. Castro became worried enough about future US intervention that he began to cooperate even more closely with the Soviet Union. He persuaded the Russians to build missile bases in Cuba.

In October 1962, American U-2 spy planes photographed the missile installations. The resulting **Cuban Missile Crisis** brought the superpowers closer to nuclear war than at any other time in history. Although Soviet ICBMs located in Russia and on Russian submarines could have easily targeted anyplace they wanted in the United States, the Cuban missile sites seemed a direct threat because they were so close to American shores. From the Russian point of view, though, they were merely imitating American policy: US missiles based in Turkey were just as close and threatening to the Russian border as those in Cuba were to America.

Kennedy, however, was determined to remove the missiles from Cuba. Nonetheless, he took the moderate step of declaring a "quarantine" of Cuba, meaning that while any military technology bound for Cuba would be stopped at sea by the US Navy, other ships could continue. This measure was not quite a blockade, which would have technically been an act of war. The Soviets declined to push the United States into shooting. Instead of forcing the issue, both sides reached an agreement, because nobody wanted World War III. The Russian missiles left Cuba. Similarly, although less publicized, the American missiles left Turkey. Thus, while both sides gained something, the resolution of the crisis appeared to the public as an American victory. The United States also promised never to invade Cuba again (although the CIA made some halfhearted and harebrained attempts at assassination with exploding cigars). Fidel Castro retired in 2008 because of declining health, while his brother Raúl followed him as president until he himself stepped aside in 2018 (although he remains first secretary of the Communist Party). Cuba remains one of the few avowedly communist regimes.

Cold War rivalries continued in other countries throughout Latin America. Juntas suppressed their opponents in the name of fighting communism. Communists organized revolts in the name of liberating the poor from capitalist oppression. US and European corporations dominated the economy to provide exports for themselves. The lower classes saw too little profit from that trade. These ideological differences guaranteed that Cold War tensions would continue to find their way into political and social divisions.

Review: How was Latin America entangled in the Cold War?

Response:

THE UNEASY UNDERSTANDING

Under the protection of NATO, the Western European nations had managed to create stable parliamentarian, democratic governments that represented most people within each state through fair and competitive elections. Alternating coalitions of conservative, liberal, or social democratic parties, with occasional participation by regional, nationalist, or communist parties on the fringes, governed in most countries. Only tiny states such as Liechtenstein and Monaco remained ruled by princes with broad powers. The last fascist dictatorships, in Greece, Spain, and Portugal, ended in the 1970s with almost no violence during the transition to parliamentary democracies.

The only serious threat to stability broke out in the year 1968. Student riots and revolts broke out in cities from Warsaw to Madrid, Berlin to Paris, Chicago to Mexico City. The students protested against the Vietnam War (see below) or nuclear weapons; for improving university conditions; for women, ethnic minorities, or indigenous peoples to gain civil rights; or for more democracy. In France, after striking workers joined student riots, the government almost fell. By the end of the year, though, most governments remained firmly in control, enforced by police using clubs and tear gas, sometimes guns, and a few tanks. A "spirit" of 1968 nevertheless continued to inspire young people to question authority. In the next few years, sporadic attacks by terrorist groups, such as Red Brigades in Italy and Baader-Meinhof in West Germany, or by organized criminals, such as the Mafia, caused feelings of insecurity rather than any actual instability.

Although European economic prosperity recovered from World War II, Europe's standing as a center of military power did not. The Western Europeans had grown used to being the center of world affairs since the neo-imperialism of the nineteenth century. Western Europe found the Cold War duality of the United States versus the Soviet Union hard to deal with. These concerns led them to take a surprising step toward peace and cooperation with one another. For a thousand years, since the collapse of Charlemagne's empire, rival states had been fighting over which share of the European heartland each should reign supreme. The horrors of the last such conflict, World War II, convinced Western European leaders to take a new path.

In the early 1950s, the leaders of West Germany and France began to promote mutual cooperation. They started in Germany in 1950 with the nationalized coal and steel industries, creating an organization to regulate and supervise the joint Coal and Steel Authority of both France and West Germany. This arrangement succeeded so well that it expanded the next year into the European Coal and Steel Community, bringing in Italy and the Benelux countries (the Lowland nations of Belgium, the Netherlands, and Luxembourg).

Within a few years, these nations integrated their economic and political systems more intensively. They agreed to the Treaty of Rome on 25 March 1957, which founded the **Common Market** or the **European Economic Community**. Soon this international organization aimed at closer political as well as economic union, reflected in its name change to the European Community in 1967. Several neutral countries, such as Sweden, Switzerland, Finland, and Austria, formed themselves into a rival European Free Trade Association. At first the United Kingdom of Great Britain hesitated to join the Common Market, relying on its special friendship with the United States and the economic ties and trade with the Commonwealth. Still, Great Britain gained membership by 1973. Rivalries, political grudges, and inflation in the European Community took longer than hoped for to overcome, but the improving prosperity of its members slowly made the European Community a serious competitor in the international economy. In addition, the European Community's unity has changed the nature of international politics. Combined with NATO, the European Community has greatly reduced, if not outright eliminated, the chances of war among Europeans for the first time in history.

Nevertheless, a possible outbreak of a global World War III remained a concern for Europeans. NATO troops based all over Western Europe provided some reassurance of slowing down a possible Russian land invasion. Moreover, the nuclear weapons possessed by the United States, Britain, and France deterred possible

Soviet aggression. Still, President de Gaulle of France remained resentful of American hegemony and vainly tried to assert French leadership by asking US forces to leave France in 1966. NATO headquarters moved from Paris to Brussels, the capital of both Belgium and the European Community. Germany felt most painfully the divisions of the Cold War, separated into its East and West parts and aware that it was on the front line of any conventional war. To reduce the possibility of war, Social Democratic leaders of West Germany began a concentrated **Ostpolitik** (East politics) in the early 1970s. They began to talk with the leader of the Social Unity Party in East Germany, hoping to improve relations between communists and capitalists.

The real turning point in Cold War relations resulted from the United States' involvement in its **Vietnam War** (1964–1973), which the Vietnamese call the "Resistance War against America." In 1956, anticolonial and communist insurgencies forced the French out of their colonies of Laos, Cambodia, and Vietnam in Indochina, despite America's secret bankrolling of the French. A fragile Vietnam was left divided between the communists, led by Ho Chi Minh, in power in the north, and westernized (and Roman Catholic) elites running the south. The Americans feared, rightly, that Ho Chi Minh would unite the country and make it part of the Communist bloc. They believed, mistakenly, in the domino theory—which asserted that if one state fell to communism, so would its neighbor, followed by the next state, and so on, just like domino blocks knocking one another down. Thus, after Vietnam would go the rest of Indochina, followed by Thailand, the Philippines, and, perhaps, the rest of the world. An alleged attack in the Gulf of Tonkin that killed or injured not a single American provided the US president Lyndon Johnson with the "justification" to commit combat troops, beginning in 1964. Congress gave him a blank check to defend American interests as he saw fit, although without declaring war.

As more American troops poured in to protect South Vietnam, it seemed inconceivable that North Vietnam could defeat the strongest empire in world history. Yet the Russians quickly claimed protection of North Vietnam under their nuclear umbrella. A troubling guerrilla war developed, one that the United States could not win as long as Russia and China supplied North Vietnam. By 1968, protesters in Europe and, more importantly, a majority of Americans called for US troops to pull out of Vietnam.

In 1968 **Richard Nixon** (r. 1969–1974) won the US presidential election partly because he claimed to have a secret plan to end the fighting in Vietnam. By that time the Cold War had been ongoing for twenty years. Again and again the superpowers had managed to annoy and provoke each other and frighten the globe with the risk of World War III. Nixon came to power mired in the unwinnable Vietnam conflict and looking for "peace with honor." The United States' heavy bombings of North Vietnam had failed. Indeed, over the course of the conflict, the US military dropped more bombs on Indochina (over 7.7 million tons) than American planes had on both Germany and Japan in all of World War II (under 2.2 million tons).

Suddenly and surprisingly, Nixon and his foreign policy advisors, especially the German immigrant Henry Kissinger, came to the realization that they had been mistaken about the Cold War. They finally figured out that China and Russia were

not allies; the two communist states had not gotten along for years and were enemies and rivals themselves. Thus, the Americans began a new strategy to exploit
Sino-Soviet tensions and increase the level of peace. Strangely enough, touring
ping-pong or table-tennis teams paved the way for American and Chinese diplomats
to begin talking. Soon the former anticommunist crusader Nixon was visiting China,
toasting and treating the despot Mao as a respected equal. Next, Nixon visited Russia, toasting and treating Brezhnev, who had crushed Czechoslovakia, as a col-
league. These leaders of the three most powerful nations on the planet then agreed
to disagree on many ideological issues, except for working together to create order
and stability. They called this policy **détente**, using a French term for a outwardly
cordial yet distrusting relationship.

Securing the cooperation of China and Russia to manage their North Vietnamese ally, the United States was able to withdraw its armed forces from Vietnam in
1974. When the shooting stopped, more than fifty thousand US troops were dead,
as were several million Vietnamese. Two years later, the communist North easily
overran the South. When Laos and Cambodia also were seized by communists,
some feared that the domino theory was about to succeed after all and that communism would roll through Southeast Asia and the Pacific. But the stability of Thailand
and the quarrels among the communists halted any further toppling of regimes.

Unexpectedly, the Cold War afflicted Cambodia with the worst disaster of the
Cold War. The communist group called **Khmer Rouge** (red Cambodians) seized
power, renaming their country Kampuchea. They then pushed certain Western
ideas of anarchism and revolution further than any other political movement. In a
wild reaction against capitalism and industrialized society (and even Marxist ideology), the Khmer Rouge agriculturalized the nation, driving urban populations into
the countryside to become farmers or to die trying in the notorious "killing fields."
The Khmer Rouge burned and desecrated all past culture to create their version
of modernity. Exalting equality, they rooted out all traditional or industrial social
differences. They eliminated most scientists, teachers, artists, intellectuals, and
priests. Even families were broken up. The Khmer Rouge slaughtered as much as a
third of its own population in this self-inflicted genocide. By 1979, the communist
government in Vietnam was so disgusted that it invaded Cambodia, drove the
Khmer Rouge into the jungles, and installed a satellite regime. The United States,
because of its dislike of communist Vietnam, then hypocritically found itself supporting the exiled communist Khmer Rouge in its attempts to throw the Vietnamese
out. Once more, Western ideologies confronted and confused one another.

Still, détente continued as a policy among the major states of the world
throughout the 1970s. The linkup of a Soviet Soyuz and an American Apollo space-
craft symbolized the high-flying spirit of cooperation. Détente peaked in August
1975 when in the capital of Finland representatives of most European states and
the United States fashioned documents to provide a basis for future cooperation.
These **Helsinki Accords** finally ended World War II, thirty years after the shooting
had stopped. A new body, the Conference for Security and Cooperation in Europe
(CSCE), provided a forum for representatives from all European states (along with
the United States) to prevent any accidental outbreak of violence or war. The Helsinki Accords also asserted basic human rights of liberty and freedom for all the
signatory states.

Détente provided a new way for the industrialized world to live with its ideological differences. Nonetheless, this uneasy truce could not have lasted for the long term. Sooner or later, ideological hostility would have provoked the Russians and Americans to shoot at or even annihilate each other. Instead, détente's collapse resulted in an American victory in the Cold War.

Review: *How did the policies of détente ease Cold War tensions?*

Response:

Make your own timeline.

1945   1980

CHAPTER

Into the Future

The Contemporary Era, 1980 to the Present

The end of the Cold War startled most intelligence analysts, politicians, and pundits (a new kind of commentator in modern media who relied more on opinion than analysis). A conflict that had framed international actions and domestic policies for more than four decades came to a close with little warning. Nevertheless, the increasing interaction of the earth's peoples challenged the place of westerners and their wealth as never before. International commerce, science, industry, and politics still guaranteed that Western civilization would continue—and would also continue to change.

THE WALLS COME DOWN

The end of the Cold War followed directly from the collapse of the policy of détente. A support for coexistence weakened first when the Soviet Union sent troops to Afghanistan in December 1979 to prop up a recently installed communist regime. Afghanistan soon became the Soviet equivalent of Vietnam, as Muslim warriors (*mujahideen*) resisted the atheistic communists. Their guerrilla warfare fought in difficult terrain with supplies from the United States kept the Russian occupying forces in turmoil.

Second, a number of labor strikes in Soviet-dominated Poland in late summer 1980 sparked a labor union movement called Solidarność (**Solidarity**). An ordinary worker, the mustachioed Lech Walesa, became the symbol of the conflict as he organized strikers from the barricades. The need for laborers in a socialist state to form a union for their own self-protection showed the failures of Soviet socialism. The Russians, though, made Polish authorities declare martial law in December 1981, which pushed the movement underground and put Walesa under house arrest. These actions made the Soviet Union and its system look both oppressive and incompetent.

Third, new leadership in the West became determined to take a harder line against Soviet domination. In Great Britain the Conservative Party's new prime minister, **Margaret Thatcher** (r. 1979–1990), disliked socialism in all its forms. She began to scale back the British welfare state, reprivatizing many businesses and industries and breaking unions. She also sharply criticized the totalitarian state of the Soviet Union. Meanwhile, in 1981, the former movie star **Ronald Reagan** (r. 1981–1989) became president of the United States. He resolved to resist Soviet expansionism and even threatened the USSR, which he called an "evil empire," with the possibility of World War III. Some Americans were shocked that the Reagan administration could suggest that a nuclear war with the Soviet Union was winnable. Reagan proposed the Strategic Defense Initiative (SDI), a new high-tech antimissile system to shield the United States from ICBMs. Since the technology for such a program was decades away from being invented, much less activated, critics named this initiative "Star Wars" (after the popular science-fiction film). Even if successful, SDI would have left America's allies in Europe defenseless against Russian mid-range missiles. To counter this real threat, Reagan and NATO leaders installed mid-range nuclear weapons in Western Europe. Many Western citizens protested, their resentment of American domination outweighing their fear of Russian invasion.

Reagan also continued the buildup of conventional armed forces of ships, planes, weapons, and soldiers in an effort to prevent possible Russian aggression anywhere. The vast US economy could afford this expensive effort, although the country went deeply into debt to do so. The United States went from being the biggest creditor nation in the world to being the biggest debtor nation during Reagan's presidency.

Fourth, the new Reagan administration disliked the new Sandinista socialist regime in Nicaragua backed by Cuba and the Soviet Union. After the US Congress refused to intervene, Reagan officials secretly and illegally financed a counterinsurgency by the "Contras" (right-wing paramilitary groups that were "against" the left-wing Sandinistas). The Reagan administration raised money for the Contras by selling weapons to Iran, a country the United States considered an international threat. In the civil war that followed, one side's "terrorists" were the other side's "freedom fighters" and vice versa. The Iran-Contra affair exposed the secret deals, but the president's authority was left intact by his subordinates' taking the blame. The American military also defied international law by mining Nicaragua's harbors, technically an act of war. In the end, the leftist regime lost by the ballot box, not bullets. In 1990, the Sandinistas allowed free elections, which restored a tentative democracy. Recently, the leader of the Sandinistas, Daniel Ortega (r. 1979–1990, 2007–), has begun a fourth term as president, despite criticisms of his growing authoritarianism.

The Cold War finally ended in the 1990s after **Mikhail Gorbachev** (r. 1985–1991) became secretary general of the Communist Party in the Soviet Union. He saw the flaws and corruption of the centralized communist system and attempted to reform Soviet society in order to save it. First, he promoted *perestroika* (restructuring) to allow more free-market competition within the economy. Second, he declared *glasnost* (openness). The regime reduced censorship, allowed more foreign travel, and imported more Western goods and entertainment. Third, Gorbachev allowed rival political parties to begin to organize, thus allowing a democratic process for the first time since the short-lived Russian Republic of 1917.

Despite Gorbachev's reform efforts, his communist state crumbled around him. The people resented their increasingly poor standard of living compared with that of Western Europe. The transition to a market economy created shortages and unemployment. Political reform was clumsy because the Communist Party resisted giving up its privileged position. Finally, repression of protests in the Soviet Union's Baltic provinces of Latvia, Lithuania, and Estonia started to resemble the Hungarian Revolt in 1956 and the Prague Spring of 1968.

The Soviet satellite states in Eastern Europe ultimately forced Gorbachev to prove his sincerity about openness by ending Soviet domination. Gorbachev finally decided against using force and violence to uphold the Brezhnev Doctrine and Soviet domination. As a result, the satellite system collapsed swiftly, without much bloodshed. First, in 1988, workers' strikes in Poland pressured the military/communist government to launch reforms and organize free elections. Big changes came in the year 1989. In September, Solidarity came to power, and the next year Lech Walesa became president. Months earlier, the Hungarians held free elections. By the summer, they had torn down their portion of the Iron Curtain where it bordered Austria. It was just a barbed wire fence with an electrified alarm system. In November, the totalitarian leader in Bulgaria, Zhivkov, resigned, beginning that country's transition to democracy. At the same time, protests in Czechoslovakia began to frighten the dictatorial regime. By December, Czechoslovakia had embraced its Velvet Revolution, so called because the separation from communism happened with comparatively little violence. The former political prisoner and playwright Václav Havel became president.[1] Finally, Romanians rejected the old system in a quick coup in which the long-reigning dictator Nicolae Ceaușescu and his wife were shot on Christmas Day, after which video of their corpses was broadcast to the nation (see figure 15.1).

The most important sign of the Cold War's end was the reunification of Germany in 1990. The East German hard-liners began to lose control in August 1989 as East German citizens began fleeing across the new open border between Hungary and Austria. Through Austria they reached West Germany, where they were welcomed as free citizens. At home in East Germany, mass demonstrations organized by churches also began to seek openness. The communist dictator of many years was deposed, and moderates tried to find new directions. On the evening of 9 November 1989, after a bureaucrat on television mentioned that some travel restrictions would be lifted, thousands of hopeful East Germans began to gather at crossing points at the Berlin Wall. They talked the guards into letting them through. By the next morning there was no sealing up the wall again. Indeed, the most potent symbol of the conflict, the Berlin Wall, was soon pounded into rubble as souvenirs for tourists. Within a year, the West German political leadership negotiated unification. On 3 October 1990, the Communist East German state officially disappeared, absorbed into the Federal Republic of Germany.

---

1. Just four years after the Velvet Revolution, Czechoslovakia went through the "Velvet Divorce." Extremist politicians, with minimal popular support, arranged to divide the country into its two main parts, which became the Czech Republic and the Slovak Republic (although usually called Slovakia). Havel resigned during the process rather than oversee the dissolution, but he then served as the first president of the Czech Republic.

Figure 15.1. These statues of communist founders Marx and Engels were relegated to a museum outside Budapest, Hungary, after the Cold War.

In 1991, a failed coup by communist hard-liners in the Soviet Union led to the defeat of Gorbachev but not of the reforms. By 1992, the Soviet Union was in the "dustbin of history." The Russian Federation replaced the USSR. The new Russia remained linked with a few former Soviet republics, as part of a so-called Commonwealth of Independent States. This association included new nations in the Caucasus (Azerbaijan, Armenia, and Georgia, for a time), the Turkish states in Central Asia (Kazakhstan, Uzbekistan, Turkmenistan, Kyrgyzstan, and Tajikistan), and Eastern Europe (Moldavia and Byelorussia or Belarus). Ukraine and the Baltic states of Estonia, Latvia, and Lithuania left completely. The Warsaw Pact was soon gone as well. The Cold War was over.

The former Soviet satellite states in Europe quickly converted to much in the Western capitalist style. Indeed, in 2004 NATO expanded to include most former Eastern European satellite states, right up to Russia's doorstep. The former Warsaw Pact members of Poland, Hungary, Romania, Bulgaria, the Czech Republic, Slovakia, and the three former Baltic "republics" of the Soviet Union (Estonia, Latvia, and Lithuania) officially entered the defensive military alliance with the West. Many of these states raised their standard of living to be comparable to those of their new Western allies, uniting their economies and destinies to the West's (see below).

The Cold War's resolution even reached to the Union of South Africa and its repressive regime of apartheid. Over the years, the government had tortured, imprisoned, and killed members of the African National Congress. International pressure of boycotts, absence of a communist threat, and worsening social strife all convinced the white racist regime to dismantle apartheid. In 1990, the regime released Nelson Mandela, leader of the African National Congress, who had been in prison since 1962. Mandela and his party won an overwhelming victory in free and fair elections in 1993. President Mandela (r. 1994–1999) passed a law that protected whites' property and advocated forgiveness rather than avenging decades of oppression. The Truth and Reconciliation Commission granted amnesty to the perpetrators of cruelty and violence in return for their honest accounts. South Africans descended from the "white" British and Dutch as well as the "colored" Indians stayed to maintain the Western industrialized culture, although poverty and violence still plagued too many descendants of the "black" native South Africans.

Despite these successes, the collapse of communism had not resulted in the pristine victory dreamed of by many in the West. A few communist dictatorships, such as those in North Korea and Cuba, still held on to their ideology, despite no longer receiving subsidies from the Soviet Union. Although Russia no longer posed an invasion threat to Europe, it was armed with the nuclear weapons capable of destroying civilization. And Russia itself transitioned away from totalitarianism only with difficulty. During the switch from communism to capitalism, Russia saw much of its wealth fall into the hands of a few well-connected politicians and friends of the elites, since the rule of law and political institutions had been insufficiently established. Pollution, job loss, and military impotence lost the nation its superpower status. Soon, however, President Vladimir Putin (r. 2000–2008, 2012–) began to concentrate power in his own hands. He had been a KGB agent stationed in East Germany as it collapsed. Nostalgic for the Soviet Union, he drew support from loyal oligarchs (now defined as hugely wealthy beneficiaries of monopolies) and boosted Russian pride by promoting nationalistic feelings.

Regretting the loss of superpower status, Russian imperialists still wanted to have dominance over fringe peoples in neighboring states that had been part of the former USSR. The new Russian Federation clung to Chechnya, despite continuing rebellion and terrorist attacks. The former Soviet republics of Georgia and Ukraine in particular felt the pain of Russian interventions. In 2008, Russia won a brief war in support of Abkhazia's and South Ossetia's secession from Georgia. In 2014, Ukrainian demonstrations forced their president into exile because he leaned too much in favor of Russia. In reaction, Russia supported separatist movements by ethnic Russians in the Ukraine, especially promoting turmoil in the eastern part of that country. The Russian Federation armed rebels and sent in Russian troops, who disavowed Russian interference by claiming to be "volunteers." Russia also successfully seized the Ukrainian peninsula of Crimea by cutting it off from the Ukraine and declaring it as Russian territory. Minor sanctions by Western nations did little to deter Putin's re-expansionism. European states may have been reluctant to take more aggressive action because they depended on natural gas imports from Russia. And, of course, no one wanted World War III. Meanwhile, other states that had fragmented from the Soviet Empire, especially in Turkish Central Asia, established mini-dictatorships of their own. Their new authoritarian rulers commanded with the language of Islam and with nationalism rather than the communist rhetoric of Marx. Thus, ethnic and nationalist hatreds were revived (see below).

Review: *How did the Cold War come to an end?*

Response:

SEARCHING FOR STABILITY

As the Soviet Union was splitting apart, Europe was coming together. After a thousand years of warfare in Europe, war among Western states had become inconceivable instead of inevitable. Since the fall of Rome in the West in 476 and the failure of the Carolingians in the ninth century to replace it, rival states had quarreled with one another in one bloody conflict after another. The rivalries had contributed to making some European states great powers, but World War I, World War II, and the Cold War had then shown the risks of mutual destruction. NATO now mutually protected the European nations. The United States remained NATO's and the world's foremost military and economic nation, the sole superpower. But by the end of the century, US military installations shut down, no longer necessary for preventing a Soviet invasion, and thousands of American troops left Europe.

The political and economic unification of Europe that had begun with the Common Market accelerated after the Cold War. In 1991, the Maastricht Treaty turned the weak European Community into the stronger **European Union** (see map 15.1). Some politicians thought the various nations of Europe could become a United States of Europe. In 2002, the union established its Common Security and Defense Policy (CSDP), which began missions to troubled countries around the world, such as the Congo, Indonesia, and Georgia. Today, its various operations support police and courts in maintaining law and order, monitor elections, try to prevent smuggling and piracy, and protect refugees and civilians in areas with violent conflict.

The European Union's greatest success remains in economics, although it values its culture as well. Its motto since 2000 has been "United in diversity." The EU removed trade and labor barriers among its members. Brussels's subsidies to the poorer member states, such as Ireland and Portugal, helped their economies to grow and to compare well with the more prosperous members, such as Germany.

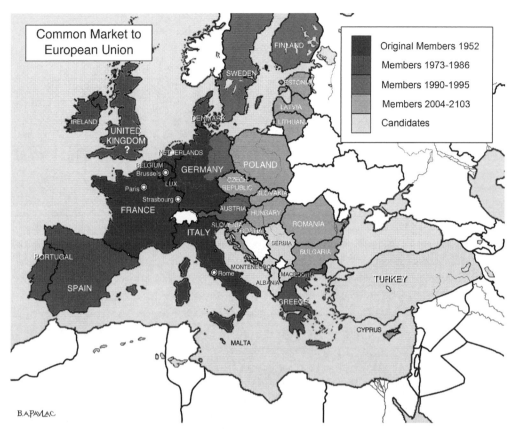

Map 15.1.   Common Market to European Union.
How do the entrance dates or locations of various countries reflect their
economic power and participation in the European Union? (Note that the
United Kingdom of Great Britain and Northern Ireland is in the process of
leaving the EU).

In 2002, a dozen competing monetary currencies within the EU countries, from the
French franc to the Italian lira to the German mark, vanished into history and were
replaced by a new common unit, the euro. By 2014, eighteen countries belonged
to the "eurozone," with several other small countries also using the euro as a currency. While many economists expected the euro to fail, it has usually remained
strong against its international rival, the American dollar.

Ongoing economic success tempted still more countries to join the European
Union. First, in 1995, the former neutral nations of Austria, Finland, and Sweden,
with their advanced Western economies, were welcomed. The Schengen Agreement, put into action in 1995, created a "Europe without borders" that allowed free
movement between the member states without going through customs and identity
checks. Next, many of the newly freed Soviet satellites were eager to join the European Union, although they had to develop their market economies and parliamentary democracies before they could be fully integrated. On 1 May 2004, the EU
welcomed new Eastern European members, including the former Soviet republics
of Estonia, Latvia, and Lithuania and the Soviet satellites of Hungary, Poland, the

Czech Republic, Slovakia, and Slovenia, along with the island states of Malta and (non-Turkish-occupied) Cyprus. The most recent to join were Romania and Bulgaria in 2007 and Croatia in 2013. Candidates as of 2018 include Montenegro, Serbia, the Former Yugoslav Republic of Macedonia, and Albania, with potential candidates of Bosnia-Herzegovina and Kosovo. Turkey with its foothold in Europe applied for candidacy back in 1987. Still, several members of the European Union oppose Turkey's membership amid doubts that Turkey is, or ever will be, "Western" enough. Growing concerns about the authoritarian measures of President Recep Tayyip Erdoğan (r. 2014–) have only complicated the relations between Turkey and the EU.

Other obstacles slowed the path to true European unity. Some "Euroskeptics" saw the dangers of a vast bureaucracy in Brussels that demanded conformity and ignored local differences. The European Parliament in Strasbourg seemed to have little power or purpose. Many Europeans wanted to see more *subsidiarity*, in which decisions are made at the regional and local levels rather than by the European Commission in Brussels (see figure 15.2). While English grew more popular as a unified *lingua franca*, Europeans continued to speak more than fifty different regional and local languages and even more dialects. Some Europeans only reluctantly accepted new member states, afraid of the cost of supporting less-developed economies and opening up borders to more intra-European immigration, competition from cheap labor, redirection of agricultural subsidies, or lack of "proper" values. Even Germany had trouble integrating Germans from the former East Germany, especially as many businesses in the former socialist state failed to adapt to the new capitalist economy.

The wealth and peace of Europe made it a magnet to poor people and ethnic minorities from former colonies all over the world. "Economic" immigrants sought a better life through better employment in Europe's land of plenty. "Political" refugees sought asylum, according to international treaties, in Europe's land of law. The fear that foreigners could not adapt to Western culture over generations is nonsense, given the right conditions. But since European governments and societies made few efforts to assimilate the newcomers, diverse immigrants often retained their own cultural attitudes. Modern communications meant they received newspapers, radio, pamphlets, and television all in their own languages. The perceived danger of Islam became a particular concern even though the percentage of Muslims in Europe had only grown from less than 2 percent in 1950 to less than 4 percent in 2008. That was about seventeen million out of a total of almost five hundred million. Some countries, like Portugal and Poland, had virtually no Muslims, while the highest percentages in Western Europe were just over 8 percent in France and Sweden. Nonetheless some Europeans began to warn of "Eurabia": that Europe would convert into a Muslim territory. The call of the muezzin from minarets competed with the church bells from steeples amid the traffic noise in streets. Thus, the European practice of tolerance allowed Muslim extremists to preach intolerance and resistance to assimilation. Would they be integrated, like metal in a melting pot, or stay separated, as an assortment of fruits in a basket? Would these peoples from Asia and Africa become westernized, or would they change the West?

Figure 15.2. The Atomium built for the 1958 World's Fair in Brussels now dominates a park that celebrates the European Union with models of cultural icons from all over Europe. Replicas shown include buildings from Pisa and Venice.

Nation-states now found it difficult to define their populations according to unified ethnicity. The European Union bureaucracy called for better treatment and human rights for Sinti and Romany (formerly called Gypsy) people, while local governments discriminated and local mobs intimidated. School officials in France, Germany, and Britain called for Muslim women and girls to stop wearing head-scarves. For many females who wore them, they were acts of religious obedience or symbols of their ethnic identity. For the opponents, the scarves, veils, and burkas subordinated women, insulted secularism (*laïcité*) or Christianity (in ways that nuns' wimples supposedly did not). Worried about the "traditional" populations of Europe, nativist or nationalistic parties campaigned to expel the growing number of non-Europeans. In the Netherlands, two killings changed politics: an environmentalist assassinated the politician Pim Fortuyn in 2002 and a Dutch Moroccan killed film director Theo van Gogh in 2004. These acts spurred the founding of the extreme nationalist Party for Freedom (PVV) under Geert Wilders. His open criticisms of Muslim culture eventually led to his being charged with (but not punished for) hate speech. Other politicians such as Marine Le Pen (daughter of Jean-Marie Le Pen) in France and Joseph Haider in Austria sought both to limit the rights of these foreigners and to resist the centralized control of the EU in Brussels. Most politicians and voters still saw these nationalists as part of an extremist fringe, sure to fade away.

As modern politics were called into question, so also did some doubt the value of Enlightenment rationalism. In the 1980s, two French intellectuals proposed new techniques to interpret Western culture, called ***postmodernism***. Jacques Derrida and Michel Foucault "deconstructed" texts to show how elites often camouflaged power and exploitation. Their postmodern critique sought to undermine the modern assertion that true knowledge can be obtained through human reason. Postmodernism criticism contributed to further uncertainty about truth and Western culture.

A concrete answer to the meaning of Western culture in Europe was supposed to be part of the Convention on the Future of the European Union in 2002. But as some politicians tried to enshrine the position of Christianity in the document, others successfully rejected the notion. Either way, the cumbersome and complicated constitution failed to win endorsement by 2005. Instead, European leaders reformed the EU through the Lisbon Treaty, which after delays went into effect in 2009. While the constitutional structures of Europe seemed stronger than ever, ethnic conflict and economic mistakes still troubled the EU's future. Of course, Europeans had no one to blame but themselves for immigrants. They had bound the world together in their practice of imperialism and capitalism since the fifteenth century. Inevitably, some foreign culture began to weave its way into European sensibilities, especially through cuisine. Curry became as standard for British food as fish and chips, while Germans and Austrians ate *doner kebabs* as an alternative to wurst.

Review: *How did the European Union attempt to provide a new economic and political basis separate from the United States?*

Response:

DIFFERENT FOLKS

The Cold War's end and the European Union's success at bringing diverse people together paradoxically encouraged some ethnic groups to seek separatist autonomy. The Cold War had huddled Western Europeans together in fear of Soviet totalitarianism. With the Cold War over, some pundits predicted that communism's collapse meant a victory for liberal democracy and for prosperity under capitalism. Many did not realize how separatist movements would actually increase. Nationalism remained a potent political ideology, although in ever smaller units. While the Cold War's end drained wars of their communist versus capitalist energy, tensions within nation-states were still empowered by cultural and tribal rivalries.

Even during the Cold War, two areas of ongoing British imperialism illustrated how nationalist conflicts divided and killed. In **Cyprus** the deep divisions between ethnic Greeks (about 80 percent of the population) and Turks (the other 20 percent) degenerated into terrorist attacks, especially by those who wanted unification with Greece. Britain pulled out in 1959, but the new Cyprus was forbidden to unify with Greece. Greeks and Turks never quite managed to live peaceably, relying on UN peacekeepers. In 1967, though, Greece's anticommunist military dictatorship decided to annex Cyprus as a distraction from its repression of domestic protests. In a preemptive strike, however, Turkish troops occupied the northern third of Cyprus. Tens of thousands of ethnic Greek Cypriots fled to the south. The two NATO allies, Greece and Turkey, just barely managed to avoid war (see figure 15.3). The whole island became a member of the European Union in 2004, but union authority does not quite apply to the northern third under Turkish rule.

In another example, Northern Ireland, which had remained part of the United Kingdom of Great Britain after independence for the rest of Ireland, experienced renewed violence between Protestants and Roman Catholics. Roman Catholics in Northern Ireland saw themselves as oppressed. They often lived in ghettoes, had worse jobs, were paid less, and were allowed fewer political rights than Protestants in the same province. The "**Troubles**" began in 1968 when a splinter group of the long-dormant Irish Republican Army calling itself the **Provisional IRA**, or Provos, began terrorist attacks. The London government at first tried to be neutral but eventually sent in thousands of troops to maintain order. The British shooting of more than a dozen Roman Catholic demonstrators on "Bloody Sunday" (30 January 1972) convinced many Catholics to consider the English part of the enemy. In the following decades, violence among British troops, Ulster constabularies, and IRA fighters killed three thousand people and injured many more. Finally, the Good Friday Agreement of 1998 brought the Republic of Ireland, Great Britain, and parties in Northern Ireland toward a permanent, peaceful resolution.

During the Cold War, such ethnic fighting had been secondary to the larger possibility of World War III. To fight the Cold War on many fronts, both communist and capitalist industrialized states had spread modern military technology to many technologically primitive societies around the globe, whether they were ready for it or not. At first, the superpowers had supplied various dictators, tyrants, juntas, rebels, insurgents, and even terrorists with various kinds of advanced weapons:

Figure 15.3. A sign by peacekeepers of the United Nations marks the division of Cyprus.

automatic rifles, grenades, land mines, plastic explosives, antitank rockets, and anti-aircraft missiles. After the Cold War, when the superpower rivals reduced their gifts of arms, international drug trading provided money for weapons. As weapons became cheaper and widespread, more people possessed an easy ability to kill others. The result was increased violence for reasons of money, ideology, or power.

Much of this violence was nationalist in nature. Terrorists periodically bombed, hijacked, kidnapped, and murdered to create ethnic states and enclaves during the Cold War. In Western Europe, terrorists lashed out in defense of their minorities, including the Basques against Spain, the Corsicans against France, and even some South Tyroleans against Italy. In 1954 a few Puerto Ricans shot members of the US Congress in the Capitol to draw attention to freeing their island from the United States. In other places of the world, civil wars and massacres broke out, giving the Western powers the choice of either standing by or intervening to stop the killing. After the Portuguese withdrew from their colony of East Timor in Indonesia, it was independent for only nine days (November–December 1975). Then Indonesians moved in and brutalized the native population, killing hundreds of thousands and sending more into exile. Only in 1999 did Australian troops backed by the United Nations begin to stabilize East Timor, creating a sovereign nation by 2002. In 1994, in the former Belgian colonies in Africa of Rwanda and Burundi, the legacy of ethnic rivalry stoked by colonial imperialism burst out in horrible slaughter. Hutu regimes started butchering lighter-skinned ethnic Tutsis with machetes. By the time they were halted a few weeks later, after a small response by the United Nations, they had killed eight hundred thousand men, women, and children.

Europeans confronted their own massacres in the Balkans of the 1990s. During the Cold War, Soviet troops maintained stability in the nations of Hungary, Romania, and Bulgaria. Bulgarian communists in the 1980s were particularly extreme in enforcing ethnic conformity. They forced Turks to change their names and give up their customs or go into exile, which hundreds of thousands did. Although the postcommunist regime cut back on such discrimination against Turks, other politicians enflamed ethnic tensions as a way to win elections.

The ethnic breakup of Yugoslavia set in motion the worst violence in Europe since World War II. During that war, communist partisans led by Josep Broz, called **Tito** (r. 1945–1980), fought both the Serbian fascist Chetnik insurgents and the Croatian fascist Ustaša regime installed by the Nazis. At war's end, Tito ruled the country.

Yet he avoided becoming a Soviet puppet and instead crafted his own brand of communist dictatorship. For his People's Republic of Yugoslavia, Tito maintained a beneficial balance in the Cold War rivalry. Officially a communist state, Tito's Yugoslavia broke quite early with Stalin and pursued friendship with capitalist Western European states. At home, he calmed the ethnic disputes that had transformed the prewar Kingdom of Serbs, Croats, and Slovenes into the Serbian fascist dictatorship of Yugoslavia. Half Croat and half Slovene himself, Tito deemphasized ethnic identity. He set up a federal system of six states: Slovenia, Croatia, Montenegro, Bosnia-Herzegovina, Serbia, and Macedonia. Each state remained somewhat autonomous from any potential Serbian bullying. Serbian nationalism was further weakened with carving out of Serbia the two autonomous provinces of Vojvodina and **Kosovo**, each with non-Serbian ethnic majorities (Hungarian and Albanian, respectively). Having dissolved ethnic tensions and situated between East and West, Yugoslavia became one of the more prosperous Eastern European countries.

Tito's death in 1980 changed little at first. The presidents of the six republics rotated the central presidency. Already in 1981, however, disturbances began in Kosovo, where Albanians, who made up 90 percent of the population, wanted more use of their own languages and better living conditions. As the Cold War ended in 1989, the president of the Serbian federal state, Slobodan Milošević, decided to use ethnic tensions for his own political gain. A Serb himself, he fueled ethnic resentment of the small Orthodox Christian Serbian minority in the province of Kosovo against the Muslim Albanian majority. He proclaimed that Serbians would not tolerate subservience in their own historic homeland.

With this revival of ethnic divisiveness the leaders of the other federal states within Yugoslavia worried about a possible Serbian takeover that would repeat the legacy of 1929. In June 1991, **Slovenia** and **Croatia** preemptively proclaimed independence. When an invasion by the Serbian-dominated Yugoslav army failed, both countries were internationally recognized as sovereign states. Nonetheless, Serbian-Croatian warfare was intense, and atrocities became the order of the day. The new term *ethnic cleansing* was coined, as both sides used threats, destruction of homes and businesses, murder, and rape to drive away rival ethnic groups from villages and districts each wanted to claim as its own.

By early 1992, **Bosnia-Herzegovina** began its own attempt at independence. Unhappily for that state, Bosnia was the most ethnically divided of all. The dual province included Roman Catholic Croats, Orthodox Serbs, and large numbers of "Bosniaks," namely Serbo-Croatian Muslims. Croatia and the Serbian-dominated remnant of Yugoslavia both attacked. A siege from 1992 to 1996 shelled the provincial capital of Sarajevo. As recently as 1984, the historic town had hosted the Winter Olympics as a symbol of peaceful competition and excellence. After the bombardment, it lay in ruins. Meanwhile, **Macedonia** used the opportunity to negotiate independence, leaving Serbia and Montenegro as the rump of the Yugoslav Federation. Greek objections to the use of the name *Macedonia*, with its Hellenistic heritage from Philip II and Alexander, forced that country to call itself officially the "Former Yugoslav Republic of Macedonia" (FYROM). A compromise to settle on the name "Republic of North Macedonia" in 2018 still faced violent opposition from extremists on both sides.

Russia's sympathies with its old ally Serbia limited what the United Nations could achieve to stop the violence in the former Yugoslavia. UN peacekeepers stood by as Serb militias and military raped and murdered. Consequently, Western powers decided to realign the mission of NATO. The end of the Cold War and the breakup of the Warsaw Pact had removed the need to defend Europe against the extinct Soviet Union. Now the Western military alliance system took up peacekeeping in Europe. In August 1995 NATO planes began air strikes intended to reduce the warfare in Bosnia. After the Dayton Accords of November 1995, NATO sent in sixty thousand troops, who successfully ended the fighting there. Subsequently, Western troops slowly shrank in number, until by 2004 the European Union took over the mission. By 2018, a few hundred EU troops and bureaucrats remained stationed in Bosnia-Herzegovina to help with stabilization and state building. Some Bosnians even hoped to enter candidacy to the EU like its fellow Balkan states. Despite this success, many Bosnians remained frustrated with ongoing slow implementation of legal reforms, quarreling politicians, high unemployment, official corruption, organized crime, and the desire of some ethnic Serbs and Croats to break up the state.

Another conflict exploded in the late 1990s over ethnic Albanians in Kosovo, where Milošević's nationalist ranting about Yugoslavia had begun. The self-proclaimed Kosovo Liberation Army launched a rebellion in that province on behalf of the Albanian majority. Milošević's Yugoslav Federation retaliated for what it saw as Kosovar terrorism and began ethnic cleansing in January 1999. NATO then launched an aerial bombing campaign to stop the killings and expulsions. Soon NATO troops occupied the province, allowing the Kosovar Albanians to frame their own self-government. A few thousand European Union bureaucrats in the "Rule of Law Mission in Kosovo" (EULEX) and several thousand NATO troops have kept the peace and worked toward building up local political institutions. Nevertheless, several EU members still do not recognize Kosovo's independence, declared in 2008. Finally, Montenegro abandoned the Yugoslav Federation in 2005, leaving Serbia to its own destiny. But even though the fighting was over, the consequences were not. The United Nations Security Council, concerned about past atrocities and anxious to prevent future violence, set up an International Criminal Tribunal in The

Hague to hold leaders of the former Yugoslavia accountable for war crimes. Ninety war criminals were found guilty; Serbia's Milošević died while awaiting trial; only a few trials still continue. Overall, these conflicts and policies have reduced ethnic differences in the Balkan states, but at the cost of much blood and destruction. The breakup of Yugoslavia demonstrated again how the passionate lures of separatism can thwart even honest efforts toward integration and unity.

Western states, for example, continued to confront world problems made worse by nationalism and ethnic differences. Russian domination of Chechnya provoked open, nasty military strikes and terrorism. When Russian authorities used poison gas to resolve a hostage situation in a Moscow theater in 2002, they killed over a hundred of the hostages along with the several dozen Chechen gunmen. Beginning in 1994, the ethnic minority of Mayan descent in the Mexican province of Chiapas organized a revolt under the Zapatistas. That conflict is still simmering today. Other states suffered divisions with less violence but important consequences. In Canada, beginning in the 1960s, the Québecois insisted on their own ethnic French identity, driving millions of citizens of non-French heritage out of the province. Tensions were eased as Canada actually, although carefully, promoted immigration to diversify national identity beyond Francophone versus Anglophone. Prime Minister Pierre Trudeau in 1971 fostered diversity rather than uniformity as the model for Canadian patriotism.

In Australia, immigration of tens of thousands per year, especially from India and China, grew the population more than birthrates by citizens. But when hundreds of refugees began to arrive by sea in 2001, they provoked anger and opposition. Refused entry, the Australian government offshored them into costly concentration camps on remote islands until resettlement. Racial tensions against Lebanese and other ethnic immigrants from the Eastern Mediterranean sparked riots in the Sydney suburb of Cronulla in 2005. As for the Aboriginal and Torres Strait Islander peoples, policies called Stolen Generations that took children from native families to be Europeanized finally ended in the 1970s. But despite a court decision in 1996 that recognized native title to land, the government sharply restricted those rights. Efforts to have Aboriginal people recognized in the Australian constitution continue to limp along. The ongoing challenge of nationalism has been how to balance desires for ethnic diversity with ideals of nationalist conformity.

Review: *How did nationalism resurge after the Cold War?*

Response:

HAVES AND CANNOTS

In addition to ethnic divisions, economic inequalities troubled the industrialized Western states at the end of the twentieth and beginning of the twenty-first centuries. Starting in the 1970s, the West's economic success began to falter, ending years of unheard of growth after World War II. The oil embargo by OPEC in 1974 marked a turning point. High fuel prices, international competition, inflation, the cost of good wages and benefits, and environmental regulations weakened the profits made in Western nations. Unemployment rates of between 5 and 10 percent burdened Western economies, even though such levels were well below the levels of the Great Depression. Increasingly, capitalists invested in factories built in Third World nations, where they could pay a fraction of the wages expected by Western workers organized in unions. Many Western nations saw high-wage manufacturing jobs disappear, to be replaced by low-wage service jobs (cooking, cleaning, or clerking). Some economists considered this as mere "creative destruction," as described by the Austrian Joseph Schumpeter. Others worried that this postindustrial economy slowed the rise in standard of living for the lower middle class compared with the upper and upper middle classes.

Different Western governments followed varying economic advice (see diagram 15.1). Sweden and Norway developed the welfare state to the highest possible degree outside communist regimes. Cradle-to-grave benefits supplied sufficient security and prosperity for many Scandinavians, if not quick economic expansion. Many other countries tried to cut back on some state-managed benefits. By the 1980s, even the socialist leaders of France (Mitterand) and Austria (Vranitzky) trimmed social programs. To compensate for lower wages, Western European regimes increased vacation time, while the Americans encouraged more women and immigrants into the workforce at lower wages.

By the late 1970s the welfare-state concept had come under attack by economists and politicians. Most famously, the "Chicago Boys," led by Milton Friedman, promoted a stronger, renewed laissez-faire attitude, encouraging governments to abandon ideas based on Keynesian economic theory. According to them, the only significant economic role government should have was balancing the money supply to prevent inflation. Otherwise, the economy worked best when government avoided imposing regulations and spending on social programs. Instead, participants in markets should be as free as possible to make economic decisions. Prime Minister Thatcher of Britain led the way, cutting welfare benefits and reprivatizing nationalized industries. Experiments with laissez-faire economics by Latin American regimes in Chile and Argentina failed to bring the predicted prosperity. In the United States, conservatives claimed to adopt similar policies, leading President Reagan to reduce some tax rates. Yet his Republican administration actually spent more on both social and military programs than the previous Democratic administration, making up the difference by borrowing money from abroad. With all this new borrowing and debt, and new competition from Germany and Japan, America's singular economic dominance of the West and the world was much reduced by the end of the 1980s.

MERCANTILISM

LAISSEZ-FAIRE / CLASSICAL
LIBERAL ECONOMICS

SOCIALISM

KEYNESIAN ECONOMICS

SUPPLY-SIDE / TRICKLE-DOWN / REAGANOMICS

Diagram 15.1.   Economic Theories of Capitalism. To summarize the various proposals dealing with the challenges of capitalism, these cartoons highlight the alleged role of government (the man with the crown) in dealing with capital (the bag of $) and contracts (the paper): 1. In mercantilism (1600s), the government and businessmen work together by establishing monopolies to benefit the state's balance of trade. 2. In laissez-faire (early 1800s), the government takes a hands-off approach, allowing the businessmen to make money according to enlightened self-interest. 3. In socialism (late 1800s), the workers demand a share of the wealth (an appeal usually resisted by government and business). 4. In Keynesian economics (1930s), the government steps in with regulations and capital investment to help the economy recover from or to prevent a depression. 5. In supply-side or trickle-down economics, or Reaganomics (1980s), a laissez-faire approach allows businesses to make their own decisions with the expectation that profits will spread to government and workers.

A new electronics industry based on computers did create new jobs. The Allies had invented computers during World War II in order to break secret codes of the Axis powers, and the computational ability of computers quickly increased. As new technologies such as transistors and the microchip were invented, computers became cheaper and smaller. The computer revolution accelerated with the invention of the **personal computer**. By the 1980s, desktop or personal computers became a consumer product in the West. First used as advanced typewriters, they soon expanded into drawing, graphics, spreadsheets, and databases, as well as games from simple solitaire to first-person shooter to multiplayer strategy and tactics simulations.

Soon computer users were connected by new global communication provided through the **Internet** (connecting local computers), the World Wide Web (structuring access to some of the information on the Internet), and e-mail (sending and receiving personal messages). In modern industrialized societies, computers control and regulate our lives more than any human bureaucrat ever could. Also, for those who can afford to spend the time to learn to use them, computers help with the acquisition of new knowledge, which is power. With wireless and cellular technologies for phones and computers developed by the end of the twentieth century, people on the move easily connected both to each other and to a vast amount of data. Through search engines, most importantly Google since the turn of the century, users have more knowledge at their fingertips than anyone ever in history. Between 2004 and 2007 three new **social media** platforms, YouTube, Twitter, and Facebook, followed by the iPhone as the first "smartphone," connected users more intimately and empowered them to be more creative than almost any previous communications technology in history.

The ease with which words and images could be electronically distributed set an example for marketing goods and services. Beginning in the 1980s, *globalization* became the slogan of those who wanted to make more money by relying on the worldwide grasp of the modern corporation, cheap transportation and communication, and low or nonexistent trade barriers and regulations. Globalization's advocates suggested that worldwide marketing strategies for material goods would be more important than the nation-state and its politics, while a worldwide trade system would benefit rich and poor nations alike. Recognizing the new reality of globalization as early as 1975, leaders of the most important economic powers began to hold such annual summit meetings as the G7 (the United States, Japan, West Germany, Great Britain, France, Italy, and Canada).[2] These leaders coordinated select economic, social, and political policies as they coped with increasing global trade.

Some economists, politicians, and citizens warned about the negatives of globalization, where unchecked markets ignored social needs. Citizens concerned about issues of social justice and human rights began to organize NGOs (nongovernmental organizations), ranging from Amnesty International (to stop torture and

---

2. It became the G8 in the 1990s with the addition of Russia, although Russia's economy was the smallest of the members. It became the G7 again when they disinvited Russia after Putin's illegal seizure of the Crimea in 2014.

cruelty) to Greenpeace (to protect the environment). They objected to Western corporations who paid low wages to impoverished natives for their country's natural resources while charging high prices to their comparatively wealthy Western customers. Exploitation was simply the price of pursuing profit. An accidental explosion of an American chemical plant in Bhopal, India, in 1984, for example, killed four thousand people and injured tens of thousands of others. Broken wells and wrecked tankers spilled crude oil regularly, ruining pristine coastlines. Multinational or transnational enterprises seemed to show more loyalty to their managers and stockholders than patriotism or sympathy toward any one country or even general human welfare.

Meanwhile, inexpensive products poured into the West from Asia. Several Asian states modernized their economic policies to compete with the dominant Western nations. Japan had led the way in the 1970s with exports of automobiles and electronics, supported by activist government policies working with major manufacturing cartels. By the 1990s, the so-called Asian Tigers (Singapore, South Korea, Nationalist China/Taiwan, and the British colony of Hong Kong) likewise became competitive.

At the end of the twentieth century, communist China had recovered from the mistakes of Mao and was becoming an economic powerhouse driven by a Western-style economy. The regime did not, however, allow Western-style democracy. In 1989, popular protests in Tiananmen Square in Beijing built a crude copy of the Statue of Liberty and demanded more representative government. The totalitarian, one-party regime dispersed the demonstrators, refusing to acknowledge how many it arrested or killed. Despite political repression, China opened economic opportunities.

China's dynamism accelerated after 1997, when the British finally returned to China their colony of Hong Kong, which Britain had held since the Opium Wars in the 1840s. China began its own version of the Commercial and Industrial Revolutions, becoming an attractive business partner to Western companies, drawing on Western capital to rapidly industrialize. Many in the West invested capital in this industrialization, or even dismantled actual factories in their home countries and shipped them to China (firing, of course, the Western workers). This new Industrial Revolution likewise exploited Chinese workers as the West had a century before. The Chinese also had child and prison laborers, long hours, high quotas, and spartan dormitories behind walls with barbed wire. As in the West in the nineteenth century, the government forbade workers to organize but was itself slow to protect workers. Still, since factory workers' wages were superior to those offered by the collapsing rural economy, many Chinese had little choice but to adapt to this new revolution. And westerners willingly paid for cheap bedding, toothbrushes, clothing, toys, and many other items at their discount warehouse stores, all "Made in China." China has used its new wealth to increase its international prestige and intervention. Once a second-rate nuclear power, China has the potential to become the world's most powerful state, militarily and economically, in the twenty-first century.

Consumerism and industrialization's impact on the environment raised concerns about their impact on our planet. Chemical emissions seemed to have opened a hole over the Antarctic in the ozone layer that protects the earth's surface from destructive ultraviolet rays. Children of European descent in Australia and New Zealand were soon required to protect their light skin with sunscreen and floppy hats. Recent scientific studies also suggest that air pollution, carbon dioxide emissions, energy production, and deforestation have produced a greenhouse effect that is heating up the atmosphere. Millions of acres of arable land in Africa and Asia have turned into desert, as rivers, lakes, and even the entire Aral Sea have dried up. The overwhelming number of scientific studies about **global climate change** have concluded that "global warming" is melting the glaciers and polar ice caps and then raising water levels to flood coastal areas. Many politicians and economists, however, are reluctant to initiate reforms that would be costly and so might threaten standards of living. Yet in 2015, states began signing on to the Paris Agreement, supplementing the Kyoto Protocol of 2005, to cut carbon emissions that damage the environment. By 2018, over 175 governments had ratified the agreement, although President Trump notified the UN of the US government's intention to withdraw. Should the global climate continue to warm as predicted, conflicts over water and land should correspondingly increase.

Even as industrialization hurts the planet, it also harms human bodies. Greater urbanization has created problematic cities in Asia and Africa. Even our food supply has become mechanized. Modern factories for food crowd thousands of caged pigs or chickens into warehouses. There they dwell in darkness and consume hormones (to speed their growth), antibiotics (to prevent diseases that would normally destroy creatures living so closely together in filth), the recycled remnants of their fellow creatures (as cheap food), and laxatives (to make their excrement more manageable). On the one hand, genetically modified foodstuffs offer the potential to provide still cheaper and more nutritious edibles. On the other hand, some believe that such artificial constructs may seriously damage our basic genetic structure and wreak havoc in natural ecosystems.

Indeed, advances in genetic science promise change at the foundation of our being. The biggest leap in the study of life since Darwin was the discovery in 1953 of deoxyribonucleic acid, or DNA. That double helix of molecules is the basic building block of life. DNA science is now used in fighting crime, having replaced fingerprints or dental impressions as the best means for identification of criminals or victims. Its real future, however, lies in scientists' tinkering with DNA's molecular structure. In 1988, the US Patent Office granted a patent on a genetically engineered mouse. Since then, synthetic organs, hormones, and compounds of all kinds for humans are being worked on. Corporations promoted GMOs (genetically modified organisms), which changed plants to be resistant to disease and pesticides or more rich in nutrients. Those opposed to their widespread use noted problems of the lack of long-term studies on their effects or the increased corporate control of agriculture. They tried to restrict the use of GMOs or at least have them clearly labeled when used in food products.

Just as with our genes, the sex lives of our bodies has become increasingly commercialized. The end of the Cold War brought the West's sexual revolution to the newly liberated Soviet bloc and also to the former colonial regions of the Third World. Business interests using the Internet and globalization provided more access to pornography for more people than ever before in history. Westerners traveled to poor countries in Asia and Eastern Europe for "sex tourism." The demands for the sex trade led organized criminals to virtually enslave women and children from poor countries to serve in brothels. While much of such commercial sex activity is done behind closed doors and outside the law, new liberties for people attracted to members of the same sex came into the open. In 1989, Denmark opened the door for homosexuals to enter civil unions, with rights similar to those of heterosexual marriage. After the Netherlands allowed legal marriage for same-sex couples in 2001, more than a dozen other Western nations in Europe and the Americas, as well as New Zealand and South Africa, also did so, with more surely to follow.

Nevertheless, Third World peoples, especially in Africa, resisted the Western openness about sexuality. On one side, modernists asserted that all people were inherently equal, regardless of sex or sexual orientation. On the other side, fundamentalists argued that men and women had different roles and that homosexuality was a sin. Many African Christians protested when Western churches ordained women and homosexuals, although the South African Anglican archbishop Desmond Tutu was a notable exception. Indeed, societies throughout Africa substantially opposed civil rights for women and homosexuals, encouraged by politicians and abetted by fundamentalist Western Christians. Ironically, leaders have claimed that their former Western imperialist masters are undermining "traditional" African identities about sex and sexuality, when colonial laws first codified rigid sex roles and punishment for deviation therefrom.

Review: How did Western economic practices dominate world trade?

Response:

SOURCES ON FAMILIES: SUPREME COURT OF THE UNITED STATES, *OBERGEFELL V. HODGES* (2015)

A decision handed down by the Supreme Court is a combination effort among the main justice (in this case, Anthony Kennedy) who delivers the opinion, those who concur, those who dissent, and the law clerks who work for them. In the following decision the court legalized same-sex marriages throughout the United States. This selection explains some of the rationale for doing so, providing context through the history of the institution.

From their beginning to their most recent page, the annals of human history reveal the transcendent importance of marriage. The lifelong union of a man and a woman always has promised nobility and dignity to all persons, without regard to their station in life. Marriage is sacred to those who live by their religions and offers unique fulfillment to those who find meaning in the secular realm. Its dynamic allows two people to find a life that could not be found alone, for a marriage becomes greater than just the two persons. Rising from the most basic human needs, marriage is essential to our most profound hopes and aspirations.

The centrality of marriage to the human condition makes it unsurprising that the institution has existed for millennia and across civilizations. Since the dawn of history, marriage has transformed strangers into relatives, binding families and societies together. . . . This wisdom was echoed . . . by Cicero, who wrote, "The first bond of society is marriage; next, children; and then the family." . . . It is fair and necessary to say these references were based on the understanding that marriage is a union between two persons of the opposite sex.

That history is the beginning of these cases. The respondents [those who oppose the petitioners or plaintiffs who brought the case] say it should be the end as well. To them, it would demean a timeless institution if the concept and lawful status of marriage were extended to two persons of the same sex. Marriage, in their view, is by its nature a gender-differentiated union of man and woman. This view long has been held—and continues to be held—in good faith by reasonable and sincere people here and through-out the world.

The petitioners acknowledge this history but contend that these cases cannot end there. Were their intent to demean the revered idea and reality of marriage, the petitioners' claims would be of a different order. But that is neither their purpose nor their submission. To the contrary, it is the enduring importance of marriage that underlies the petitioners' contentions. This, they say, is their whole point. . . .

Recounting the circumstances of three of these cases illustrates the urgency of the petitioners' cause from their perspective. Petitioner James Obergefell, a plaintiff in the Ohio case, met John Arthur over two decades ago. They fell in love and started a life together, establishing a lasting, committed relation. In 2011, however, Arthur was diagnosed with amyotrophic lateral sclerosis, or ALS. . . . Two years ago, Obergefell and Arthur decided . . . to marry before Arthur died. To fulfill their mutual promise, they traveled from Ohio to Maryland, where same-sex marriage was legal. It was difficult for Arthur to move, and so the couple were wed inside a medical transport plane as it remained on the tarmac in Baltimore. Three months later, Arthur died. . . . By statute, they must remain strangers even in death, a state-imposed separation Obergefell deems "hurtful for the rest of time." He brought suit to be shown as the surviving spouse on Arthur's death certificate.

April DeBoer and Jayne Rowse are co-plaintiffs in the case from Michigan. They celebrated a commitment ceremony to honor their permanent relation in 2007. They both work as nurses, DeBoer in a neonatal unit and Rowse in an emergency unit. In 2009, DeBoer and Rowse fostered and then adopted a baby boy. Later that same year, they welcomed another son into their family. The new baby, born prematurely and abandoned by his biological mother, required around-the-clock care. The next year, a baby girl with special needs joined their family. Michigan, however, permits only opposite-sex married couples or single individuals to adopt, so each child can have only one woman as his or her legal parent. If an emergency were to arise, schools and hospitals may treat the three children as if they had only one parent. And, were tragedy to befall either DeBoer or Rowse, the other would have no legal rights over the children she had not been permitted to adopt. This couple seeks relief from the continuing uncertainty their unmarried status creates in their lives.

Army Reserve Sergeant First Class Ijpe DeKoe and his partner Thomas Kostura, co-plaintiffs in the Tennessee case, fell in love. In 2011, DeKoe received orders to deploy to Afghanistan. Before leaving, he and Kostura married in New York. . . . Their lawful marriage is stripped from them whenever they reside in Tennessee, returning and disappearing as they travel across state lines. . . .

No union is more profound than marriage, for it embodies the highest ideals of love, fidelity, devotion, sacrifice, and family. In forming a marital union, two people become something greater than once they were. As some of the petitioners in these cases demonstrate, marriage embodies a love that may endure even past death. It would misunderstand these men and women to say they disrespect the idea of marriage. Their plea is that they do respect it, respect it so deeply that they seek to find its fulfillment for themselves. Their hope is not to be condemned to live in loneliness, excluded from one of civilization's oldest institutions. They ask for equal dignity in the eyes of the law. The Constitution grants them that right.

Questions:

- *How does the source place marriage in a historical context?*
- *How does the source use the personal experiences of the plaintiffs to make a case?*
- *How does the source argue against those who disagree with the decision?*

Responses:

Citation

Obergefell v. Hodges. 576 US (2015). Supreme Court of the United States. https:// www.supremecourt.gov/opinions/14pdf/14–556_3204.pdf.

For more on this source, go to http://www.concisewesternciv.com/sources/sof15.-html.

VALUES OF VIOLENCE

Nationalist terrorism seemed on the decline by the 1990s in much of the West. The IRA in Northern Ireland and the ETA in Spain slowly stopped their bombings. In the United States, some homegrown terrorists struck against Planned Parenthood clinics, African Americans, and the government itself (such as the 1995 bombing of the Oklahoma City Federal Building that killed 168 people). But most Americans worried more about crime directly caused by the illegal drug trade. Victory in the Cold War seemed to herald a new triumph of what some saw as Western values of democracy, global capitalism, and the nation-state.

Nevertheless, tensions about Israel and restlessness in the Middle East provided fuel for new fires. The West's dependence on oil imports continued to force its attention toward the region. Many people there disliked both Western ideology, with its acceptance of changing social attitudes, and economic exploitation, with profits flowing out of Arab and Muslim nations. Certain fundamentalist Muslims, as individuals and as groups, began to oppose the West with force.[3]

The West could, of course, take much of the blame for the growing opposition of some Muslims. The West did not leave Islam to flourish on its own. When westerners took over much of the Middle East in the nineteenth and early twentieth centuries, they were confident enough in their worldview to try to force both Christianity and secularism on their imperialist subjects. It was merely unexpected good fortune for many Arab nations that geologists discovered petroleum beneath their desert sands just as the imperialist experiment failed. To more easily get at cheap oil without direct colonial control, Western leaders propped up local despots and dictators with whom they could conveniently make economic arrangements. Meanwhile, many people in those countries resented both foreign intervention and the authoritarian governments it supported.

The tensions between aspects of Islamic civilization and a modern world created by Western civilization were revealed with the **Iranian Revolution** (1978–1980). Through much of the Cold War, the shah of Iran, Mohammed Reza Pahlavi, had ruled as a near-absolute monarch. The CIA had put the shah in power in 1953 by overthrowing the democratically elected but socialist prime minister Mohammad Mossadegh. Serving as a loyal ally of the United States in the region, the shah had been somewhat progressive, carrying out land reform in the 1970s and promoting

---

3. No one has yet come up with a satisfactory name for describing the wide range of different political agents who have recently combined Islam and terrorism. "Islamofascist" misapplies the nationalistic and state- or corporate-based ideology of fascism. "Jihadist" validates those who believe *jihad* is compatible with slaughter and suicide. "Islamist" may associate the name of the religion "Islam" too closely with indiscriminate killing. But it seems to work to distinguish "Islamic" as a term for those groups that are clearly fundamentalist. The Obama administration rejected the label "radical Islamic terrorists" as feeding into propaganda to increase hostility toward Muslims.

secular modernization and westernization. By the end of the 1970s, ironically, the rising wealth and education of the middle classes made them disgusted with the shah's secret police and absolutism. From exile in Paris, a religious leader, the Ayatollah Khomeini, orchestrated a revolution that forced the shah into exile in January 1979. Khomeini then created a new religious dictatorship, or theocracy, based on his interpretation of Islam.

The Iranian Revolution kept the science needed to maintain oil wealth and military power, but it rejected much of the rest of Western culture. After American president Jimmy Carter (r. 1977–1981) allowed the shah into the United States for medical treatment, Iranian students attacked the American embassy in Iran's capital of Tehran. They seized what they called a "spy den" and held its staff hostage for 444 days. Carter's failure to gain release or rescue of the hostages contributed to his defeat in his reelection campaign. The new Iran championed anti-Western civilization and called on other Muslims to support its expansionist Shiite agenda.

While the United States could not take direct action against Iran, it encouraged another friendly and more secular dictator of Iraq, Saddam Hussein (r. 1979–2004), to attack Iran, supporting him with intelligence and weapons. The resulting Iran-Iraq War (1980–1988) killed hundreds of thousands, reviving trench warfare and even the use of poison gas. After the war ended as a draw, Saddam looked toward his wealthy neighbor Kuwait as a way to pay for the war's costs. The British had carved Kuwait out of the Ottoman Empire in the nineteenth century. From Saddam Hussein's point of view, he just wanted to take back what had rightfully belonged to Iraq before the Western surge of imperialism. In August 1990 his armies invaded the tiny principality.

Kuwait was, however, a sovereign state and a member of the United Nations, which had been created to prevent such wars. Under the leadership of American president George H. W. Bush (r. 1989–1993), the United Nations intervened. During the **First Persian Gulf War** (1990–1991), half a million American and allied troops liberated Kuwait at the disproportionate cost of about eight hundred lives for the United States and its allies, versus probably one hundred thousand Iraqis. The UN forces left Saddam Hussein in power, though, since the United Nations does not intervene in the internal affairs of its members.

The First Gulf War only helped the new militant version of Islam to grow. Saddam Hussein, though his political base had always been largely secularist, began to reframe his position as one of Muslims against westerners. Many Muslims in other Islamic countries also had become hostile against their own secular regimes as well as against Israel, the United States, and Western civilization as a whole. The dictator Muammar Gaddafi (r. 1969–2011) in Libya, for example, had sponsored the bombing of a Pan Am flight to the United States which exploded over Lockerbie, Scotland, in 1988. In 1997, the so-called Islamic Group killed dozens of tourists at Luxor in Egypt.

The unending struggle between the Palestinians and Israelis fueled other acts of terror. Israeli governments had failed to implement real Palestinian self-government as agreed in the Camp David Accords, while Western governments did little to force them to do so. Instead, Israel continued to dispossess Palestinians and encouraged Jewish settlers to create fortified enclaves within occupied areas.

An attack in 1983 by Hezbollah blowing up US Marines in their barracks frightened the United States into reducing its direct involvement in the region. By the 1990s, Palestinians in the occupied territories carried out *intifadas* (uprisings), consisting of boycotts of Israeli businesses, strikes, demonstrations, and "wars of stones," or rock throwing. The Israelis responded by restricting Palestinian movements (thus preventing them from working), demolitions (bulldozing homes and villages), and force (such as rocket assassination attacks on Palestinian leaders). In a Second Intifada (2001–2005), Palestinian suicide bombers were regularly blowing up themselves and numerous Israelis on buses and in cafés. Divisions among Palestinians led to Fatah, a successor to the PLO, as the authority in the West Bank, while the rival Hamas (Islamic Resistance Group) in the Gaza Strip regularly launched chaotic missile attacks that killed a few Israelis. Israel usually responded disproportionately with its own missiles and invasions that demolished many buildings and killed hundreds. Neither Palestinian leaders nor Israeli politicians seemed able to end mutual exchanges of violence, while Western regimes likewise failed to engage.

Another nest of hostility to the West developed in Afghanistan. When the Americans had armed the Muslim militant *mujahideen* in Afghanistan to fight the Soviets in the 1980s, they did not foresee possible awful consequences. After the Cold War had ended, some religious students, or **Taliban**, became so disgusted with the ongoing violence that they organized their own attacks on everyone else, using the arms America had given them. Their devotion and discipline helped them to take over the country. They then imposed their own Islamist dictatorship, even harsher in the cultural imperatives than Iran's. Their most notorious actions included both the forcible confinement and sexual abuse of women and iconoclastically destroying priceless ancient sculptures.

The Taliban provided a haven to yet another new kind of international Islamist terrorist group, **al-Qa'ida** (the Base). Founded and financed by a Saudi former oil and construction magnate, Osama bin Laden, al-Qa'ida promoted his militant version of Islam. He was especially resentful of American intervention in the Middle East, whether in support of Israel or against Saddam Hussein. His Islamist organization launched the boldest terrorist attack in history on 11 September 2001 (**9/11**). Two hijacked airliners hit the twin towers of the World Trade Center in New York City, symbol of Western commerce and capitalism. The resulting fires led to the skyscrapers' collapse. A third plane damaged the Pentagon (the US military's command center near Washington, DC), while a fourth crashed into a field in Pennsylvania after its hostage passengers fought back against their hijackers. All told, about three thousand people (mostly Americans, but also dozens from other nations) died on that day from these attacks.

In response, President George W. Bush (r. 2001–2009) declared a "War on Terrorism." This declaration, unfortunately, was a muddy concept. For one, only Congress could constitutionally declare war. For another, terrorism has been a tactic, not an enemy against whom a state can easily fight using traditional armed forces. Since the end of the nineteenth century, terrorists have used small-scale violence to achieve their political goals. Such terrorist attacks are hard to stop. As access to weapons becomes easier and grudges against specific state systems do not fade, terrorism offers an affordable substitute for sustained guerrilla war or conventional armies. Typical armed forces have been ill suited to combat terrorists, who blended so easily into the civilian population, both before and after they struck. Even in industrialized Western nations, such as Britain facing the IRA in Northern Ireland or Spain facing the ETA in the Basque regions, authorities could not completely crush terrorist cells. But by using the term *war*, the United States has become permanently, but vaguely, stuck "at war."

Since 9/11, some success against terrorism has come from addressing the root political complaints and using approaches similar to criminal investigations, expanding intelligence and police agencies. Some laws threatened to remove civil rights and legal due process from both citizens and aliens as they increased surveillance of public places, private computer and phone communications, and even persons' homes. Western states tended to favor security over civil liberty, invasive technology versus personal privacy, and ethnic intolerance against economic generosity.

Militarily, Article 5 of NATO's mutual self-defense agreement went into effect: an attack on one member was an attack on all. The United States and allied troops retaliated for 9/11 by invading Afghanistan, where the Taliban had sheltered bases of al-Qa'ida. The United States and its allies won a quick victory. Yet most al-Qa'ida leaders, including Osama bin Laden, managed to escape. Unfortunately for peace, Afghanistan did not stabilize either, as warlords reasserted their domination against tens of thousands of troops from NATO members and fifty partner states.

Then, despite being the world's lone superpower, the United States found itself unable to lead the West in dealing with terrorism, despite sympathy generated by the 9/11 attacks. Instead of finishing off al-Qa'ida, President Bush's attention turned to removing Saddam Hussein from power in Iraq. The Bush administration listened to "neoconservative" theorists who promoted a renewed American exceptionalism, believing that the United States could unilaterally intervene in troubled spots around the world to create Western-style capitalist democracies.

In this context, the American administration asserted that invading Iraq was part of that vague wider "War on Terrorism." They suggested that Saddam had connections with al-Qa'ida and the attacks of 9/11 (which was not true). Specifically, the United States claimed that Iraq had defied UN resolutions about eliminating weapons of mass destruction (**WMDs**, a new name for the category "ABC" or atomic, biological, chemical weapons). The failure of UN inspectors to find any evidence of such weapons notwithstanding, Bush pushed toward invasion. Neither the United Nations, nor NATO, nor most of the world's nations supported this action. Many westerners actively protested what they saw as the American rush into a distracting war. Nevertheless, the application of new bombing technology and rapid mobile forces, called "shock and awe," won the United States and its "Coalition of the Willing" (with Great Britain as the only serious participant) a quick military conquest in the **Iraq or Second Persian Gulf War** (2003–2011). Many countries in Asia and Africa, however, saw America's mission, called "Operation Iraqi Freedom," as a violation of international law, reinforcing a fear that America could and would invade wherever it wanted, at will.

The quick mission accomplishment, however, did not end the conflict, as American and allied forces faced serious hostility to their occupation. Iraqi insurgents regularly killed coalition troops with sniping and IEDs (improvised explosive devices) while terrorizing their own fragile government and weary population with kidnappings and beheadings. Human rights organizations and defenders sharply criticized the American government for its actions, including torture of "enemy combatants," which was against international law. Al-Qa'ida's terrorist bombings of commuter trains in Madrid on 13 March 2004 or subway bombings in London in 2005 proved that it could operate despite the loss of bases in Afghanistan. Osama bin Laden himself remained at large until 2011, when American commandos under the orders of the next president, Barack Obama (r. 2009–2017), shot him in his secret refuge in Pakistan. By the end of that year, Obama carried out an agreement made by the previous Bush administration to pull out all American combat troops from Iraq, leaving it severely divided between Sunni, Shia, and Kurds.

The official end of America's Iraq War celebrated very little of a victory for "Western" values, much less American power. People of course feared terrorist kidnappings, shootings, hijackings, and suicide bombings. They resented the randomness, fatalities, and ultimate futility of most terrorist attacks. Yet many around the world also condemned the US course of preemptive war, torture, and bombing from the skies, especially since it had not created functional and prosperous democracies in its wake.

Review: How did Western and non-Western societies use violence to achieve political and cultural ends?

Response:

THE WALLS GO UP AGAIN

One of the sad ironies of history in the past few years has been the reappearance of walls. When the Berlin Wall and Iron Curtain fell at the end of the Cold War, many people hoped for a new age of toleration and prosperity (see figure 15.4). New and old fears, however, have brought back wall building with a vengeance. The mentality of using barriers had never quite disappeared. Militarized frontiers had continued between the Koreas, and in parts of Asia and Africa. In Northern Ireland the "Peace Lines" or "Peace Walls" which had gone up during the Troubles remained standing, even if in 2007 a functional coalition government called for them to come

Figure 15.4. Fragments of the Berlin Wall live on as art. This painting originated in 1979, when a photographer captured the moment when Soviet premier Leonid Brezhnev embraced East German president Erich Honecker in a "socialist fraternal kiss." After the Wall's fall in 1989, Russian artist Dmitri Vrubel re-created the kiss on one section, with the title in Russian and German, "My God, help me to survive this deadly love." In 2009, twenty years after the fall, the wall remnant was cleaned, repaired, and repainted to be a more durable "gallery." The kiss painting survives today, covered with graffiti and blocked behind parked cars—somewhat symbolic of the messiness of the West.

down. At the turn of the century Israel had begun its currently roughly 25-foot-high and 440-mile-long "West Bank Barrier." Ostensibly it prevented suicide bombings, even if Palestinians considered that its purpose was to reduce their economic and political freedoms and concretize the theft of their territory. Some critics thought the wall more reminiscent of the ghettoes of the Renaissance or Third Reich.

A new barricade mentality began, however, after the globalized economy suffered a severe blow in 2008. In the years just before, many businesspeople and economists boasted from their towering skyscrapers that the constant capitalist cycle of boom and bust had been forever broken. Since market bubbles and bursts were a relic of history, financial barriers prohibiting banks from speculating were torn down. Capitalists deregulated, increased debt, failed to require sufficient collateral, and encouraged both incautious investing and rampant profit reaping. The remnants of the Reagan and Thatcher economic favoritism toward profit drew in even Democrats under Bill Clinton (r. 1993–2001), Labour under Tony Blair (r. 1997–2007), and other social democratic parties. Most regimes agreed to loosening regulations for health and safety, lowering taxes on the wealthy, encouraging companies to merge and monopolize, allowing exploitative interest rates on loans and credit cards, attacking trade unionism, and transferring capital and industry easily between and outside Western nations. Free trade agreements and cheaper transportation of goods in containers led to the dismantling of factories. Left behind were many unemployed workers unwilling or unable to follow jobs across country or overseas.

Naïve confidence in the wisdom of markets proved false, since many investments were not as safe as advertised. In America, stock markets and hedge funds had become overinflated with risky products called derivatives. In Europe, poor countries were showered with loans that would be difficult to repay, economic downturn or not. In 2008 the markets suddenly collapsed when investors realized how much bad debt had piled up. Trillions of euros and dollars and pounds completely disappeared over the following year in what some call the "Great Recession." The major banks of Iceland, for example, which had grown bigger than the rest of the national economy, completely crashed. That ruined that country's economy and stalled its admission to the European Union.

The eurozone itself added to its own crisis in 2009 after the Greek government admitted that it had ignored required limits on its national debt. The euro had been created with a significant flaw: the dominant Deutsche Bundesbank (German Central Bank) largely controlled its value, which meant that individual nations could not manipulate currency rates to help them recover from debt, as they had done before the currency union. As a result, Greece threatened to default. There was even talk of "Grexit," or Greece exiting from the European Union. To prevent widespread economic devastation, the EU poured billions of euros in as bailouts while imposing strict austerity measures (increasing taxes and cutting social welfare). The Greek economy still weakened and drove unemployment numbers to over a quarter of the workforce. Soon Portugal, Ireland, Italy, and Spain joined in admitting to serious debt and needing bailouts and other aid. Their failures earned those countries the insulting acronym of PIIGS.

How Europe, the West, and the global economic powers dealt with this crisis exposed the complex strengths and tensions that still lay within Western civilization. The responses to the collapse alternated between two economic theories. On one side, policies of massive Keynesian spending, careful monitoring, and regulation faced off on the other side against "reforms" of increasing privatization of public enterprises and austerity by cutting social services, government pensions, and civil services. Each side claimed theirs was the right course.

In the United States, after the bankruptcy of Lehman Brothers, an investment company, the government threw taxpayer money at other "too big to fail" corporations and banks, allowing investors and owners to stay wealthy. Executives paid themselves and major investors with the bailouts rather than fund pensions or raise wages for middle-class jobs. Except in Iceland, financial executives avoided jail (unlike in some previous financial mismanagement crises). Corporation managements used shareholder money to pay off the few fines levied against them as punishment. After ten years, Western economies seemed to be healing, and the wealthy had accumulated a greater share of wealth than ever, while the middle class seemed threatened by the high costs of living on stagnant wages and by a rising revolution in robotics. But which lessons, if any, governments and capitalists would learn from these failures remained unknown (see Primary Source Project 15).

The many common citizens themselves seemed to lose confidence in the elites who led them into economic disaster. Populations reacted to rising unemployment and social welfare cutbacks by demonstrating, striking, and voting for extremist parties. Many became anti-globalization, anti–European Union, or anti–Wall Street. That somehow made sense, since their policies had largely caused the economic failure. Much of privately owned and increasingly consolidated broadcast and print media deflected the blame for people's problems elsewhere: against minorities, the poor, "foreigners," and migrants.

Sudden increases of migrants from Muslim countries helped to trigger a panic. The escalation originated in the so-called Arab Spring of 2011. As we have seen, many Arab states were ruled by authoritarian governments that rejected participation of the people around nationalist "traditions." In the Arab Spring, however, revolts broke out inspired by the hope that certain Western ideas of free speech, open and fair elections with choice, checks and balances on authority, and honest and efficient bureaucracies might be good for their countries as well. The conflicts began in December 2010, when police abuse in Tunisia on behalf of its dictator provoked riots, which then encouraged people in various other North African and Middle East countries to demonstrate, protest, and agitate for democratic change. Dictators toppled in Tunisia, Libya, Egypt, Syria, Bahrain, and Yemen. In many of the elections that followed, however, Islamist parties such as the Muslim Brotherhood tended to win and then tried to entrench themselves in power, while enforcing fundamentalist religious conformity. Rather than bringing freedom, therefore, the elections merely brought a different form of repression.

Revolutions went even more wrong in Libya and Syria. With the overt intervention of NATO through air support, Libyans overthrew Colonel Muammar Gaddafi after decades of rule. But their inability to restore order left a failed state. In Syria a civil war broke out, in which Western powers declined at first to intervene. The dictator Bashar al-Assad (r. 2000–), who had inherited power from his father, had failed to address the crisis of a massive drought. In reaction to protests, Assad had tens of thousands of Syrians arrested, tortured, and killed while reducing many neighborhoods to rubble.

These two failed regimes led to thousands, then millions of "economic" and "political" refugees heading toward Europe through Libya and from Syria. In 2013 and 2014, Italian border facilities became so overwhelmed with tens of thousands of migrants crossing the Mediterranean in ramshackle boats that they could only be housed in near concentration camp conditions. At first, other European Union members offered little help for Italy's border problem. As migrant numbers climbed in 2015, however, leaders and citizens of some European countries, especially Chancellor Angela Merkel of Germany (r. 2005–), welcomed refugees. Confronted with these humanitarian crises, the European Commission required all Union members to accept set quotas of refugees. Germany generously took in the most, a million refugees in 2015 alone (measured against a population of eighty-one million).

Then a reaction flared up. The seemingly never-ending flood of immigrants and a few incidents of cultural conflict provoked xenophobia, especially in the former East Germany, which still suffered from comparatively low income levels and high unemployment. Then Hungary, Poland, Slovakia, and the Czech Republic banded together and refused to take any refugees, even while Spain, Greece, and Italy were overburdened. And several states, such as Hungary and Austria, began constructing barriers, mostly chain-link fences with barbed or razor wire, enforced by border guards, to control or prevent immigrants from entering their countries. Walls had returned.

These populist and nativist political movements worried about the loss of their various ethnic identities within and across Europe. Even though studies show that immigrants do not increase crime, perception has been different. And even though studies show that immigrants often enrich an economy, people resent their cost in social benefits. In France an "identitarian" movement had been growing in reaction to Muslim immigrants. Identitarians promoted chauvinism and hostility to foreigners and rejected cosmopolitanism. Each country itself should be ethnically homogeneous, agreeing with nationalist ideas going back to the 1800s. It does seem paradoxical, though, that foreigners who were characterized as ignorant and inferior were simultaneously believed to be a threat capable of taking over the powerful complex industrialized states of Europe.

Two Eastern European countries openly embraced fascism, as they had between World Wars I and II. In Hungary, Prime Minister Viktor Orbán since 2010 and in Poland Jaroslaw Kaczyński of the PiS (Law and Justice Party) since 2015 have moved toward authoritarian regimes based on paranoid nationalism. Orbań and Kaczyński have followed Putin's success in Russia: restricting opposition parties, packing courts with subservient jurists, hiring cronies and partisans for the civil service, funneling public contracts to family and friends, and limiting freedom of speech. In November 2017 tens of thousands of Poles gathered to chant "White Europe, Europe must be white," while only a few thousand protested to "Stop fascism." In his reelection in 2018, Hungary's Orbań increased his popular support by campaigning against immigration. His government then made it a crime to help migrants who lack proper documentation. Politicians openly questioned who belonged in any country or to Europe itself (see map 15.2).

A new terrorist group soon bolstered fears. It arose, in part, because the Western-backed regimes in Iraq and Afghanistan had difficulty sustaining democracies, despite having trillions of dollars poured into the effort. Anti-Western forces began to counterattack the weak democracies. In early 2014, a Sunni-inclined group called ISIS or ISIL (Islamic State in Iraq and Greater Syria, or the Levant) used the ongoing civil war in Syria to seize control of parts of that country and invade Iraq. ISIL, considered overly extreme even by the weakened al-Qa'ida, proclaimed its hostility to Western values. Their anger went back to the arbitrary borders drawn by the victorious Allies after the fall of the Ottoman Empire at the end of World War I. As its name implies, ISIL aspired to establish a new transnational caliphate that eliminated the modern borders. The group began its acts of terrorism by broadcasting video of the beheadings of infidels. Soon, however, it seized US weapons from retreating Iraqi troops and used them in its own army. Several victories won ISIL wide territory across Syria and Iraq, where group members blew up Christian, Yazidi, and Shiite homes and sacred places. US and Western military responses, in cooperation with Russia, broke up ISIL's army, especially through the

Map 15.2. Europe, 2018.
How many countries belong to Europe? (Note that ongoing conflict in the Ukraine may change its borders, including the internationally unrecognized takeover of the Crimea by Russia).

use of **drones** (see figure 15.5). This latest advance in military technology enabled remote-controlled flying machines to fire missiles from a safe distance to blow up targets. Drones are more precise than traditional strategic bombing, but nevertheless they have targeted and killed innocent victims as well, albeit in smaller numbers.

ISIL responded to its military loss by launching terrorist attacks against the West, helped by new members recruited through social media on the Internet. Trucks became the new weapon of terrorists, plowing into crowds on streets, on bridges, and in marketplaces. Attacks in Nice, in 2016, followed by Ohio State University, Berlin, Jerusalem, London (twice in 2017), Stockholm, Barcelona, Edmonton, and New York, killed and injured several innocent people each time.

Things were somewhat better in the Western alliance's war in Afghanistan, where American-led NATO forces briefly stabilized the country by deploying a record high number of 130,000 troops by 2012. After that, the Bush administration started to wind down American involvement, handing over frontline combat to the Afghan military and leaving only about 13,000 NATO troops in advisory, training,

Figure 15.5. A predator drone armed with Hellfire missiles on patrol over Afghanistan. (US Air Force photo/Lt. Col. Leslie Pratt)

and support roles. But a resurgence of Taliban forces (with links to Iran and Russia) complicated the withdrawal. After November 2017, NATO troop numbers increased by a few thousand, with an additional 14,000 from the United States. Already Afghanistan is the longest war in American (although not European) history. In the face of continuing resistance, in 2018 NATO committed to funding its military presence through 2024. Yet without a clear plan or aggressive commitment to reinforcements, the Western alliance seemed unable to bring either peace or liberal democracy to the region, much less halt terrorism.

In 2016 those who feared foreign immigrants began to make their numbers felt at the polls. Since many of those immigrants were pouring into the EU, politicians in Great Britain decided to hold a plebiscite on whether the United Kingdom should remain part of the European Union. The supporters of "Brexit" (an abbreviation for British Exit) compared the European Union with the Roman Empire, and not in a good way (see Primary Source Project 5). They airily boasted that the departure would be easy and would enable Britain to make its own decisions. Pro-EU voices pointed out that extricating the United Kingdom would be very complicated and unprofitable.

On the day of the referendum, 23 June 2016, many Britons went to bed expecting that the Brexit option would be defeated. Everyone woke to find that a slim majority of votes had won for leaving the EU. The pro-EU prime minister immediately announced his resignation. Elsewhere, many Scots, who had overwhelmingly voted against Brexit, even began to renew talk of independence from the United Kingdom in order to remain in the EU. The new pro-Brexit prime minister, Theresa

May (r. 2016–), the United Kingdom's second woman in that position, began negotiations to withdraw Britain from the European Union. Unsurprisingly, talks did not
go as smoothly as the Brexit advocates had claimed they would.

Meanwhile, anti-immigration voices in the United States also gained political
control. On 8 November 2016, the real estate magnate and former reality-show host
Donald Trump won a surprise victory to become president of the United States. He
had begun his campaign in 2015 by disparaging immigrants from Mexico as drug
users, criminals, and rapists. His blustery rhetoric thrilled cheering crowds as he
boasted that only he could make America great again. At his new golf course in
Scotland the day after the Brexit vote, the presidential candidate cheered the
results, saying people were angry at open borders and had taken back their country.
His unique tweets on social media won him more fans. As a large part of his campaign platform, Trump repeatedly promised to build a wall on the Mexican border
to stop illegal immigration. His wall would cover at least half of the two thousand-
mile-long border, would be "big and beautiful," and would not cost Americans
anything: Mexico would pay for it.

Upon assuming office in 2017, one of Trump's first executive acts was to ban
citizens from seven Muslim countries from traveling to the United States. He also
reduced the number of refugees that would be accepted from states like Syria that
were torn by violence and civil war. In 2018 his administration implemented a
zero-tolerance policy for anyone entering the country illegally (see figure 15.6). To

Figure 15.6. Prototypes of the new bigger, taller, see-through border
wall for the US-Mexican border are shown to the public in the fall of 2017.
(Mani Albrecht for U.S. CBP)

enforce the policy, government agents at the border separated thousands of children from their parents and put some within pens or cages, also called "walls [made] out of chain-link fences." Very little planning was made about how family members could be reunited.

After the 2016 votes in Great Britain and the United States, Western intelligence services began to reveal the extent of malicious interference from a new form of warfare: cyberattacks. Evidence made increasingly clear that Russian officials had worked to influence the voting in Britain and America through infiltration of politicians' e-mail servers, probing of voting machines and databases, and made-up memes posted in social media. President Trump's confused pronouncements on whether or not he accepted the findings of the Western intelligence agencies helped to erode the Western alliance system.

Trump also proclaimed policies of "America First" that echoed the position of isolationists before both World War I and World War II. He discontinued work on international trade agreements and instead initiated protectionist trade wars with other economies, including longtime American allies. He called the European Union a "foe" of the United States and regularly criticized his fellow NATO members. To many observers, Trump seemed to disrespect known allies and instead defend Russia, in spite of its cyberattacks, its continued illegal occupation of Crimea, and its continuing intervention in Ukraine. Nevertheless, Trump often contradicted or denied his own recorded words and actions, leading to confusion both in the United States and abroad. His convenient practice for avoiding accountability was to accuse his opponents of "fake news" about any information or reports with which he disagreed, while his own people used "alternative facts." The Republican administration's new troubled relationship with both reality and allies in Europe undermined the idea of the West.

Within the United States, Trump's policy of "America First" helped to launch a new cultural war that questioned what it was to be a citizen in the twenty-first century. Advocates of multiculturalism continued to call for the acceptance of more diversity and additional help for the disadvantaged. The Black Lives Matter movement challenged the system about how too many young black men were shot by police. They partly blamed "white privilege," the idea that Americans whose ancestors came from Europe had certain inherent social advantages because of their race and identity. The #MeToo movement drew attention to misogyny, sexual harassment, and "rape culture." Opponents, however, attacked these ideas as overextensions of "political correctness." Instead, the "alt-right" argued that "white" men themselves were being sidelined in their own country by those who failed to recognize the inherent differences either between men and women or among various "races." Neo-Nazis openly marched at the University of Virginia in Charlottesville in August 2017, bearing tiki torches and shouting about "Blood and Soil" and that "the Jews will not replace us." Increasing numbers both in the United States and in Europe voted against politicians who favored democracy's usual system of compromise between opposing parties and views through the use of civil discourse. Instead they supported total victory for their own point of view by electing "their" strongmen (and occasional strongwomen), leading to further division and polarization rather than consensus.

Nationalist parties in France, the Netherlands, Austria, Germany, Sweden, Denmark, and Finland have surged in popularity and expanded their representation in parliaments. Nativist candidates were vocal in bashing European unity, as well as immigration, free trade, and deficit spending. The May 2017 presidential election in France required the cooperation of leftists, liberals, and moderates to unite around conservative Emmanuel Macron in order to defeat the Front National candidate Marine Le Pen. In October 2017 Catalonian nationalists tried to secede from Spain. The two nationalist parties in Germany, AfD (Alternative for Germany) and Pegida (Patriotic Europeans against the Islamization of the West), won seats in the German Reichstag in November 2017, weakening Merkel's ability to govern (see figure 15.7). A conservative-nationalist coalition government in Austria formed in late 2017, which proclaimed "Austria first!" In the Italian elections of 2018, the populist M5S (Five Star Movement) party, only recently formed in 2009, won the most votes and was able to form a government with the League party. Both parties showed hostility to the European Union.

Thus the post–Cold War consensus has been attacked from both sides of the political spectrum. From the left came complaints of freewheeling economic policies that enriched the few at the expense of the many. From the right, populism and nationalism resisted international cooperation and immigration. From the left multiculturalism and socialism continued to criticize dominant elites. A soft voice of reconciliation was Pope Francis I (r. 2013–), a Jesuit and former archbishop from Argentina, the first-ever head of the Roman Catholic Church to be chosen from the Americas. Like his namesake, the medieval Francis of Assisi, the pope called on people to build bridges, not walls.

Figure 15.7. Almost every Monday, as shown here in July 2017, protestors have been marching in Dresden to protest the Merkel government and show their alignment with right-wing movements. The law forbids displaying actual Nazi symbols, but not criticizing politicians. So protestors carry flags of various nationalist associations and signs with political commentary. The sign with Chancellor Merkel's hands altered into a large circle reads: "Who still votes for me and my accomplices, has an asshole at least this wide open."

Western civilization must decide how it is going to continue to manage its own, and the world's, affairs. Does it follow the lead of a unilateral United States of America? Try to promote international law and multilateral interventions? Is it united at all in the face of geopolitical dangers from varied terrorist groups and rogue nations? Does it turn back to its own religious roots? Are those roots fanatical or tolerant? Can the West spread prosperity with more fairness and less exploitation? Will the rest of the world accept any of this? How will the West continue to adapt to the rapid change created by science, capitalism, industry, transportation, and communication? How will the West adjust to the growing power of Asian nations? Of course, Western civilization is not one single entity but rather a collection of its individual citizens, who in turn are grouped into class, ethnicity, and citizenship. All of us, individually and together, must confront each of these questions.

Review: *What tensions and attitudes have weakened the unity of the Western alliances?*

Response:

PRIMARY SOURCE PROJECT 15: THE EUROPEAN CENTRAL BANK VERSUS THE NATIONAL FRONT ABOUT THE EU

The global economic crisis beginning in 2008 presented challenges for the European Union. A leading figure in the union, Yves Mersch, the former governor of the Banque Central du Luxembourg (BCL) and a current member of the executive board of the European Central Bank (ECB), offers his largely positive views on European integration. In opposition, a program paper of the Front National, a nationalistic party in France, criticizes the EU's economic policies.

Source 1: Speech by Yves Mersch (15 May 2014)

[The first of] May this year, exactly two weeks ago, was more than just Labor Day. It was the tenth anniversary of the accession of no fewer than ten countries to the European Union. Three other countries—Bulgaria, Romania and, most recently, Croatia—have since joined. The European Union, despite its shortcomings, remains respected and influential. It also remains an aspiration for non-members and maybe even, in other ways, an inspiration. The Union has been and is a successful undertaking.

The EU has become a role model for regional cooperation. It has achieved its original objectives, namely to ensure peace and prosperity in a notoriously conflict-ridden part of the world. . . . Throughout its almost 60-year history, the EU has shown its ability to overcome important economic and political challenges. In fact, the euro area, the most integrated part of the Union, has grown since 1999 and the number of member states continues to increase—despite the challenges and setbacks of the recent crisis. Having started out with eleven countries, it has expanded over the years and now comprises eighteen. Most of them have experienced a slow but steady improvement in their economies. The number of countries having recently reset a target date for the adoption of the euro is a witness of unabated attraction of our common project subject to the agreed convergence path and criteria.

In many ways, EU membership and the prospect of euro adoption provided an impetus for reforms in these countries. . . . EU accession has also helped in the development of stronger institutions and a more business-friendly environment. Last but not least, EU funds, on a significant scale, have been invested in these countries, bringing noticeable improvements to the transport infrastructure and other domains. . . .

As the past few years of Economic and Monetary Union (EMU) have shown, temporary fulfillment of the convergence criteria does not, by itself, guarantee trouble-free membership of the euro area. Large and persistent macroeconomic imbalances accumulated in several euro area countries and were partly to blame for the economic and financial crisis which broke out in 2008.

In some countries, high public spending since the adoption of the euro has resulted in extremely high public deficits and an unsustainable accumulation of public debt. Other countries however have experienced excessive growth in private debt based on buoyant capital imports and low interest rates. This has resulted in surging imports and large current account deficits rather than strong trend potential growth. In some instances, excessive credit growth—closely associated with an unsustainable boom in real estate markets—has undermined the soundness of some financial institutions and given rise to an excessive accumulation of private debt. . . .

The EU has learnt its lessons. We now know what did not work properly. We have all realized that there needs to be a stronger set of institutions and rules to support the euro, that a monetary union needs to be accompanied by a banking union and a fiscal union, that, in the end, economic integration and political integration in Europe go hand in hand. . . .

In today's highly interconnected and competitive world, it means thinking beyond national economic interests and instead exploiting synergies and comparative advantages together. In short, it means working together to hold our own.

Source 2: "A Controlled End to Stimulate Growth" by the National Front (2014)

Ten years after its introduction into the daily life of the French, the euro as a single currency is proving to be a complete failure, despite the blindness of the proponents of Europe in Brussels and Frankfurt who refuse to admit the obvious. In fact, the euro is going to disappear, because the cost of maintaining it is every day becoming more unsupportable for the nations for which it is totally unsuitable. Since its inception, the euro has been an economic aberration, denounced by numerous economists. The tinkering and successive plans for bail-outs to save the euro will not solve the crisis. Therefore, an orderly plan for suspending the euro needs to be started now.

The single currency has become a symbol of a European federalist policy of an absurd brinksmanship by elite financiers ready to sacrifice the people on the altar of their own interests. Money should be put in its proper place, becoming once again an economic instrument in the service of growth and employment.

The euro was doomed from the start. At the time it was launched, the American Nobel Prize winner Milton Friedman, for example, predicted the failure of the euro, the crisis that would follow, and demonstrated the unsurpassable efficacy of monetary freedom. . . .

Today, the balance sheet of the euro is disastrous. The promises of prosperity, of growth, and of employment have not been kept. Since the creation of the single currency, the euro zone is the region of the world that has known the slowest growth. The exchange rate is much too high for France, accelerating outsourcing and de-industrialization of our country, which has also suffered for the last ten years from the non-union wage policy of Germany. . . . The euro did nothing to protect Europe from the first great crisis of 2008. . . .

It is advisable at present to refuse to engage in pointless policies of austerity in the name of preserving a currency that is stifling Europe. These successive plans for austerity always hit the same people: the working and middle classes, retirees, and civil servants. . . . France should therefore veto useless and ruinous plans for bailing-out countries that are victims of the euro. French money should stay in France.

France must prepare, along with its European partners, for the end of the unhappy experience with the euro and for the beneficial return of national currencies that permit competitive devaluation, in order to breathe life into our economy and rediscover the path to prosperity.

The team of France and Germany should perform the driving role in this consultation and in the planned suspension of the euro experience. The team must rediscover the initiative and allow the euro zone to escape stagnation. . . . A majority of Germans (54% in October 2011) favor a return to the mark. Abandoning the euro is a technical challenge, but in no way will it provoke the cataclysm described by ideologues and other fanatics of the single currency. Well prepared, coordinated with the other European nations, the orderly end of the euro is the requirement for the economic revival of France. To stay with the euro is to condemn ourselves "to die by inches," in the words of economist Alain Cotta.

Questions:

- *What details does each source use to prove its argument, positive or negative, for the euro?*
- *What specific changes does each source call for?*
- *On the basis of these two sources, without substantiating background, citations, or studies, how is one to decide which view is more credible?*

Responses:

Make your own timeline.

1980   **2020**

Citations

Mersch, Yves. Speech at the conference "The World Isn't Flat—Why Place Matters and What It Means for Us," organized by ASPIRE, Kraków, 15 May 2014. European Central Bank, n.d. Accessed 1 September 2014, http://www.ecb.europa.eu/press/key/date/2014/html/sp140515_2.en.html.

"Une fin maitrisée pour libérer la croissance." Translated by Elizabeth S. Lott. The Official Site of the *Front National*, n.d. Accessed 1 September 2014, http://www.frontnational.com/le-projet-de-marine-le-pen/redressement-economique-et-so cial/euro.

For more on these sources, go to http://www.concisewesternciv.com/sources/psc15.html.

Epilogue

Why Western Civilization?

Several hundred years ago, Western civilization took the worldwide lead in politics (often by success in war), economics (by accumulating wealth), and science and technology (by using machines to help with the first two). In each of these areas, states and social groups in the West gained more efficiency and effectiveness than organized societies elsewhere in the world. On the one hand, westerners used the power from these advantages to intimidate and oppress other human cultures and civilizations. On the other hand, westerners brought knowledge to those other societies that, in time, enabled some of them to become powerful in their own right by adopting parts of Western civilization. Cultures around the world are still deciding what to keep from the West and what to use against its dominance. Some would argue that Western values are uniquely essential to those who have inherited them. Others argue that anyone can adopt Western values, that they can be universal. And certainly what some consider to be values can be seen by others as vices. Regardless, the dynamism generated by the West guarantees that tomorrow will be different from today. Therein lie the difficulties of applying historical understanding. In a changing world, what should we ourselves choose to learn from the past of Western civilization?

A couple of decades ago, students at Stanford University chanted the phrase "Western Civ has got to go." They were saying that a Western civilization course requirement in their curriculum was more harmful than helpful. Although the incident was hardly significant, defenders of Western culture sometimes point to this specific incident as a signal of doom for the study of Western Civ. For the West exists only as long as many of its members and opponents say it exists. It becomes real through self-identification or from labeling by others. Without being defined, no civilization has inherent cohesion.

501

In the last few years people have been arguing about "the West" more than ever. Such is not unexpected, since every civilization has come under attack. The West has confronted external enemies, from Viking, Saracen, and Magyar hordes plundering the Carolingian Empire to al-Qa'ida blowing up commuters in New York, Madrid, and London. The West has also faced internal enemies, who have caused peasant rebellions, civil wars about the role of government, the attempted genocide of Jews, criminal organizations taking the streets, and white supremacists committing mass shootings and blowing up buildings. All civilizations define themselves by the extent of their supremacy over their own subjects or against their neighbors, the "others." All cultures have, at one time or another, confronted new people and ideas and faced the necessity of either absorbing them or eliminating them. Since Western civilization is so widespread today, it cannot help but provoke opposition from those who do not accept the extent of its reach or agree with its values.

It is also important to remember that "the West" has never, at any time, been one single, monolithic entity. As described in this book, a long historical process of human choices about those values, many of them contradictory, have resulted in a divided West. In its belief systems, the West has experienced everything from myths to monotheisms, philosophical speculation to scientific secularism. In its culture, the West has expressed itself in everything from epic poetry to prose history, theatricals and spectacles, novels and newspapers, which have been transmitted on everything from stone and bone, clay and canvas, parchment and paper, to celluloid film and streams of electrons. In its power over nature, the West is historically rooted with all other worldwide cultures in the knife and knapsack of the hunter-gatherers to the plow and pottery of agriculturists. The West progressed further, with the steam engine and steel cruiser to today's computers and cars. But none of these inventions or attitudes necessarily made the West's culture better or superior. Nonetheless, through the power of its militaries, ideas, discoveries, and economies, it is indisputable that the West came to reign supreme over world affairs by the nineteenth century.

Like any powerful civilization in world history, the West achieved its ascendancy most obviously by wielding weapons and wealth. Yet the West has never spoken with one unified voice. Both a strength and a weakness of Western civilization has been its division into many sovereign states. Their rivalries with one another spurred innovation and growth as well as destruction and death. This variety also enabled democratic and republican ideals to survive against prevailing absolutism and authoritarianism. The cooperation of individuals and groups in capitalism financed political growth and further fostered responsive government.

Some people believe that the West is based on freedom of the individual, but its own history shows an ambivalent interaction with that ideal. The nation-state as the primary way to organize people easily subsumes individuals, who only really matter when connected to larger social groups of family, class, and corporation. And when any state goes to war, few support the freedom of the individual to opt out from the collectivism of military service. Nation-states rose to great powers when, ironically, some individual states grew strong enough to create overseas empires. Western guns and galleons gave Europeans a lethal advantage over many other peoples in Asia, Africa, and the Americas. Imperialist Spain and Portugal were joined by France and England, then the Netherlands and Russia, next Germany and Italy, and finally, the United States and even Japan, re-created in the West's own image. The official empires of the West largely collapsed in the twentieth century, partly because the West was drained by three global conflicts: World War I, World War II, and the Cold War.

At the end of these conflicts, the United States of America stood above all others as a superpower. The United States had achieved a unique global superiority through its money, media, and military. An economy and financial system allowed less than 5 percent of the world's population to consume more than 20 percent of its resources. Since World War II, the United States has wielded an influence without precedent. Its ideas have spread in television and movies, games, music, and fashion, while the power of its armed forces reflects a budget larger than about the next seven most-powerful nations combined.

One of the most uncertain directions of Western civilization today is the extent to which the United States of America will either continue to dominate it or separate from it. Some American exceptionalists have suggested that its hegemony should allow the United States alone to define what the world should be in the future, acting unilaterally. To make the USA number one is to focus on its interests at the expense of other nations. Those who critique American exceptionalism wish the United States to work with the nations of Europe, and even the world, funneling war and power through the multilateral international institutions (such as NATO and the UN) created by the West in the second half of the twentieth century. President Obama proposed, "I believe in American exceptionalism, just as I suspect that the Brits believe in British exceptionalism and the Greeks believe in Greek exceptionalism." For true believers, his view was tantamount to a contempt for the West. President Trump has said, "I declare today for the world to hear that the West will never ever be broken; our values will prevail; our people will thrive; and our civilization will triumph." Can the West remain "special," however, without asserting superiority?

The study of the West has thus been undermined due to cultural warfare over which aspect of its past (and present) truly represents its traditional values and virtues. Some who argue for Western exceptionalism like to draw up little lists about what makes this civilization so special, worthy of emulation. This is history written by the victors. But, if the losers have any history of their own at all, they often nurse their grudges until they can try to vanquish their oppressors. Should history remind us of our nobility or force us to acknowledge our crimes? People want their heroes and villains—although usually we want the heroes to resemble us and the villains to appear like some "other." It is hard to cope when the roles are reversed. Christianity had pacifists like Jesus, Saint Francis, and Martin Luther King Jr., as well as murderers like schismatics, crusaders, and inquisitors. Nations had their largely successful, yet flawed, rulers (King Henry II, King Louis XIV, and Chancellor Bismarck), as well as their failure-ridden, yet human, leaders (King John, King Louis XVI, and Adolf Hitler). Each has had, and will have, at least some proponents and some opponents. Good historians try to sort out the greatness and the failures that belong to each of us, recording all facets of events and people, both good and bad.

More important than the leaders of the past may have been the different ideologies that informed their choices. Various factions in our culture identify some beliefs as vices, others as virtues, and vice versa. The Enlightenment consensus of reason and science has never completely overwhelmed religious and superstitious viewpoints. Ongoing resistance to Darwinian evolution by those who assert a literal interpretation of the Bible illustrates this lack of success. Yet Christianity has not been able to beget its "City of God." Neither has rationalism built its utopia, because people have never been able to agree on priorities. Some argue that capitalism should sanctify the pursuit of profit only by corporations, while others call for society to embrace all persons as active economic agents. Elites redefine democracy as the mere holding of elections, in which money makes some voices louder than votes. The masses often seek to be heard but speak in many different voices (quite literally, in the many languages from Basque to Bulgarian still spoken in the European Union). Most people want to win, which means usually that other people lose. Few people seem willing to compromise or forgive.

All these tensions among competing ideas interacted to create Western civilization. Fights over causation, civil rights, capitalism, class, high culture, and Christianity have all driven historical change. Influences from neighboring cultures and civilizations, small and large, from Mesopotamians, Egyptians, Assyrians, Persians, Muslims, North Africans, Byzantines, Slavs, Magyars, East Asians, South Asians, Central Asians, Native Americans, sub-Saharan Africans, Pacific Islanders, and others helped to shape Western civilization over the centuries.

While advocates of *multiculturalism* have attacked Western expressions of power, history shows that the West has always been multicultural. In its earliest phases, Hebrews tried to Judaize their Canaanite neighbors in Palestine; the Greeks began to hellenize the peoples conquered by Alexander; the Romans romanized everyone from the Iberians to the Britains, Germans, Greeks, Mesopotamians, and Egyptians. They also subjugated the Etruscans, Carthaginians, Druids, and others. In the early Middle Ages, the church Christianized the ruling Germans and their neighbors. None of these "-izations" succeeded completely—elements of earlier cultures always survived. The alleged unity of medieval Christendom actually rested on the different "nations" of English, French, Germans, Italians, Spanish, and others. Then, from the Middle Ages into the nineteenth century, the diverse Germanic invaders who had toppled the western half of the Roman Empire melded into their conquered populations, in the process transforming and spreading new cultures. The Gothic Germans and old Romans (and Celts and a few others) diversified into the French, the English, the Italians, the Spanish, the Portuguese, the Scandinavians, the Scots, the Irish, the Dutch, the Swiss, the Belgians, and others, including even Luxembourgers, Liechtensteiners, Andorrans, and Austrians. The Slavic states of eastern Europe connected with the West after the fall of the Byzantines and the Ottomans (although complicated by the Russians and their ambivalent attitude to "westernness"). As many of these westerners trekked into the world, colonizing and colonized peoples organized as Latin Americans, "North" Americans, Australians, New Zealanders, South Africans, and others. All of them reflect multiculturalism; all of them share in Western civilization, insofar as they have appropriated large parts of it. Yet some people claim that Latin America is not "Western," even though the majority of the people believe in Christianity, speak European languages, are organized into industrial-age classes, apply economic theories, use modern science and technology, and live under modern nation-state political systems.

Does Western civilization have a future? At several moments in its past, Western civilization almost did not. Persia might have conquered Greece. The Romans might have self-destructed in their republican civil wars. The Germans might have resisted Christianity. Norse, Magyar, or Saracen invaders might have overwhelmed the Christendom of Charlemagne. The Mongols might have wiped out the West, as they did many societies that opposed them. Asian armies might have conquered Europe anytime up to the seventeenth century. Nuclear war might have ended it all during the Cold War (and still may).

Up to now, Western civilization has become a historical force by surviving numerous challenges and developing overwhelming power, partly because of the revolutions it has experienced and assimilated. It has been held together in the last few decades by a group of institutions such as NATO for a military alliance, and for economics, the International Monetary Fund, the World Bank, many trade agreements, the EU, and the G7. But nothing is stable, ever since the many Western revolutions committed to constant change. The Commercial Revolution, the intellectual revolutions of the Renaissance and Enlightenment, the religious revolution of the Reformation, the Scientific Revolution, the Industrial Revolution, and the political revolutions of England, America, and France all guarantee that tomorrow is different from today. These revolutions encourage human creativity and the application of the "new" to improve people's lives.

Change has not been common to all historical views. Some cultures, such as the Hindu in India or the Mayan in Central America, see a cyclical turn to history, looking to revive or maintain traditional orders, resisting anything new or different. The ancient Egyptian and early Chinese civilizations valued the unchanging permanence of a society that mirrored an eternal heavenly order. The monarchs and nobles ruled from their fine palaces, the priests prayed in their gilded temples, and the peasants shoveled manure in the fields. So it had been; so it always should be. Any disruptions—an invasion by foreigners, the end of a dynasty and civil war, a natural disaster—should be overcome so that the elites could restore the right order of things. These attitudes and concepts are also found in Western civilization.

But from the Jews, through the Greeks and Romans, and to the Germans, the West began to embrace change, even when its leaders would not admit it to themselves. The Jews appealed to the eternal law of God but adapted to changing circumstances as they went from wandering tribes, to kingdoms, to a people scattered across the world. Now, some of them are building the national state of Israel and confronting hostility within and without. The Greeks cleverly expanded outward from their homeland and briefly achieved cultural predominance in the Eastern Mediterranean and the Middle East, only to lose it through their failure to include other cultures. They regained a brief ascendancy with the surviving remnant of Rome known as the Byzantine Empire, only to lose that empire to the Turks. The Romans did so well at learning from the Greeks that they passed on an imperialist legacy to the Byzantine East, Islam, and the West. The Germans who inadvertently destroyed Rome in the fifth century AD bound the cultures of the Greeks and

Romans to their own, tolerated a Jewish presence, and embraced Christianity. Although the Germanic barbarians failed to unite the West under one government, the common appeal to Christianity, Greece, and Rome combined with the eagerness of the states in western Europe to learn from one another, their neighbors, and immigrants to invent the great revolutions in economics, learning, religion, science, and politics.

The themes of supremacy and diversity reveal these ongoing changes. Some leaders and societies have sought domination, which bound allegiances into a unity that strengthened. Arguments over what justified supremacy recast societies: a divine mandate (decided upon by whose God?), tradition (choosing which part of the assorted past?), knowledge (as taught by whom?), power (with what degree of violence?). Over time, though, supremacies have often stifled creativity. They demanded mere obedience and often oppressed. At the same time, humans obviously have sought diversity, fracturing into smaller unities while striving for what is new. Yet emphasis on too many differences, or focusing too much on them, has fragmented people into mutual hostilities, if not armed camps. Recent conflicts show clearly: there are no fundamental assumptions about which everyone agrees. The tendency toward diversity subverts supremacy.

Today, international and multiregional organizations continue to expand, while nationalistic groups persistently cling to their separate constructed identities. As the world economy binds peoples together, nationalists want to restrict immigration; local patriotism resists international solidarity among human beings. Most people still fail to empathize with either the exploited or the enemy, although modern media zap their words, sounds, and images into our living rooms every day. And with anyone able to put information on the Internet, people who look can easily find both facts and falsehoods that confirm their convictions. Our collapsing world seems both smaller and more conflict ridden.

Where does that leave Western civilization? Globalization of all markets and cultures is taking place under pervasive Western methodologies of investment and profit. Superficially, Western culture is everywhere, in the commercial products of food, drink, and clothing, in the machines that make life easier and regulated, in the entertainment of music, games, and visual images. Those countries where Western civilization runs deepest are those whose populations largely descend from western Europe: in North America, both Canada and the United States, and in the South Pacific, Australia, and New Zealand. The states of Latin America through the Caribbean, Central America, and South America are all Western, although with large doses of Native American and some African influences. Substantially westernized countries are also in Eastern Europe, including Russia.

In the Middle East, Israel is largely Western, although increasingly at odds with Arab Palestinians inside and outside its borders. Oil riches have brought Western concepts to many other Muslim countries, provoking the hostility behind much of modern Islamist terrorism. On the African continent, South Africa with its British and Afrikaaner minority is most thoroughly westernized. Yet other African nations bear the scars and retain some of the benefits of Western colonialism while trying to adapt to a global economy run on Western principles. Japan has become largely a Western nation. Contemporary China has exploited Western capitalist policies, while it retains officially a Communist authoritarian system (Western in its mechanisms). In the rest of the world, all former colonial areas of the West, the depth of Western penetration varies. Some nations have strong elements of rejection, while others are eagerly trying to assimilate.

What does it mean to be Western? Take your choice: science or supernaturalism, democracy or dictatorship, socialism or self-interest, class consciousness or ethnic identification, virtuosity or vulgarity, religiosity or rationality. All are rooted in our tradition, and all have flaws, at least according to those who choose one over the other. Perhaps the most significant Western value is a beautiful and dreadful ambiguity (see figure E.1).

I once found a graffito written on a desk in a classroom where I taught history: "If history is so important, how come it is gone?" The writer obviously did not fully understand the point of studying history. The past isn't gone. History is all around us. And not just in dusty museums, crumbling monuments, or misty memories of

Figure E.1. The city of Salzburg represents many of the varied aspects of Western civilization. It uses modern technology of electricity and automobiles, yet encourages pedestrians (with the footbridge across the river); its economy was once centered around its namesake salt, mined in the mountains in the distance, while today tourism dominates; also its river has been canalized to control flooding and increase property. Its politics have gone through many stages since the initial Stone Age settlement: a town under the Celts; a city under the Romans; a town refounded under the German Carolingians after being abandoned in late antiquity; a spiritual principality ruled by prince-bishops in the Holy Roman Empire, who built the powerful fortress; a province fought over by various powers; and finally a federal state today in Austria. Salzburg once had social structures of aristocrats, townspeople, and peasants, and now it has celebrities, professionals, laborers, and the poor. Some of its culture can be seen in the visible churches and their spires and heard in its music festivals. These churches indicate the traditional belief system of Christianity, but they seem increasingly as tourist attractions rather than centers of faith.

old-timers. Could you understand your own self without remembering your childhood? The past is in the baggage of our minds, in the frameworks of our institutions, in the complexity of our problems. We cannot escape history. We may ignore it only at our peril, since it frames all events around us. Our common heritage has shaped the institutions and structures within which we live. Every significant event instantly becomes history the moment it is over.

Because of Western developments, more people have more choices to affect their politics, economics, and culture than ever before in history. The ability to choose is, of course, limited by one's position in society. The rich usually have more options than the middle class, while the poor struggle with even fewer choices. Legitimate authorities (through law enforcement and war) as well as extralegal organized groups (through crime and terrorism) have the ability to restrict choices of disconnected individuals. Nevertheless, many of us have some freedom to decide our own future because of the success of certain Western values.

Our future depends on the choices we make today. Those people who made decisions in the past changed the course of events to restrict our choices. All kinds of people have appeared in the past of the West, whether forward looking or backward leaning, tolerant or closed-minded, humanist or pragmatic, cruel or kind, tyrannical or populist. This diversity allows almost anyone to claim they are defending tradition, whether proposing a liberating innovation or clinging to oppressive preservation.

You should understand what you believe, whether inherited from family, imposed by society, or freely accepted as your own. You should then act according to your beliefs within our global society. This book offers one path to understanding the world's Western heritage. You can either learn more on your own, benefit from study of other scholars and teachers, be satisfied with what has been offered here, or forget it all. You can benefit, or not, from historical examples of wisdom, stupidity, greatness, and failure. It is ultimately up to you. Choose your story and how to live into it.

Review: *How should one shape one's own worldview by picking and choosing from the key legacies of Western civilization?*

Response:

Timelines

Note: The timelines present key names, events, ideas, institutions, and inventions in chronological order, roughly according to their first appearance in history. Numbers along each side of the timelines indicate time segments and the name of the general historical period; older dates are at the top, more recent toward the bottom. Additionally, terms placed within the white and shaded boxes between the horizontal lines are in approximate chronological order. The six vertical columns spread across each timeline divide data according to categories explained in chapter 1. In the Politics column, information from similar geographic areas tends to be grouped together within the cells, aligned left, center, or right. For example, in timeline C, most of the Politics terms aligned at the left relate to Great Britain. Terms given in all capital letters are states or nations when they first appear, important wars, or regimes. Although some terms in the Culture column are not explained in the text, key works, genres, artists, and writers through history are listed to provide context. Book titles are italicized.

Timeline A. The Ancient Middle East and West before 500 BC

	SCIENCE & TECHNOLOGY	ECONOMY	POLITICS
Prehistory			
	Paleolithic Age clothing tools	hunter-gatherers	*Homo sapiens*
30,000 Y.A.			
	Neolithic Age	trade/commerce slavery	
7000 B.C.			
	animal domestication agriculture copper Bronze Age	Neolithic Agricultural Revolution property	villages, towns, cities Mesopotamian city states war absolutism monarchy kings kingdoms MIDDLE-EASTERN CIVILIZATIONS Sumerians
2900 B.C.	writing		Egypt
	mathematics astronomy	taxes	pharaohs
	calendar		dynasty
2600 B.C.			
2300 B.C.			empires
2000 B.C.			Hebrews
			Middle Kingdom of Egypt Amorites/Babylonians
1700 B.C.			
			New Kingdom of Egypt
1400 B.C.			
			Hatshepsut Ahkenaton Exodus "Dark Age"
1100 B.C.	alphabet Iron Age		Phoenicians Israel & Judea colonialism
		money	
800 B.C.			*polis/poleis* Greek Archaic Age Rome
	hoplites-phalanx *thetes*-trireme		ASSYRIAN EMPIRE militarism Babylonian Captivity of the Hebrews PERSIAN EMPIRE
500 B.C.			

Ancient History (spanning from 2900 B.C. to 500 B.C.)

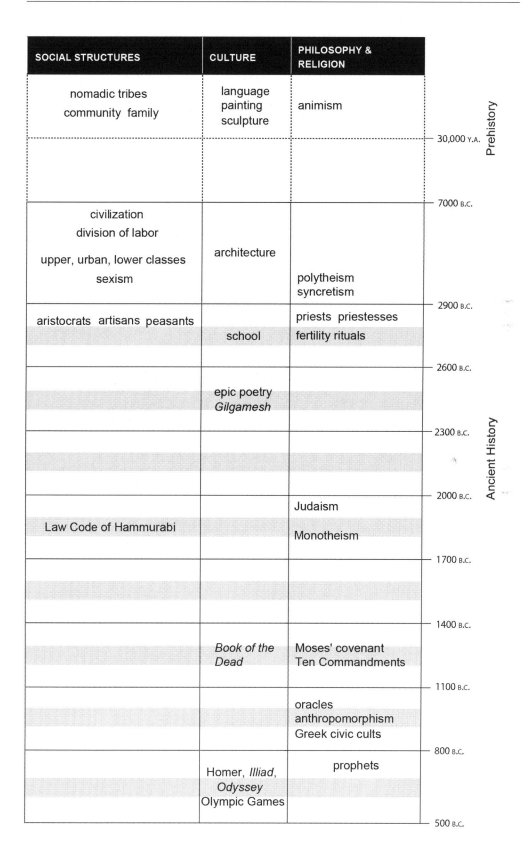

SOCIAL STRUCTURES	CULTURE	PHILOSOPHY & RELIGION	
nomadic tribes community family	language painting sculpture	animism	
			— 30,000 Y.A.
			— 7000 B.C.
civilization division of labor upper, urban, lower classes sexism	architecture	polytheism syncretism	
aristocrats artisans peasants	school	priests priestesses fertility rituals	— 2900 B.C.
			— 2600 B.C.
	epic poetry *Gilgamesh*		
			— 2300 B.C.
			— 2000 B.C.
Law Code of Hammurabi		Judaism Monotheism	
			— 1700 B.C.
			— 1400 B.C.
	Book of the Dead	Moses' covenant Ten Commandments	
			— 1100 B.C.
		oracles anthropomorphism Greek civic cults	
			— 800 B.C.
	Homer, *Illiad*, *Odyssey* Olympic Games	prophets	
			— 500 B.C.

Prehistory

Ancient History

Timeline B. The Ancient Middle East and West, 550 BC to AD 530

	SCIENCE & TECHNOLOGY	ECONOMY	POLITICS
	hoplites-phalanx *thetes*-trireme	land reform	aristocracy- -oligarchy- -tyranny- -democracy *polis* citizenship
500 B.C.			Athenian democracy ostracism ROMAN REPUBLIC
	rationalism		PERSIAN WARS Senate, consuls Delian League, Athenian Empire
400 B.C.	concrete		PELOPONNESIAN WARS demagogues
	Aristotle		Gauls/Celts sack Rome tribunes
	dialectic logic aqueduct		Philip II of Macedon proscription Alexander III "the Great" ROMAN EMPIRE
300 B.C.	Roman legion Roman roads		Hellenistic kingdoms
200 B.C.			PUNIC WARS
		latifundia	Hannibal ROMAN CIVIL WARS Tiberius & Gaius Gracchus
100 B.C.	Julian calendar		Julius Caesar
B.C. A.D.			Antony & Cleopatra PRINCIPATE
			Octavian "Augustus" Caesar *princeps, imperator*, Praetorian Guard
			Pax Romana Goths/Germans natural law, lawyers
A.D.100	geocentric and heliocentric theories		Five Good Emperors adoption and designation
A.D.200		wage/price freeze	DOMINATE Diocletian
A.D.300			Constantine I "the Great"
			Huns Germanic barbarian migrations
A.D.400			Franks, Merovingians Second Sack of Rome
			Anglo-Saxons
			Fall of the Roman Empire in the West
A.D.500			Justinian Byzantine Empire

Classical/Ancient History

SOCIAL STRUCTURES	CULTURE	PHILOSOPHY & RELIGION	
	GREEK CLASSICAL AGE		
	lyric poetry		
patricians & plebians	Greek Golden Age theater history Parthenon	mystery religious cults philosophy Sophists	500 B.C.
		humanism	
	Lysistrata Oedipus	Socrates	
		Plato idealism	400 B.C.
	Hellenistic Age	Aristotle Jews	
Alexandria		Diaspora anti-Semitism	
cosmopolitan		Epicureanism stoicism	300 B.C.
		rabbis	
proletariat			200 B.C.
optimates vs *populares*			
	Gallic War Vergil, *Aeneid*	Hebrew scriptures (Old Testament) deification	100 B.C.
		Yeshua of Nazareth Christianity martyrs	B.C. A.D.
		Paul of Tarsus gospels councils apostolic succession	
		clergy mass saints apologists sacraments excommunication	A.D. 100
			A.D. 200
			A.D. 300
Constantinople		Edict of Milan Council of Nicaea Christian Bible (New Testament) orthodoxy heresy	
		Augustine of Hippo *City of God*	A.D. 400
		monasticism regular clergy	
Justinian's Law Code			A.D. 500

Classical/Ancient History

Timeline C. The Medieval West, 500–1640

	SCIENCE & TECHNOLOGY	ECONOMY	POLITICS
			Franks, Merovingians
			Clovis Justinian
			Justinian's Law Code
600		manorial economics	"Do-nothing kings"
			Anglo-Saxon kingdoms
700			CAROLINGIAN EMPIRE
	stirrups		mayors of the palace
			Pippin "the Short"
800		three-field planting	Charlemagne
			Vikings, Magyars, Moslems
	horse collars		Alfred "the Great"
			ENGLAND FRANCE GERMANY
			FEUDAL POLITICS
900	castles		SCOTLAND
			Otto I "the Great"
	knights		HOLY ROMAN EMPIRE
1000			HUNGARY DENMARK NORWAY SWEDEN
	reconquest of Toledo		
	Arab science in West	*Domesday Book*	William "the Conqueror"
		commune	Crusades Henry IV
1100		revival of towns & trade	Concordat of Worms
		industrialization	
	windmills	putting out/cottage guilds	Henry II PORTUGAL
		master, journeyman, apprentice	Philip II "Augustus"
1200			John Teutonic knights
	Scholasticism		Magna Carta
			Philip IV "the Fair"
1300			Parliament
	mini ice age begins		Estates-General
	pikes		OTTOMAN EMPIRE
	gunpowder, firearms	COMMERCIAL	SWITZERLAND
	cannons	REVOLUTION	Hundred Years War
1400		capitalism	Joan of Arc
		banks	Peace of Lodi
	printing press	public debt	AUSTRIA
			Habsburg dynasty Ferdinand & Isabella
	Columbus		SPAIN
	Vasco da Gama		Western European colonial imperialism
1500			Henry VIII Charles V
		Atlantic/African slave trade	DUTCH NETHERLANDS
		bourse, stock exchange	
			Elizabeth I St. Bart's Massacre Philip II
		mercantilism	Spanish Armada
1600			Wars of Religion
			Henry IV
			Thirty Years War
			English Civil War Peace of Westphalia

Left margin labels: Early Middle / Dark Ages · High Middle Ages · Later Middle Ages

SOCIAL STRUCTURES	CULTURE	PHILOSOPHY & RELIGION		
clan, kin, tribe, people, folk		monasticism Benedictine Rule		
free-unfree	Gregorian chant	caesaro-papism	600	
personal justice vendetta/feud	Latin literature	Pope Gregory I Islam: Mohammed Qu'ran		
trial by ordeal customary law			700	Early Middle / Dark Ages
	Carolingian Renaissance	Frankish-Papal Alliance Iconoclastic Controversy	800	
	minuscule seven liberal arts			
seigneur & serf feudal society	Romanesque art		900	
		Cluniac Reform		
	Gothic art	Peace & Truce of God	1000	
nobility chivalry courtesy	tournaments rise of vernacular *Chanson de Roland*	"Great Schism" Eastern Orthodox Gregorian Reform Pope Gregory VII Investiture Struggle Crusades	1100	
burghers, bourgeois patrician, artisan, common	universities Romance Goliards	Cistercian Reform canon law Peter Abelard Thomas Becket	1200	High Middle Ages
	colleges	Cathars, dualism Mendicants Francis of Assisi Inquisition Thomas Aquinas	1300	
BLACK DEATH peasant revolts	Dante, *Divine Comedy* Chaucer Christine de Pizan	Pope Boniface VIII "Babylonian Captivity" "Great Western Schism"	1400	
	RENAISSANCE textual criticism humanism Leonardo, Raphael	mysticism witch hunts Christian humanism Erasmus Spanish Inquisition	1500	
	Machiavelli, *The Prince* Michelangelo Shakespeare	REFORMATION Martin Luther Jean Calvin Anabaptists English Reformation	1600	Later Middle Ages
		Counter-Reformation Council of Trent Loyola, Jesuits Inquisition, *Index*		

Timeline D. Early Modern West, 1540–1914

Left margin era labels: **Renaissance & Reformation**, **Early Modern Europe**, **Nineteenth Century**
Date markers: 1600, 1700, 1800, 1900

SCIENCE & TECHNOLOGY	ECONOMY	POLITICS
Copernicus		Wars of Religion
heliocentric theory astronomy SCIENTIFIC REVOLUTION Gregorian calendar	COMMERCIAL REVOLUTION mercantilism	RUSSIA Elizabeth I DUTCH NETHERLANDS Philip II REPUBLICANISM divine right CONSTITUTIONALISM ABSOLUTISM
scientific method empiricism	joint-stock company	DUTCH REPUBLIC GREAT BRITAIN Henry IV "of Navarre" Thirty Years War Cardinal Richelieu
Galileo physics		English Civil War Cromwell Peace of Westphalia sovereign nation-state balance of power
scientific academies Newton	Scientific Agricultural Revolution	PRUSSIA Louis XIV "the Sun King" Glorious Revolution ancien régime Peter I "the Great"
mini ice age ends spinning jenny		cabinet, prime minister British Empire enlightened despotism Frederick II "the Great" War of Austrian Succession Maria Theresa
canals steam engine encyclopedia	INDUSTRIAL REVOLUTION mill/factory system laissez-faire Adam Smith classical liberal economics	Seven Years War American Revolution partitions of POLAND USA federalism, president Louis XVI FRENCH REVOLUTION National Assembly, Bastille, Reign of Terror, Thermidor Wars of the Coalitions
railways	"iron law of wages" Luddites utopian socialism	Napoleon Bonaparte guerrilla warfare Battle of Waterloo Metternich Congress of Vienna liberalism nationalism conservatism Monroe Doctrine LATIN AMERICAN STATES
geology uniformitarianism evolution indoor plumbing	consumerism corporations	British reform bills GREECE Afrikaaners neo-imperialism Rev of 1830 US-Indian removals BELGIUM Mexico-US War Opium Wars Rev of 1848
biology Darwin natural selection	Marxism trade/labor unions	Napoleon III Crimean War Sepoy Mutiny Meiji Restoration American Civil War ITALY Risorgimento Cavour Garibaldi Paris Commune Bismark 2nd GERMAN EMPIRE Third Republic
oil chemicals electricity Pasteur, germ theory internal combustion engine	social democracy neo-mercantilism state socialism Christian socialism	SERBIA, BULGARIA, RUMANIA terrorism anarchism US-Plains Indian Wars Dollar Diplomacy pan-slavism yugo-slavism Hawaii partition of Africa Spanish American War Zionism
automobile airplane atomic theory Freud	cartels, trusts	Boer War SOUTH AFRICA Boxer Rebellion Balkan Wars Franz Ferdinand

SOCIAL STRUCTURES	CULTURE	PHILOSOPHY & RELIGION		
		Roman Catholicism		Renaissance & Reformation
estates clergy		Counter-Reformation Council of Trent		
nobility common-peasant	Shakespeare BAROQUE	Wars of Religion	1600	
	orchestra, opera Rembrandt Rubens			
westernization	Rococo art			
	ENLIGHTENMENT *philosophes*		1700	Early Modern Europe
	novels Bach	humanitarianism skepticism Pietism deism agnosticism atheism progress Great Awakening		
	Neoclassicism			
	newspapers			
Wollstonecraft male suffrage *Declaration of the Rights of Man and the Citizen*	Rousseau Voltaire Mozart symphony ROMANTICISM		1800	
upper/middle/lower classes urbanization	Beethoven			
		materialism		Nineteenth Century
police public sanitation	Goethe, *Faust* Turner REALISM			
"family values"	Dickens professional sports	"higher criticism" Social Darwinism		
	naturalism Richard Wagner impressionism	Christian fundamentalism		
social sciences sociology anthropology	Monet, Rodin, Van Gogh	Christian modernism	1900	
concentration camps		Pope Leo XIII		

Timeline E. The Twentieth Century, 1900–present

Twentieth Century	SCIENCE & TECHNOLOGY	ECONOMY	POLITICS
	telegraph, telephone Freud's subconscious auto	neo-mercantilism laissez-faire socialism consumer economy trade unions	neo-imperialism conservative, liberal, socialist political parties terrorism militarism Zionism "open door" policy, Boxer Rebellion
1900	airplane atomic theory Einstein's relativity plastic	"robber barons" trusts cartels department stores	Theodore Roosevelt alliance system progressivism
1910	gas warfare U-boats tanks bombers/fighters influenza pandemic	"war socialism"	Balkan crises ALBANIA WORLD WAR I genocide Russian Revolution USSR Wafd CZECHO-SLOVAKIA ESTONIA LATVIA LITHUANIA HUNGARY AUSTRIA FINLAND KINGDOM OF SERBS, CROATS, and SLOVENES
1920	radio air conditioning Heisenberg's Principle	era of big business USSR: NEP USSR: 5-year plans collectivization Wall Street Crash	IRELAND totalitarianism, authoritarianism League of Nations TURKEY "Red scare" "Yellow Peril" Mussolini fascism Jiang, KMT Stalinism YUGOSLAVIA Mao Zedong
1930	antibiotics radar	Great Depression New Deal Keynesian Economics	Hitler Naziism FDR Spanish Civil War Munich Conference Atlantic Charter WORLD WAR II
1940	jet computer atomic bomb nuclear bomb television genetics Sputnik space flight Space Race	Great Leap Forward baby boomers	Blitzkrieg Pearl Harbor United Nations Peron Israel Berlin Blockade apartheid Maoism Nehru NATO COLD WAR CYPRUS McCarthyism Korean Police Action Warsaw Pact
1950	ICBMs	shopping malls	Treaty of Rome Suez Crisis EEC Castro decolonization
1960	laser transistor	German & Japanese economic "miracles"	Kennedy Berlin Wall Congo Crisis Cuban Missile Crisis Johnson race riots Vietnam War Northern Ireland troubles Six-Day War PLO
1970	moon landing Earth Day pocket calculators	OPEC oil embargo G7	Nixon Allende détente Helsinki Accords Greens Sandinistas Solidarity Iranian Revolution
1980	Three Mile Island personal computer Chernobyl	Reaganomics global debt	Reagan Thatcher Iran-Iraq War Falklands War Gorbachev glasnost End of the COLD WAR
1990	Internet cell phones	globalization G8	SLOVENIA, CROATIA, BELARUS, UKRAINE, BOSNIA, MACEDONIA MOLDAVIA First Persian Gulf War European Union Mandela Chinese Capitalist Revolution
2000	drones smartphones	global recession	9/11 invasion of Afghanistan and Iraq MONTENEGRO, SERBIA, KOSOVO

SOCIAL STRUCTURES	CULTURE	PHILOSOPHY & RELIGION	
industrialization urbanization	advertising	Christian fundamentalism	
	fin de siècle	Christian modernism	— 1900
suffragettes	ragtime realism, naturalism		
	primitivism		
	cubism expressionism		— 1910
	abstract art movies		
Ku Klux Klan race riots	dada		
aristocracy depoliticized	Jazz Age sports Roaring Twenties	"Lost Generation" "monkey" trial	— 1920
women's suffrage			
Prohibition Lindbergh	surrealism		
		mass evangelists	— 1930
	International School		
gulags	socialist realism	Gandhi	
	Picasso		
	abstract expressionism	Holocaust	— 1940
	pop art	existentialism	
welfare state			— 1950
	television		
suburbanization desegregation	"Coca-colanization"	Islamic fundamentalism	
civil rights movement	rock'n'roll		
sexual revolution 1968 student protests	The Beatles op art	Vatican II Martin Luther King, Jr.	— 1960
women's liberation	rock concerts	drug culture cults	
abortion debate			— 1970
NGOs	video games	televangelists	
AIDS	music videos	The "Religious Right" Pope John Paul II	— 1980
ethnic cleansing	postmodernism		— 1990
homosexual rights			
immigration debate	global climate change debate		— 2000

Twentieth Century

Common Abbreviations

AD   anno Domini, in the Year of the Lord (some historians instead use CE, Common Era)

b.   born

BC   Before Christ (some historians instead use BCE, Before the Common Era)

ca.   circa, around or about

cent.   century

d.   died

fl.   flourished

r.   ruled

Glossary

The terms below cover many of the important ideas that Western civilization has either developed on its own, borrowed from others, or interacted with. The terms often end in *-ism* or *-ation* (and are ***boldface italicized*** in the text). Some of these ideas have been discredited by dominant attitudes of political institutions, social pressures, intellectual fashions, or religious organizations. Still, all of these diverse ideas, many of which contradict one another, are options to be adopted and practiced.

absolutism: The idea and practice that one person should dominate in authority and decision making within a state. Historians and political theorists most often apply the term to European monarchs of the seventeenth and eighteenth centuries AD, although the concept does apply to all ages.

agnosticism: The belief that the existence of God or of any supernatural beings is impossible to prove.

American exceptionalism: A point of view that sees Americans as different from their fellow westerners or other peoples, usually as being more virtuous or free. The source of this alleged virtue ranges from a special relationship with God to the unique genius of the Founding Fathers. *See also* **Western exceptionalism**.

Anabaptism: A religious belief that rejects infant baptism, an idea that united diverse groups of Christians during the Reformation. *See also* **Christianity**; **Protestantism**.

anarchism: A political idea that calls for the destruction of industrialized and bureaucratized societies so that a utopian agricultural society can appear. *See also* **terrorism**.

Anglicanism: A branch of Christians formed during the Reformation, first organized as the Church of England, which defines itself as a middle path between Protestantism and Roman Catholicism. British imperialism planted numerous Anglican churches around the world, now loosely connected to one another as the Anglican Communion. *See also* **Christianity**.

animism: The religious belief that nature is alive with spirits and ghosts that affect our natural world. Animism was probably the first religion, and many remaining hunter-gatherers still practice some form of it.

523

anthropomorphism: The idea that gods and deities look and act like human beings. Much of ancient Greek and Roman mythology was based on this concept.

anti-intellectualism: The criticism of the thoughts and opinions of educated elites as less useful than those of the "common" uneducated masses. *See also* **intellectualism**.

antisemitism: A euphemism for the hatred of Jews. *See also* **Judaism**; **racism**; **Zionism**.

apostolic poverty: The belief that it is virtuous for Christians to live like the poor, since Jesus and his followers did so. The height of its influence was in the Middle Ages with the Waldensians and Francis of Assisi's monasticism of the mendicants. See also **asceticism**.

apostolic succession: The belief in some parts of Christianity that the true church requires its leaders (bishops and priests) to be ordained in a direct line from Jesus and his apostles.

arabization: The process of making people conform to Arabic culture, especially Islam and its associated traditions. *See also* **islamization**.

Arianism: A religious belief in the third century AD that distinguished the human nature of Jesus from the divine. Most denominations of Christianity officially reject this division and see Jesus as fully human and fully divine at the same time. *See also* **heresy**.

aristocracy: The idea and practice that a few families are of a higher status than others and therefore should rule society.

asceticism: The avoidance of worldly pleasures in living one's life.

assassination: The political practice of murdering leaders in order to force change.

atheism: The belief that denies the existence of the supernatural. *See also* **supernaturalism**.

atomic theory: The scientific idea that the smallest indivisible part of a unique substance is an atom (Greek for "not able to be cut"). Ancient Greek philosophers first suggested the idea, which was scientifically verified in the late nineteenth and early twentieth century.

authoritarianism: The modern political practice of a dictatorship, where a ruler and their party significantly control mass communication and bureaucracy while maintaining order through secret police, paramilitary, and military groups. *See also* **absolutism**; **dictatorship**; **fascism**; **Leninism**; **Stalinism**; **totalitarianism**; **tyranny**.

balance of power: A foreign policy idea most popular between 1648 and 1945 that the nations of Europe should league together against any state that tried to dominate the Continent.

balkanization: The practice of carving up larger empires into smaller states, as done after World War I in eastern Europe. Often it is used in a negative sense.

baptism: The religious idea in Christianity that a ritual with water binds one to that belief system.

barbarian: (1) A term used by civilized urban peoples to describe other peoples who are not civilized (that is, living in pastoral or hunter-gatherer economies);

(2) a term used by one people to insult another as unjustifiably cruel, regardless of either's level of socioeconomic development.

Bolshevism: The name for the communist movement in early twentieth-century Russia led by Lenin. *See also* **communism**; **Leninism**.

bureaucracy: The practice of governing by means of written records and offices that issue, administer, and store them.

caesaro-papism: The practice of the medieval Eastern Roman or Byzantine emperors of helping to organize and supervise the hierarchy and belief system of the Christian church in their empire. *See also* **Orthodox Christianity**.

Calvinism: The belief system held by churches formed during the Reformation that followed the theology of Jean Calvin. Predestination, the belief that God has already chosen who is saved or damned, is its most distinctive doctrine. *See also* **determinism**; **Protestantism**.

capitalism: In its simplest form, the practice of reinvesting profits. As part of our modern ideological conflicts, the term often refers to private ownership of the means of production using free markets, as opposed to communism, where the government carries out central planning of the economy. *See also* **communism**; **Marxism**.

catastrophism, theory of: A scientific idea that explains geology or the history and structures of the earth according to rare and unusual events of enormous power, resembling divine intervention. *See also* **uniformitarianism, theory of**.

Catharism: The medieval religion that mixed Christianity and dualism and was therefore identified by the Christian church as a heresy. *See also* **dualism**; **heresy**.

Christianity: The monotheistic religion that asserts that God became incarnate as his son, Jesus of Nazareth. The Romans executed Jesus, but as the Messiah, or Christ, he returned from the dead to offer salvation, or entrance into heaven for his followers. Since the first century, Christians have divided into many groups: a few who did not define Jesus as fully God and human, as well as the vast majority who have. *See also* **Anabaptism**; **Anglicanism**; **Arianism**; **Calvinism**; **heresy**; **Lutheranism**; **Orthodox Christianity**; **Pietism**; **Protestantism**; **Roman Catholicism**; **schism**.

Christian socialism: A socialist idea adopted by Christians, especially Roman Catholics, using religious ideology as a basis to improve conditions for workers while still respecting the private property rights of capitalists.

civilization: The practice of people living in cities, which supported rich political, social, and cultural lifestyles that could spread over vast territories and many peoples. Distinct governments, social structures, art and literature, and belief systems indicate differences among civilizations.

classical liberal economics, theory of: Also called laissez-faire, the idea that the least interference by government provides the best opportunities for economic growth. It was developed in the eighteenth century in opposition to mercantilism. *See also* **mercantilism, economic theory of**; **socialism**.

collectivization: The practice of Stalin during the 1930s, where the state confiscated land from peasants and consolidated the large tracts into communal farms. Communists in other states, such as China and Cambodia/Kampuchea, later undertook similar policies. *See also* **communism**; **Leninism**; **Marxism**; **Stalinism**.

colonialism: The action of one state sending out some of its people to settle in another place. A colony may or may not retain close connections with the homeland. *See also* **imperialism**.

communism: The utopian idea proposed by Karl Marx in the nineteenth century of a perfect society where the means of production would be shared by all. *See also* **Leninism**; **Stalinism**.

conciliarism: The idea and practice that church councils should be the ultimate authority in resolving conflicts among Christians.

conservatism: A political direction, developed into parties during the nineteenth century, that stands for resisting change in order to preserve political, social, and cultural advantages of the elites. Today conservatism often calls for reducing the role of government in the economy.

constitutionalism: The political idea that law limits a government's powers, whether formally written in an explicit document or by the precedent of tradition.

constitutional monarchy: The practice of having a democratically structured government while keeping a royal dynasty as a stabilizing force. *See also* **democracy**; **parliamentarianism**; **republicanism**.

cynicism: A philosophy originating among the ancient Greeks advocating the rejection of common social rules and human comforts. Today it often describes a pessimism that people's intentions are based on self-interest rather than the common good.

deification: The belief that a human being, usually a powerful leader, can be transformed into a god.

deism: The religious belief that God is the creator of the universe, although it deemphasizes the Christian dogma of Jesus's incarnation.

democracy: The political idea and practice that the best form of government involves the largest possible number of citizens making decisions. Democracies usually involve checks and balances upon authority and factions or parties that dispute and compromise about different political viewpoints. Direct democracy in ancient Athens included all male citizens. Modern democracies usually use elected representatives. A democrat is not necessarily to be confused with a member of the modern American political party. *See also* **parliamentarianism**; **republicanism**.

democratic socialism: Also called social democracy, the effort of revisionists of Marxism to work through the political process instead of through a proletarian revolution. The various modern labor and social democratic political parties were the result.

denazification: The policy after World War II to purge members of the Nazi Party from leadership positions in occupied Germany. *See also* **Naziism**.

determinism: A philosophy that asserts humans have very little free will in deciding their fate. *See also* **Calvinism**.

dialectical materialism: The theoretical model of history suggested by Karl Marx, where a dominant class conflicts with an exploited class. *See also* **Marxism**.

dialectic logic: A method of gaining knowledge that uses two pieces of known data to produce or confirm other information. *See also* **Scholasticism**; **syllogism**.

dictatorship: The practice of one person seizing power in a government. While today the term is used in a negative way, the Romans originally used the method during political crises. *See also* **authoritarianism**; **totalitarianism**; **tyranny**.

diversity: The term used in this text to describe the creative impulse as a force in history. New ideas and groupings of people create change.

divine right: The political idea that God has placed kings in power as part of his divine order.

dualism: A religious philosophy that sees the universe as divided between two powerful beings, one a good force inspired by spirit and ideas, the other an evil influence based on matter and flesh. *See also* **Catharism**; **Gnosticism**; **Zoroastrianism**.

ecumenism: The effort by religions, usually those of Christianity, to tolerate one another, work together, and perhaps unify. It was most influential in the mid-twentieth century. *See also* **toleration**.

egalitarianism: The idea that the best society tries to equalize the wealth, influence, and opportunities of all its citizens. It is exemplified by ancient Sparta, the radicals of the French Revolution, and much Marxist ideology.

empiricism: The idea that observations by our senses are both accurate and reasonable. It is the starting point of scientific knowledge. *See also* **rationalism**; **science**.

enlightened despotism: The political idea and practice that asserted that one person, usually a benevolent dynastic monarch, should rule, since unity encouraged simplicity and efficiency.

environmentalism: The idea and practice since the 1960s of reducing human interference with and damage upon the natural world.

Epicureanism: A philosophy that suggests that the best way of life is to avoid pain. The good life lay in withdrawal into a pleasant garden to discuss the meaning of life with friends. Epicureanism originated among the Hellenistic Greeks and was popularized by the Romans.

ethnicity: The idea of grouping humans into categories based on certain physical and behavioral differences. Ethnocentrism means that certain members of ethnic groups view members of other groups as inferior and dangerous. What separates ethnicity from race is the idea that race is unchangeable, while ethnicity is more fluid and open. *See also* **racism**.

evolution: The observed scientific phenomenon about the increasing diversity and complexity of life on earth from millions of years ago to the present. Darwin's theory of natural selection is the framework under which most scientists today understand the process of evolution. *See also* **natural selection, theory of**.

excommunication: The practice of various Christian churches of disciplining members by shunning them from society and cutting them off from the sacraments.

factionalism: The practice of refusing to cooperate with opposing political and social groups.

fascism: A political ideology, most popular in the 1920s and 1930s, where an extreme nationalist dictatorship seemed the best form of government. Fascist authoritarian and totalitarian regimes offered alternatives to socialism, communism, and parliamentary democracy. Many capitalists were able to accept fascist regimes, despite their violent tendencies toward outsiders, since fascism's concept of the corporate state still allowed some private property and profit. *See also* **authoritarianism**; **dictatorship**; **Naziism**; **totalitarianism**.

federalism: The political practice in republics of separating governmental power within a country, where a strong central administration competes and shares power with provincial or state and local governments. It contrasts with a confederate system, where the central administration is weaker than the local governments.

feminism: The idea that women are not inferior to men, but rather should have equal access to education, political participation, and economic independence. Today it is often mischaracterized as hostility or sexism against men. *See also* **women's liberation**.

feudal politics: The system where knights bound one another together by oaths and rituals to rule society after AD 1000. The term *feudalism* should be avoided because of its many confusing meanings.

fundamentalism: A belief that values traditional, often preindustrial customs and attitudes, especially regarding religion. Fundamentalists reject modern ways of knowing based on the skepticism of literary criticism and the scientific and historical methods. In Christianity, it includes those who support an allegedly literal interpretation of the Bible rather than an interpretation through higher criticism. *See also* **higher criticism**; **textual criticism**.

germanization: The policy of making people conform to German culture. Used by some princes in the Holy Roman Empire, bureaucrats in the Second German Empire, and the Nazis of the Third Reich. *See also* **Naziism**; **pan-germanism**.

germ theory of disease: The scientific theory, argued by Pasteur in the nineteenth century, that microscopic organisms, such as bacteria and viruses, cause many sicknesses. While very successful as a means to understand illness, it does not, however, explain all disease.

globalization: The recent practice of the world's economies being tied more closely together, often bypassing the interests of nations, regions, and localities.

Gnosticism: The ancient philosophy or religion that drew on dualism and argued that its followers held secret knowledge about the meaning of life. Gnostics tried to influence early Christianity. *See also* **dualism**.

heathenism: A religion of polytheism. It was once a term of insult in late Rome applied to poor peasants (living in the countryside) who were ignorant of Christianity; since the Early Middle Ages, heathen has meant any non-Christian in or outside Christendom. *See also* **paganism**; **polytheism**.

hedonism: A philosophy originating among the ancient Greeks that suggested success came to those who pursued pleasure as the highest good.

hellenization: The policy of making people under Greek authority conform to Greek institutions and culture. Practiced especially by the Greek rulers of the Hellenistic Age, after the death of Alexander "the Great."

heresy: Literally, a "choice" or a "sect," the term with which winners in a cultural or religious debate label the ideas of the losers. *See also* **orthodoxy**.

higher criticism: The practice of applying modern scholarly techniques to examining the Bible. *See also* **fundamentalism**; **textual criticism**.

history: The idea that the past is a product of human activity that needs to be interpreted. Since the eighteenth century, the historical method practiced by academics has been the most reliable way to produce objective and accurate versions of the past.

humanism: The philosophy begun by the ancient Greeks that the world is to be understood by and for humans. It gained a significant revival in the Renaissance, including a version called Christian humanism, inspired by the faith in Jesus. Recently some Christians attack what they call "secular humanism" which they believe undermines lives based on religion.

humanitarianism: The idea that humans ought to treat one another well. It is sometimes incorporated in Christianity and was promoted by many intellectuals of the Enlightenment.

idealism: Also known as the doctrine of ideas, idealism is a philosophical explanation of reality that proposed that particular things in the observable world are reflections of universal truths. It is famously formulated by Plato in his "Allegory of the Cave."

imperialism: The practice of taking over different peoples in other countries and communities in order to build an empire. Empires often surpass kingdoms or nations in the diversity of their subject peoples. *See also* **colonialism**; **neo-imperialism**.

individualism: The idea that political and social policies should favor opportunities for single human beings over those in collectives or groups. *See also* **collectivization**.

intellectualism: The idea that educated elites should be respected. *See also* **anti-intellectualism**.

Islam: The religion begun by Muhammad in Arabia. Muslims believe that the one, true God has established a special relationship to those who submit to his will, as explained in the Qur'an.

islamization: The policy of making people conform to Islam and live as Muslims.

Judaism: The religion begun by the ancient Hebrews. Jews believe that the one, true God has established a special relationship with them, as revealed in their sacred scriptures (called by Christians the Old Testament). *See also* **antisemitism**; **Zionism**.

Keynesian economic theory: An economic theory, part of which says that massive government spending can rescue a nation's economy from a depression. It is named after its creator, twentieth-century British economist John Maynard Keynes.

kleptocracy: The practice of government public officials using their authority to increase their personal wealth (rule by those who steal).

Leninism: The ideological and political program put in place by Lenin through the Russian Revolution. He established a dictatorship enforced by secret police, had the state take over substantial portions of the economy (a policy called war communism), and carried out land reform. See also **Bolshevism**; **communism**; **Marxism**.

lesbianism: The practice of women being sexually attracted to and involved with other women. The term comes from the island Lesbos, where Sappho, the ancient Greek poet, had her school (although she herself was not strictly lesbian). *See also* **sapphism**.

liberalism: A political direction that developed into parties during the nineteenth century. It generally stands for changing laws in order to broaden political, social, and cultural opportunities for the middle classes. Today liberalism often calls for accepting a role of government in the economy.

liberation theology: A religious idea in Latin America of the twentieth century that called for Christianity to look after the poor in this world and not merely preach about salvation for the next.

Lutheranism: The version of Christianity that originated with Martin Luther during the Reformation emphasizing justification through faith. *See also* **Christianity**; **Protestantism**.

manorial economics: The economic system in which serfs worked the lands of their seigneurial lords in exchange for the use of farmland for themselves; preferred instead of *manorialism*, a term to be avoided because of its confusing meanings.

Marxism: The particular socialist ideology developed by Karl Marx in the mid-nineteenth century that advocated a proletarian revolution to overthrow bourgeois capitalist society. Since then, Marxism has been used as a synonym for communism. *See also* **Bolshevism**; **communism**; **dialectical materialism**; **Leninism**; **socialism**; **Stalinism**.

materialism: The idea that the physical goods and pleasures in this observable world should take priority over any possible spiritual virtues or destinies.

McCarthyism: A belief usually characterized as a paranoid and unfair attempt to persecute innocent people for their allegedly dangerous political views. It is named after a US senator who during the 1950s wanted to purge alleged communists from the government, politics, and the media.

mercantilism, economic theory of: The idea that government intervention provides the best opportunities for economic growth, especially in establishing monopolies and a favorable balance of trade. It was developed in the sixteenth century in order to manage early capitalism. *See also* **classical liberal economics, theory of**; **neo-mercantilism, theory of**.

militarism: The idea and practice that virtues such as discipline, obedience, courage, and willingness to kill for the state are the highest values a civilized society can hold. It is exemplified by the ancient Assyrians, the Spartans, and the modern Prussians.

Mithraism: An ancient religion, originating in Persia but most popular among the Roman military. Its cultic followers believed that Mithras was the son of the sun god, born on December 25, who killed the heavenly bull to bring fertility and whose own death helped human souls to an afterlife. *See also* **Zoroastrianism**.

modernism: A belief that accepts changes brought by the Enlightenment and the Commercial and Industrial Revolutions toward a more secular and materialistic society. In Christianity, it includes those who support rigorous scholarly examination of scripture. *See also* **higher criticism**.

monasticism: A religious way of life in which people live in a cloistered setting under strict rules, usually involving renunciation of property, physical pleasure, and freedom of choice.

monotheism: The religious belief that only one God exists and should be worshipped.

multiculturalism: The idea that knowledge of and appreciation for diverse ways of life is beneficial for society.

nationalism: The political idea that asserts that states should be organized exclusively around ethnic unities. The problem is, few states only have only one ethnic group living within their borders. Nationalists often try to cultivate patriotism, or love of one's country, which can, but does not necessarily, lead to hostility between nations. An extreme form of nationalism is called chauvinism, named after an apocryphal French patriot. The word chauvinism is also applied to male sexism.

nativism: The political movement that promotes fears that foreigners and immigrants threaten the economic opportunities and social positions of the resident population. "Natives" usually means those of European ancestry: not the oppressed native indigenous or aboriginal peoples.

naturalism: (1) The movement in classical sculpture and art since the Renaissance to portray objects exactly as they appear in nature rather than with an abstract interpretation; (2) the movement in literature since the late nineteenth century to focus on suffering caused by modern society. *See also* **realism**.

natural selection, theory of: Also called "survival of the fittest," Darwin's theory explains how the fact of evolution took place. The theory proposes that the struggle of creatures for food and reproduction encouraged change as organisms adapted to their environment, competed with others, and then passed on useful characteristics to offspring. Thus some species went extinct while many living things become increasingly diverse and more complex. *See also* **evolution**.

Naziism or **national socialism:** The uniquely German version of fascism. Formulated by Adolf Hitler and brought into action during the Third Reich (1933–1945), it fulfilled many Germans' need for nationalistic pride. Its extreme germanization, however, aimed for the Nazi domination of Eurasia and the enslavement or extermination of non-German peoples, especially Jews. *See also* **authoritarianism**; **fascism**; **germanization**; **pan-germanism**; **totalitarianism**.

neo-imperialism: The political practice of Western industrialized states that built up overseas colonial empires between 1830 and 1914. *See also* **colonialism**; **imperialism**.

neo-mercantilism, theory of: The economic idea in Western industrialized states between 1830 and 1914 that combined neo-imperialism abroad with laissez-faire practices at home. *See also* **mercantilism, economic theory of**.

nominalism: The medieval philosophy that proposed that only particular material things in the observable world exist, while collective ideas and categories are mere "names" created by the human mind. *See also* **idealism**.

objectivity: The attempt to remain neutral or interpret disagreements from an unbiased point of view. *See also* **subjectivity**.

oligarchy: The political idea that states are best run by the economic and social elites. *See also* **aristocracy**; **plutocracy**.

Orthodox Christianity: The version of Christianity originally centered in the Byzantine Empire. It became a separate branch after the Great Schism with Western Latin Christianity beginning in 1054. *See also* **Christianity**; **Protestantism**; **Roman Catholicism**; **schism**.

orthodoxy: Literally, the "right teaching," it is the label adopted by groups whose ideas win a cultural debate. *See also* **heresy**.

ostracism: The political practice in ancient Athens of exiling politicians who were considered too dangerous. Today it often means a social practice of shunning. *See also* **excommunication**.

pacifism: The political idea that wars are not a proper activity of states. Instead of warmongering, efforts to maintain peace should be prioritized. Some Christians and Christian groups promoted the idea in Western civilization.

paganism: A religion of polytheism. It was once a term of insult in late Rome leveled at poor peasants who were ignorant of Christianity; since the Early Middle Ages it has meant any non-Christian in or outside Christendom. *See also* **heathenism**; **polytheism**.

pan-germanism: The ideology that all German peoples should be ruled together. As a policy of Adolf Hitler and his Third Reich, it had some success in the 1930s until Hitler showed his determination to rule non-Germans also. *See also* **Naziism**.

pan-hellenism: The idea that all Greeks should be united, at least culturally.

pan-slavism: The political idea that called for all Slavs to live together in one nation-state. The Russians, as the dominant Slavic group, were most behind this movement. *See also* **yugo-slavism**.

pan-turkism: A version of Turkish nationalism that sought to promote unity among diverse Turkish peoples. "Young Turks" toward the end of the Ottoman Empire tried to encourage all subject peoples to become more like Turks.

parliamentarianism: The political idea and practice that elected representatives with limited terms are the best means of governing a state. Structurally, the person who leads the majority in the parliament, usually called a prime minister or a chancellor, is the most powerful political official in the government. *See also* **constitutionalism**; **democracy**; **republicanism**.

particularism: The political and social idea that specific local variations in institutions and beliefs are the best way to organize the state and society. *See also* **diversity**; **universalism**.

philosophy: Literally, "love of wisdom," any intellectual system that proposes explanations for the nature of the universe and the purpose of human beings. While a philosophy may or may not have a supernatural dimension, it should rely on rationalism.

Pietism: A form of Christianity that arose during the eighteenth century, especially among Lutherans, in which believers dedicated themselves to prayer and charity.

plutocracy: A government run by and for the interests of the wealthy. *See also* **oligarchy**.

polytheism: The belief in many gods and goddesses. Divine beings usually reflected the values and needs of farming communities. *See also* **heathenism**; **paganism**.

populism: A political ideology that believes the masses of people (usually rural and middle and lower class) have more wisdom and virtue than elites (usually professionals, intellectuals, and capitalists), career politicians, and several social institutions (such as cities, the Roman Catholic Church, and secretive fraternal organizations). Its leaders often resort to demagoguery. *See also* **anti-intellectualism**; **fascism**; **nativism**.

postmodernism: The academic practice of "deconstructing" texts and ideas to understand both how dominant elites perpetuate power and resisting "others" subvert authority. Such postmodernist relativism disputes the Enlightenment effort toward attaining objective truth.

progress: The idea that people should work to improve political, social, and living conditions in this world. It has been an important Western idea since the Enlightenment.

Protestantism: Any version of Christianity that appeared after Luther's Reformation and its break from Roman Catholicism and Orthodox Christianity; the name originates with those who protested the imperial attacks upon Luther. *See also* **Anabaptism**; **Anglicanism**; **Calvinism**; **Christianity**; **Lutheranism**; **Orthodox Christianity**; **Pietism**.

racism: The social and political belief that people inherit immutable characteristics within racial categories as if they were a species and that some "races" are superior to others. There is no good scientific proof of significant differences among these constructed racial groups. Racism developed as an influential political ideology in the nineteenth century.

rationalism: The concept that the human mind can comprehend the natural world.

realism: (1) The movement in art since the Renaissance to make paintings and sculptures portray objects as human eyes see them; (2) the movement in literature since the late nineteenth century to focus on social problems. *See also* **naturalism**.

Realpolitik: The political practice of both pragmatically making compromise and using force to achieve desired ends, usually the strengthening of the state. Conservative nationalists promoted it in the nineteenth century.

regionalism: The political idea that people are best organized within smaller geographic areas rather than the typical large nation-state or centralized empire. *See also* **particularism**; **subsidiarity**.

religion: From the word "to bind," a belief system that proposes a supernatural explanation for the nature of the universe and the purpose of human beings.

republicanism: The political idea and practice that elected representatives with limited terms are the best means of governing a state. Republicanism paired with the checks and balances of constitutionalism are the foundation of most modern democratic states. In its strict form, a republic elects all significant political figures, thus excluding constitutional monarchy. A republican is not necessarily to be confused with a member of the modern American political party. *See also* **constitutional monarchy**; **democracy**; **parliamentarianism**.

Roman Catholicism: The version of Christianity that originally centered in the western portion of the ancient Roman Empire. It is characterized by being under the authority of the bishop of Rome, eventually called the pope. It defined itself as uniquely Roman after the schism from Orthodox Christianity in 1054 and with the rise of Protestantism in the sixteenth century. *See also* **Christianity**; **Orthodox Christianity**; **Protestantism**; **schism**.

romanization: The process carried out by ancient Romans of conforming their subject peoples, institutions, and attitudes to those of the Roman Empire.

Romantic movement: The intellectual movement begun in the nineteenth century that appreciated nature, admired the Middle Ages, and emphasized emotion as a reaction against the rationalism of the Enlightenment.

sapphism: The practice of women being sexually attracted to and involved with other women. The term comes from Sappho, the ancient Greek poet (although she herself was not strictly lesbian). *See also* **lesbianism**.

schism: Literally, a "rip," usually used to describe one religious group splitting away from another. *See also* **heresy**; **Orthodox Christianity**; **orthodoxy**.

Scholasticism: The medieval philosophy "of the schools," which applied Aristotle's dialectic logic to better explain Christianity. *See also* **dialectic logic**; **syllogism**.

science: The idea that knowledge of nature can best be gained through rigorous experimentation and observation according to the scientific method. Scientific theories provide coherent explanations for the facts of natural phenomena. Science's many successes have made it the dominant modern methodology. *See also* **empiricism**.

sexism: The belief that one sex (usually the male) is better than the other (usually the female). *See also* **feminism**; **women's liberation**.

skepticism: The intellectual idea of doubting everything and trusting only what can be tested through reason.

Social Darwinism: The idea of understanding human society through perspectives influenced by the debate over evolution. Social Darwinists usually rationalized the supremacy of rich European elites over the impoverished masses both in the West (through laissez-faire policies) and around the world (through colonialism). *See also* **colonialism**; **classical liberal economics, theory of**; **evolution**; **imperialism**; **natural selection, theory of**; **neo-imperialism**; **racism**.

socialism: Several ideas and practices that have developed since the Industrial Revolution to address the political, social, and economic inequalities between capitalists and workers. In principle, socialism stands for helping the workers. Over time, socialist theories and systems have developed in many directions. *See also* **Christian socialism**; **classical liberal economics, theory of**; **communism**; **democratic socialism**; **Marxism**; **Naziism**; **state socialism**; **trade unionism**; **utopian socialism**; **war socialism**.

sovietization: The practice of the Soviet Union during the Cold War of transforming states under their influence to conform to Stalinism. *See also* **Stalinism**.

Stalinism: The developments in the early Soviet Union that both modernized state and society and created a totalitarian dictatorship based on Stalin's cult of personality. *See also* **Leninism**; **Marxism**.

state socialism: The practice of conservative governments legislating practices to improve the condition of workers. *See also* **socialism**.

stoicism: A philosophy that calls for people to do their duty in difficult circumstances. It originated among the Hellenistic Greeks and was popularized by the Romans.

subjectivity: The inclination to take sides or interpret disagreements from a biased point of view. *See also* objectivity.

subsidiarity: The political idea and practice that decisions should be made at the regional and local levels rather than by a distant national, imperial, or global authority. *See also* **particularism**; **regionalism**.

suburbanization: The process of moving people to live in areas around cities that mixed traditional urban dwellings with rural landscapes. It became common in the late twentieth century with the increasing use of automobiles.

supernaturalism: The belief that another realm exists apart from the reality that can be empirically observed and sensed. Forces or beings in the supernatural realm are often believed to have influence or power within the natural world.

supremacy: A term used in this text to indicate historical change through the enforced domination of ideas or by those with power.

syllogism: An element of dialectic logic as developed by the ancient Greek philosopher Aristotle, where two pieces of known information are compared in order to reach new knowledge. *See also* **dialectic logic**; **Scholasticism**.

syncretism: The process in which elements of an idea, philosophy, or religion are blended with those of another.

terrorism: The political idea and practice of using small-scale violence, usually against civilians, to achieve specific political ends. Large-scale violence becomes guerrilla war, rebellion, or actual war. *See also* **anarchism**.

textual criticism: The intellectual tool developed during the Renaissance of comparing different manuscript versions of an author in order to find the best, most accurate text. *See also* **higher criticism**.

theocracy: The political idea and practice that religious leaders should rule the state.

toleration: The idea that people and society should accept other people who believe in different worldviews, philosophies, or religions. *See also* **diversity**; **ecumenism**.

totalitarianism: The modern political practice of a strong dictatorship, where a ruler and his party substantially control mass communication, bureaucracy, and the economy and maintain order through secret police and a strong military. *See also* **authoritarianism**; **dictatorship**; **fascism**; **Leninism**; **Stalinism**.

trade unionism: The practice of organizing labor unions (trade unions in Britain, syndicalism in France) to help workers. At first illegal, unions often successfully improved conditions for workers to the point that much of the working class blended into the middle class during the twentieth century. *See also* **socialism**.

tyranny: The practice of one person seizing power in a government. While today the term is used in a negative way, tyrants among the ancient Greeks often opened politics to become more egalitarian and democratic. *See also* **dictatorship**.

uniformitarianism, theory of: A scientific theory to explain the history of the earth. It states that the same (uniform) processes that are shaping the earth today have always acted to mold the planet. *See also* **catastrophism, theory of**; **science**.

universalism: The attitude that the same beliefs and practices should be applied or open to everyone. *See also* **particularism**; **supremacy**.

urbanization: The process of moving rural people to live in ever-larger cities, carried out after the Industrial Revolution. Today most people live in urban areas.

utopian socialism: The first version of socialism, which called on capitalists to improve conditions for workers. *See also* **socialism**.

vandalism: The practice of writing on or damaging property, either out of spite or to make a statement. It is named after the Vandal sack of Rome in AD 455, perhaps unfairly since later sacks were worse.

war socialism: A common policy during World War I and World War II when governments took control of large sectors of the economy, creating a new military-industrial complex. In doing so, they often had to appease workers to prevent strikes. *See also* **socialism**.

Western exceptionalism: A point of view that sees Europeans as better than peoples in Asia, Africa, or the Americas. The source of this alleged virtue ranges from the success of Western imperial colonialism, through superior moral upbringing, to divine favor.

westernization: The process of conforming non-European institutions and attitudes to those of Western civilization.

women's liberation: A movement in the 1960s and 1970s that promoted the rights of women to education, political participation, and economic independence. It was largely successful in Western industrialized states. *See also* **feminism**; **sexism**.

yugo-slavism: The political idea that called for all southern (*yugo*) Slavs to live together in one nation-state. The Serbs, as the dominant group of southern Slavs, were most behind this movement. *See also* **pan-slavism**.

zairianization: A political idea of Congolese nationalism, where the authoritarian kleptocrat Mobuto in the 1960s rejected European culture and tried to readapt his country to more native African ways. *See also* **kleptocracy**.

Zionism: Originally the idea of Jewish nationalism, namely that Jews, like any other nationality, should have their own nation-state. Zionism culminated in the modern state of Israel in 1948. Ever since, the term has sometimes been used to describe the alleged racist and imperialist policies of Israel against Arab Palestinians. *See also* **antisemitism**; **Judaism**.

Zoroastrianism: A dualistic religion in ancient Persia founded by the legendary Zoroaster or Zarathustra. *See also* **dualism**.

Index

Letters after page numbers indicate the following: d = diagram; f = figure; m = map; n = note; ps = primary source; sf = sources on families; t = timeline; tb = table. Terms in **boldface** designate a person.

Aachen, 160
Abbasid Caliphate, 176
abbot/abbess, 148, 164, 178
ABC weapons, 426, 485
Abdullah, king of Trans- jordan, 394
Abelard, Peter, 193, 193n3, 515*t*
Abkhazia, 463
abolitionism, 264
Aboriginal people, 473
abortion, 434, 519*t*
Abraham, 54
absolute monarchy, 268–76, 313
absolutism, 28, 28n2, 86, 104–12, 268–76, 285–86, 312–13, 384, 510*t*, 516*t*
abstract art, 519*t*
abstract expressionism, 519*t*
Abyssinia, 252, 344, 398
acculturation, 12
Achilles, 71
acquired immune deficiency syndrome (AIDS), 435, 519*t*
AD, 7, 121, 121n1
Adam, 54
Adelaide of Italy, 171
adoption and designation policy, 110–11, 512*t*
Adowa, battle of, 344, 398
advertising, 308, 380, 519*t*

Aeneid (Vergil), 116, 513*t*
Afghanistan, 459–60, 484–85, 491–92, 518*t*
Africa: and Arab Spring, 489; decolonization and, 445–47; economic issues, 447; imperialism and, 245–46, 252, 340–42, 392; and Italy, 398; and jazz, 380; Partition of, 342, 516*t*; and sexual morality, 479; and slavery, 250; and West, 506; and World War I, 370; and World War II, 415
African National Congress, 344, 436, 463
African peoples. *See* blacks
Afrikaaners, 340–41, 344, 516*t*
afterlife: Christianity on, 123; Dante on, 195; Egyptians on, 41, 42*f*; Jews on, 60, 62; Marx on, 322
Agincourt, battle of, 216
Agnes, saint, 131
agnosticism, 262, 517*t*
Agricola, 112–14*ps*
agriculture, 35, 69–70, 510*t*; development of, 25–30; and global economy, 447; interwar years, 382; Khmer Rouge and, 457; medieval,

165, 205; Romans and, 103; science and, 259, 299–300, 516*t*
Agrippina, 107
Ahab, 63
AIDS, 435, 519*t*
air conditioning, 518*t*
airplanes, 309, 366, 370, 381, 394, 413, 415, 516*t*, 518*t*
Akhenaton, pharaoh, 42, 510*t*
Alaric, 138
al-Assad, Bashar, 489
Albania, 366–67, 410, 466, 518*t*
Albanians, 363, 471–73
Albigensians, 203–4
alcohol, 382
Alcuin Albinus, 160
Alexander, king of Yugo- slavia, 398
Alexander II, tsar of Russia, 360
Alexander VI, pope, 229
Alexander the Great of Macedon, 63, 82, 82n1, 83*m*, 86, 91, 512*t*
Alexandra, tsarina of Russia, 385, 387
Alexandria, 91, 513*t*
Alfred the Great, 150, 514*t*
Algeria, 445–46

About the Author

Brian A. Pavlac is professor of history at King's College in Wilkes-Barre, Pennsylvania, where he has served as chair of the department, director of the Center for Excellence in Learning and Teaching, and a Herve A. LeBlanc Distinguished Service Professor. He is the author of *Witch Hunts in the Western World: Persecution and Punishment from the Inquisition through the Salem Trials* and articles on Nicholas of Cusa and excommunication, editor of and contributor to *Game of Thrones versus History: Written in Blood*, co-author of the forthcoming *The Holy Roman Empire: A Historical Encyclopedia*, and translator of Balderich's *A Warrior Bishop of the 12th Century: The Deeds of Albero of Trier*.